Excel® 2010

FOR

DUMMIES®

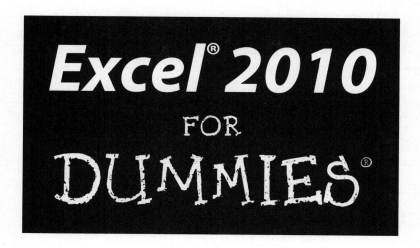

by Greg Harvey, PhD

John Wiley & Sons, Inc.

Excel® 2010 For Dummies®

Published by
John Wiley & Sons, Inc.
111 River Street
Hoboken, NJ 07030-5774

www.wiley.com

Copyright © 2010 by John Wiley & Sons, Inc., Hoboken, New Jersey

Published by John Wiley & Sons, Inc., Hoboken, New Jersey

Published simultaneously in Canada

For general information on our other products and services, please contact our Customer Care Department within the U.S. at 877-762-2974, outside the U.S. at 317-572-3993, or fax 317-572-4002.

For technical support, please visit www.wiley.com/techsupport.

Wiley publishes in a variety of print and electronic formats and by print-on-demand. Some material included with standard print versions of this book may not be included in e-books or in print-on-demand. If this book refers to media such as a CD or DVD that is not included in the version you purchased, you may download this material at http://booksupport.wiley.com. For more information about Wiley products, visit www.wiley.com.

Library of Congress Control Number: 2010923559

ISBN 978-0-470-48953-6 (pbk); ISBN 978-0-470-63468-4 (ebk); ISBN 978-0-470-63469-1 (ebk); ISBN 978-0-470-63470-7 (ebk)

Manufactured in the United States of America

10 9 8 7 6 5

WILEY

About the Author

Greg Harvey has authored tons of computer books, the most recent being *Excel Workbook For Dummies* and *Roxio Easy Media Creator 8 For Dummies,* and the most popular being *Excel 2003 For Dummies* and *Excel 2003 All-in-One Desk Reference For Dummies.* He started out training business users on how to use IBM personal computers and their attendant computer software in the rough and tumble days of DOS, WordStar, and Lotus 1-2-3 in the mid-80s of the last century. After working for a number of independent training firms, Greg went on to teach semester-long courses in spreadsheet and database management software at Golden Gate University in San Francisco.

His love of teaching has translated into an equal love of writing. For Dummies books are, of course, his all-time favorites to write because they enable him to write to his favorite audience: the beginner. They also enable him to use humor (a key element to success in the training room) and, most delightful of all, to express an opinion or two about the subject matter at hand.

Greg received his doctorate degree in Humanities in Philosophy and Religion with a concentration in Asian Studies and Comparative Religion last May. Everyone is glad that Greg was finally able to get out of school before he retired.

Dedication

An Erucolindo melindonya

Author's Acknowledgments

Let me take this opportunity to thank all the people, both at Wiley Publishing, Inc., and at Mind over Media, Inc., whose dedication and talent combined to get this book out and into your hands in such great shape.

At Wiley Publishing, Inc., I want to thank Andy Cummings and Katie Feltman for their encouragement and help in getting this project underway and their ongoing support every step of the way. These people made sure that the project stayed on course and made it into production so that all the talented folks on the production team could create this great final product.

At Mind over Media, I want to thank Christopher Aiken for his review of the updated manuscript and invaluable input and suggestions on how best to restructure the book to accommodate all the new features and, most importantly, present the new user interface.

Publisher's Acknowledgments

We're proud of this book; please send us your comments at `http://dummies.custhelp.com`. For other comments, please contact our Customer Care Department within the U.S. at 877-762-2974, outside the U.S. at 317-572-3993, or fax 317-572-4002.

Some of the people who helped bring this book to market include the following:

Acquisitions and Editorial

Project Editor: Nicole Sholly

Senior Acquisitions Editor: Katie Feltman

Copy Editor: Brian Walls

Technical Editors: Mike Talley,
   Joyce Nielsen

Editorial Manager: Kevin Kirschner

Editorial Assistant: Amanda Graham

Senior Editorial Assistant: Cherie Case

Cartoons: Rich Tennant
   (`www.the5thwave.com`)

Composition Services

Project Coordinator: Patrick Redmond

Layout and Graphics: Ashley Chamberlain,
   Joyce Haughey, Christine Williams

Proofreader: Linda Seifert

Indexer: Sharon Shock

Publishing and Editorial for Technology Dummies

   Richard Swadley, Vice President and Executive Group Publisher

   Andy Cummings, Vice President and Publisher

   Mary Bednarek, Executive Acquisitions Director

   Mary C. Corder, Editorial Director

Publishing for Consumer Dummies

   Kathleen Nebenhaus, Vice President and Executive Publisher

Composition Services

   Debbie Stailey, Director of Composition Services

Contents at a Glance

Table of Contents

Introduction

● ●

I'm very proud to present you with *Excel 2010 For Dummies,* the latest version of everybody's favorite book on Microsoft Office Excel for readers with no intention whatsoever of becoming spreadsheet gurus.

Excel 2010 For Dummies covers all the fundamental techniques you need to know in order to create, edit, format, and print your own worksheets. In addition to showing you around the worksheet, this book also exposes you to the basics of charting, creating data lists, and performing data analysis. Keep in mind, though, that this book just touches on the easiest ways to get a few things done with these features — I don't attempt to cover charting, data lists, or data analysis in the same definitive way as spreadsheets: This book concentrates on spreadsheets because spreadsheets are what most regular folks create with Excel.

About This Book

This book isn't meant to be read cover to cover. Although its chapters are loosely organized in a logical order (progressing as you might when studying Excel in a classroom situation), each topic covered in a chapter is really meant to stand on its own.

Each discussion of a topic briefly addresses the question of what a particular feature is good for before launching into how to use it. In Excel, as with most other sophisticated programs, you usually have more than one way to do a task. For the sake of your sanity, I have purposely limited the choices by usually giving you only the most efficient ways to do a particular task. Later, if you're so tempted, you can experiment with alternative ways of doing a task. For now, just concentrate on performing the task as I describe.

As much as possible, I've tried to make it unnecessary for you to remember anything covered in another section of the book. From time to time, however, you will come across a cross-reference to another section or chapter in the book. For the most part, such cross-references are meant to help you get more complete information on a subject, should you have the time and interest. If you have neither, no problem. Just ignore the cross-references as if they never existed.

How to Use This Book

This book is similar to a reference book. You can start by looking up the topic you need information about (in either the Table of Contents or the index) and then refer directly to the section of interest. I explain most topics conversationally (as though you were sitting in the back of a classroom where you can safely nap). Sometimes, however, my regiment-commander mentality takes over, and I list the steps you need to take to accomplish a particular task in a particular section.

What You Can Safely Ignore

When you come across a section that contains the steps you take to get something done, you can safely ignore all text accompanying the steps (the text that isn't in bold) if you have neither the time nor the inclination to wade through more material.

Whenever possible, I have also tried to separate background or footnote-type information from the essential facts by exiling this kind of junk to a sidebar (look for blocks of text on a gray background). Often, these sections are flagged with icons that let you know what type of information you will encounter there. You can easily disregard text marked this way. (I'll scoop you on the icons I use in this book a little later.)

Foolish Assumptions

I'm going to make only one assumption about you (let's see how close I get): You have access to a PC (at least some of the time) that is running Windows 7, Windows Vista, or Windows XP and on which Microsoft Office Excel 2010 is installed. Having said that, I don't assume that you've ever launched Excel 2010, let alone done anything with it.

This book is intended for users of Microsoft Office Excel 2010. If you're using Excel for Windows version Excel 97 through 2003, the information in this book will only confuse and confound you because only Excel 2007 works similar to the 2010 version that this book describes.

If you're working with a version of Excel earlier than Excel 2007, please put this book down slowly and pick up a copy of *Excel 2003 For Dummies* instead.

How This Book Is Organized

This book is organized in six parts (which gives you a chance to see at least six of those great Rich Tennant cartoons!). Each part contains two or more chapters (to keep the editors happy) that more or less go together (to keep you happy). Each chapter is divided further into loosely related sections that cover the basics of the topic at hand. However, don't get hung up on following the structure of the book; ultimately, it doesn't matter whether you find out how to edit the worksheet before you learn how to format it, or whether you figure out printing before you learn editing. The important thing is that you find the information — and understand it when you find it — when you need to perform a particular task.

In case you're interested, a synopsis of what you find in each part follows.

Part 1: Getting In on the Ground Floor

As the name implies, in this part I cover such fundamentals as how to start the program, identify the parts of the screen, enter information in the worksheet, save a document, and so on. If you're starting with absolutely no background in using spreadsheets, you definitely want to glance at the information in Chapter 1 to discover the secrets of the Ribbon interface before you move on to how to create new worksheets in Chapter 2.

Part 11: Editing without Tears

In this part, I show you how to edit spreadsheets to make them look good, including how to make major editing changes without courting disaster. Peruse Chapter 3 when you need information on formatting the data to improve the way it appears in the worksheet. See Chapter 4 for rearranging, deleting, or inserting new information in the worksheet. Read Chapter 5 for the skinny on printing your finished product.

Part 111: Getting Organized and Staying That Way

Here I give you all kinds of information on how to stay on top of the data that you've entered into your spreadsheets. Chapter 6 is full of good ideas on how to keep track of and organize the data in a single worksheet. Chapter 7 gives you the ins and outs of working with data in different worksheets in the same workbook and gives you information on transferring data between the sheets of different workbooks.

Part IV: Digging Data Analysis

This part consists of two chapters. Chapter 8 introduces performing various types of what-if analysis in Excel, including setting up data tables with one and two inputs, performing goal seeking, and creating different cases with Scenario Manager. Chapter 9 introduces Excel's vastly improved pivot table and pivot chart capabilities that enable you to summarize and filter vast amounts of data in a worksheet table or data list in a compact tabular or chart format.

Part V: Life beyond the Spreadsheet

In Part V, I explore some of the other aspects of Excel besides the spreadsheet. In Chapter 10, you find out just how ridiculously easy it is to create a chart using the data in a worksheet. In Chapter 11, you discover just how useful Excel's data list capabilities can be when you have to track and organize a large amount of information. In Chapter 12, you find out about using add-in programs to enhance Excel's basic features, adding hyperlinks to jump to new places in a worksheet, to new documents, and even to Web pages, as well as how to record macros to automate your work.

Part VI: The Part of Tens

As is the tradition in *For Dummies* books, the last part contains lists of the top ten most useful and useless facts, tips, and suggestions. In this part, you find three chapters. Chapter 13 provides my top ten list of the best new features in Excel 2010 (and boy was it hard keeping it to just ten). Chapter 14 gives you the top ten beginner basics you need to know as you start using this program. Chapter 15 gives you the King James Version of the Ten Commandments of Excel 2010. With this chapter under your belt, how canst thou goest astray?

Conventions Used in This Book

The following information gives you the lowdown on how things look in this book. Publishers call these items the book's *conventions* (no campaigning, flag-waving, name-calling, or finger-pointing is involved, however).

Throughout the book, you'll find Ribbon command sequences (the name on the tab on the Ribbon and the command button you select) separated by a command arrow, as in:

Home⇨Copy

This shorthand is the Ribbon command that copies whatever cells or graphics are currently selected to the Windows Clipboard. It means that you click the Home tab on the Ribbon (if it isn't displayed already) and then click the Copy button (that sports the traditional side-by-side page icon).

Some of the Ribbon command sequences involve not only selecting a command button on a tab but then also selecting an item on a drop-down menu. In this case, the drop-down menu command follows the name of the tab and command button, all separated by command arrows, as in:

Formulas⇨Calculation Options⇨Manual

This shorthand is the Ribbon command sequence that turns on manual recalculation in Excel. It says that you click the Formulas tab (if it isn't displayed already) and then click the Calculation Options button followed by the Manual drop-down menu option.

Although you use the mouse and keyboard shortcut keys to move your way in, out, and around the Excel worksheet, you do have to take some time to enter the data so that you can eventually mouse around with it. Therefore, this book occasionally encourages you to type something specific into a specific cell in the worksheet. Of course, you can always choose not to follow the instructions. When I tell you to enter a specific function, the part you should type generally appears in **bold** type. For example, **=SUM(A2:B2)** means that you should type exactly what you see: an equal sign, the word **SUM**, a left parenthesis, the text **A2:B2** (complete with a colon between the letter-number combos), and a right parenthesis. You then, of course, have to press Enter to make the entry stick.

Occasionally, I give you a *hot key combination* that you can press in order to choose a command from the keyboard rather than clicking buttons on the Ribbon with the mouse. Hot key combinations are written like this: Alt+FS or Ctrl+S (both of these hot key combos save workbook changes).

With the Alt key combos, you press the Alt key until the hot key letters appear in little squares all along the Ribbon. At that point, you can release the Alt key and start typing the hot key letters (by the way, you type all lowercase hot key letters — I only put them in caps to make them stand out in the text).

Hot key combos that use the Ctrl key are of an older vintage and work a little bit differently. You have to hold down the Ctrl key while you type the hot key letter (though again, type only lowercase letters unless you see the Shift key in the sequence, as in Ctrl+Shift+C).

Excel 2010 uses only one pull-down menu (File) and one toolbar (the Quick Access toolbar). You open the File pull-down menu by clicking the File tab or pressing Alt+F. The Quick Access toolbar with its four buttons appears to the immediate right of the File tab.

Finally, if you're really observant, you may notice a discrepancy in how the names of dialog box options (such as headings, option buttons, and check boxes) appear in the text and how they actually appear in Excel on your computer screen. I intentionally use the convention of capitalizing the initial letters of all the main words of a dialog box option to help you differentiate the name of the option from the rest of the text describing its use.

Icons Used in This Book

The following icons are placed in the margins to point out stuff you may or may not want to read.

This icon alerts you to nerdy discussions that you may well want to skip (or read when no one else is around).

This icon alerts you to shortcuts or other valuable hints related to the topic at hand.

This icon alerts you to information to keep in mind if you want to meet with a modicum of success.

This icon alerts you to information to keep in mind if you want to avert complete disaster.

Where to Go from Here

If you've never worked with a computer spreadsheet, I suggest that, right after getting your chuckles with the cartoons, you first go to Chapter 1 and find out what you're dealing with. If you're someone with some experience with earlier versions of Excel, I want you to head directly to the section, "Migrating to Excel 2010 from Earlier Versions Using Pull-down Menus" in Chapter 1, where you find out how to stay calm as you become familiar and, yes, comfortable with the Ribbon user interface.

Then, as specific needs arise (such as, "How do I copy a formula?" or "How do I print just a particular section of my worksheet?"), you can go to the Table of Contents or the index to find the appropriate section and go right to that section for answers.

Part I
Getting In on the Ground Floor

The 5th Wave   By Rich Tennant

OVER-SPREADSHEETING

@RICHTENNANT

"According to your current physical symptoms, you'll be bald well before you're fat."

In this part . . .

In this part, I break down the Excel user interface and make sense of the tabs and command buttons you're going to face day after day after day. Of course, it does you no good just to know what's what onscreen; you need to be able to use all these bells and whistles (or buttons and boxes in this case). Therefore, I also show you how to use some of the more prominent buttons and boxes to enter your spreadsheet data. From this humble beginning, it's a quick trip to total screen mastery.

Chapter 1

The Excel 2010 User Experience

*T*he Excel 2010 user interface, like Excel 2007, scraps its reliance on a series of pull-down menus, task panes, and multitudinous toolbars. Instead, it uses a single strip at the top of the worksheet called the Ribbon that puts the bulk of the Excel commands you use at your fingertips at all times.

Add to the Ribbon a File tab and a Quick Access toolbar — along with a few remaining task panes (Clipboard, Clip Art, and Research) — and you end up with the handiest way to crunch your numbers, produce and print polished financial reports, as well as organize and chart your data. In other words, to do all the wonderful things for which you rely on Excel.

Best of all, this new and improved Excel user interface includes all sorts of graphical improvements. Foremost is Live Preview that shows you how your actual worksheet data would appear in a particular font, table formatting, and so on before you actually select it. Additionally, Excel 2010 supports an honest to goodness Page Layout View that displays rulers and margins along with headers and footers for every worksheet and has a zoom slider at the bottom of the screen that enables you to zoom in and out on the spreadsheet data instantly. Finally, Excel 2010 is full of pop-up galleries that make spreadsheet formatting and charting a real breeze, especially in tandem with Live Preview.

Excel's Ribbon User Interface

When you launch Excel 2010, the program opens the first of three new worksheets (named Sheet1) in a new workbook file (named Book1) inside a program window like the one shown in Figure 1-1.

Quick Access toolbar   Worksheet area   Formula bar   Ribbon

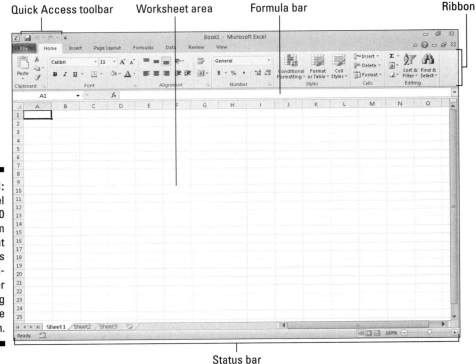

Figure 1-1:
The Excel
2010
program
window that
appears
immedi-
ately after
launching
the
program.

Status bar

The Excel program window containing this worksheet of the workbook contains the following components:

- ✔ **File tab** that when clicked opens the new Backstage View — a menu on the left that contains all the document- and file-related commands, including Info (selected by default), Save, Save As, Open, Close, Recent, New, Print, and Save & Send. Additionally, there's a Help option with add-ins, an Options item that enables you to change many of Excel's default settings, and an Exit option to quit the program.

- ✔ Customizable **Quick Access toolbar** that contains buttons you can click to perform common tasks, such as saving your work and undoing and redoing edits.

✔ **Ribbon** that contains the bulk of the Excel commands arranged into a series of tabs ranging from Home through View.

✔ **Formula bar** that displays the address of the current cell along with the contents of that cell.

✔ **Worksheet area** that contains the cells of the worksheet identified by column headings using letters along the top and row headings using numbers along the left edge; tabs for selecting new worksheets; a horizontal scroll bar to move left and right through the sheet; and a vertical scroll bar to move up and down through the sheet.

✔ **Status bar** that keeps you informed of the program's current mode and any special keys you engage, and enables you to select a new worksheet view and to zoom in and out on the worksheet.

Going Backstage via File

To the immediate left of the Home tab on the Ribbon right below the Quick Access toolbar, you find the File tab.

When you click File, the new Backstage View opens. This view contains a menu similar to the one shown in Figure 1-2. When you open the Backstage View with the Info option selected, Excel displays at-a-glance stats about the workbook file you have opened and active in the program.

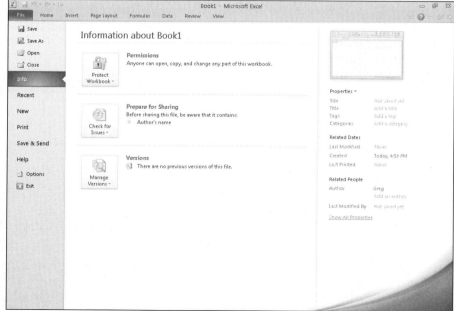

Figure 1-2: Open Backstage View to get at-a-glance information about the current file, access all file-related commands, and modify the program options.

This information panel is divided into two panes. The pane on the left contains large buttons that enable you to modify the workbook's permissions, distribution, and versions. The pane on the right contains a thumbnail of the workbook followed by a list of fields detailing the workbook's various Document Properties, some of which you can change (such as Title, Tags, Categories, and Author), and many of which you can't (such as Size, Last Modified, Created, and so forth).

Above the Info option, you find the commands (Save, Save As, Open, and Close) you commonly need for working with Excel workbook files. Near the bottom, the File tab contains a Help option that, when selected, displays a Support panel in the Backstage View. This panel contains options for getting help on using Excel, customizing its default settings, as well as checking for updates to the Excel 2010 program. Below Help, you find options that you can select to change the program's settings, along with an Exit option that you can select when you're ready to close the program.

 Click the Recent option to continue editing an Excel workbook you've worked on of late. When you click the Recent option, Excel displays a panel with a list of all the workbook files recently opened in the program. To re-open a particular file for editing, all you do is click its filename in this list.

To close the Backstage View and return to the normal worksheet view, you can click the File tab a second time or simply press the Escape key.

Bragging about the Ribbon

The Ribbon (shown in Figure 1-3) changes the way you work in Excel 2010. Instead of having to memorize (or guess) on which pull-down menu or toolbar Microsoft put the particular command you want to use, their designers and engineers came up with the Ribbon that shows you the most commonly used options needed to perform a particular Excel task.

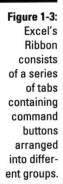

Figure 1-3: Excel's Ribbon consists of a series of tabs containing command buttons arranged into differ-ent groups.

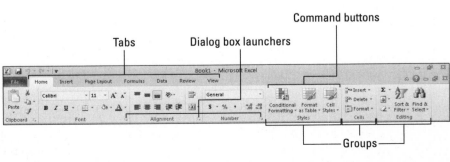

The Ribbon contains the following components:

- ✔ **Tabs** for each of Excel's main tasks that bring together and display all the commands commonly needed to perform that core task.

- ✔ **Groups** that organize related command buttons into subtasks normally performed as part of the tab's larger core task.

- ✔ **Command buttons** within each group that you select to perform a particular action or to open a gallery from which you can click a particular thumbnail. *Note:* Many command buttons on certain tabs of the Ribbon are organized into mini-toolbars with related settings.

- ✔ **Dialog box launcher** in the lower-right corner of certain groups that opens a dialog box containing a bunch of additional options you can select.

To display more of the Worksheet area in the program window, you can minimize the Ribbon so that only its tabs display. Simply click the Minimize the Ribbon button, the first button with what looks like a greater than symbol pointing upward in the group of buttons for minimizing, maximizing, and closing the current worksheet window to the right of the Ribbon tabs and to the immediate left of the Help button. You can also double-click any one of the Ribbon's tabs, or just press Ctrl+F1. To redisplay the entire Ribbon, and keep all the command buttons on its tabs displayed in the program window, click the Expand the Ribbon button, double-click one of the tabs, or press Ctrl+F1 a second time.

When you work in Excel with the Ribbon minimized, the Ribbon expands each time you click one of its tabs to show its command buttons, but that tab stays open only until you select one of the command buttons. The moment you select a command button, Excel immediately minimizes the Ribbon again and just displays its tabs.

Keeping tabs on the Excel Ribbon

The first time you launch Excel 2010, its Ribbon contains the following tabs from left to right:

- ✔ **Home** tab with the command buttons normally used when creating, formatting, and editing a spreadsheet, arranged into the Clipboard, Font, Alignment, Number, Styles, Cells, and Editing groups.

- ✔ **Insert** tab with the command buttons normally used when adding particular elements (including graphics, PivotTables, charts, hyperlinks, and headers and footers) to a spreadsheet, arranged into the Tables, Illustrations, Charts, Sparklines, Filter, Links, Text, and Symbols groups.

- ✔ **Page Layout** tab with the command buttons normally used when preparing a spreadsheet for printing or re-ordering graphics on the sheet, arranged into the Themes, Page Setup, Scale to Fit, Sheet Options, and Arrange groups.

✔ **Formulas** tab with the command buttons normally used when adding formulas and functions to a spreadsheet or checking a worksheet for formula errors, arranged into the Function Library, Defined Names, Formula Auditing, and Calculation groups. *Note:* This tab also contains a Solutions group when you activate certain add-in programs, such as Analysis ToolPak and Euro Currency Tools. See Chapter 12 for more on using Excel add-in programs.

✔ **Data** tab with the command buttons normally used when importing, querying, outlining, and subtotaling the data placed into a worksheet's data list, arranged into the Get External Data, Connections, Sort & Filter, Data Tools, and Outline groups. *Note:* This tab also contains an Analysis group when you activate add-ins, such as Analysis ToolPak and Solver. See Chapter 12 for more on Excel add-ins.

✔ **Review** tab with the command buttons normally used when proofing, protecting, and marking up a spreadsheet for review by others, arranged into the Proofing, Language, Comments, and Changes groups. *Note:* This tab also contains an Ink group with a sole Start Inking button when you're running Office 2010 on a Tablet PC or a computer equipped with a digital ink tablet.

✔ **View** tab with the command buttons normally used when changing the display of the Worksheet area and the data it contains, arranged into the Workbook Views, Show, Zoom, Window, and Macros groups.

In addition to these standard seven tabs, Excel has an eighth, optional Developer tab that you can add to the Ribbon if you do a lot of work with macros and XML files. See Chapter 12 for more on the Developer tab.

Although these standard tabs are the ones you always see on the Ribbon when it displays in Excel, they aren't the only things that can appear in this area. Excel can display contextual tools when you're working with a particular object that you select in the worksheet, such as a graphic image you've added or a chart or PivotTable you've created. The name of the contextual tools for the selected object appears immediately above the tab or tabs associated with the tools.

For example, Figure 1-4 shows a worksheet after you click the embedded chart to select it. As you can see, doing this adds the contextual tool called Chart Tools to the very end of the Ribbon. The Chart Tools contextual tool has its own three tabs: Design (selected), Layout, and Format. Note, too, that the command buttons on the Design tab are arranged into groups Type, Data, Chart Layouts, Chart Styles, Location, and Mode.

The moment you deselect the object (usually by clicking somewhere outside the object's boundaries), the contextual tool for that object and all its tabs immediately disappear from the Ribbon, leaving only the regular tabs — Home, Insert, Page Layout, Formulas, Data, Review, and View — displayed.

Chart Tools contextual tab

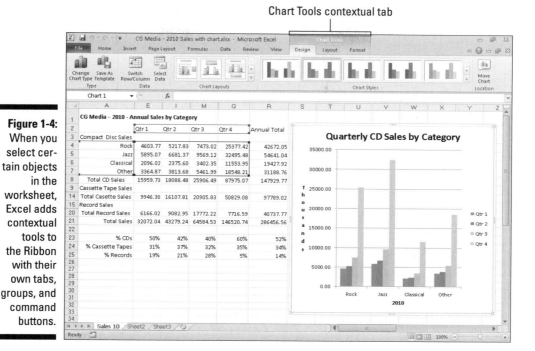

Figure 1-4:
When you
select cer-
tain objects
in the
worksheet,
Excel adds
contextual
tools to
the Ribbon
with their
own tabs,
groups, and
command
buttons.

Selecting commands from the Ribbon

The most direct method for selecting commands on the Ribbon is to click the
tab that contains the command button you want and then click that button in
its group. For example, to insert a piece of clip art into your spreadsheet, you
click the Insert tab and then click the Clip Art button to open the Clip Art task
pane in the Worksheet area.

The easiest method for selecting commands on the Ribbon — if you know
your keyboard well — is to press the Alt key and then type the sequence of
letters designated as the hot keys for the desired tab and associated command buttons.

When you press and release the Alt key, Excel displays the hot keys for all
the tabs on the Ribbon. When you type one of the Ribbon tab hot keys to
select it, all the command button hot keys appear along with the hot keys
for the dialog box launchers (see Figure 1-5). To select a command button or
dialog box launcher, simply type its hot key letter(s).

Figure 1-5:
Excel hot
keys for
selecting
command
buttons and
dialog box
launchers.

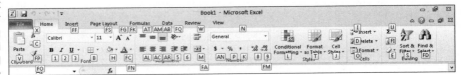

If you know the old Excel shortcut keys from versions Excel 97 through 2003, you can still use them. For example, instead of going through the rigmarole of pressing Alt+HC to copy a cell selection to the Office Clipboard and then Alt+HV to paste it elsewhere in the sheet, you can still press Ctrl+C to copy the selection and then press Ctrl+V when you're ready to paste it. Note, however, that when using a hot key combination with the Alt key, you don't need to keep the Alt key depressed while typing the remaining letter(s) as you do when using a shortcut key combo with the Ctrl key.

Customizing the Quick Access toolbar

When you start using Excel 2010, the Quick Access toolbar contains only the following few buttons:

- ✔ **Save** to save any changes made to the current workbook using the same filename, file format, and location

- ✔ **Undo** to undo the last editing, formatting, or layout change you made

- ✔ **Redo** to reapply the previous editing, formatting, or layout change that you just removed with the Undo button

The Quick Access toolbar is very customizable because Excel makes it easy to add any Ribbon command to it. Moreover, you're not restricted to adding buttons for just the commands on the Ribbon; you can add any Excel command you want to the toolbar, even the obscure ones that don't rate an appearance on any of its tabs.

By default, the Quick Access toolbar appears above the Ribbon tabs immediately to the right of the Excel program button (used to resize the workbook window or quit the program). To display the toolbar beneath the Ribbon immediately above the Formula bar, click the Customize Quick Access Toolbar button (the drop-down button to the right of the toolbar with a horizontal bar above a down-pointing triangle) and then click Show Below the Ribbon on its drop-down menu. You will definitely want to make this change if you start adding more buttons to the toolbar so that the growing Quick Access toolbar doesn't start crowding the name of the current workbook that appears to the toolbar's right.

Adding command buttons on the Customize Quick Access Toolbar's drop-down menu

When you click the Customize Quick Access Toolbar button, a drop-down menu appears containing the following commands:

- ✔ **New** to open a new workbook

- ✔ **Open** to display the Open dialog box for opening an existing workbook

- ✔ **Save** to save changes to your current workbook

- ✔ **E-mail** to open your mail

- ✔ **Quick Print** to send the current worksheet to your default printer

- ✔ **Print Preview and Print** to open the Print panel in Backstage View with a preview of the current worksheet in the right pane

- ✔ **Spelling** to check the current worksheet for spelling errors

- ✔ **Undo** to undo your latest worksheet edit

- ✔ **Redo** to reapply the last edit that you removed with Undo

- ✔ **Sort Ascending** to sort the current cell selection or column in A to Z alphabetical order, lowest to highest numerical order, or oldest to newest date order

- ✔ **Sort Descending** to sort the current cell selection or column in Z to A alphabetical order, highest to lowest numerical order, or newest to oldest date order

When you open this menu, only the Save, Undo, and Redo options are selected (indicated by the check marks); therefore, these buttons are the only buttons to appear on the Quick Access toolbar. To add any of the other commands on this menu to the toolbar, you simply click the option on the drop-down menu. Excel then adds a button for that command to the end of the Quick Access toolbar (and a check mark to its option on the drop-down menu).

To remove a command button that you add to the Quick Access toolbar in this manner, click the option a second time on the Customize Quick Access Toolbar button's drop-down menu. Excel removes its command button from the toolbar and the check mark from its option on the drop-down menu.

Adding command buttons on the Ribbon

To add a Ribbon command to the Quick Access toolbar, simply right-click its command button on the Ribbon and then click Add to Quick Access Toolbar on its shortcut menu. Excel then immediately adds the command button to the very end of the Quick Access toolbar, immediately in front of the Customize Quick Access Toolbar button.

If you want to move the command button to a new location on the Quick Access toolbar or group it with other buttons on the toolbar, click the Customize Quick Access Toolbar button and then click the More Commands option near the bottom of its drop-down menu.

Excel then opens the Excel Options dialog box with the Quick Access Toolbar tab selected (similar to the one shown in Figure 1-6). On the right side of the dialog box, Excel shows all the buttons added to the Quick Access toolbar. The order in which they appear from left to right on the toolbar corresponds to the top-down order in the list box.

Figure 1-6:
Use the buttons on the Quick Access Toolbar tab of the Excel Options dialog box to customize the appearance of the Quick Access toolbar.

To reposition a particular button on the toolbar, click it in the list box on the right and then click either the Move Up button (the one with the black triangle pointing upward) or the Move Down button (the one with the black triangle pointing downward) until the button is promoted or demoted to the desired position on the toolbar.

You can add vertical separators to the toolbar to group related buttons. To do this, click the <Separator> option in the list box on the left and then click the Add button twice to add two. Then, click the Move Up or Move Down button to position one of the two separators at the beginning of the group and the other at the end.

To remove a button added from the Ribbon, right-click it on the Quick Access toolbar and then click the Remove from Quick Access Toolbar option on its shortcut menu.

Adding non-Ribbon commands to the Quick Access toolbar

You can also use the options on the Quick Access Toolbar tab of the Excel Options dialog box (refer to Figure 1-6) to add a button for any Excel command even if it isn't one of those displayed on the tabs of the Ribbon:

1. **Click the type of command you want to add to the Quick Access toolbar in the Choose Commands From drop-down list box.**

   The types of commands include the Popular Commands pull-down menu (the default) as well as each of the tabs that appear on the Ribbon. To display only the commands that are not displayed on the Ribbon, click Commands Not in the Ribbon near the top of the drop-down list. To display a complete list of the Excel commands, click All Commands near the top of the drop-down list.

2. **Click the command whose button you want to add to the Quick Access toolbar in the list box on the left.**

3. **Click the Add button to add the command button to the bottom of the list box on the right.**

4. **(Optional) To reposition the newly added command button so that it isn't the last one on the toolbar, click the Move Up button until it's in the desired position.**

5. **Click the OK button to close the Excel Options dialog box.**

If you've created favorite macros (see Chapter 12) that you routinely use and want to be able to run directly from the Quick Access toolbar, click Macros in the Choose Commands From drop-down list box in the Excel Options dialog box and then click the name of the macro to add followed by the Add button.

Having fun with the Formula bar

The Formula bar displays the cell address (determined by a column letter(s) followed by a row number) and the contents of the current cell. For example, cell A1 is the first cell of each worksheet at the intersection of column A and row 1; cell XFD1048576 is the last cell of each worksheet at the intersection of column XFD and row 1048576. The type of entry you make determines the contents of the current cell: text or numbers, for example, if you enter a heading or particular value, or the details of a formula if you enter a calculation.

The Formula bar has three sections:

- ✔ **Name box:** The left-most section that displays the address of the current cell address.

- ✔ **Formula bar buttons:** The second, middle section that appears as a rather nondescript button displaying only an indented circle on the left (used to narrow or widen the Name box) and the Insert Function button (labeled *fx*) on the right. When you start making or editing a cell entry, Cancel (an *X*) and Enter (a check mark) buttons appear between them.

- ✔ **Cell contents:** The third, right-most white area to the immediate right of the Insert Function button takes up the rest of the bar and expands as necessary to display really long cell entries that won't fit in the normal area.

The cell contents section of the Formula bar is important because it *always* shows you the contents of the cell even when the worksheet does not. (When you're dealing with a formula, Excel displays only the calculated result in the cell in the worksheet and not the formula by which that result is derived.) Additionally, you can edit the contents of the cell in this area at anytime. Similarly, when the cell contents area is blank, you know that the cell is empty as well.

How you assign 26 letters to 16,384 columns

When it comes to labeling the 16,384 columns of an Excel 2010 worksheet, our alphabet with its measly 26 letters is simply not up to the task. To make up the difference, Excel doubles the letters in the cell's column reference so that column AA follows column Z (after which you find column AB, AC, and so on) and then triples them so that column AAA follows column ZZ (after which you get column AAB, AAC, and the like). At the end of this letter tripling, the 16,384th and last column of the worksheet ends up being XFD so that the last cell in the 1,048,576th row has the cell address XFD1048576!

What to do in the Worksheet area

The Worksheet area is where most of the Excel spreadsheet action takes place because it's the place that displays the cells in different sections of the current worksheet and it's right inside the cells that you do all your spreadsheet data entry and formatting, not to mention a great deal of your editing.

To enter or edit data in a cell, that cell must be current. Excel indicates that a cell is current in three ways:

- ✔ The cell cursor — the dark black border surrounding the cell's entire perimeter — appears in the cell.
- ✔ The address of the cell appears in the Name box of the Formula bar.
- ✔ The cell's column letter(s) and row number are shaded (in a kind of an orange-beige color on most monitors) in the column headings and row headings that appear at the top and left of the Worksheet area, respectively.

Moving around the worksheet

An Excel worksheet contains far too many columns and rows for all a worksheet's cells to be displayed at one time regardless of how large your personal computer monitor screen is or how high the screen resolution. (After all, we're talking 17,179,869,184 cells total!) Therefore, Excel offers many methods for moving the cell cursor around the worksheet to the cell where you want to enter new data or edit existing data:

- ✔ Click the desired cell — assuming that the cell is displayed within the section of the sheet visible in the Worksheet area.

  Click the Name box, type the address of the desired cell, and then press the Enter key.
- ✔ Press F5 to open the Go To dialog box, type the address of the desired cell into its Reference text box, and then click OK.
- ✔ Use the cursor keys, as shown in Table 1-1, to move the cell cursor to the desired cell.
- ✔ Use the horizontal and vertical scroll bars at the bottom and right edge of the Worksheet area to move the part of the worksheet that contains the desired cell and then click the cell to put the cell cursor in it.

Keystroke shortcuts for moving the cell cursor

Excel offers a wide variety of keystrokes for moving the cell cursor to a new cell. When you use one of these keystrokes, the program automatically scrolls a new part of the worksheet into view, if this is required to move the cell pointer. In Table 1-1, I summarize these keystrokes, including how far each one moves the cell pointer from its starting position.

Table 1-1	Keystrokes for Moving the Cell Cursor
Keystroke	*Where the Cell Cursor Moves*
→ or Tab	Cell to the immediate right.
← or Shift+Tab	Cell to the immediate left.
↑	Cell up one row.
↓	Cell down one row.
Home	Cell in Column A of the current row.
Ctrl+Home	First cell (A1) of the worksheet.
Ctrl+End or End, Home	Cell in the worksheet at the intersection of the last column that has data in it and the last row that has data in it (that is, the last cell of the so-called active area of the worksheet).
Page Up	Cell one full screen up in the same column.
Page Down	Cell one full screen down in the same column.
Ctrl+→ or End, →	First occupied cell to the right in the same row that is either preceded or followed by a blank cell. If no cell is occupied, the pointer goes to the cell at the very end of the row.
Ctrl+← or End, ←	First occupied cell to the left in the same row that is either preceded or followed by a blank cell. If no cell is occupied, the pointer goes to the cell at the very beginning of the row.
Ctrl+↑ or End, ↑	First occupied cell above in the same column that is either preceded or followed by a blank cell. If no cell is occupied, the pointer goes to the cell at the very top of the column.
Ctrl+↓ or End, ↓	First occupied cell below in the same column that is either preceded or followed by a blank cell. If no cell is occupied, the pointer goes to the cell at the very bottom of the column.
Ctrl+Page Down	The cell pointer's location in the next worksheet of that workbook.
Ctrl+Page Up	The cell pointer's location in the previous worksheet of that workbook.

Note: In the case of those keystrokes that use arrow keys, you must either use the arrows on the cursor keypad or else have the Num Lock disengaged on the numeric keypad of your keyboard.

The keystrokes that combine the Ctrl or End key with an arrow key listed in Table 1-1 are among the most helpful for moving quickly from one edge to the other in large tables of cell entries or for moving from table to table in a section of a worksheet with many blocks of cells.

When you use Ctrl and an arrow key to move from edge to edge in a table or between tables in a worksheet, you hold down Ctrl while you press one of the four arrow keys (indicated by the + symbol in keystrokes, such as Ctrl+→).

When you use End and an arrow-key alternative, you must press and then release the End key *before* you press the arrow key (indicated by the comma in keystrokes, such as End, →). Pressing and releasing the End key causes the End Mode indicator to appear on the status bar. This is your sign that Excel is ready for you to press one of the four arrow keys.

Because you can keep the Ctrl key depressed while you press the different arrow keys that you need to use, the Ctrl-plus-arrow-key method provides a more fluid method for navigating blocks of cells than the End-then-arrow-key method.

You can use the Scroll Lock key to "freeze" the position of the cell pointer in the worksheet so that you can scroll new areas of the worksheet in view with keystrokes, such as PgUp (Page Up) and PgDn (Page Down), without changing the cell pointer's original position. (In essence, making these keystrokes work in the same manner as the scroll bars.)

After engaging Scroll Lock, when you scroll the worksheet with the keyboard, Excel does not select a new cell while it brings a new section of the worksheet into view. To "unfreeze" the cell pointer when scrolling the worksheet via the keyboard, you just press the Scroll Lock key again.

Tips on using the scroll bars

To understand how scrolling works in Excel, imagine its humongous worksheet as a papyrus scroll attached to rollers on the left and right. To bring into view a section of papyrus hidden on the right, you crank the left roller until the section with the cells that you want to see appears. Likewise, to scroll into view a worksheet section hidden on the left, you crank the right roller until the section of cells appears.

You can use the horizontal scroll bar at the bottom of the Worksheet area to scroll back and forth through the columns of a worksheet and the vertical scroll bar to scroll up and down through its rows. To scroll a column or a row at a time in a particular direction, click the appropriate scroll arrow at the ends of the scroll bar. To jump immediately back to the originally displayed area of the worksheet after scrolling through single columns or rows in this fashion, simply click the area in the scroll bar that now appears in front of or after the scroll bar.

You can resize the horizontal scroll bar making it wider or narrower by dragging the button that appears to the immediate left of its left scroll arrow. Just keep in mind when working in a workbook that contains a whole bunch of worksheets that widening the horizontal scroll bar can hide the display of the workbook's later sheet tabs.

To scroll very quickly through columns or rows of the worksheet, hold down the Shift key and then drag the scroll button in the appropriate direction within the scroll bar until the columns or rows that you want to see appear on the screen in the Worksheet area. When you hold down the Shift key while you scroll, the scroll button within the scroll bar becomes skinny and a ScreenTip appears next to the scroll bar, keeping you informed of the letter(s) of the columns or the numbers of the rows that you're whizzing through.

If your mouse has a wheel, you can use it to scroll directly through the columns and rows of the worksheet without using the horizontal or vertical scroll bars. Simply position the white cross mouse pointer in the center of the Worksheet area and then hold down the wheel button of the mouse. When the mouse pointer changes to a four-pointed arrow with a black dot in its center, drag the mouse pointer in the appropriate direction (left and right to scroll through columns or up and down to scroll through rows) until the desired column or row comes into view in the Worksheet area.

The only disadvantage to using the scroll bars to move around is that the scroll bars bring only new sections of the worksheet into view — they don't actually change the position of the cell cursor. If you want to start making entries in the cells in a new area of the worksheet, you still have to remember to select the cell (by clicking it) or the group of cells (by dragging through them) where you want the data to appear before you begin entering the data.

Surfing the sheets in a workbook

Each new workbook you open in Excel 2010 contains three blank worksheets, each with its own 16,384 columns and 1,048,576 rows (giving you a truly staggering 51,539,607,552 blank cells!). But, that's not all. If ever you need more worksheets in your workbook, you can add them simply by clicking the Insert Worksheet button that appears to the immediate right of the last sheet tab (see Figure 1-7) or by pressing Shift+F11.

Figure 1-7:
The Sheet
Tab scroll
buttons,
sheet tabs,
and Insert
Worksheet
button
enable you
to activate
your work-
sheets and
add to them.

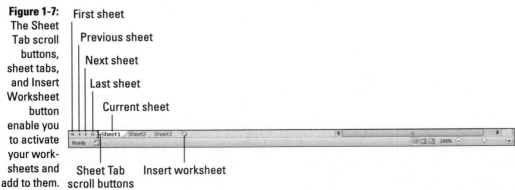

First sheet

Previous sheet

Next sheet

Last sheet

Current sheet

Sheet Tab   Insert worksheet
scroll buttons

One reason for adding extra sheets to a workbook

You may wonder why anyone would ever need more than three worksheets given just how many cells each individual sheet contains. The truth is that it's all about how you choose to structure a particular spreadsheet rather than running out of places to put the data. For example, suppose that you need to create a workbook that contains budgets for all the various departments in your corporation, you may decide to devote an individual worksheet to each department (with the actual budget spreadsheet tables laid out in the same manner on each sheet) rather than placing all the tables in different sections of the same sheet. Using this kind of one-sheet-per-budget layout makes it much easier for you to find each budget, print each one as a separate page of a report, and, if ever necessary, to consolidate the data in a separate summary worksheet.

On the left side of the bottom of the Worksheet area, the Sheet Tab scroll buttons appear followed by the actual tabs for the worksheets in your workbook and the Insert Worksheet button. To activate a worksheet for editing, you select it by clicking its sheet tab. Excel lets you know what sheet is active by displaying the sheet name in boldface type and making its tab appear on top of the others.

Don't forget the Ctrl+Page Down and Ctrl+Page Up shortcut keys for selecting the next and previous sheet, respectively, in your workbook.

If your workbook contains too many sheets for all the tabs to display at the bottom of the Worksheet area, use the Sheet Tab scroll buttons to bring new tabs into view (so that you can then click them to activate them). You click the Next Sheet button to scroll the next hidden sheet tab into view or the Last Sheet button to scroll the last group of completely or partially hidden tabs into view.

Showing off the Status bar

The Status bar is the last component at the very bottom of the Excel program window (see Figure 1-8). The Status bar contains the following:

- **Mode indicator** that shows the current state of the Excel program (Ready, Edit, and so on) as well as any special keys that are engaged (Caps Lock, Num Lock, and Scroll Lock).

- **AutoCalculate indicator** that displays the average and sum of all the numerical entries in the current cell selection along with the count of every cell in the selection.

✔ **Layout selector** that enables you to select between three layouts for the Worksheet area: Normal, the default view that shows only the worksheet cells with the column and row headings; Page Layout View that adds rulers, page margins, and shows page breaks for the worksheet; and Page Break Preview that enables you to adjust the paging of a report. (See Chapter 5 for details.)

✔ **Zoom slider** that enables you to zoom in and out on the cells in the Worksheet area by dragging the slider to the right or left, respectively.

Figure 1-8:
The Status bar displays the program's current standing and enables you to select new worksheet views.

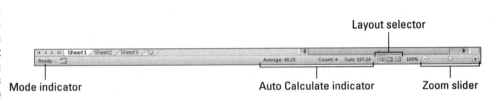

Layout selector

Mode indicator   Auto Calculate indicator   Zoom slider

The Num Lock indicator tells you that you can use the numbers on the numeric keypad for entering values in the worksheet. This keypad will most often be separate from the regular keyboard (on the right side if you're using a separate keyboard) and embedded in keys on the right side of the keyboard on almost all laptop computers where the keyboard is built in to the computer.

Launching and Quitting Excel

Excel 2010 runs under both the older Windows XP operating system and the newer Vista and Windows 7 operating systems. Because of changes made to the Start menu in Windows Vista and Windows 7, the procedure for starting Excel from these versions of Windows is a bit different from Windows XP.

Starting Excel from the Start menu

You can use the Start Search box at the bottom of the Windows Vista Start menu or the Search Programs and Files search box on the Windows 7

Start menu to locate Excel on your computer and launch the program in no time at all:

1. **Click the Start button on the Windows taskbar to open the Windows Start menu.**

2. **Click the Start menu's search text box and type the letters** exc **to have Windows locate Microsoft Office Excel 2010 on your computer.**

3. **Click the Microsoft Excel 2010 option that now appears in the left Programs column on the Start menu.**

If you have more time on your hands, you can also launch Excel from the Windows Start menu by going through the rigmarole of clicking Start➪All Programs➪Microsoft Office➪Microsoft Excel 2010.

Starting Excel from the Windows XP Start menu

When starting Excel 2010 from the Windows XP Start menu, you follow these simple steps:

1. **Click the Start button on the Windows taskbar to open the Windows Start menu.**

2. **With the mouse, highlight All Programs on the Start menu and then Microsoft Office on the Start continuation menu before clicking the Microsoft Excel 2010 option on the Microsoft Office continuation menu.**

Pinning a Microsoft Excel 2010 option on your Windows Start menu

If you use Excel all the time, you may want to make its program option a permanent part of the Windows Start menu. To do this, you pin the program option to the Start menu (and the steps for doing this are the same in Windows XP as they are in Windows Vista and Windows 7):

1. **Click the Windows Start button and then highlight the All Programs option on the Start menu.**

   Windows XP opens a continuation menu from its Start menu and Windows Vista and Windows 7 display a new menu of program options on their Start menus.

2. **Highlight the Microsoft Office option on the Windows XP continuation menu or click the Microsoft Office option on the Windows Vista/7 Start menu.**

   Windows XP displays a continuation menu with a list of all the Office 2010 programs installed on your computer. Windows Vista and Windows 7 display a submenu listing the Office 2010 programs.

3. **Right-click Microsoft Excel 2010 on the Windows continuation or submenu to open its shortcut menu.**

4. **Click Pin to Start Menu on the shortcut menu.**

 After pinning Excel in this manner, the Microsoft Excel 2010 option always appears in the upper section of the left-hand column of the Windows Start menu and you can then launch Excel simply by clicking the Windows Start button and then clicking this menu option.

 After you pin the Microsoft Excel 2010 option on to the Windows 7 Start menu, whenever you highlight this menu item, Windows 7 automatically expands the Start menu to display a list of your recently opened Excel workbook files. You can then open one of these files for further editing at the same time you launch the Excel 2010 program by clicking its filename on the Start menu.

Adding a Microsoft Excel 2010 shortcut to your Windows desktop

Some people prefer having the Excel program icon appear on the Windows desktop so that they can launch the program from the desktop by double-clicking this program icon. To create a Microsoft Excel 2010 program shortcut for your Windows desktop, you follow these steps:

1. **Click the Windows Start button and then highlight the All Programs option on the Start menu.**

   Windows XP opens a continuation menu from its Start menu and Windows Vista and Windows 7 display a new menu of program options on their Start menus.

2. **Highlight the Microsoft Office option on the Windows XP continuation menu or click the Microsoft Office option on the Windows Vista/ Windows 7 Start menu.**

   Windows XP displays a continuation menu with a list of all the Office 2010 programs installed on your computer. Windows Vista and Windows 7 display a submenu listing the Office 2010 programs.

3. **Right-click Microsoft Excel 2010 on the Windows continuation or sub-menu to open its shortcut menu.**

4. **Highlight the Send To option on this menu and then click Desktop (Create Shortcut) on the continuation shortcut menu.**

   Windows adds a Microsoft Excel 2010 shortcut icon to your Windows desktop that launches the program when you double-click it or right-click it and then click the Open option.

Adding Excel to the Windows Quick Launch toolbar

If you want to be able to launch Excel 2010 by clicking a single button, drag the Excel icon for your Windows Vista or Windows XP desktop shortcut to the Quick Launch toolbar to the immediate right of the Start button at the beginning of the Windows taskbar. When you position the icon on this tool-bar, Windows indicates where the new Excel button will appear by drawing a black, vertical I-beam in front of or between the existing buttons on this bar. As soon as you release the mouse button, Windows adds an Excel 2010 button to the Quick Launch toolbar that enables you to launch the program by a single click of its icon.

Pinning an Excel icon to the Windows 7 taskbar

If your computer is running Windows 7, you can add a Microsoft Excel 2010 icon to the taskbar in addition to the standard Internet Explorer, Windows Explorer, and Windows Media Player buttons.

All you do is drag and drop the Microsoft Excel 2010 icon that either you pinned to the Windows Start menu or you added as a shortcut to the Windows desktop into its desired position on the Windows 7 taskbar. (See "Pinning a Microsoft Excel 2010 option on your Windows Start menu" and "Adding a Microsoft Excel 2010 shortcut to your Windows desktop" earlier in this chapter for details.)

After pinning a Microsoft Excel 2010 icon to the Windows 7 taskbar, the button appears on the Windows taskbar each time you start your computer, and you can launch the Excel program simply by single clicking its icon.

Exiting Excel

When you're ready to call it a day and quit Excel, you have several choices for shutting down the program:

- ✔ Choose File➪Exit.
- ✔ Press Alt+FX or Alt+F4.
- ✔ Click the Close button (the X) in the upper-right corner of the Excel program window.

If you try to exit Excel after working on a workbook and you haven't saved your latest changes, the program displays an alert box querying whether you want to save your changes. To save your changes before exiting, click the Save command button. (For detailed information on saving documents, see Chapter 2.) If you've just been playing around in the worksheet and don't want to save your changes, you can abandon the document by clicking the Don't Save button.

Help Is on the Way

You can get online help with Excel 2010 anytime that you need it while using the program. Simply click the Help button (the button with the question mark icon to the immediate right of the Minimize the Ribbon button on the right side of the program window opposite the Ribbon's tabs) or press F1 to open a separate Excel Help window. (See Figure 1-9.)

When the Excel Help window opens, Excel attempts to use your Internet connection to update its topics. The opening Help window contains links that you can click to get information on what's new in the program.

To get help with a particular command or function, use the Search text box at the top of the Excel Help window. Type keywords or a phrase describing your topic (such as "print preview" or "printing worksheets") in this text box and then press Enter or click the Search button. The Excel Help window then presents a list of links to related help topics that you can click to display the information.

To print the help topic displayed in the Excel Help window, click the Print button (with the printer icon) on its toolbar. Excel then opens a Print dialog box where you can select the printer and options to use in printing the information.

To display a table of contents with all the main categories and subtopics arranged hierarchically, click the Show Table of Contents button (with the book icon) on the toolbar.

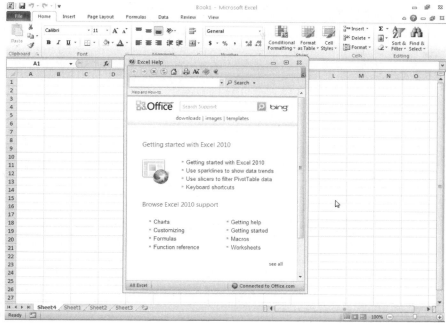

Figure 1-9:
The Excel
Help
window
automatically
connects
you to the
Internet
when you
open it.

Migrating to Excel 2010 from Earlier Versions Using Pull-down Menus

If you're a brand new Excel user or have had some experience with Excel 2007, you're going to take to Excel 2010's Ribbon User Interface like a duck to water. However, if you're coming to Excel 2010 as a dedicated user of earlier Excel versions (Excel 97 all the way through Excel 2003), the first time you launch Excel 2010 and take a gander at the Ribbon, you're probably going to feel more like someone just threw you into the deep end of the pool without a life preserver.

Don't panic! Simply use this section of the chapter as your Excel 2010 life preserver. It's intended to get you oriented, keep your head above water, and have you swimming with the new interface in no time at all. Just give me five minutes of your precious time and I promise I'll have you up and running with Excel 2010 and maybe even smiling again. Now, take a deep breath, and here we go. . . .

First, the bad news: There is *no* Classic mode in Excel 2010 that will magically turn that fat, screen real estate–stealing Ribbon back into those sleek, tried and true pull-down menus (thanks Microsoft, I needed that!). After the wonderful designers and engineers at Microsoft got through dumping all the pull-down menus and toolbars that you worked so diligently to master and on which you relied every Excel workday of your life, there was just nothing left for them to hang a Classic mode onto.

Now, for the good news: You really don't need a Classic mode — you just need to find out where those scoundrel engineers went and put all the stuff you used to do so effortlessly in versions of Excel before the Ribbon User Interface. After all, you already know what most of those pull-down menu items and toolbar buttons do; all you have to do is locate them.

Cutting the Ribbon down to size

Want to get that busy Ribbon out of your face? At this point, it's just taking up valuable space and probably making you crazy. So, please double-click any one of the tabs or press Ctrl+F1 right now to cut the Ribbon display down to only its tabs. Single-clicking a tab then temporarily redisplays the Ribbon until you select one of its command buttons, whereas pressing Ctrl+F1 a second time redisplays the Ribbon and keeps it open in all its glory.

When only the tabs — Home through View — are showing at the top of the Excel program window, you should feel a whole lot more comfortable with the screen. The Excel 2010 screen is then as clean and uncluttered, if not more, as the earlier version of Excel that you were using with only the Quick Access toolbar, Ribbon tabs, and Formula bar displayed above the Worksheet area.

Now, you're probably wondering where those Microsoft engineers moved the most important and commonly used pull-down menu commands. Table 1-2 shows the Excel 2010 equivalents for the menu commands you probably used most often in doing your work in the earlier version of Excel.

When a particular command is assigned to one of the tabs on the Ribbon, Table 1-2 lists only the tab and command button name without naming the group because the group name plays no part in selecting the command. For example, the table lists the View⇨Header and Footer command as Insert⇨Header & Footer without regard to the fact that the Header & Footer button is part of the Text group on the Insert tab.

Table 1-2	Excel 2010 Equivalents for Common Pull-down Menu Commands in Excel 2003		
Excel 2003 Command	*Excel 2010 Equivalent*	*Common Shortcut Keys*	*Excel 2010 Shortcut Keys*
File Menu			
File⇨New	File⇨New	Ctrl+N	Alt+FN
File⇨Open	File⇨Open	Ctrl+O	Alt+FO
File⇨Save	File⇨Save or Save button on the Quick Access toolbar	Ctrl+S	Alt+FS
File⇨Save As	File⇨Save As	F12	Alt+FA
File⇨Print	File⇨Print	Ctrl+P	Alt+FP
File⇨Send To⇨Mail Recipient	File⇨Share⇨ Send Using Email		Alt+FHE
File⇨Send To⇨ Recipient Using Internet Fax Service	File⇨Share⇨ Send as Internet Fax		Alt+FHIF
File⇨Close	File⇨Close	Ctrl+W	Alt+FC
Edit Menu			
Edit⇨Office Clipboard	Home⇨Clipboard group's dialog box launcher		Alt+HFO
Edit⇨Clear⇨All	Home⇨Clear (eraser icon)⇨Clear All		Alt+HEA
Edit⇨Clear⇨Formats	Home⇨Clear (eraser icon)⇨Clear Formats		Alt+HEF
Edit⇨Clear⇨Contents	Home⇨Clear (eraser icon) ⇨Clear Contents	Delete key	Alt+HEC
Edit⇨Clear⇨Comments	Home⇨Clear (eraser icon) ⇨Clear Comments		Alt+HEM
Edit⇨Delete	Home⇨Delete		Alt+HD
Edit⇨Move or Copy Sheet	Home⇨Format⇨Move or Copy Sheet		Alt+HOM
Edit⇨Find	Home⇨Find & Select⇨ Find	Ctrl+F	Alt+HFDF
Edit⇨Replace	Home⇨Find & Select⇨ Replace	Ctrl+H	Alt+HFDR

(continued)

Table 1-2 *(continued)*

Excel 2003 Command	Excel 2010 Equivalent	Common Shortcut Keys	Excel 2010 Shortcut Keys
View Menu			
View⇨Header and Footer	Insert⇨Header & Footer		Alt+NH
View⇨Full Screen	View⇨Full Screen		Alt+WE
Insert Menu			
Insert⇨Cells	Home⇨Insert⇨ Insert Cells		Alt+HII
Insert⇨Rows	Home⇨Insert⇨ Insert Sheet Rows		Alt+HIR
Insert⇨Columns	Home⇨Insert⇨ Insert Sheet Columns		Alt+HIC
Insert⇨Worksheets	Home⇨Insert⇨Insert Sheet		Alt+HIS
Insert⇨Symbol	Insert⇨Symbol		Alt+NU
Insert⇨Page Break	Page Layout⇨Breaks⇨ Insert Page Break		Alt+PBI
Insert⇨Name⇨ Define	Formulas⇨Define Name⇨Define Name		Alt+MMD
Insert⇨Name⇨ Paste	Formulas⇨Use in Formula		Alt+MS
Insert⇨Name⇨ Create	Formulas⇨Create from Selection		Alt+MC
Insert⇨Name⇨Label	Formulas⇨Name Manager		Alt+MN
Insert⇨Comment	Review⇨New Comment		Alt+RC
Insert⇨Picture	Insert⇨Picture		Alt+NP
Insert⇨Hyperlink	Insert⇨Hyperlink	Ctrl+K	Alt+NI
Format Menu			
Format⇨Cells	Home⇨Format⇨ Format Cells	Ctrl+1	Alt+HOE
Format⇨Row⇨ Height	Home⇨Format⇨ Row Height		Alt+HOH
Format⇨Row⇨ AutoFit	Home⇨Format⇨ AutoFit Row Height		Alt+HOA

Excel 2003 Command	Excel 2010 Equivalent	Common Shortcut Keys	Excel 2010 Shortcut Keys
Format⇨Row⇨ Hide/Unhide	Home⇨Format⇨Hide & Unhide⇨Hide Rows/ Unhide Rows		Alt+HOUR/ Alt+HOUO
Format⇨Column⇨ Width	Home⇨Format⇨Column Width		Alt+HOW
Format⇨Column⇨Hide/ Unhide	Home⇨Format⇨Hide & Unhide⇨Hide Columns/ Unhide Columns		Alt+HOUC/ Alt+HOUL
Format⇨Column⇨ Standard Width	Home⇨Format⇨ Default Width		Alt+HOD
Format⇨Sheet⇨Rename	Home⇨Format⇨ Rename Sheet		Alt+HOR
Format⇨Sheet⇨Hide/ Unhide	Home⇨Format⇨ Hide & Unhide⇨ Hide Sheet/Unhide Sheet		Alt+HOUS/ Alt+HOUH
Format⇨Sheet⇨ Background	Page Layout⇨Background		Alt+PG
Format⇨Sheet⇨ Tab Color	Home⇨Format⇨Tab Color		Alt+HOT
Format⇨AutoFormat	Home⇨Format as Table		Alt+HT
Format⇨Conditional Formatting	Home⇨Conditional Formatting		Alt+HL
Format⇨Style	Home⇨Cell Styles		Alt+HJ
Tools Menu			
Tools⇨Spelling	Review⇨Spelling	F7	Alt+RS
Tools⇨Research	Review⇨Research		Alt+RR
Tools⇨Error Checking	Formulas⇨Error Checking		Alt+MK
Tools⇨Speech⇨ Show Text to Speech Toolbar	*Available only as custom Speak Cells, Speak Cells - Stop Speaking Cells, Speak Cells by Columns, Speak Cells by Rows, and Speak Cells on Enter buttons added to Quick Access toolbar*		

(continued)

Table 1-2 *(continued)*

Excel 2003 Command	Excel 2010 Equivalent	Common Shortcut Keys	Excel 2010 Shortcut Keys
Tools⇨Track Changes	Review⇨Track Changes		Alt+RG
Tools⇨Protection⇨ Protect Sheet	Review⇨Protect Sheet		Alt+RPS
Tools⇨Protection⇨Allow Users to Edit Ranges	Review⇨Allow Users to Edit Ranges		Alt+RU
Tools⇨Protection⇨ Protect Workbook	Review⇨Protect Workbook		Alt+RPW
Tools⇨Protection⇨ Protect and Share Workbook	Review⇨ Protect and Share Workbook		Alt+RO
Tools⇨Macro	View⇨Macros	Alt+F8	Alt+WMV
Tools⇨Add-Ins	File⇨Options⇨Add-Ins		Alt+FTAA and then Alt+G
Tools⇨ AutoCorrect Options	File⇨Options⇨Proofing⇨ AutoCorrect Options		Alt+FTP and then Alt+A
Tools⇨Options	File⇨Options		Alt+FT
Data Menu			
Data⇨Sort	Home⇨Sort & Filter⇨ Custom Sort		Alt+HSU
Data⇨Filter⇨ AutoFilter	Data⇨Filter		Alt+AT
Data⇨Filter⇨ Advanced Filter	Data⇨Advanced		Alt+AQ
Data⇨Form	*Available only as a custom Form button added to Quick Access toolbar*		
Data⇨Subtotals	Data⇨Subtotal		Alt+AB
Data⇨Validation	Data⇨Data Validation⇨ Data Validation		Alt+AVV
Data⇨Table	Data⇨What-If Analysis⇨ Data Table		Alt+AWT

Excel 2003 Command	Excel 2010 Equivalent	Common Shortcut Keys	Excel 2010 Shortcut Keys
Data⇨Text to Columns	Data⇨Text to Columns		Alt+AE
Data⇨Consolidate	Data⇨Consolidate		Alt+AN
Data⇨Group and Outline	Data⇨Group/Ungroup		Alt+AG/ Alt+AU
Data⇨PivotTable and PivotChart Report	Insert⇨PivotTable⇨ PivotTable/PivotChart		Alt+NVT/ Alt+NVC
Data⇨Import External Data	Data⇨From Other Sources		Alt+AFO
Window Menu			
Window⇨New Window	View⇨New Window		Alt+WN
Window⇨Arrange	View⇨Arrange All		Alt+WA
Window⇨Compare Side by Side	View⇨View Side by Side (two-page icon in Window group)		Alt+WB
Window⇨Hide, Unhide	View⇨Hide/Unhide		Alt+WH/ Alt+WU
Window⇨Split	View⇨Split		Alt+WS
Window⇨Freeze Panes	View⇨Freeze Panes		Alt+WF

For the most part, the pull-down menu commands listed in Table 1-2 are logically located. The ones that take the most getting used to are the Header & Footer and PivotTable/Chart commands that are located on the Insert tab rather than the View tab and Data tab as might be expected given they inhabited, respectively, the View and Data pull-down menus in earlier Excel versions. Additionally, the worksheet background command ended up all by its lonesome on the Page Layout tab rather than going to the Home tab with all its fellow formatting commands.

Finding the Standard toolbar buttons equivalents

If you're like me, you came to rely heavily on the buttons of the Standard toolbar in doing all sorts of everyday tasks in earlier versions of Excel. Table

1-3 shows you the Excel 2010 equivalents for the buttons on the Standard toolbar in Excel 2003. As you can see from this table, most of the Standard toolbar buttons are regulated to one of these places in Excel 2010:

 ✔ **Backstage View** activated by clicking the File tab or pressing Alt+F (New, Open, Save, Print)

 ✔ **Quick Access toolbar** (Save, Undo, and Redo)

 ✔ **Home tab** in the Clipboard group (Cut, Copy, Paste, and Format Painter) and Editing group (AutoSum, Sort Ascending, and Sort Descending)

Table 1-3	Excel 2010 Equivalents for the Standard Toolbar Buttons in Excel 2003		
Toolbar Button	*Excel 2010 Equivalent*	*Common Shortcut Keys*	*Excel 2010 Shortcut Keys*
New	File⇨New	Ctrl+N	Alt+FN
Open	File⇨Open	Ctrl+O	Alt+FO
Save	File⇨Save or Save button on Quick Access toolbar	Ctrl+S	Alt+FS
Permission	*Available only as a custom Permission button added to Quick Access toolbar*		
E-mail	File⇨Save & Send⇨Send Using E-mail		Alt+FDE
Print	Quick Print button on Quick Access toolbar		
Print Preview	File⇨Print		Alt+FP
Spelling	Review⇨Spelling	F7	Alt+RS
Research	Review⇨Research		Alt+RR
Cut	Home⇨Cut (scissors icon in Clipboard group)	Ctrl+X	Alt+HX
Copy	Home⇨Copy (double-sheet icon in Clipboard group)	Ctrl+C	Alt+HC
Paste	Home⇨Paste	Ctrl+V	Alt+HV

Toolbar Button	Excel 2010 Equivalent	Common Shortcut Keys	Excel 2010 Shortcut Keys
Format Painter	Home⇨Format Painter (brush icon in Clipboard group)		Alt+HFP
Undo	Undo button on Quick Access toolbar	Ctrl+Z	
Redo	Redo button on Quick Access toolbar	Ctrl+Y	
Insert Ink Annotations	Review⇨Start Inking (appears only on Tablet PCs or computers with a digital ink tablet)		Alt+RK
Insert Hyperlink	Insert⇨Hyperlink	Ctrl+K	Alt+NI
AutoSum	Home⇨AutoSum (Σ - Sigma icon)		Alt+HU
Sort Ascending	Home⇨Sort & Filter⇨Sort A to Z		Alt+HSS
Sort Descending	Home⇨Sort & Filter⇨Sort Z to A		Alt+HSO
Chart Wizard	*Not available except as specific chart type command buttons in the Charts group on the Insert tab*		
Drawing	*Not available except as command buttons in the Illustrations and Text groups on the Insert tab, and as custom buttons added to Quick Access toolbar*		
Zoom	View⇨Zoom		Alt+WQ
Microsoft Excel Help	Microsoft Office Excel Help button to the right of the Ribbon tabs	F1	

Because Excel 2010 supports only a single toolbar (the Quick Access toolbar), the Drawing toolbar disappears completely from Excel 2010, thus the Drawing button on the Standard toolbar has no equivalent. Most of its main features, including clip art, inserting graphics files, and creating diagrams and WordArt are now on the Insert tab. Also, Excel 2010 doesn't have an equivalent to the Chart Wizard button on the Standard toolbar because you can create a chart in a split-second by clicking the Column, Line, Pie, Bar, Area, Scatter, or Other Charts command buttons on the Insert tab (see Chapter 10).

Finding the Formatting toolbar buttons equivalents

Finding the Excel 2010 equivalents for the buttons on the Formatting toolbar in earlier versions of Excel couldn't be easier: Every one of the buttons on the Formatting toolbar is displayed prominently on the Home tab of the Ribbon. They're all easy to identify because they use the same icons as before and are located in the Font, Alignment, or Number group on the Home tab (refer to Figure 1-3).

In addition to the Font, Font Size, Bold, Italic, Underline, Borders, Fill Color, and Font Color buttons from the Formatting toolbar, the Font group also contains the following two buttons:

- ✔ **Increase Font Size** button that bumps up the current font size a point
- ✔ **Decrease Font Size** button that reduces the current font size by a point

In addition to the Left Align, Center, Right Align, Decrease Indent, Increase Indent, and Merge & Center buttons, the Alignment group also contains the following buttons:

- ✔ **Top Align** button that vertically aligns the data entered into the current cell selection with the top edge of the cell
- ✔ **Middle Align** button that vertically centers the data entered into the current cell selection
- ✔ **Bottom Align** button that aligns the data entered in the current cell selection with the bottom edge of the cell
- ✔ **Orientation** button that opens a pop-menu of orientation options that enable you to change the direction of the text entered into the current cell selection (by angling it up or down, converting it to vertical text, or rotating it up or down) and open the Alignment tab of the Format Cells dialog box
- ✔ **Wrap Text** button that applies wrap text to the current cell selection so that Excel expands the row heights as needed to fit all its text within the current column widths

In addition to the Percent Style, Comma Style, Increase Decimal, and Decrease Decimal buttons from the Formatting toolbar, the Numbers group contains the following buttons:

- **Accounting Number Format** button that enables you to select among several different currency formats from U.S. dollars to Swiss Francs, as well as to open the Number tab of the Format Cells dialog box with the Accounting number format selected

- **Number Format** button that opens a pop-up menu of different number options from General through Text, as well as opens the Number tab in the Format Cells dialog box when you select its More Number Formats option

Putting the Excel Quick Access toolbar to good use during the transition

Figure 1-10 shows you the Excel 2010 program window with the Ribbon minimized and a completely customized Quick Access toolbar moved down so that it appears under the tabs and above the Formula bar. This completely custom version of the Quick Access toolbar should seem very familiar to you: It contains every button from the Standard and Formatting toolbar in Excel 2003 with the exception of the Permission, Drawing, Zoom, and Help buttons. The Permission button is so esoteric and seldom used that I didn't bother to add it. The Drawing button has no equivalent in Excel 2010. And neither the Zoom button nor the Help button is really needed because the Zoom slider that enables you to quickly select a new screen magnification percentage always displays in the lower-right corner of the Excel 2010 Status bar and the Help button always displays on the right side of the bar containing the Ribbon tabs.

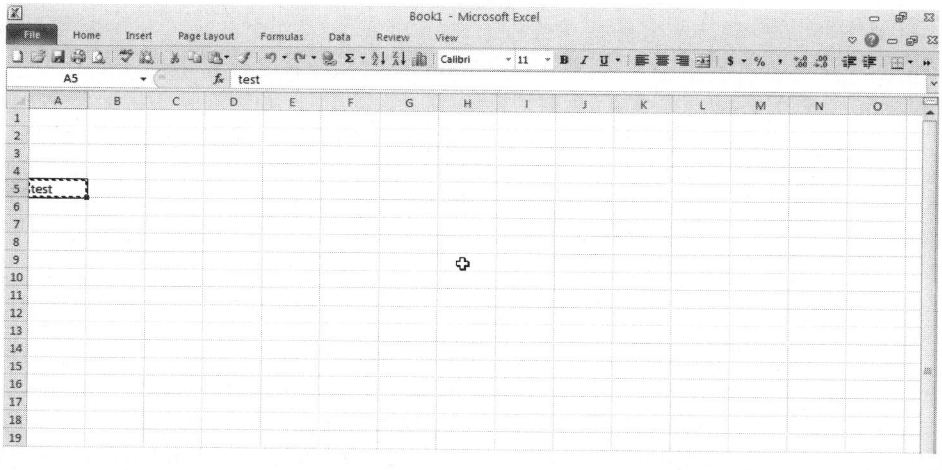

Figure 1-10: After minimizing the Ribbon and adding most of the buttons from the Standard and Formatting toolbars to the Quick Access toolbar.

To customize your Quick Access toolbar so that it matches the one shown in Figure 1-10 with every button from the Standard and Formatting toolbars except the Permission, Drawing, Zoom, and Help buttons, follow these steps:

1. **Click the Customize Quick Access Toolbar button at the end of the Quick Access toolbar and then click the Show Below the Ribbon option.**

   When filling the Quick Access toolbar with buttons, you need to place the bar beneath the Ribbon so that it won't crowd the name of the current workbook file.

2. **Click the Customize Quick Access Toolbar button again and this time click the More Commands option.**

   Excel opens the Excel Options dialog box with the Quick Access Toolbar tab selected. The Customize Quick Access Toolbar list box on the right side of this dialog box shows all three of the default buttons in the order in which they now appear on the toolbar.

3. **Click the New option in the Popular Commands list followed by the Add button.**

   Excel adds the New command button at the end of the toolbar indicated by the appearance of the New button at the bottom of the list in the Customize Quick Access Toolbar list box on the right.

4. **Click the Move Up button (with the triangle pointing upward) three times to move the New button to the top of the Customize Quick Access Toolbar list box and the first position on the Quick Access toolbar.**

   The New button is now in front of the Save button on the toolbar.

5. **Click the Open option in the Popular Commands list box on the left and then click the Add button.**

   Excel inserts the Open button in the Customize Quick Access Toolbar list box between the New and the Save buttons, which is exactly where it appears on the Standard toolbar.

6. **Click the Save button in the Customize Quick Access Toolbar list box on the right to select this button. Then, click the Quick Print option in the Popular Commands list box on the left and click the Add button.**

   Excel inserts the Quick Print button after the Save button.

7. **Click the Print Preview button near the bottom of the Popular Commands list box and then click the Add button.**

   Excel inserts the Print Preview button after the Quick Print button in the Customize Quick Access Toolbar list box.

   Now, you need to add the Spelling and Research buttons. They are located on the Review tab in Excel 2010. Before you can add the buttons to the Quick Access toolbar, you need to replace Popular Commands with Review Tab by selecting this option on the Choose Commands From drop-down list.

8. **Click the Choose Commands From drop-down button and then click Review Tab in the drop-down list.**

   Excel now displays all the command buttons on the Review tab of the Ribbon in the list box below.

9. **Add the Spelling and Research buttons from the Review Tab list box to the Customize Quick Access Toolbar list box and position them so that they appear one after the other following the Print Preview button.**

   Next, you need to add the Cut, Copy, Paste, and Format Painter buttons to the Quick Access toolbar. These command buttons are on the Home tab.

10. **Click the Home Tab option in the Choose Commands From drop-down list and then add the Cut, Copy, and Paste buttons to the Customize Quick Access Toolbar in this order in front of the Undo button.**

    Note when adding the Paste button that Choose Commands From displays two Paste buttons. The first is the regular Paste button that was on the Standard toolbar. The second is a Paste button with a drop-down button that, when clicked, opens a drop-down menu with all the special Paste options. You can add either one, although the second Paste button with the drop-down menu is much more versatile.

11. **Click the Format Painter option in the Home Tab list box and then click the Add button.**

    Excel adds the Format Painter button after the Paste button in the Customize Quick Access Toolbar list box on the right.

12. **Click the Redo button in the Customize Quick Access Toolbar list box to select its icon, click Insert Tab on the Choose Commands From drop-down list, and then add the Insert Hyperlink button to the Quick Access toolbar.**

13. **Add the remaining Standard toolbar buttons — AutoSum, Sort Ascending, Sort Descending, and Create Chart — to the Quick Access toolbar.**

    The AutoSum, Sort Ascending, and Sort Descending buttons are available in the Home Tab list box and the Create Chart button (the closest thing to the Chart Wizard in Excel 2010) is on the Insert Tab list box.

14. **Add the buttons on the Formatting toolbar to the Quick Access toolbar in the order in which they appear.**

    The Formatting toolbar contains these tools all found on the Home tab:

    • Font

    • Font Size

- Bold
- Italic
- Underline
- Align Text Left
- Center
- Align Text Right
- Merge & Center
- Accounting Number Format (corresponding to the Currency Style button)
- Percent Style
- Comma Style
- Increase Decimal
- Decrease Decimal
- Decrease Indent
- Increase Indent
- Borders
- Fill Color
- Font Color

15. Click the OK button to close the Excel Options dialog box and return to the Excel program window.

Your Quick Access toolbar should now have the same buttons as the one shown in Figure 1-10.

After adding all the buttons on the Standard and the Formatting toolbars (save the Permission button that almost nobody uses, the Drawing button that has no equivalent in Excel 2010, and the Zoom and Help buttons that are always available in the program window), the Quick Access toolbar fills the entire width of the screen on many monitors. If you add extra buttons that can't fit on the single row above the Formula bar, Excel automatically adds a More Controls button to the end of the Quick Access toolbar. You then click the More Controls button to display a pop-up menu containing the unseen buttons of the toolbar.

To add vertical separators to divide the buttons into groups, as in the original Standard and Formatting toolbars and shown in Figure 1-10, click the <Separator> option located at the top of each Choose Commands From list box followed by the Add button.

Getting good to go with Excel 2010

The version of the Excel 2010 program window shown in Figure 1-10 with the Ribbon minimized to just tabs and the Quick Access toolbar displayed above the Formula bar with all but a few of the buttons from the Standard and Formatting toolbars is as close as I can get you to any sort of Excel 2003 Classic mode.

Combine this simplified screen layout with the common shortcut keys (see Table 1-2) that you already know and you should be pretty much good to go with Excel 2010. Of course, the Ribbon can't always stay reduced to just its tabs. As you find out while you explore the features covered in the remaining chapters, there'll be times when you need the tools (especially in the form of those fantastic galleries) that a particular tab has to offer.

The only other issues that should be of any concern to you right now are the new Excel 2010 file formats and running all those Excel macros on which you've come to rely.

Dealing with the new Excel file formats

Yes, it's true that Excel 2010 naturally saves its workbooks in the XLSX file format introduced in Excel 2007 (a format that Microsoft insists is a truly "open" XML file format and not at all proprietary as were all the previous Excel file formats).

Fortunately, Excel 2010 has no trouble opening any workbook files saved in the good old XLS file format used by versions 97 through 2003. More importantly, the program automatically saves all editing changes you make to these files in this original file format.

Therefore, you don't have a worry in the world when it comes to making simple edits to existing spreadsheets with Excel 2010. Simply, open the workbook file and then make all the necessary changes. When you finish, click the Save button on the Quick Access toolbar to save your changes in the good old XLS file format that everybody in the office who is still using a previous version of Excel can still open, edit, and print. Excel also warns you should you ever add a new 2007 or 2010 element to the existing workbook that isn't supported by earlier versions.

The challenge comes when you need to use Excel 2010 to create a brand new spreadsheet. The program automatically wants to save all new workbooks in its fancy new XLSX file format (see Chapter 2 for a complete rundown on this new workbook file format and the pros and cons of using it). If you don't want to save your workbook in this format, you need to remember to click the Save as Type drop-down button in the Save As dialog box and then click the Excel 97-2003 Workbook (*.xls) option on its drop-down menu before you click Save.

If you work in an office environment where all the workbooks you produce with Excel 2010 must be saved in the old Excel 97-2003 format for compatibility sake, you can change the program's default Save setting so that the program always saves all new workbooks in the old file format. To do this, open the Save tab of the Excel Options dialog box (File➪Options➪Save or Alt+FTS) and then click Excel 97-2003 Workbook in the Save Files in This Format drop-down list box before you click OK.

Using your macros

The good news is that Excel 2010 supports the creating and running of macros, using the same Microsoft Visual Basic for Applications of earlier versions. It even enables you to edit these macros in a version of VBA Editor, if you're sufficiently skilled to do so.

The biggest problem with macros comes about if you have a tendency, as I do, to map your global macros (the ones you save in the PERSONAL.XLSB workbook so that they're available when working in any Excel workbook) onto custom pull-down menus and toolbars. Because Excel 2010 retains only the File tab and Quick Access toolbar, none of the custom menus and toolbars to which you've assigned macros comes over to Excel 2010. Although the macros are still a part of their respective workbooks and continue to run, you must now run all macros either using keyboard shortcuts you assigned to them or via the Macro dialog box (click View➪Macros➪View Macros or press Alt+WMV or Alt+F8).

You can assign macros to buttons on the Quick Access toolbar and then run them by clicking their buttons. The only problem is that all macros you assign to this toolbar use the same generic macro button icon so that the only way to differentiate the macros is through the ScreenTip that appears when you position the mouse over the button.

To assign a macro to a generic macro on the Quick Access toolbar, open the Quick Access Toolbar tab of the Excel Options dialog box (File➪Options➪ Quick Access Toolbar or Alt+FTQ) and then select Macros in the Choose Commands From drop-down list box. Excel then displays the names of all the macros in the current workbook (including all global macros saved in the PERSONAL.XLSB workbook) in the Choose Commands From list box. To assign a macro to a macro button, click its name in this list box and then click the Add button. You can then move the macro button to the desired position on the Quick Access toolbar with the Move Up and Move Down buttons and, if you so desire, make it part of a separate section on the toolbar by adding a vertical separator with the <Separator> option before and after its button.

Chapter 2

Creating a Spreadsheet from Scratch

After you know how to launch Excel 2010, it's time to find out how not to get yourself into trouble when actually using it! In this chapter, you find out how to put all kinds of information into all those little, blank worksheet cells I describe in Chapter 1. Here you find out about the Excel AutoCorrect and AutoComplete features and how they can help cut down on errors and speed up your work. You also get some basic pointers on other smart ways to minimize the drudgery of data entry, such as filling out a series of entries with the AutoFill feature and entering the same thing in a bunch of cells all at the same time.

After discovering how to fill up a worksheet with all this raw data, you find out what has to be the most important lesson of all — how to save all that information on disk so that you don't ever have to enter the stuff again!

So What Ya Gonna Put in That New Workbook of Yours?

When you start Excel without specifying a document to open — which is what happens when you start the program from the Windows 7, Windows Vista, or Windows XP Start menu (refer to Chapter 1) — you get a blank workbook in a new workbook window. This workbook, temporarily named Book1, contains three blank worksheets (Sheet1, Sheet2, and Sheet3). To begin to work on a new spreadsheet, you simply start entering information in the first sheet of the Book1 workbook window.

The ins and outs of data entry

Here are a few simple guidelines (a kind of data-entry etiquette, if you will) to keep in mind when you create a spreadsheet in Sheet1 of your new workbook:

- ✔ Whenever you can, organize your information in tables of data that use adjacent (neighboring) columns and rows. Start the tables in the upper-left corner of the worksheet and work your way down the sheet, rather than across the sheet, whenever possible. When it's practical, separate each table by no more than a single column or row.

- ✔ When you set up these tables, don't skip columns and rows just to "space out" the information. In Chapter 3, you see how to place as much white space as you want between information in adjacent columns and rows by widening columns, heightening rows, and changing the alignment.

- ✔ Reserve a single column at the left edge of the table for the table's row headings.

- ✔ Reserve a single row at the top of the table for the table's column headings.

- ✔ If your table requires a title, put the title in the row above the column headings. Put the title in the same column as the row headings. You can get information on how to center this title across the columns of the entire table in Chapter 3.

In Chapter 1, I make a big deal about how big each of the worksheets in a workbook is. You may wonder why I'm now on your case about not using that space to spread out the data that you enter into it. After all, given all the real estate that comes with each Excel worksheet, you'd think conserving space would be one of the last things you'd have to worry about.

You'd be 100 percent correct . . . except for one little, itty-bitty thing: Space conservation in the worksheet equals memory conservation. You see, while a table of data grows and expands into columns and rows in new areas of the worksheet, Excel decides that it had better reserve a certain amount of computer memory and hold it open just in case you go crazy and fill that area with cell entries. Therefore, if you skip columns and rows that you really don't need to skip (just to cut down on all that cluttered data), you end up wasting computer memory that could store more information in the worksheet.

You must remember this . . .

Now you know: The amount of computer memory available to Excel determines the ultimate size of the spreadsheet you can build, not the total number of cells in the worksheets of your workbook. When you run out of memory, you've effectively run out of space — no matter how many columns and rows are still available. To maximize the information you can get into a single worksheet, always adopt the "covered wagon" approach to worksheet design by keeping your data close together.

Doing the Data-Entry Thing

Begin by reciting (in unison) the basic rule of worksheet data entry. All together now:

> To enter data in a worksheet, position the cell pointer in the cell where you want the data and then begin typing the entry.

Before you can position the cell pointer in the cell where you want the entry, Excel must be in Ready mode (look for Ready as the Mode indicator at the beginning of the Status bar). When you start typing the entry, however, Excel goes through a mode change from Ready to Enter mode (and *Enter* replaces *Ready* as the Mode indicator).

If you're not in Ready mode, try pressing Esc.

As soon as you begin typing in Enter mode, the characters that you type in a cell in the worksheet area simultaneously appear on the Formula bar near the top of the screen. Typing something in the current cell also triggers a change to the Formula bar because two new buttons, Cancel and Enter, appear between the Name box drop-down button and the Insert Function button.

As you continue to type, Excel displays your progress on the Formula bar and in the active cell in the worksheet (see Figure 2-1). However, the insertion point (the flashing vertical bar that acts as your cursor) displays only at the end of the characters displayed in the cell.

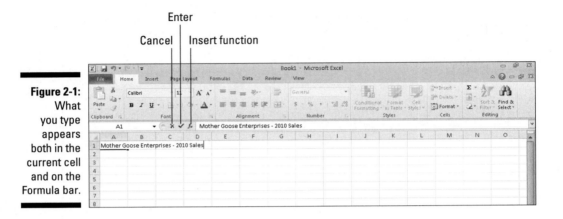

Figure 2-1:
What you type appears both in the current cell and on the Formula bar.

After you finish typing your cell entry, you still have to get it into the cell so that it stays put. When you do this, you also change the program from Enter mode back to Ready mode so that you can move the cell pointer to another cell and, perhaps, enter or edit the data there.

To complete your cell entry and, at the same time, get Excel out of Enter mode and back into Ready mode, you can click the Enter button on the Formula bar, press the Enter key, or press one of the arrow keys (↓, ↑, →, or ←) to move to another cell. You can also press the Tab key or Shift+Tab keys to complete a cell entry.

Now, even though each of these alternatives gets your text into the cell, each does something a little different afterward, so please take note:

- ✔ If you click the Enter button (the one with the check mark) on the Formula bar, the text goes into the cell, and the cell pointer just stays in the cell containing the brand-new entry.

- ✔ If you press the Enter key on your keyboard, the text goes into the cell, and the cell pointer moves down to the cell below in the next row.

- ✔ If you press one of the arrow keys, the text goes into the cell, and the cell pointer moves to the next cell in the direction of the arrow. Press ↓, and the cell pointer moves below in the next row just as it does when you finish off a cell entry with the Enter key. Press → to move the cell pointer right to the cell in the next column; press ← to move the cell pointer left to the cell in the previous column; and press ↑ to move the cell pointer up to the cell in the next row above.

Getting the Enter key to put the cell pointer where you want it

Excel automatically advances the cell pointer to the next cell down in the column every time you press Enter to complete the cell entry. If you want to customize Excel so that pressing Enter doesn't move the cell pointer when the program enters your data, or to have it move the cell pointer to the next cell up, left, or right, open the Advanced tab of the Excel Options dialog box (Alt+FTA).

To prevent the cell pointer from moving at all, select the After Pressing Enter, Move Selection check box to remove its check mark. To have the cell pointer move in another direction, click the Direction pop-up list box right below and then select the new direction you want to use (Right, Up, or Left). When you finish changing the settings, click OK or press Enter.

✔ If you press Tab, the text goes into the cell, and the cell pointer moves to the adjacent cell in the column on the immediate right (the same as pressing the → key). If you press Shift+Tab, the cell pointer moves to the adjacent cell in the column on the immediate left (the same as pressing the ← key) after putting in the text.

No matter which of the methods you choose when putting an entry in its place, as soon as you complete your entry in the current cell, Excel deactivates the Formula bar by removing the Cancel and Enter buttons. Thereafter, the data you entered continues to appear in the cell in the worksheet (with certain exceptions that I discuss later in this chapter), and every time you put the cell pointer into that cell, the data will reappear on the Formula bar as well.

If, while still typing an entry or after finishing typing but prior to completing the entry, you realize that you're just about to stick it in the wrong cell, you can clear and deactivate the Formula bar by clicking the Cancel button (the one with the X in it) or by pressing Esc. If, however, you don't realize that you had the wrong cell until after you enter your data there, you have to either move the entry to the correct cell (something you find out how to do in Chapter 4) or delete the entry (see Chapter 4) and then reenter the data in the correct cell.

It Takes All Types

Unbeknownst to you while you go about happily entering data in your spreadsheet, Excel constantly analyzes the stuff you type and classifies it into one of three possible data types: a piece of *text,* a *value,* or a *formula.*

If Excel finds that the entry is a formula, the program automatically calculates the formula and displays the computed result in the worksheet cell (you continue to see the formula itself, however, on the Formula bar). If Excel is satisfied that the entry does not qualify as a formula (I give you the qualifications for an honest-to-goodness formula a little later in this chapter), the program then determines whether the entry should be classified as text or as a value.

Excel makes this distinction between text and values so that it knows how to align the entry in the worksheet. It aligns text entries with the left edge of the cell and values with the right edge. Because most formulas work properly only when they are fed values, by differentiating text from values, the program knows which will and will not work in the formulas that you build. Suffice to say that you can foul up your formulas but good if they refer to any cells containing text where Excel expects values to be.

The telltale signs of text

A text entry is simply an entry that Excel can't pigeonhole as either a formula or value. This makes text the catchall category of Excel data types. As a practical rule, most text entries (also known as *labels*) are a combination of letters and punctuation or letters and numbers. Text is used mostly for titles, headings, and notes in the worksheet.

You can tell right away whether Excel has accepted a cell entry as text because text entries automatically align at the left edge of their cells. If the text entry is wider than the cell can display, the data spills into the neighboring cell or cells on the right, *as long as those cells remain blank* (see Figure 2-2).

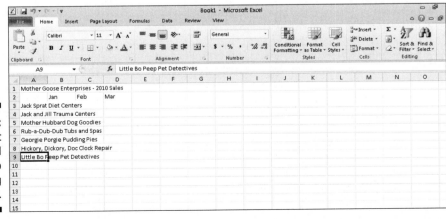

Figure 2-2:
Long text
entries spill
over into
neighboring
blank cells.

To Excel, text is nothing but a big zero

Use the AutoCalculate indicator to prove to yourself that Excel gives all text entries the value of 0 (zero). As an example, enter the number **10** in one cell and then some stupid piece of text, such as **Excel is like a box of chocolates**, in the cell directly below. Then drag up so that both cells (the one with 10 and the one with the text) are highlighted. Take a gander at the AutoCalculate indicator on the Status bar, and you see that it reads Average: 10, Count: 2, and Sum: 10, proving that the text adds nothing to the total value of these two cells.

If, sometime later, you enter information in a cell that contains spillover text from a cell to its left, Excel cuts off the spillover of the long text entry (see Figure 2-3). Not to worry: Excel doesn't actually lop these characters off the cell entry — it simply shaves the display to make room for the new entry. To redisplay the seemingly missing portion of the long text entry, you have to widen the column that contains the cell where the text is entered. (To find out how to do this, skip ahead to Chapter 3.)

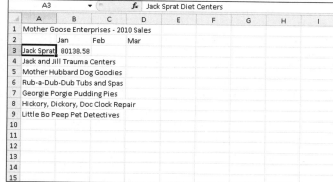

Figure 2-3:
Entries in cells to the right cut off the spillover text in cells on the left.

How Excel evaluates its values

Values are the building blocks of most of the formulas that you create in Excel. As such, values come in two flavors: numbers that represent quantities (*14* stores or *$140,000* dollars) and numbers that represent dates (*July 30, 1995*) or times (*2* p.m.).

You can tell whether Excel has accepted your entry as a value because values automatically align at the right edge of their cells. If the value that you enter is wider than the column containing the cell can display, Excel automatically converts the value to (of all things) *scientific notation*. To restore a value that's been converted into that weird scientific notation stuff to a regular number, simply widen the column for that cell. (Read how in Chapter 3.)

Making sure that Excel's got your number

When building a new worksheet, you'll probably spend a lot of your time entering numbers, representing all types of quantities from money that you made (or lost) to the percentage of the office budget that went to coffee and donuts. (You mean you don't get donuts?)

To enter a numeric value that represents a positive quantity, like the amount of money you made last year, just select a cell, type the numbers — for example, **459600** — and complete the entry in the cell by clicking the Enter button, pressing the Enter key, and so on. To enter a numeric value that represents a negative quantity, such as the amount of money the office spent on coffee and donuts last year, begin the entry with the minus sign or hyphen (–) before typing the numbers and then complete the entry. For example, **–175** (that's not too much to spend on coffee and donuts when you just made $459,600).

If you're trained in accounting, you can enclose the negative number (that's *expense* to you) in parentheses. You'd enter it like this: **(175)**. If you go to all the trouble to use parentheses for your negatives (expenses), Excel goes ahead and automatically converts the number so that it begins with a minus sign; if you enter **(175)** in the Coffee and Donut expense cell, Excel spits back –175. (Relax, you can find out how to get your beloved parentheses back for the expenses in your spreadsheet in Chapter 3.)

With numeric values that represent dollar amounts, like the amount of money you made last year, you can include dollar signs ($) and commas (,) just as they appear in the printed or handwritten numbers you're working from. Just be aware that when you enter a number with commas, Excel assigns a number format to the value that matches your use of commas. (For more information on number formats and how they are used, see Chapter 3.) Likewise, when you preface a financial figure with a dollar sign, Excel assigns an appropriate dollar-number format to the value (one that automatically inserts commas between the thousands).

When entering numeric values with decimal places, use the period as the decimal point. When you enter decimal values, the program automatically adds a zero before the decimal point (Excel inserts 0.34 in a cell when you enter **.34**) and drops trailing zeros entered after the decimal point (Excel inserts 12.5 in a cell when you enter **12.50**).

If you don't know the decimal equivalent for a value that contains a fraction, you can just go ahead and enter the value with its fraction. For example, if you don't know that 2.1875 is the decimal equivalent for 2³⁄₁₆, just type **2 3/16** (making sure to add a space between the 2 and 3) in the cell. After completing the entry, when you put the cell pointer in that cell, you see 2³⁄₁₆ in the cell of the worksheet, but 2.1875 appears on the Formula bar. As you see in Chapter 3, it's then a simple trick to format the display of 2³⁄₁₆ in the cell so that it matches the 2.1875 on the Formula bar.

If you need to enter simple fractions, such as ¾ or ⅝, you must enter them as a mixed number preceded by zero; for example, enter **0 3/4** or **0 5/8** (be sure to include a space between the zero and the fraction). Otherwise, Excel thinks that you're entering the dates March 4 (3/4) and May 8 (5/8).

When entering in a cell a numeric value that represents a percentage (so much out of a hundred), you have this choice:

- You can either divide the number by 100 and enter the decimal equivalent (by moving the decimal point two places to the left like your teacher taught you; for example, enter **.12** for 12 percent).

- You can enter the number with the percent sign (for example, enter **12%**).

Either way, Excel stores the decimal value in the cell (0.12 in this example). If you use the percent sign, Excel assigns a percentage-number format to the value in the worksheet so that it appears as 12%.

How to fix your decimal places (when you don't even know they're broken)

If you find that you need to enter a whole slew of numbers that use the same number of decimal places, you can turn on Excel's Fixed Decimal setting and have the program enter the decimals for you. This feature really comes in handy when you have to enter hundreds of financial figures that all use two decimal places (for example, for the number of cents).

To *fix* the number of decimal places in a numeric entry, follow these steps:

1. **Choose File⇨Options⇨Advanced or press Alt+FTA.**

   The Advanced tab of the Excel Options dialog box opens.

2. **Click the Automatically Insert a Decimal Point check box in the Editing Options section to fill it with a check mark.**

   By default, Excel fixes the decimal place two places to the left of the last number you type. To change the default Places setting, go to Step 3; otherwise move to Step 4.

Don't get in a fix over your decimal places!

When the Fixed Decimal setting is on, Excel adds a decimal point to all the numeric values that you enter. However, if you want to enter a number without a decimal point, or one with a decimal point in a position different from the one called for by this feature, you have to remember to type the decimal point (period) yourself. For example, to enter the number 1099 instead of 10.99 when the decimal point is fixed at two places, type **1099** followed immediately by a period (.) in the cell.

And, for heaven's sake, please don't forget to turn off the Fixed Decimal feature before you work on another worksheet or exit Excel. Otherwise, when you intend to enter values, such as 20, you'll end up with 0.2 instead, and you won't have a clue what's going on!

3. **(Optional) Type a new number in the Places text box or use the spinner buttons to change the value.**

   For example, you could change the Places setting to 3 to enter numbers with the following decimal placement: 00.000.

4. **Click OK or press Enter.**

   Excel displays the Fixed Decimal status indicator on the Status bar to let you know that the Fixed Decimal feature is now active.

After fixing the decimal place in numeric values, Excel automatically adds a decimal point to any numeric value that you enter using the number of places you selected; all you do is type the digits and complete the entry in the cell. For example, to enter the numeric value 100.99 in a cell after fixing the decimal point to two places, type the digits **10099** without adding any period for a decimal point. When you complete the cell entry, Excel automatically inserts a decimal point two places from the right in the number you typed, leaving 100.99 in the cell.

When you're ready to return to normal data entry for numerical values (where you enter any decimal points yourself), open the Advanced tab of the Excel Options dialog box (Alt+FTA), click the Automatically Insert a Decimal Point check box again, this time to clear it, and then click OK or press Enter. Excel removes the Fixed Decimal indicator from the Status bar.

Tapping on the old ten-key

You can make the Fixed Decimal feature work even better by selecting the block of cells where you want to enter numbers (see "Entries all around the block," later in this chapter) and then pressing Num Lock so that you can enter all the data for this cell selection from the numeric keypad (à la ten-key adding machine).

Using this approach, all you have to do to enter the range of values in each cell is type the number's digits and press Enter on the numeric keypad. Excel inserts the decimal point in the proper place while it moves the cell pointer down to the next cell. Even better, when you finish entering the last value in a column, pressing Enter automatically moves the cell pointer to the cell at the top of the next column in the selection.

Look at Figures 2-4 and 2-5 to see how you can make the ten-key method work for you. In Figure 2-4, the Fixed Decimal feature is turned on (using the default of two decimal places), and the block of cells from B3 through D9 are selected. You also see that six entries have already been made in cells B3 through B8 and a seventh, 30834.63, is about to be completed in cell B9. To make this entry when the Fixed Decimal feature is on, you simply type **3083463** from the numeric keypad.

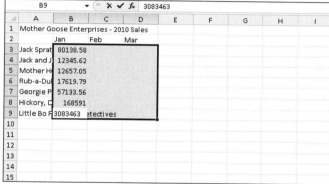

Figure 2-4: To enter the value 30834.63 in cell B9, type **3083463** and press Enter.

In Figure 2-5, check out what happens when you press Enter (on either the regular keyboard or the numeric keypad). Not only does Excel automatically add the decimal point to the value in cell B9, but it also moves the cell pointer up and over to cell C3 where you can continue entering the values for this column.

Entering dates with no debate

At first look, it may strike you a bit odd to enter dates and times as values in the cells of a worksheet rather than text. The reason for this is simple, really: Dates and times entered as values can be used in formula calculations, whereas dates and times entered as text cannot. For example, if you enter two dates as values, you can then set up a formula that subtracts the more recent date from the older date and returns the number of days between them. This kind of thing just couldn't happen if you were to enter the two dates as text entries.

	A	B	C	D	E	F	G	H	I
1	Mother Goose Enterprises - 2010 Sales								
2		Jan	Feb	Mar					
3	Jack Sprat	80138.58							
4	Jack and J	12345.62							
5	Mother H	12657.05							
6	Rub-a-Du	17619.79							
7	Georgie P	57133.56							
8	Hickory, D	168591							
9	Little Bo F	3083463							
10									
11									
12									
13									
14									
15									

Excel determines whether the date or time that you type is a value or text by the format that you follow. If you follow one of Excel's built-in date and time formats, the program recognizes the date or time as a value. If you don't follow one of the built-in formats, the program enters the date or time as a text entry — it's as simple as that.

Excel recognizes the following time formats:

3 AM or **3 PM**

3 A or **3 P** (upper- or lowercase a or p — Excel inserts 3:00 AM or 3:00 PM)

3:21 AM or **3:21 PM** (upper- or lowercase am or pm)

3:21:04 AM or **3:21:04 PM** (upper- or lowercase am or pm)

15:21

15:21:04

Excel isn't fussy, so you can enter the AM or PM designation in the date in any manner — uppercase letters, lowercase letters, or even a mix of the two.

Excel knows the following date formats. (Month abbreviations always use the first three letters of the name of the month: Jan, Feb, Mar, and so forth.)

November 6, 2008 or **November 6, 08** (appear in cell as 6-Nov-08)

11/6/08 or **11-6-08** (appear in cell as 11/6/2008)

6-Nov-08 or **6/Nov/08** or even **6Nov08** (all appear in cell as 6-Nov-08)

11/6 or **6-Nov** or **6/Nov** or **6Nov** (all appear in cell as 6-Nov)

Nov-06 or **Nov/06** or **Nov06** (all appear in cell as 6-Nov)

The dating game

Dates are stored as serial numbers that indicate how many days have elapsed from a particular starting date; times are stored as decimal fractions indicating the elapsed part of the 24-hour period. Excel supports two date systems: the 1900 date system used by Excel in Windows, where January 1, 1900 is the starting date (serial number 1) and the 1904 system used by Excel for the Macintosh, where January 2, 1904 is the starting date.

If you ever get a hold of a workbook created with Excel for the Macintosh that contains dates that seem all screwed up when you open the file, you can rectify this problem by opening the Advanced tab of the Excel Options dialog box (File⇨Options⇨Advanced or Alt+FTA) and then clicking the Use 1904 Date System check box in the When Calculating This Workbook section before you click OK.

Make it a date in the 21st Century

Contrary to what you might think, when entering dates in the 21st Century, you need to enter only the last two digits of the year. For example, to enter the date January 6, 2008, in a worksheet, I enter **1/6/08** in the target cell. Likewise, to put the date February 15, 2010, in a worksheet, I enter **2/15/10** in the target cell.

This system of having to put in only the last two digits of dates in the 21st Century works only for dates in the first three decades of the new century (2000 through 2029). To enter dates for the years 2030 on, you need to input all four digits of the year.

This also means, however, that to put in dates in the first three decades of the 20th Century (1900 through 1929), you must enter all four digits of the year. For example, to put in the date July 21, 1925, you have to enter **7/21/1925** in the target cell. Otherwise, if you enter just the last two digits (**25**) for the year part of the date, Excel enters a date for the year 2025 and not 1925!

Excel 2010 always displays all four digits of the year in the cell and on the Formula bar even when you only enter the last two. For example, if you enter **11/06/08** in a cell, Excel automatically displays 11/6/2008 in the worksheet cell (and on the Formula bar when that cell is current).

Therefore, by looking at the Formula bar, you can always tell when you've entered a 20th rather than a 21st Century date in a cell even if you can't keep straight the rules for when to enter just the last two digits rather than all four. (Read Chapter 3 for information on how to format your date entries so that only the last digits display in the worksheet.)

For information on how to perform simple arithmetic operations between the dates and time you enter in a worksheet and have the results make sense, see the information about dates in Chapter 3.

Fabricating those fabulous formulas!

As entries go in Excel, formulas are the real workhorses of the worksheet. If you set up a formula properly, it computes the correct answer when you enter the formula into a cell. From then on, the formula stays up to date, recalculating the results whenever you change any of the values that the formula uses.

You let Excel know that you're about to enter a formula (rather than some text or a value), in the current cell by starting the formula with the equal sign (=). Most simple formulas follow the equal sign with a built-in function, such as SUM or AVERAGE. (See the section "Inserting a function into a formula with the Insert Function button," later in this chapter, for more information on using functions in formulas.) Other simple formulas use a series of values or cell references that contain values separated by one or more of the following mathematical operators:

- + (plus sign) for addition
- − (minus sign or hyphen) for subtraction
- * (asterisk) for multiplication
- / (slash) for division
- ^ (caret) for raising a number to an exponential power

For example, to create a formula in cell C2 that multiplies a value entered in cell A2 by a value in cell B2, enter the following formula in cell C2: **=A2*B2**.

To enter this formula in cell C2, follow these steps:

1. **Select cell C2.**
2. **Type the entire formula** =A2*B2 **in the cell.**
3. **Press Enter.**

Or

1. **Select cell C2.**
2. **Type = (equal sign).**
3. **Select cell A2 in the worksheet by using the mouse or the keyboard.**

   This action places the cell reference A2 in the formula in the cell (as shown in Figure 2-6).

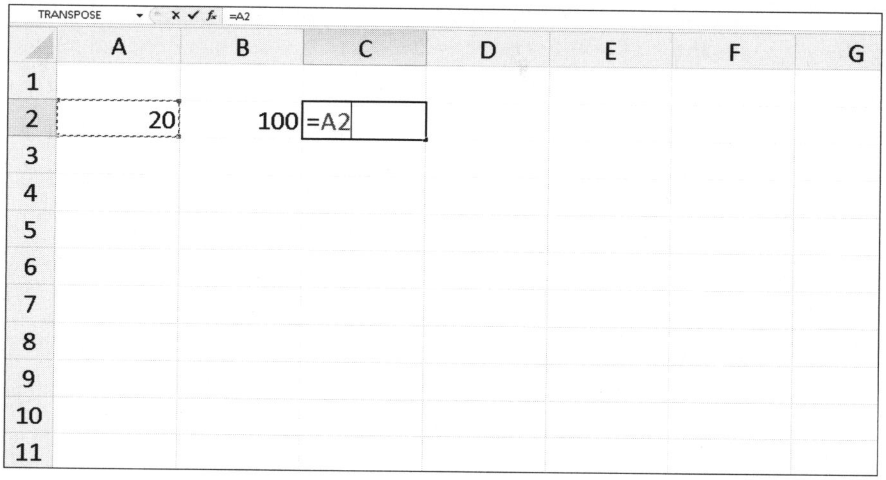

Figure 2-6:
To start the formula, type = and then select cell A2.

4. **Type * (Shift+8 on the top row of the keyboard).**

   The asterisk is used for multiplication rather than the × symbol you used in school.

5. **Select cell B2 in the worksheet by using the mouse or the keyboard.**

   This action places the cell reference B2 in the formula (as shown in Figure 2-7).

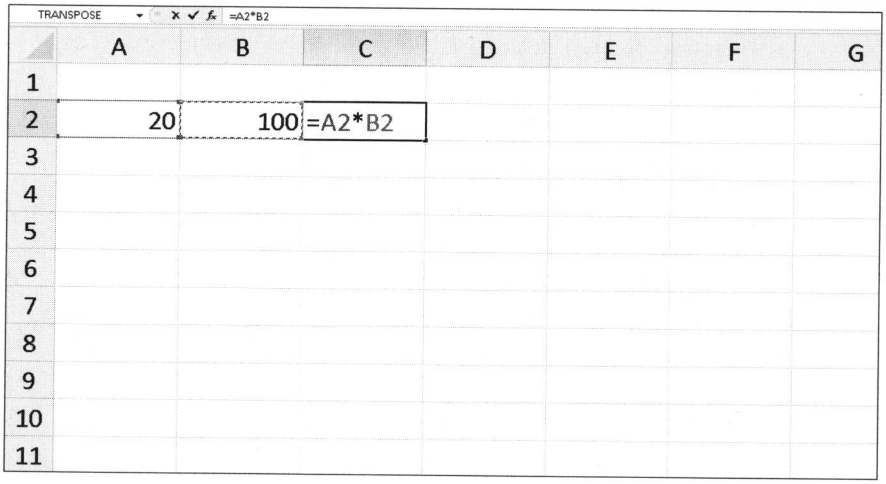

Figure 2-7:
To complete the second part of the formula, type * and select cell B2.

6. **Click the Enter button to complete the formula entry while keeping the cell pointer in cell C2.**

   Excel displays the calculated answer in cell C2 and the formula =A2*B2 in the Formula bar (as shown in Figure 2-8).

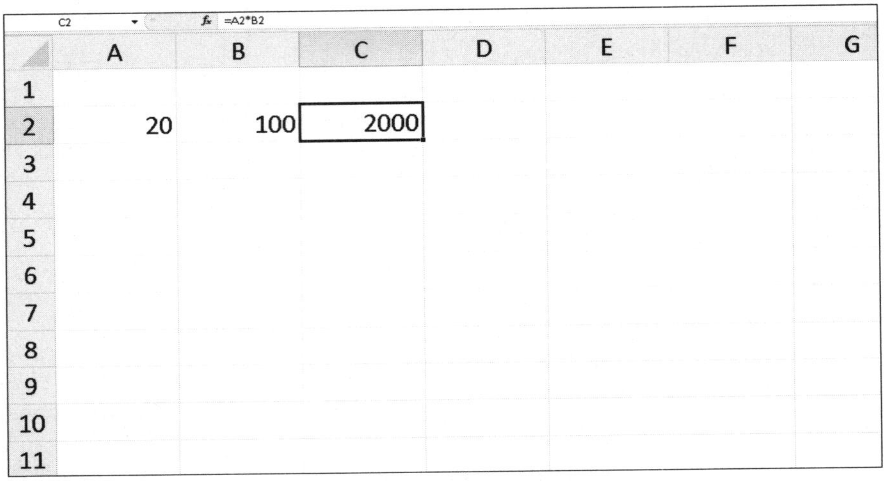

C2	▼	*fx*	=A2*B2			
	A	B	C	D	E	F	G
1							
2	20	100	2000				
3							
4							
5							
6							
7							
8							
9							
10							
11							

Figure 2-8: Click the Enter button, and Excel displays the answer in cell C2 while the formula appears in the Formula bar above.

When you finish entering the formula **=A2*B2** in cell C2 of the worksheet, Excel displays the calculated result, depending on the values currently entered in cells A2 and B2. The major strength of the electronic spreadsheet is the capability of formulas to change their calculated results automatically to match changes in the cells referenced by the formulas.

Now comes the fun part: After creating a formula like the preceding one that refers to the values in certain cells (rather than containing those values itself), you can change the values in those cells, and Excel automatically recalculates the formula, using these new values and displaying the updated answer in the worksheet! Using the example shown in Figure 2-8, suppose that you change the value in cell B2 from 100 to 50. The moment that you complete this change in cell B2, Excel recalculates the formula and displays the new answer, 1000, in cell C2.

If you want it, just point it out

The method of selecting the cells you use in a formula, rather than typing their cell references, is *pointing*. Pointing is quicker than typing and reduces the risk that you might mistype a cell reference. When you type a cell reference, you can easily type the wrong column letter or row number and not realize your mistake by looking at the calculated result returned in the cell.

If you select the cell that you want to use in a formula either by clicking it or moving the cell pointer to it, you have less chance of entering the wrong cell reference.

Altering the natural order of operations

Many formulas that you create perform more than one mathematical operation. Excel performs each operation, moving from left to right, according to a strict pecking order (the natural order of arithmetic operations). In this order, multiplication and division pull more weight than addition and subtraction and, therefore, perform first, even if these operations don't come first in the formula (when reading from left to right).

Consider the series of operations in the following formula:

    =A2+B2*C2

If cell A2 contains the number 5, B2 contains the number 10, and C2 contains the number 2, Excel evaluates the following formula:

    =5+10*2

In this formula, Excel multiplies 10 times 2 to equal 20 and then adds this result to 5 to produce the result 25.

If you want Excel to perform the addition between the values in cells A2 and B2 before the program multiplies the result by the value in cell C2, enclose the addition operation in parentheses as follows:

    =(A2+B2)*C2

The parentheses around the addition tell Excel that you want this operation performed before the multiplication. If cell A2 contains the number 5, B2 contains the number 10, and C2 contains the number 2, Excel adds 5 and 10 to equal 15 and then multiplies this result by 2 to produce the result 30.

In fancier formulas, you may need to add more than one set of parentheses, one within another (like the wooden Russian dolls that nest within each other) to indicate the order in which you want the calculations to take place. When nesting parentheses, Excel first performs the calculation contained in the most inside pair of parentheses and then uses that result in further calculations as the program works its way outward. For example, consider the following formula:

    =(A4+(B4–C4))*D4

Excel first subtracts the value in cell C4 from the value in cell B4, adds the difference to the value in cell A4, and then finally multiplies that sum by the value in D4.

Without the additions of the two sets of nested parentheses, left to its own devices, Excel would first multiply the value in cell C4 by that in D4, add the value in A4 to that in B4, and then perform the subtraction.

Don't worry too much when nesting parentheses in a formula if you don't pair them properly so that you have a right parenthesis for every left parenthesis in the formula. If you do not include a right parenthesis for every left one, Excel displays an alert dialog box that suggests the correction needed to balance the pairs. If you agree with the program's suggested correction, you simply click the Yes button. However, be sure that you only use parentheses: ( ). Excel balks at the use of brackets — [ ] — or braces — { } — in a formula by giving you an Error alert box.

Formula flub-ups

Under certain circumstances, even the best formulas can appear to have freaked out after you get them in your worksheet. You can tell right away that a formula's gone haywire because instead of the nice calculated value you expected to see in the cell, you get a strange, incomprehensible message in all uppercase letters beginning with the number sign (#) and ending with an exclamation point (!) or, in one case, a question mark (?). This weirdness, in the parlance of spreadsheets, is as an *error value*. Its purpose is to let you know that some element — either in the formula itself or in a cell referred to by the formula — is preventing Excel from returning the anticipated calculated value.

When one of your formulas returns one of these error values, an alert indicator (in the form of an exclamation point in a diamond) appears to the left of the cell when it contains the cell pointer, and the upper-left corner of the cell contains a tiny green triangle. When you position the mouse pointer on this alert indicator, Excel displays a brief description of the formula error and adds a drop-down button to the immediate right of its box. When you click this button, a pop-up menu appears with a number of related options. To access online help on this formula error, including suggestions on how to get rid of the error, click the Help on This Error item on this pop-up menu.

The worst thing about error values is that they can contaminate other formulas in the worksheet. If a formula returns an error value to a cell and a second formula in another cell refers to the value calculated by the first formula, the second formula returns the same error value, and so on down the line.

After an error value shows up in a cell, you have to discover what caused the error and edit the formula in the worksheet. In Table 2-1, I list some error values that you might run into in a worksheet and then explain the most common causes.

Table 2-1	Error Values That You May Encounter from Faulty Formulas
What Shows Up in the Cell	**What's Going On Here?**
#DIV/0!	Appears when the formula calls for division by a cell that either contains the value 0 or, as is more often the case, is empty. Division by zero is a no-no in mathematics.
#NAME?	Appears when the formula refers to a *range name* (see Chapter 6 for info on naming ranges) that doesn't exist in the worksheet. This error value appears when you type the wrong range name or fail to enclose in quotation marks some text used in the formula, causing Excel to think that the text refers to a range name.
#NULL!	Appears most often when you insert a space (where you should have used a comma) to separate cell references used as arguments for functions.
#NUM!	Appears when Excel encounters a problem with a number in the formula, such as the wrong type of argument in an Excel function or a calculation that produces a number too large or too small to be represented in the worksheet.
#REF!	Appears when Excel encounters an invalid cell reference, such as when you delete a cell referred to in a formula or paste cells over the cells referred to in a formula.
#VALUE!	Appears when you use the wrong type of argument or operator in a function, or when you call for a mathematical operation that refers to cells that contain text entries.

Fixing Those Data Entry Flub-Ups

We all wish we were perfect, but alas, because so few of us are, we are best off preparing for those inevitable times when we mess up. When entering vast quantities of data, it's easy for those nasty little typos to creep into your work. In your pursuit of the perfect spreadsheet, here are things you can do. First, get Excel to correct certain data entry typos automatically when they happen with its AutoCorrect feature. Second, manually correct any disgusting little errors that get through, either while you're still in the process of making the entry in the cell or after the entry has gone in.

You really AutoCorrect that for me

The AutoCorrect feature is a godsend for those of us who tend to make the same stupid typos over and over. With AutoCorrect, you can alert Excel 2010 to your own particular typing gaffes and tell the program how it should automatically fix them for you.

When you first install Excel, the AutoCorrect feature already knows to automatically correct two initial capital letters in an entry (by lowercasing the second capital letter), to capitalize the name of the days of the week, and to replace a set number of text entries and typos with particular substitute text.

You can add to the list of text replacements at any time when using Excel. These text replacements can be of two types: typos that you routinely make along with the correct spelling, and abbreviations or acronyms that you type all the time along with their full forms.

To add to the replacements:

1. **Choose File⇨Options⇨Proofing or press Alt+FTP and then click the AutoCorrect Options button or press Alt+A.**

   Excel opens the AutoCorrect dialog box shown in Figure 2-9.

2. **On the AutoCorrect tab in this dialog box, enter the typo or abbreviation in the Replace text box.**

3. **Enter the correction or full form in the With text box.**

4. **Click the Add button or press Enter to add the new typo or abbreviation to the AutoCorrect list.**

5. **Click the OK button to close the AutoCorrect dialog box.**

Figure 2-9:
Use the Replace and With options in the AutoCorrect dialog box to add all typos and abbreviations you want Excel to automatically correct or fill out.

Cell editing etiquette

Despite the help of AutoCorrect, some mistakes are bound to get you. How you correct them really depends upon whether you notice before or after completing the cell entry.

- ✔ If you catch the mistake before you complete an entry, you can delete it by pressing your Backspace key until you remove all the incorrect characters from the cell. Then you can retype the rest of the entry or the formula before you complete the entry in the cell.

- ✔ If you don't discover the mistake until after you've completed the cell entry, you have a choice of replacing the whole thing or editing just the mistakes.

- ✔ When dealing with short entries, you'll probably want to take the replacement route. To replace a cell entry, position the cell pointer in that cell, type your replacement entry, and then click the Enter button or press one of the arrow keys.

- ✔ When the error in an entry is relatively easy to fix and the entry is on the long side, you'll probably want to edit the cell entry rather than replace it. To edit the entry in the cell, simply double-click the cell or select the cell and then press F2.

- ✔ Doing either one reactivates the Formula bar by displaying the Enter and Cancel buttons once again and placing the insertion point in the cell entry in the worksheet. (If you double-click, the insertion point positions itself wherever you click; press F2, and the insertion point positions itself after the last character in the entry.)

- ✔ Notice also that the mode indicator changes to Edit. While in this mode, you can use the mouse or the arrow keys to position the insertion point at the place in the cell entry that needs fixing.

In Table 2-2, I list the keystrokes that you can use to reposition the insertion point in the cell entry and delete unwanted characters. If you want to insert new characters at the insertion point, simply start typing. If you want to delete existing characters at the insertion point while you type new ones, press the Insert key on your keyboard to switch from the normal insert mode to overtype mode. To return to normal insert mode, press Insert a second time. When you finish making corrections to the cell entry, you must complete the edits by pressing Enter before Excel updates the contents of the cell.

While Excel is in Edit mode, you must reenter the edited cell contents by either clicking the Enter button or pressing Enter. You can use the arrow keys as a way to complete an entry only when the program is in Enter mode. When the program is in Edit mode, the arrow keys move the insertion point only through the entry that you're editing, not to a new cell.

A tale of two edits: Cell versus Formula bar editing

Excel gives you a choice between editing a cell's contents either in the cell or on the Formula bar. Whereas most of the time, editing right in the cell is just fine, when dealing with really long entries (like humongous formulas that go on forever or text entries that take up paragraphs), you may prefer to do your editing on the Formula bar. This is because Excel 2010 automatically adds up and down scroll arrow buttons to the end of the Formula bar when a cell entry is too long to display completely on a single row. These scroll arrow buttons enable you to display each line of the cell's long entry without expanding the Formula bar (as in earlier versions of Excel) and thereby obscuring the top part of the Worksheet area.

To edit the contents in the Formula bar rather than in the cell itself, click the appropriate scroll arrow button to display the line with the contents that needs editing and then click the I-beam mouse pointer at the place in the text or numbers that requires modification to set the insertion cursor.

Table 2-2	Keystrokes for Fixing Those Cell Entry Flub-Ups
Keystroke	*What the Keystroke Does*
Delete	Deletes the character to the right of the insertion point
Backspace	Deletes the character to the left of the insertion point
→	Positions the insertion point one character to the right
←	Positions the insertion point one character to the left
↑	Positions the insertion point, when it is at the end of the cell entry, to its preceding position to the left
End or ↓	Moves the insertion point after the last character in the cell entry
Home	Moves the insertion point in front of the first character of the cell entry
Ctrl+→	Positions the insertion point in front of the next word in the cell entry
Ctrl+←	Positions the insertion point in front of the preceding word in the cell entry
Insert	Switches between insert and overtype mode

Taking the Drudgery out of Data Entry

Before leaving the topic of data entry, I feel duty-bound to cover some of the shortcuts that really help to cut down on the drudgery of this task. These data-entry tips include AutoComplete and AutoFill features as well as doing data entry in a preselected block of cells and making the same entry in a bunch of cells all at the same time.

I'm just not complete without you

The AutoComplete feature in Excel 2010 is not something you can do anything about, just something to be aware of while you enter your data. In an attempt to cut down on your typing load, our friendly software engineers at Microsoft came up with the AutoComplete feature.

AutoComplete is like a moronic mind reader who anticipates what you might want to enter next based on what you just entered. This feature comes into play only when you're entering a column of text entries. (It does not come into play when entering values or formulas or when entering a row of text entries.) When entering a column of text entries, AutoComplete looks at the kinds of entries that you make in that column and automatically duplicates them in subsequent rows whenever you start a new entry that begins with the same letter as an existing entry.

For example, suppose that I enter **Jack Sprat Diet Centers** (one of the companies owned and operated by Mother Goose Enterprises) in cell A2 and then move the cell pointer down to cell A3 in the row below and press **J** (lowercase or uppercase, it doesn't matter). AutoComplete immediately inserts the remainder of the familiar entry — *ack Sprat Diet Centers* — in this cell after the J, as shown in Figure 2-10.

Now this is great if I happen to need Jack Sprat Diet Centers as the row heading in both cells A2 and A3. Anticipating that I might be typing a different entry that just happens to start with the same letter as the one above, AutoComplete automatically selects everything after the first letter in the duplicated entry it inserted (from *ack* on, in this example). This enables me to replace the duplicate text supplied by AutoComplete just by continuing to type. For example, after capturing the Excel screen that you see in Figure 2-10, I entered Jack and Jill Trauma Centers — another of Mother's companies — in cell A3.

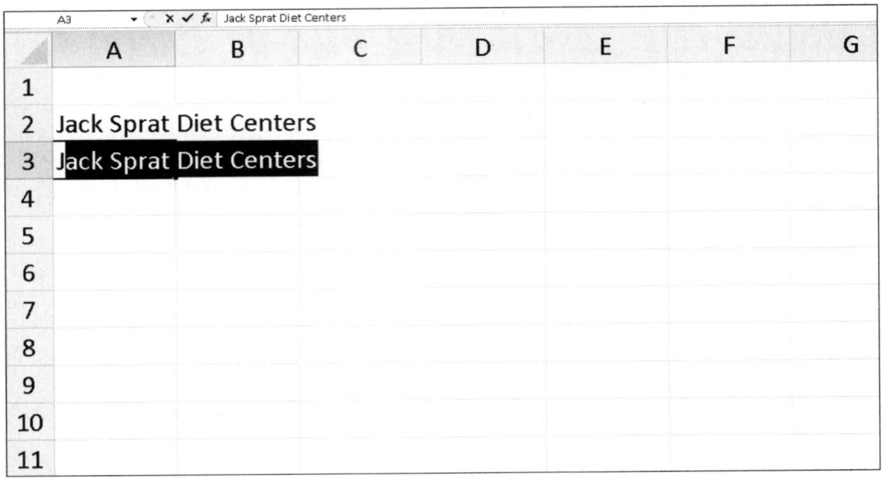

A3	▾	✕ ✓ ƒx	Jack Sprat Diet Centers			
	A	B	C	D	E	F	G

	A	B	C	D	E	F	G
1							
2	Jack Sprat Diet Centers						
3	Jack Sprat Diet Centers						
4							
5							
6							
7							
8							
9							
10							
11							

Figure 2-10:
Auto
Complete
duplicates
a previous
entry if you
start a new
entry in
the same
column that
begins with
the same
letter.

If you override a duplicate supplied by AutoComplete in a column by typing one of your own (as in my example with changing Jack Sprat Diet Centers to Jack and Jill Trauma Centers in cell A3), you effectively shut down its ability to supply any more duplicates for that particular letter. For instance, in my example, after changing Jack Sprat Diet Centers to Jack and Jill Trauma Centers in cell A3, AutoComplete doesn't do anything if I then type **J** in cell A4. In other words, you're on your own if you don't continue to accept AutoComplete's typing suggestions.

If you find that the AutoComplete feature is really making it hard for you to enter a series of cell entries that all start with the same letter but are otherwise not alike, you can turn off the AutoComplete feature. Click File➪Options➪Advanced or press Alt+FTA to select the Advanced tab of the Excel Options dialog box. Then, select the Enable AutoComplete for Cell Values check box in the Editing Options section to remove its check mark before clicking OK.

Fill 'er up with AutoFill

Many of the worksheets that you create with Excel require the entry of a series of sequential dates or numbers. For example, a worksheet may require you to title the columns with the 12 months, from January through December, or to number the rows from 1 to 100.

Excel's AutoFill feature makes short work of this kind of repetitive task. All you have to enter is the starting value for the series. In most cases, AutoFill is smart enough to figure out how to fill out the series for you when you drag the fill handle to the right (to take the series across columns to the right) or down (to extend the series to the rows below).

REMEMBER

The AutoFill handle looks like this — + — and appears only when you position the mouse pointer on the lower-right corner of the active cell (or the last cell, when you've selected a block of cells). If you drag a cell selection with the white cross mouse pointer rather than the AutoFill handle, Excel simply extends the cell selection to those cells you drag through (see Chapter 3). If you drag a cell selection with the arrowhead pointer, Excel moves the cell selection (see Chapter 4).

When creating a series with the fill handle, you can drag in only one direction at a time. For example, you can fill the series or copy the entry to the range to the left or right of the cell that contains the initial values, or you can fill the series or copy to the range above or below the cell containing the initial values. You can't, however, fill or copy the series to two directions at the same time (such as down and to the right by dragging the fill handle diagonally).

While you drag the mouse, the program keeps you informed of whatever entry will be entered into the last cell selected in the range by displaying that entry next to the mouse pointer (a kind of AutoFill tips, if you will). When you release the mouse button after extending the range with the fill handle, Excel either creates a series in all of the cells that you select or copies the entire range with the initial value. To the right of the last entry in the filled or copied series, Excel also displays a drop-down button that contains a shortcut menu of options. You can use this shortcut menu to override Excel's default filling or copying. For example, when you use the fill handle, Excel copies an initial value into a range of cells. But, if you want a sequential series, you could do this by selecting the Fill Series command on the AutoFill Options shortcut menu.

In Figures 2-11 and 2-12, I illustrate how to use AutoFill to enter a row of months, starting with January in cell B2 and ending with June in cell G2. To do this, you simply enter **January** in cell B2 and then position the mouse pointer on the fill handle in the lower-right corner of this cell before you drag through to cell G2 on the right (as shown in Figure 2-11). When you release the mouse button, Excel fills in the names of the rest of the months (February through June) in the selected cells (as shown in Figure 2-12). Excel keeps the cells with the series of months selected, giving you another chance to modify the series. (If you went too far, you can drag the fill handle to the left to cut back on the list of months; if you didn't go far enough, you can drag it to the right to extend the list of months further.)

Also, you can use the options on the AutoFill Options drop-down menu (opened by clicking the drop-down button that appears on the fill handle to the right of June) to override the series created by default. To have Excel copy January into each of the selected cells, choose Copy Cells on this menu. To have the program fill the selected cells with the formatting used in cell B2 (in this case, the cell has had bold applied to it — see Chapter 3 for details on formatting cells), you select Fill Formatting Only on this menu. To have Excel fill in the series of months in the selected cells without copying the formatting used in cell B2, you select the Fill without Formatting command from this shortcut menu.

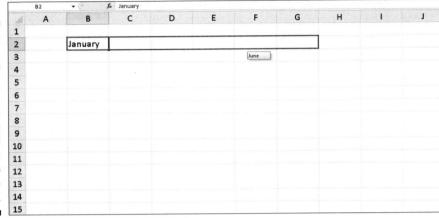

Figure 2-11:
To enter a series of months, enter the first month and then drag the Fill handle in a direction to add sequential months.

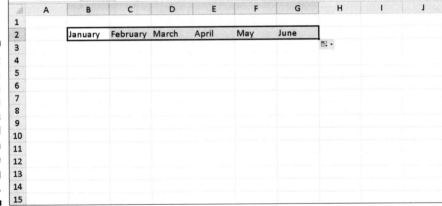

Figure 2-12:
Release the mouse button, and Excel fills the cell selection with the missing months.

See Table 2-3 in the following section to see some of the different initial values that AutoFill can use and the types of series that Excel can create from them.

Working with a spaced series

AutoFill uses the initial value that you select (date, time, day, year, and so on) to design the series. All the sample series I show in Table 2-3 change by a factor of one (one day, one month, or one number). You can tell AutoFill to create a series that changes by some other value: Enter two sample values in neighboring cells that describe the amount of change you want between each value in the series. Make these two values the initial selection that you extend with the fill handle.

For example, to start a series with Saturday and enter every other day across a row, enter **Saturday** in the first cell and **Monday** in the cell next door. After selecting both cells, drag the fill handle across the cells to the right as far as you need to fill out a series based on these two initial values. When you release the mouse button, Excel follows the example set in the first two cells by entering every other day (Wednesday to the right of Monday, Friday to the right of Wednesday, and so on).

Table 2-3	Samples of Series You Can Create with AutoFill
Value Entered in First Cell	*Extended Series Created by AutoFill in the Next Three Cells*
June	July, August, September
Jun	Jul, Aug, Sep
Tuesday	Wednesday, Thursday, Friday
Tue	Wed, Thu, Fri
4/1/99	4/2/99, 4/3/99, 4/4/99
Jan-00	Feb-00, Mar-00, Apr-00
15-Feb	16-Feb, 17-Feb, 18-Feb
10:00 PM	11:00 PM, 12:00 AM, 1:00 AM
8:01	9:01, 10:01, 11:01
Quarter 1	Quarter 2, Quarter 3, Quarter 4
Qtr2	Qtr3, Qtr4, Qtr1
Q3	Q4, Q1, Q2
Product 1	Product 2, Product 3, Product 4

Copying with AutoFill

You can use AutoFill to copy a text entry throughout a cell range (rather than fill in a series of related entries). To copy a text entry to a cell range, hold down the Ctrl key while you click and drag the Fill handle. When you hold down the Ctrl key while you click the fill handle, a plus sign appears to the right of the Fill handle — your sign that AutoFill will *copy* the entry in the active cell instead of creating a series using it. You can also tell because the entry that appears as the AutoFill tip next to the mouse pointer while you drag contains the same text as the original cell. If you decide after copying an initial label or value to a range that you should have used it to fill in a series, click the drop-down button that appears on the fill handle at the cell with the last copied entry and then select the Fill Series command on the AutoFill Options shortcut menu that appears.

Although holding down Ctrl while you drag the fill handle copies a text entry, just the opposite is true when it comes to values! Suppose that you enter the number **17** in a cell and then drag the fill handle across the row — Excel just copies the number 17 in all the cells that you select. If, however, you hold down Ctrl while you drag the fill handle, Excel then fills out the series (17, 18, 19, and so on). If you forget and create a series of numbers when you only need the value copied, rectify this situation by selecting the Copy Cells command on the AutoFill Options shortcut menu.

Creating custom lists for AutoFill

In addition to varying the increment in a series created with AutoFill, you can also create your own custom series. For example, say your company has offices in the following locations and you get tired of typing the sequence in each new spreadsheet that requires them:

- ✔ New York
- ✔ Chicago
- ✔ Atlanta
- ✔ Seattle
- ✔ San Francisco
- ✔ San Diego

After creating a custom list with these locations, you can enter the entire sequence of cities simply by entering New York in the first cell and then dragging the Fill handle to the blank cells where the rest of the companies should appear.

To create this kind of custom series, follow these steps:

1. **Choose File➪Options➪Advanced or press Alt+FTA and then click the Edit Custom Lists button in the General section to open the Options dialog box (as shown in Figure 2-13).**

   If you've already gone to the time and trouble of typing the custom list in a range of cells, go to Step 2. If you haven't yet typed the series in an open worksheet, go to Step 5.

2. **Click inside the Import List from Cells text box and then click the Collapse Dialog Box button (the one with the picture of the tiny grid to the right of the Import List from Cells text box) so that you can see your list and drag through the range of cells to select them (see Chapter 3 for details).**

3. **After selecting the cells in the worksheet, click the Expand Dialog Box button.**

   This button automatically replaces the Collapse Dialog Box button.

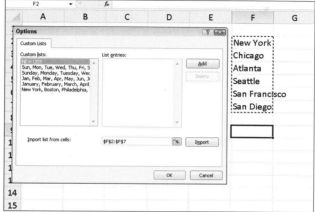

Figure 2-13:
Creating
a custom
company
location
list from a
range of
existing cell
entries.

4. **Click the Import button to copy this list into the List Entries list box.**

   Skip to Step 7.

5. **Click inside the List Entries list box and then type each entry (in the desired order), being sure to press Enter after typing each one.**

   When all the entries in the custom list appear in the List Entries list box in the order you want them, proceed to Step 6.

6. **Click the Add button to add the list of entries to the Custom Lists list box.**

   Finish creating all the custom lists you need, using the preceding steps. When you're done, move to Step 7.

7. **Click OK twice, the first time to close the Options dialog box and the second to close the Excel Options dialog box and return to the current worksheet in the active workbook.**

After adding a custom list to Excel, from then on you need only enter the first entry in a cell and then use the fill handle to extend it to the cells below or to the right.

If you don't even want to bother with typing the first entry, use the AutoCorrect feature — refer to the section "You really AutoCorrect that for me," earlier in this chapter — to create an entry that will fill in as soon as you type your favorite acronym for it (such as *ny* for New York).

Inserting special symbols

Excel makes it easy to enter special symbols, such as foreign currency indica-tors, and special characters, such as the trademark and copyright symbols, into your cell entries. To add a special symbol or character to a cell entry you're making or editing, click Insert⇨Symbol on the Ribbon or press Alt+NU to open the Symbol dialog box (similar to the one shown in Figure 2-14).

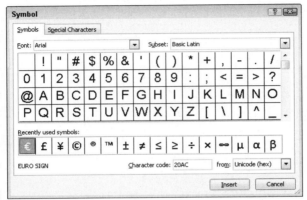

Figure 2-14: Use the Symbol dialog box to insert special symbols and characters into your cell entries.

The Symbol dialog box contains two tabs: Symbols and Special Characters. To insert a mathematical or foreign currency symbol on the Symbols tab, click its symbol in the list box and then click the Insert button. (You can also do this by double-clicking the symbol.) To insert characters, such as foreign language or accented characters from other character sets, click the Subset drop-down button, click the name of the set in the drop-down list, and then click the desired characters in the list box. You can also insert commonly used currency and mathematical symbols, such as the pound or plus-or-minus symbol, by clicking them in the Recently Used Symbols section at the bottom of this tab.

To insert special characters, such as the registered trademark, paragraph symbol, and ellipsis, click the Special Characters tab of the Symbol dialog box, locate the symbol in the scrolling list, click it, and then click the Insert button. (You can insert one of these special characters by double-clicking it also.)

When you finish inserting special symbols and characters, close the Symbol dialog box by clicking its Close button in its upper-right corner.

Entries all around the block

When you want to enter a table of information in a new worksheet, you can simplify the job of entering the data if you select all the empty cells in which you want to make entries before you begin entering any information. Just position the cell pointer in the first cell of what is to become the data table and then select all the cells in the subsequent columns and rows. (For information on the ways to select a range of cells, see Chapter 3.) After you select the block of cells, you can begin entering the first entry.

When you select a block of cells (also known as a *range*) before you enter information, Excel restricts data entry to that range as follows:

- ✔ The program automatically advances the cell pointer to the next cell in the range when you click the Enter button or press Enter to complete each cell entry.

- ✔ In a cell range that contains several different rows and columns, Excel advances the cell pointer down each row of the column while you make your entries. When the cell pointer reaches the cell in the last row of the column, the cell pointer advances to the first selected row in the next column to the right. If the cell range uses only one row, Excel advances the cell pointer from left to right across the row.

- ✔ When you finish entering information in the last cell in the selected range, Excel positions the cell pointer in the first cell of the now-completed data table. To deselect the cell range, click the mouse pointer on one of the cells in the worksheet (inside or outside the selected range — it doesn't matter) or press one of the arrow keys.

Be sure that you don't press one of the arrow keys to complete a cell entry within a preselected cell range instead of clicking the Enter button or pressing Enter. Pressing an arrow key deselects the range of cells when Excel moves the cell pointer. To move the cell pointer around a cell range without deselecting the range, try these methods:

- ✔ Press Enter to advance to the next cell down each row and then across each column in the range. Press Shift+Enter to move up to the previous cell.

- ✔ Press Tab to advance to the next cell in the column on the right and then down each row of the range. Press Shift+Tab to move left to the previous cell.

- ✔ Press Ctrl+. (period) to move from one corner of the range to another.

Data entry express

You can save a lot of time and energy when you want the same entry (text, value, or formula) to appear in many cells of the worksheet; you can enter the information in all the cells in one operation. You first select the cell ranges to hold the information. (Excel lets you select more than one cell range for this kind of thing — see Chapter 3 for details.) Then you construct the entry on the formula bar and press Ctrl+Enter to put the entry into all the selected ranges.

The key to making this operation a success is to hold the Ctrl key while you press Enter so that Excel inserts the entry on the formula bar into all the selected cells. If you forget to hold Ctrl and you just press Enter, Excel places the entry in the first cell only of the selected cell range.

You can also speed up data entry in a list that includes formulas by making sure that the Extend Data Range Formats and Formulas check box is selected in the Editing Options section of the Advanced tab in the Excel Options dialog box. (Choose File⇨Options⇨Advanced or press Alt+FTA.) When this check box is selected, Excel automatically formats new data that you type in the last row of a list to match that of like data in earlier rows and copies down formulas that appear in the preceding rows. Note, however, that for this new feature to kick in, you must manually enter the formulas and format the data entries in at least three rows preceding the new row.

How to Make Your Formulas Function Even Better

Earlier in this chapter, I show you how to create formulas that perform a series of simple mathematical operations, such as addition, subtraction, multiplication, and division. (See the section "Fabricating those fabulous formulas!") Instead of creating complex formulas from scratch out of an intricate combination of these operations, you can find an Excel function to get the job done.

A *function* is a predefined formula that performs a particular type of computation. All you have to do to use a function is supply the values that the function uses when performing its calculations. (In the parlance of the Spreadsheet Guru, such values are the *arguments of the function*.) As with simple formulas, you can enter the arguments for most functions either as a numerical value (for example, **22** or **–4.56**) or, as is more common, as a cell reference (**B10**) or as a cell range (**C3:F3**).

Just as with a formula you build yourself, each function you use must start with an equal sign (=) so that Excel knows to enter the function as a formula rather than as text. Following the equal sign, you enter the name of the function (in uppercase or lowercase — it doesn't matter, as long as you spell the name correctly). Following the name of the function, you enter the arguments required to perform the calculations. All function arguments are enclosed in a pair of parentheses.

If you type the function directly in a cell, remember not to insert spaces between the equal sign, function name, and the arguments enclosed in parentheses. Some functions use more than one value when performing their designated calculations. When this is the case, you separate each function with a comma (not a space).

After you type the equal sign and begin typing the first few letters of the name of the function you want to use, a drop-down list showing all the functions that begin with the letters you've typed appears immediately beneath the cell. When you see the name of the function you want to use on this list, double-click it and Excel will finish entering the function name in the cell and on the Formula bar as well as add the left parenthesis that marks the beginning of the arguments for the function.

Excel then displays all the arguments that the function takes beneath the cell and you can indicate any cell or cell range that you want to use as the first argument by either pointing to it or typing its cell or range references. When the function uses more than one argument, you can point to the cells or cell ranges or enter the addresses for the second argument right after you enter a comma (,) to complete the first argument.

After you finish entering the last argument, you need to close off the function by typing a right parenthesis to mark the end of the argument list. The display of the function name along with its arguments that appeared beneath the cell when you first selected the function from the drop-down list then disappears. Click the Enter button or press Enter (or the appropriate arrow key) to then insert the function into the cell and have Excel calculate the answer.

Inserting a function into a formula with the Insert Function button

Although you can enter a function by typing it directly in a cell, Excel provides an Insert Function button on the Formula bar you can use to select any of Excel's functions. When you click this button, Excel opens the Insert Function dialog box (shown in Figure 2-15) where you can select the function you want to use. After you select your function, Excel opens the Function Arguments dialog box. In this dialog box, you can specify the function arguments. The real boon comes when you're fooling with an unfamiliar function or one that's kind of complex (some of these puppies can be hairy). You can get loads of help in completing the argument text boxes in the Function Arguments dialog box by clicking the Help on This Function link in the lower-left corner.

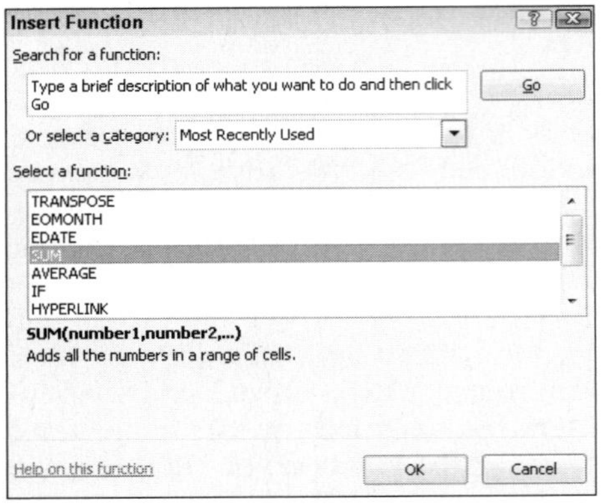

Figure 2-15:
Select the
function you
want to use
in the Insert
Function
dialog box.

The Insert Function dialog box contains three boxes: a Search for a Function text box, an Or Select a Category drop-down list box, and a Select a Function list box. When you open the Insert Function dialog box, Excel automatically selects Most Recently Used as the category in the Select a Category drop-down list box and displays the functions you usually use in the Select a Function list box.

If your function isn't among the most recently used, you must then select the appropriate category of your function in the Select a Category drop-down list box. If you don't know the category, you must search for the function by typing a description of its purpose in the Search for a Function text box and then press Enter or click the Go button. For example, to locate all the Excel functions that total values, you enter **total** in the Search for Function list box and click the Go button. Excel then displays its list of recommended functions for calculating totals in the Select a Function list box. You can peruse the recommended functions by selecting each one. While you select each function in this list, the Insert Function dialog box shows you the required arguments followed by a description, at the bottom of the dialog box, of what the function does.

After you locate and select the function that you want to use, click the OK button to insert the function into the current cell and open the Function Arguments dialog box. This dialog box displays the required arguments for the function along with any that are optional. For example, suppose that you select the SUM function (the crown jewel of the Most Recently Used function category) in the Select a Function list box and then click OK. As soon as you do, the program inserts

SUM()

in the current cell and on the Formula bar (following the equal sign), and the Function Arguments dialog box showing the SUM arguments appears on the screen (as shown in Figure 2-16). This is where you add the arguments for the SUM function.

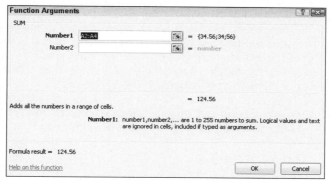

Figure 2-16:
Specify the arguments to use in the selected function in the Function Arguments dialog box.

As shown in Figure 2-16, you can sum up to 255 numbers in the Function Arguments dialog box. What's not obvious, however (there's always some trick, huh?), is that these numbers don't have to be in single cells. In fact, most of the time you'll be selecting a whole slew of numbers in nearby cells (in a multiple cell selection — that range thing) that you want to total.

To select your first number argument in the dialog box, you click the cell (or drag through the block of cells) in the worksheet while the insertion point is in the Number1 text box. Excel then displays the cell address (or range address) in the Number1 text box while, at the same time, showing the value in the cell (or values, if you select a bunch of cells) in the box to the right. Excel displays the total near the bottom of the Function Arguments dialog box after the words *Formula result=*.

When selecting cells, you can minimize this arguments dialog box to just the contents of the Number1 text box by dragging the cell pointer through the cells to sum in the worksheet. After you minimize the arguments dialog box while selecting the cells for the first argument, you can then expand it again by releasing the mouse button.

You can also reduce the dialog box to the Number1 argument text box by clicking the Minimize Dialog Box button on the right of the text box, selecting the cells, and then clicking the Maximize Dialog Box button (the only button displayed on the far right) or by pressing the Esc key. Instead of minimizing the dialog box, you can also temporarily move it out of the way by clicking on any part and then dragging the dialog box to its new destination on the screen.

If you're adding more than one cell (or bunch of cells) in a worksheet, press the Tab key or click the Number2 text box to move the insertion point to that text box. (Excel responds by extending the argument list with a Number3 text box.) Here is where you specify the second cell (or cell range) to add to the one now showing in the Number1 text box. After you click the cell or drag through the second cell range, the program displays the cell address(es), the numbers in the cell(s) to the right, and the running total near the bottom of the Function Arguments dialog box after *Formula result=* (as shown in Figure 2-16). You can minimize the entire Function Arguments dialog box down to just the contents of the argument text box you're dealing with (Number2, Number3, and so on) by clicking its particular Minimize Dialog Box button if the dialog box obscures the cells that you need to select.

When you finish pointing out the cells or bunch of cells to sum, click the OK button to close the Function Arguments dialog box and put the SUM function in the current cell.

Editing a function with the Insert Function button

You can also use the Insert Function button to edit formulas that contain functions right from the Formula bar. Select the cell with the formula and function to edit before you click the Insert Function button (the one sporting the *fx* that appears immediately in front of the current cell entry on the Formula bar).

As soon as you click the Insert Function button, Excel opens the Function Arguments dialog box where you can edit its arguments. To edit just the arguments of a function, select the cell references in the appropriate argument's text box (marked Number1, Number2, Number3, and so on) and then make whatever changes are required to the cell addresses or select a new range of cells.

Excel automatically adds any cell or cell range that you highlight in the worksheet to the current argument. If you want to replace the current argument, you need to highlight it and remove its cell addresses by pressing the Delete key before you highlight the new cell or cell range to use as the argument. (Remember that you can always minimize this dialog box or move it to a new location if it obscures the cells you need to select.)

When you finish editing the function, press Enter or click the OK button in the Function Arguments dialog box to put it away and update the formula in the worksheet.

I'd be totally lost without AutoSum

Before leaving this fascinating discussion on entering functions, I want you to get to the AutoSum tool in the Editing group on the Home tab of the Ribbon.

Look for the Greek sigma (Σ) symbol. This little tool is worth its weight in gold. In addition to entering the SUM, AVERAGE, COUNT, MAX, or MIN functions, it also selects the most likely range of cells in the current column or row that you want to use as the function's argument and then automatically enters them as the function's argument. Nine times out of ten, Excel selects (with the *marquee* or moving dotted line) the correct cell range to total, average, count, and so forth. For that tenth case, you can manually correct the range by simply dragging the cell pointer through the block of cells to sum.

Simply click the AutoSum button on the Home tab when you want to insert the SUM function into the current cell. If you want to use this button to insert another function, such as AVERAGE, COUNT, MAX, or MIN, you need to click its drop-down button and select the name of the desired function on its pop-up menu (click Count Numbers on the menu to insert the COUNT function). If you select the More Functions command on this menu, Excel opens the Insert Function dialog box as though you had clicked the *fx* button on the Formula bar.

In Figure 2-17, check out how to use the AutoSum tool to total the sales of Jack Sprat Diet Centers in row 3. Position the cell pointer in cell E3 where the first-quarter total is to appear and then click the AutoSum tool. Excel inserts SUM (equal sign and all) onto the Formula bar; places a marquee around the cells B3, C3, and D3; and uses the cell range B3:D3 as the argument of the SUM function.

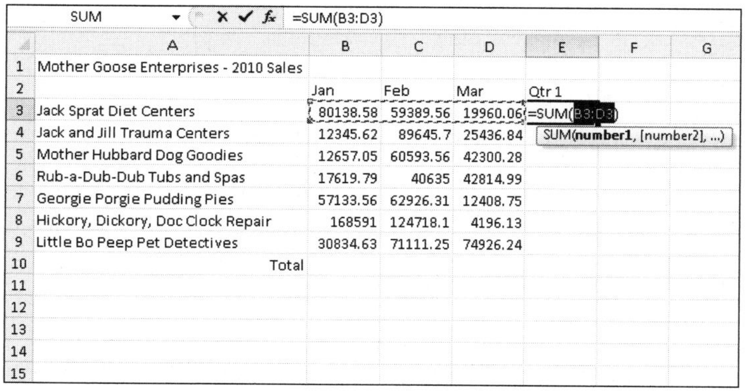

Figure 2-17:
To total Jack Sprat Diet Centers first quarter sales for row 3, click the AutoSum button in cell E3 and press Enter.

	SUM	▼	✕ ✔ *fx*	=SUM(B3:D3)			
	A	B	C	D	E	F	G
1	Mother Goose Enterprises - 2010 Sales						
2		Jan	Feb	Mar	Qtr 1		
3	Jack Sprat Diet Centers	80138.58	59389.56	19960.06	=SUM(B3:D3)		
4	Jack and Jill Trauma Centers	12345.62	89645.7	25436.84	SUM(**number1**, [number2], ...)		
5	Mother Hubbard Dog Goodies	12657.05	60593.56	42300.28			
6	Rub-a-Dub-Dub Tubs and Spas	17619.79	40635	42814.99			
7	Georgie Porgie Pudding Pies	57133.56	62926.31	12408.75			
8	Hickory, Dickory, Doc Clock Repair	168591	124718.1	4196.13			
9	Little Bo Peep Pet Detectives	30834.63	71111.25	74926.24			
10	Total						
11							
12							
13							
14							
15							

Now look at the worksheet after you insert the function in cell E3 (see Figure 2-18). The calculated total appears in cell E3 while the following SUM function formula appears in the Formula bar:

```
=SUM(B3:D3)
```

Figure 2-18: The worksheet with the first quarter totals calculated with AutoSum.

	E3			fx	=SUM(B3:D3)		
	A	B	C	D	E	F	
1	Mother Goose Enterprises - 2010 Sales						
2		Jan	Feb	Mar	Qtr 1		
3	Jack Sprat Diet Centers	80138.58	59389.56	19960.06	159488.2		
4	Jack and Jill Trauma Centers	12345.62	89645.7	25436.84			
5	Mother Hubbard Dog Goodies	12657.05	60593.56	42300.28			
6	Rub-a-Dub-Dub Tubs and Spas	17619.79	40635	42814.99			
7	Georgie Porgie Pudding Pies	57133.56	62926.31	12408.75			
8	Hickory, Dickory, Doc Clock Repair	168591	124718.1	4196.13			
9	Little Bo Peep Pet Detectives	30834.63	71111.25	74926.24			
10	Total						
11							
12							
13							
14							
15							

After entering the function to total the sales of Jack Sprat Diet Centers, you can copy this formula to total sales for the rest of the companies by dragging the fill handle down column E until the cell range E3:E10 is highlighted.

Look at Figure 2-19 to see how you can use the AutoSum tool to total the January sales for all the Mother Goose Enterprises in column B. Position the cell pointer in cell B10 where you want the total to appear. Click the AutoSum tool, and Excel places the marquee around cells B3 through B9 and correctly enters the cell range B3:B9 as the argument of the SUM function.

Figure 2-19: Click the AutoSum button in cell B10 and press Enter to total the January sales for all companies in column B.

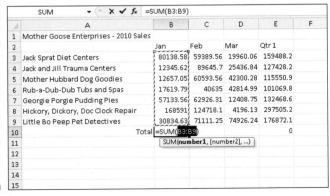

	SUM			X ✔ fx	=SUM(B3:B9)		
	A	B	C	D	E	F	
1	Mother Goose Enterprises - 2010 Sales						
2		Jan	Feb	Mar	Qtr 1		
3	Jack Sprat Diet Centers	80138.58	59389.56	19960.06	159488.2		
4	Jack and Jill Trauma Centers	12345.62	89645.7	25436.84	127428.2		
5	Mother Hubbard Dog Goodies	12657.05	60593.56	42300.28	115550.9		
6	Rub-a-Dub-Dub Tubs and Spas	17619.79	40635	42814.99	101069.8		
7	Georgie Porgie Pudding Pies	57133.56	62926.31	12408.75	132468.6		
8	Hickory, Dickory, Doc Clock Repair	168591	124718.1	4196.13	297505.2		
9	Little Bo Peep Pet Detectives	30834.63	71111.25	74926.24	176872.1		
10	Total	=SUM(B3:B9)			0		
11		SUM(**number1**, [number2], ...)					
12							
13							
14							
15							

In Figure 2-20, you see the worksheet after inserting the function in cell B10 and using the AutoFill feature to copy the formula to cells C10 and D10 to the right. (To use AutoFill, drag the fill handle through the cells to the right until you reach cell D10. Release the mouse button.)

	B10			f_x	=SUM(B3:B9)		
	A		B	C	D	E	F
1	Mother Goose Enterprises - 2010 Sales						
2			Jan	Feb	Mar	Qtr 1	
3	Jack Sprat Diet Centers		80138.58	59389.56	19960.06	159488.2	
4	Jack and Jill Trauma Centers		12345.62	89645.7	25436.84	127428.2	
5	Mother Hubbard Dog Goodies		12657.05	60593.56	42300.28	115550.9	
6	Rub-a-Dub-Dub Tubs and Spas		17619.79	40635	42814.99	101069.8	
7	Georgie Porgie Pudding Pies		57133.56	62926.31	12408.75	132468.6	
8	Hickory, Dickory, Doc Clock Repair		168591	124718.1	4196.13	297505.2	
9	Little Bo Peep Pet Detectives		30834.63	71111.25	74926.24	176872.1	
10		Total	379320.2	509019.5	222043.3	1110383	
11							
12							
13							
14							
15							

Figure 2-20: The worksheet after copying the SUM function formulas using the fill handle.

Making Sure That the Data Is Safe and Sound

All the work you do in any of the worksheets in your workbook is at risk until you save the workbook as a disk file, normally on your computer's hard drive. Should you lose power or should your computer crash for any reason before you save the workbook, you're out of luck. You have to re-create each keystroke — a painful task, made all the worse because it's so unnecessary. To avoid this unpleasantness altogether, adopt this motto: Save your work any time that you enter more information than you could possibly bear to lose.

To encourage frequent saving on your part, Excel even provides you with a Save button on the Quick Access toolbar (the one with the picture of a 3¼" floppy disk, the very first on the toolbar). You don't even have to take the time and trouble to choose the Save command from the File pull-down menu (opened by choosing File) or even press Ctrl+S; you can simply click this tool whenever you want to save new work on disk.

When you click the Save button, press Ctrl+S, or choose File➪Save for the first time, Excel displays the Save As dialog box. Use this dialog box to replace the temporary document name (Book1, Book2, and so forth) with a more descriptive filename in the File Name text box, select a new file format in the Save As Type drop-down list box, and select a new drive and folder before you save the workbook as a disk file.

When you finish making changes in the Save As dialog box, click the Save button or press Enter to have Excel 2010 save your work. When Excel saves your workbook file, the program saves all the information in every worksheet in your workbook (including the last position of the cell cursor) in the designated folder and drive.

You don't have to fool with the Save As dialog box again unless you want to rename the workbook or save a copy of it in a different folder. If you want to do these things, you must choose File⇨Save As or press Alt+FA to choose the Save As command rather than clicking the Save button on the Quick Access toolbar or pressing Ctrl+S.

The Save As dialog box in Windows 7 and Windows Vista

Figure 2-21 shows you the Save As dialog box as it appears in Excel 2010 when running the program under Windows 7. Here, you can replace the temporary filename (Book1, Book2, and so on) with a more descriptive name by clicking the File Name text box and typing in the new name (up to 255 characters total, including spaces).

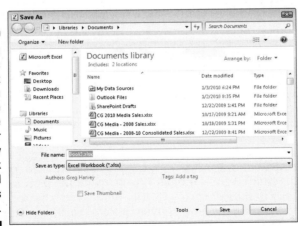

Figure 2-21:
The Save As
dialog box
enables you
to select the
filename
and folder
for the new
workbook
file as well
as add tags
to it.

To select a new folder in which to save the new workbook file, follow these steps:

1. **In the Navigation Pane, click the name of the folder in the Favorites, Libraries, Computer, or Network section in which you want to save the workbook file.**

2. To save the workbook file within a subfolder of one of the folders now displayed in the main pane of the Save As dialog box, double-click its folder icon to open it up.

3. (Optional) If you want to save the workbook file inside a new subfolder within the folder currently open in the Save As dialog box, click the New Folder button on the toolbar, replace the suggested New Folder name by typing the actual name of the folder, and then press Enter.

4. Click the Save button to save the file in the selected folder.

When the Save As dialog box is expanded by clicking the Browse Folders button, you can modify the authors or add tags to the new workbook file by clicking the Add an Author or Add a Tag text boxes. You can then use this information later when searching for the workbook. (See Chapter 4 for details on searching.)

The Save As dialog box in Windows XP

The Windows XP version of the Save As dialog box contains a bunch of large buttons that appear on the left side of the dialog box: My Recent Documents, Desktop, My Documents, My Computer, and My Network Places. Use these buttons to select the following folders in which to save your new workbook file:

✔ Click the My Recent Documents button to save your workbook in the Recent folder. The Recent folder resides in this hierarchy: Windows folder (on your hard drive)\Application Data folder\Microsoft folder\Office folder\Recent folder.

✔ Click the Desktop button to save your workbook on your computer's desktop.

✔ Click the My Documents button to save your workbook in the My Documents folder.

✔ Click the My Computer button to save your workbook on one of the disks on your computer or in your own or a shared documents folder on your hard drive.

✔ Click the My Network Places button to save your workbook in one of the folders on your company's network.

To save your workbook in a new subfolder within the folder open in the Save As dialog box, click the Create New Folder button on the toolbar (or press Alt+4) and then type the name for the folder in the New Folder dialog box before you click OK.

Changing the default file location

Whenever you open the Save As dialog box to save a new workbook file, Excel 2010 automatically selects the folder listed in the Default File Location text box on the Save tab of the Excel Options dialog box (File⇨Options⇨Save or Alt+FTS).

When you first start using Excel, the default folder is either the My Documents (Windows XP) or the Documents folder (Windows 7 and Windows Vista) under your user name on your hard drive. For example, the directory path of the default folder where Excel 2010 automatically saves new workbook files on my computer running Windows XP is

```
C:\Documents and Settings\Greg\My Documents
```

However, the directory path of the default folder where Excel 2010 automatically saves new workbook files on my other computer running Windows 7 is

```
C:\Users\Greg\Documents
```

The very generic My Documents or Documents folder may not be the places on your hard drive where you want all the new workbooks you create automatically saved. To change the default file location to another folder on your computer, follow these steps:

1. **Choose File⇨Options⇨Save or press Alt+FTS to open the Save tab of the Excel Options dialog box.**

   The Default File Location text box displays the directory path to the current default folder.

2. **Click the Default File Location text box.**

   To edit part of the path (such as the My Documents or Documents folder name after your user name), click the mouse pointer at that place in the path to set the insertion point.

3. **Edit the existing path or replace it with the path to another folder in which you want all future workbooks to save to automatically.**

4. **Click OK to close the Excel Options dialog box.**

The difference between the XLSX and XLS file format

Excel 2010 supports the use of the XML-based file format first introduced in Excel 2007 (which Microsoft officially calls the Microsoft Office Open XML format). This default file format is touted as being more efficient in saving data resulting in smaller file size and offering superior integration with external data sources (especially, when these resources are Web-based ones supporting XML files). This XML-based file format carries the filename extension `.xlsx` and is the file format in which Excel automatically saves any new workbook you create.

The only problem with this newfangled XML-based file format is that it can't be opened by earlier Excel versions (before Excel 2007). Therefore, if someone who needs to work with the workbook you've just created isn't using Excel 2007 or hasn't yet upgraded to Excel 2010, you need to save the new workbook in the earlier file format used in Excel versions 97 through 2003 with the old `.xls` filename extension.

To do this, click the Save As Type drop-down button in the Save As dialog box and then click Excel 97-2003 Workbook (*.xls) on the drop-down menu. (If you work in an office where all workbooks must be backwardly compatible with earlier versions, see "Dealing with the new Excel file formats" in Chapter 1 for a tip on making the Excel 97-2003 workbook file format the default format for Excel 2010.)

Filename extensions, such as `.xlsx` and `.xls`, do not appear as part of the filename (even though they are appended) in the File Name text box in the Excel Save As dialog box unless you've specifically changed Windows' folder options to show them. To make this change, open the Folder Options dialog box in Windows Explorer and then deselect the Hide Extensions for Known File Types check box on the View tab. To open the Folder Options dialog box, select Tools➪Options on the Explorer window's pull-down menus in Windows XP or click the Organize button and then select Folder and Search Options on its drop-down menu in Windows 7 and Windows Vista.

Excel 2010 also supports a special binary file format called Excel Binary Workbook that carries the `.xlsb` filename extension. Select this binary format for huge spreadsheets that you create that have to be compatible with earlier versions of Excel.

Saving the Workbook as a PDF File

The PDF (Portable Document File) file format developed by Adobe Systems Incorporated enables people to open up and print documents without access to the original programs with which the documents were created.

Excel 2010 enables you to save your workbook files directly in this special PDF file format. You can readily share your Excel 2010 workbooks with users who don't have Excel installed on their computers by saving them as PDF files. All they need to open and print the PDF copy of the workbook file is the free Adobe Reader software (which they can download from the Adobe Web site at www.adobe.com).

To save your workbook as a PDF file, you simply select the PDF option on the Save as Type drop-down list in the Save As dialog box. Excel then adds PDF-specific options to the bottom of the Save As dialog box, with the Standard (Publishing Online and Printing) button under the Optimize For heading and the Open File after Publishing check box selected.

If you want to make the resulting PDF file as small as possible (because your worksheet is so large), click the Minimum Size (Publishing Online) button under the Optimize For heading. If you want to change which parts of the workbook are saved in the resulting PDF (Excel automatically saves all ranges in the active worksheet of the workbook), click the Options button directly beneath the Minimum Size (Publishing Online) option and make the appropriate changes in the Options dialog box before you click OK.

If you don't need to edit the filename (Excel automatically appends .pdf to the current filename) or the folder location in the Save As dialog box, simply click the Save button. Excel then saves a copy of the workbook in a PDF file format and, provided you don't deselect the Open File after Publishing check box, automatically opens the workbook for your inspection in Adobe Reader. After viewing the PDF version in Adobe Reader, you can then return to your worksheet in Excel by clicking Reader's Close button (or pressing Alt+F4).

If you create an Excel 2010 workbook that incorporates new features not supported in earlier versions of Excel, instead of saving the workbook as an .xls file, thereby losing all of its 2010 enhancements, consider saving it as a PDF file. That way, co-workers still using pre-2010 Excel versions can still access the data in all its glory via Adobe Reader.

Document Recovery to the Rescue

Excel 2010 offers a document recovery feature that can help you in the event of a computer crash because of a power failure or some sort of operating system freeze or shutdown. The AutoRecover feature saves your workbooks at regular intervals. In the event of a computer crash, Excel displays a Document Recovery task pane the next time you start Excel after rebooting the computer.

When you first start using Excel 2010, the AutoRecover feature is set to automatically save changes to your workbook (provided that the file has already been saved) every ten minutes. You can shorten or lengthen this interval as you see fit. Choose File➪Options➪Save or press Alt+FTS to open the Excel Options dialog box with the Save tab selected. Use the spinner buttons or enter a new automatic save interval into the text box marked Save AutoRecover Information Every 10 Minutes before clicking OK.

After re-launching Excel 2010 after a computer crash that prevents you from saving your workbook file, the program opens with the Document Recovery task pane on the left side of the screen. This Document Recovery task pane shows the available versions of the workbook files that were open at the time of the computer crash. The original version of the workbook file is identified, including when it was saved, as is the recovered version of the file (displaying an .xlsb file extension) and when it was saved.

To open the recovered version of a workbook (to see how much of the work it contains that was unsaved at the time of the crash), position the mouse pointer over the AutoRecover version, click its drop-down menu button, and then click Open. After you open the recovered version, you can then (if you choose) save its changes by clicking the Save button on the Quick Access toolbar or by choosing File⇨Save.

To save the recovered version of a workbook without bothering to first open it, place your mouse over the recovered version in the task pane, click its drop-down button, and then choose Save As. To abandon the recovered version permanently (leaving you with *only* the data in the original version), click the Close button at the bottom of the Document Recovery task pane. When you click the Close button, an alert dialog box appears, giving you the chance to retain the recovered versions of the file for later viewing. To retain the files for later viewing, select the Yes (I Want to View These Files Later) radio button before clicking OK. To retain only the original versions of the files shown in the task pane, select the No (Remove These Files. I Have Saved the Files I Need) radio button instead.

The AutoRecover features only work on Excel workbooks that you've saved at least one time (as explained in the earlier section "Making Sure That the Data Is Safe and Sound"). In other words, if you build a new workbook and don't bother to save and rename it prior to experiencing a computer crash, the AutoRecover feature will not bring back any part of it. For this reason, it is very important that you get into the habit of saving new workbooks with the Save button on the Quick Access toolbar very shortly after beginning to work on its worksheets. Or use the trusty keyboard shortcut Ctrl+S.

Part II
Editing without Tears

The 5th Wave
By Rich Tennant

"I've used several spreadsheet programs, but this is the best one for designing quilt patterns."

In this part . . .

The business world wouldn't be half-bad if it weren't for the fact that right around the time you master your job, somebody goes and changes it on you. When your life must always be flexible, changing gears and "going with the flow" can really grate on a person! The sad truth is that a big part of the work you do with Excel 2010 is changing the stuff you slaved so hard to enter into the spreadsheet in the first place.

In Part II, I break down this editing stuff into three phases: formatting the raw data; rearranging the formatted data or in some cases deleting it; and spitting out the final formatted and edited data in printed form. Take it from me, after you know your way around editing your spreadsheets (as presented in this part of the book), you're more than half-way home with Excel 2010.

Chapter 3

Making It All Look Pretty

*I*n spreadsheet programs like Excel, you normally don't worry about how the stuff looks until after you enter all the data in the worksheets of your workbook and save it all safe and sound (see Chapters 1 and 2). Only then do you pretty up the information so that it's clearer and easy to read.

After you decide on the types of formatting that you want to apply to a portion of the worksheet, you can select all the cells to beautify and then click the appropriate tool or choose the menu command to apply those formats to the cells. However, before you discover all the fabulous formatting features you can use to dress up cells, you need to know how to pick the group of cells that you want to apply the formatting to — that is, *selecting the cells* or, alternately, *making a cell selection*.

Be aware, also, that entering data into a cell and formatting that data are two completely different things in Excel. Because they're separate, you can change the entry in a formatted cell, and new entries assume the cell's formatting. This enables you to format blank cells in a worksheet, knowing that when you get around to making entries in those cells, those entries automatically assume the formatting you assign to those cells.

Choosing a Select Group of Cells

Given the monotonously rectangular nature of the worksheet and its components, it shouldn't come as a surprise to find that all the cell selections you make in the worksheet have the same kind of cubist feel to them. After all, worksheets are just blocks of cells of varying numbers of columns and rows.

A *cell selection* (or *cell range*) is whatever collection of neighboring cells you choose to format or edit. The smallest possible cell selection in a worksheet is just one cell: the so-called *active cell.* The cell with the cell cursor is really just a single cell selection. The largest possible cell selection in a worksheet is all the cells in that worksheet (the whole enchilada, so to speak). Most of the cell selections you need for formatting a worksheet will probably fall somewhere in between, consisting of cells in several adjacent columns and rows.

Excel shows a cell selection in the worksheet by highlighting in color the entire block of cells within the extended cell cursor except for the active cell that keeps its original color. (Figure 3-1 shows several cell selections of different sizes and shapes.)

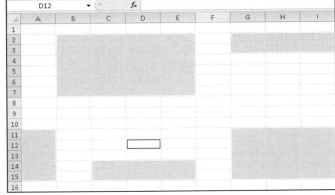

Figure 3-1:
Several cell
selections
of various
shapes and
sizes.

In Excel, you can select more than one cell range at a time (a phenomenon somewhat ingloriously called a *noncontiguous* or *nonadjacent selection*). In fact, although Figure 3-1 appears to contain several cell selections, it's really just one big, nonadjacent cell selection with cell D12 (the active one) as the cell that was selected last.

Point-and-click cell selections

The mouse is a natural for selecting a range of cells. Just position the mouse pointer (in its thick, white cross form) on the first cell and then click and drag in the direction that you want to extend the selection.

- ✔ To extend the cell selection to columns to the right, drag your mouse to the right, highlighting neighboring cells as you go.
- ✔ To extend the selection to rows to the bottom, drag your mouse down.
- ✔ To extend the selection down and to the right at the same time, drag your mouse diagonally toward the cell in the lower-right corner of the block you're highlighting.

Shifty cell selections

To speed up the old cell-selection procedure, you can use the Shift+click method, which goes as follows:

1. **Click the first cell in the selection.**

   This selects that cell.

2. **Position the mouse pointer in the last cell in the selection.**

   This is kitty-corner from the first cell in your selected rectangular block.

3. **Press the Shift key and hold it down while you click the mouse button again.**

   When you click the mouse button the second time, Excel selects all the cells in the columns and rows between the first cell and last cell.

The Shift key works with the mouse like an *extend* key to extend a selection from the first object you select through to, and including, the second object you select. See the section "Extend that cell selection," later in this chapter. Using the Shift key enables you to select the first and last cells, as well as all the intervening cells in a worksheet or all the document names in a dialog list box.

If, when making a cell selection with the mouse, you notice that you include the wrong cells before you release the mouse button, you can deselect the cells and resize the selection by moving the pointer in the opposite direction. If you already released the mouse button, click the first cell in the highlighted range to select just that cell (and deselect all the others) and then start the whole selection process again.

Nonadjacent cell selections

To select a nonadjacent cell selection made up of more than one non-touching block of cells, drag through the first cell range and release the mouse button. Then hold down the Ctrl key while you click the first cell of the second range and drag the pointer through the cells in this range. As long as you hold down Ctrl while you select the subsequent ranges, Excel doesn't deselect any of the previously selected cell ranges.

The Ctrl key works with the mouse like an *add* key to include non-neighboring objects in Excel. See the section "Nonadjacent cell selections with the keyboard," later in this chapter. By using the Ctrl key, you can add to the selection of cells in a worksheet or to the document names in a dialog list box without having to deselect those already selected.

Going for the "big" cell selections

You can select the cells in entire columns or rows or even all the cells in the worksheet by applying the following clicking-and-dragging techniques to the worksheet frame:

- To select every single cell in a particular column, click its column letter on the frame at the top of the worksheet document window.

- To select every cell in a particular row, click its row number on the frame at the left edge of the document window.

- To select a range of entire columns or rows, drag through the column letters or row numbers on the frame surrounding the workbook.

- To select more than entire columns or rows that are not right next to each other (that old noncontiguous stuff, again), press and hold down the Ctrl key while you click the column letters or row numbers of the columns and rows that you want to add to the selection.

- To select every cell in the worksheet, press Ctrl+A or click the Select All button, which is the button with the triangle pointing downward on the diagonal (reminding me of the corner of a dog-eared book page). It's in the upper-left corner of the workbook frame, formed by the intersection of the row with the column letters and the column with the row numbers.

Selecting the cells in a table of data, courtesy of AutoSelect

Excel provides a quick way (called AutoSelect) to select all the cells in a table of data entered as a solid block. To use AutoSelect, simply follow these steps:

1. **Click the first cell of the table to select it.**

   This is the cell in the table's upper-left corner.

2. **Hold down the Shift key while you double-click the right or bottom edge of the selected cell with the arrowhead mouse pointer. (See Figure 3-2.)**

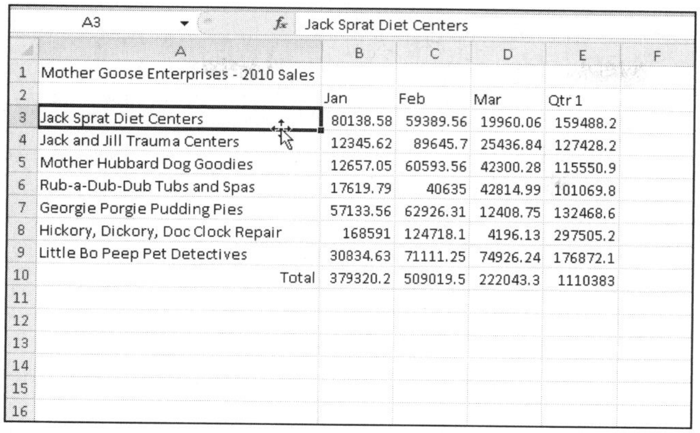

Figure 3-2:
Position
the mouse
pointer on
the first
cell's bot-
tom edge
to select all
cells of the
table's first
column.

Double-clicking the bottom edge of the cell causes the cell selection to
expand to the cell in the last row of the first column (as shown in Figure
3-3). If you double-click the right edge of the cell, the cell selection
expands to the cell in the last column of the first row.

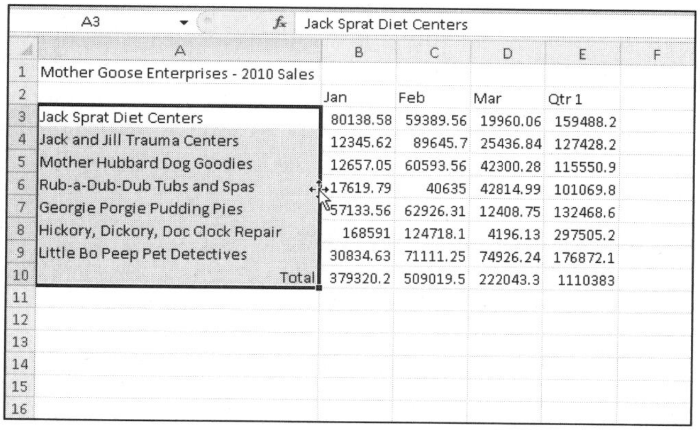

Figure 3-3:
Hold down
Shift while
you double-
click the
bottom
edge of the
first cell to
extend the
selection
down the
column.

**3a. Double-click somewhere on the right edge of the cell selection (refer
to Figure 3-3) if the cell selection now consists of the first column of
the table.**

This selects all the remaining rows of the table of data (as shown in
Figure 3-4).

**3b. Double-click somewhere on the bottom edge of the current cell selec-
tion if the cell selection now consists of the first row of the table.**

This selects all the remaining rows in the table.

Figure 3-4:
Hold down
Shift as you
double-click
the right
edge of
the current
selection
to extend it
across the
rows of the
table.

	A3	▼	ⓒ	*fₓ*	Jack Sprat Diet Centers		
	A		B	C	D	E	F
1	Mother Goose Enterprises - 2010 Sales						
2			Jan	Feb	Mar	Qtr 1	
3	Jack Sprat Diet Centers		80138.58	59389.56	19960.06	159488.2	
4	Jack and Jill Trauma Centers		12345.62	89645.7	25436.84	127428.2	
5	Mother Hubbard Dog Goodies		12657.05	60593.56	42300.28	115550.9	
6	Rub-a-Dub-Dub Tubs and Spas		176⟳79	40635	42814.99	101069.8	
7	Georgie Porgie Pudding Pies		57133.56	62926.31	12408.75	132468.6	
8	Hickory, Dickory, Doc Clock Repair		168591	124718.1	4196.13	297505.2	
9	Little Bo Peep Pet Detectives		30834.63	71111.25	74926.24	176872.1	
10		Total	379320.2	509019.5	222043.3	1110383	
11							
12							
13							
14							
15							
16							

TIP Although the preceding steps may lead you to believe that you have to select the first cell of the table when you use AutoSelect, you can actually select any of the cells in the four corners of the table. Then, when expanding the cell selection in the table with the Shift key depressed, you can choose whatever direction you like to either select the first or last row of the table or the first or last column. (Choose left, by clicking the left edge; right, by clicking the right edge; up, by clicking the top edge; or down, by clicking the bottom edge.) After expanding the cell selection to include either the first or last row or first or last column, you need to click whichever edge of that current cell selection that will expand it to include all the remaining table rows or columns.

Keyboard cell selections

If you're not keen on using the mouse, you can use the keyboard to select the cells you want. Sticking with the Shift+click method of selecting cells, the easiest way to select cells with the keyboard is to combine the Shift key with other keystrokes that move the cell cursor. (I list these keystrokes in Chapter 1.)

Start by positioning the cell cursor in the first cell of the selection and then holding the Shift key while you press the appropriate cell-pointer movement keys. When you hold the Shift key while you press direction keys — such as the arrow keys ($\uparrow$, $\rightarrow$, $\downarrow$, $\leftarrow$), PgUp, or PgDn — Excel anchors the selection on the current cell, moves the cell cursor, and highlights cells as it goes.

TIP When making a cell selection this way, you can continue to alter the size and shape of the cell range with the cell-pointer movement keys as long as you don't release the Shift key. After you release the Shift key, pressing any of the cell-pointer movement keys immediately collapses the selection, reducing it to just the cell with the cell cursor.

Extend that cell selection

If holding the Shift key while you move the cell cursor is too tiring, you can place Excel in Extend mode by pressing (and promptly releasing) F8 before you press any cell-pointer movement key. Excel displays the Extend Selection indicator on the left side of the Status bar — when you see this, the program will select all the cells that you move the cell cursor through (just as though you were holding down the Shift key).

After you highlight all the cells you want in the cell range, press F8 again (or Esc) to turn off Extend mode. The Extend Selection indicator disappears from the status bar, and then you can once again move the cell cursor with the keyboard without highlighting everything in your path. In fact, when you first move the pointer, all previously selected cells are deselected.

AutoSelect keyboard style

For the keyboard equivalent of AutoSelect with the mouse (see the "Selecting the cells in a table of data, courtesy of AutoSelect" section), you combine the use of the F8 key (Extend key) or the Shift key with the Ctrl+arrow keys or End+arrow keys to zip the cell cursor from one end of a block to the other and merrily select all the cells in that path.

To select an entire table of data with a keyboard version of AutoSelect, follow these steps:

1. **Position the cell cursor in the first cell.**

   That's the cell in the upper-left corner of the table.

2. **Press F8 (or hold the Shift key) and then press Ctrl+→ to extend the cell selection to the cells in the columns on the right.**

3. **Then press Ctrl+↓ to extend the selection to the cells in the rows below.**

The directions in the preceding steps are somewhat arbitrary — you can just as well press Ctrl+↓ before you press Ctrl+→. Just be sure (if you're using the Shift key instead of F8) that you don't let up on the Shift key until after you finish performing these two directional maneuvers. Also, if you press F8 to get the program into Extend mode, don't forget to press this key again to get out of Extend mode after the table cells are all selected, or you'll end up selecting cells that you don't want included when you next move the cell cursor.

Nonadjacent cell selections with the keyboard

Selecting more than one cell range is a little more complicated with the keyboard than it is with the mouse. When using the keyboard, you alternate between *anchoring* the cell cursor and moving it to select the cell range and *unanchoring* the cell cursor and repositioning it at the beginning of the next range. To unanchor the cell cursor so that you can move it into position for selecting another range, press Shift+F8. This puts you in Add to Selection mode, in which you can move to the first cell of the next range without selecting any more cells. Excel lets you know that the cell cursor is unanchored by displaying the Add to Selection indicator on the left side of the Status bar.

To select more than one cell range by using the keyboard, follow these general steps:

1. **Move the cell cursor to the first cell of the first cell range that you want to select.**

2. **Press F8 to get into Extend Selection mode.**

   Move the cell cursor to select all the cells in the first cell range. Alternatively, hold the Shift key while you move the cell cursor.

3. **Press Shift+F8 to switch from Extend Selection mode to Add to Selection mode.**

   The Add to Selection indicator appears in the Status bar.

4. **Move the cell cursor to the first cell of the next nonadjacent range that you want to select.**

5. **Press F8 again to get back into Extend Selection mode and then move the cell cursor to select all the cells in this new range.**

6. **If you still have other nonadjacent ranges to select, repeat Steps 3, 4, and 5 until you select and add all the cell ranges that you want to use.**

Cell selections à la Go To

If you want to select a large cell range that would take a long time to select by pressing various cell-pointer movement keys, use the Go To feature to extend the range to a far distant cell. All you gotta do is follow this pair of steps:

1. **Position the cell cursor in the first cell of the range and then press F8 to anchor the cell cursor and get Excel into Extend Selection mode.**

2. **Press F5 or Ctrl+G to open the Go To dialog box, type the address of the last cell in the range (the cell kitty-corner from the first cell), and then click OK or press Enter.**

Because Excel is in Extend Selection mode at the time you use the Go To feature to jump to another cell, the program not only moves the cell cursor to the designated cell address but selects all the intervening cells as well. After selecting the range of cells with the Go To feature, don't forget to press F8 (the Extend Selection key) again to prevent the program from messing up your selection by adding more cells the next time you move the cell cursor.

Having Fun with the Format as Table Gallery

Here's a formatting technique that doesn't require you to do any prior cell selecting. (Kinda figures, doesn't it?) The Format as Table feature is so automatic that the cell cursor just has to be within the table of data prior to you clicking the Format as Table command button in the Styles group on the Home tab. Clicking the Format as Table command button opens its rather extensive Table gallery with the formatting thumbnails divided into three sections — Light, Medium, and Dark — each of which describes the intensity of the colors used by its various formats.

As soon as you click one of the table formatting thumbnails in this Table gallery, Excel makes its best guess as to the cell range of the data table to apply it to (indicated by the marquee around its perimeter) and the Format As Table dialog box, similar to the one shown in Figure 3-5, appears.

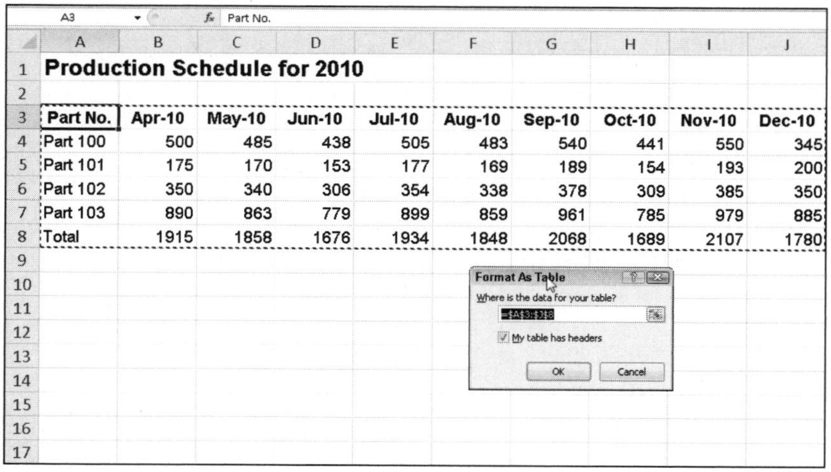

Figure 3-5: Selecting a format from the Table gallery and indicating its range in the Format As Table dialog box.

	A	B	C	D	E	F	G	H	I	J
1	Production Schedule for 2010									
2										
3	Part No.	Apr-10	May-10	Jun-10	Jul-10	Aug-10	Sep-10	Oct-10	Nov-10	Dec-10
4	Part 100	500	485	438	505	483	540	441	550	345
5	Part 101	175	170	153	177	169	189	154	193	200
6	Part 102	350	340	306	354	338	378	309	385	350
7	Part 103	890	863	779	899	859	961	785	979	885
8	Total	1915	1858	1676	1934	1848	2068	1689	2107	1780

A3   *fx* Part No.

Format As Table
Where is the data for your table?
=$A$3:$J$8
☑ My table has headers
OK   Cancel

This dialog box contains a Where Is the Data for Your Table text box that shows the address of the cell range currently selected by the marquee and a My Table Has Headers check box.

If Excel does not correctly guess the range of the data table you want to format, drag through the cell range to adjust the marquee and the range address in the Where Is the Data for Your Table text box. If your data table doesn't use column headers or, if the table has them, but you still don't want Excel to add Filter drop-down buttons to each column heading, deselect the My Table Has Headers check box before you click the OK button.

The table formats in the Table gallery are not available if you select multiple nonadjacent cells before you click the Format as Table command button on the Home tab.

After you click the OK button in the Format As Table dialog box, Excel applies the format of the thumbnail you clicked in the gallery to the data table. Additionally, the Design tab appears under the Table Tools contextual tab at the end of the Ribbon, as shown in Figure 3-6.

Production Sch 2010.xlsx - Microsoft Excel
Table Tools
File
Home
Insert
Page Layout
Formulas
Data
Review
View
Design
Table Name:
Table1
Resize Table
Properties
Summarize with PivotTable
Remove Duplicates
Convert to Range
Tools
Export
Refresh
External Table Data
Header Row
Total Row
Banded Rows
First Column
Last Column
Banded Columns
Table Style Options
Table Styles
A3
Part No.
Production Schedule for 2010
Part No | Apr-10 | May-10 | Jun-10 | Jul-10 | Aug-10 | Sep-10 | Oct-10 | Nov-10 | Dec-10
Part 100 | 500 | 485 | 438 | 505 | 483 | 540 | 441 | 550 | 345
Part 101 | 175 | 170 | 153 | 177 | 169 | 189 | 154 | 193 | 200
Part 102 | 350 | 340 | 306 | 354 | 338 | 378 | 309 | 385 | 350
Part 103 | 890 | 863 | 779 | 899 | 859 | 961 | 785 | 979 | 885
Total | 1915 | 1858 | 1676 | 1934 | 1848 | 2068 | 1689 | 2107 | 1780
Sheet1
Sheet2
Sheet3
Ready
140%

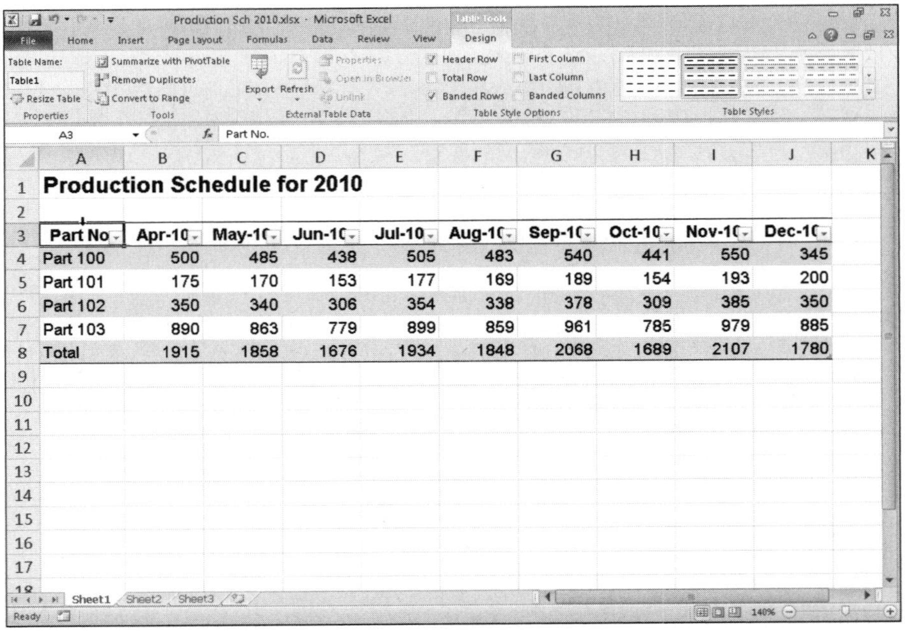

Figure 3-6: After you select a format from the Table gallery, the Design tab appears under the Table Tools contextual tab.

The Design tab enables you to use Live Preview to see how your table would appear. Simply position the mouse pointer over any of the format thumbnails in the Table Styles group to see the data in your table appear in that table format. Click the button with the triangle pointing downward to scroll up new rows of table formats in the Table Styles group and the button with the triangle pointing upward to scroll down rows without opening the Table gallery and possibly obscuring the actual data table in the Worksheet area. Click the More button (the one with the horizontal bar above the downward pointing triangle) to redisplay the Table gallery and then mouse over the thumbnails in the Light, Medium, and Dark sections to have Live Preview apply them to the table.

In addition to enabling you to select a new format from the Table gallery in the Table Styles group, the Design tab contains a Table Style Options group containing a bunch of check boxes that enable you to customize the look of the selected table format even further:

- ✔ **Header Row** to add special formatting and Filter buttons to each of the column headings in the first row of the table.

- ✔ **Total Row** to have Excel add a Total Row to the bottom of the table that displays the sums of each column that contains values. To apply another Statistical function to the values in a particular column, click the cell in that column's Total Row to display a drop-down list button and then select the function — Average, Count, Count Numbers, Max, Min, Sum, StdDev (Standard Deviation), or Var (Variance).

- ✔ **First Column** to have Excel display the row headings in the first column of the table in bold.

- ✔ **Last Column** to have Excel display the row headings in the last column of the table in bold.

- ✔ **Banded Rows** to have Excel apply shading to every other row in the table.

- ✔ **Banded Columns** to have Excel apply shading to every other column in the table.

Whenever you assign a format in the Table gallery to one of the data tables in your workbook, Excel automatically assigns that table a generic range name (Table1, Table2, and so on). You can use the Table Name text box in the Properties group on the Design tab to rename the data table by giving it a more descriptive range name. (See Chapter 6 for all you need to know about naming cell ranges.)

When you finish selecting and/or customizing the formatting of your data table, click a cell outside of the table to remove the Table Tools contextual tab (with its Design tab) from the Ribbon. If later, you decide that you want to further experiment with the table's formatting, click any of the table's cells to redisplay the Table Tools' Design tab at the end of the Ribbon.

Cell Formatting from the Home Tab

Some spreadsheet tables or ranges within them require a lighter touch than the Format as Table command button offers. For example, you may have a data table where the only emphasis you want to add is to make the column headings bold at the top of the table and to underline the row of totals at the bottom (done by drawing a borderline along the bottom of the cells).

The formatting buttons that appear in the Font, Alignment, and Number groups on the Home tab enable you to accomplish just this kind of targeted cell formatting. Figures 3-7, 3-8, and 3-9 identify all the formatting buttons in these three groups on the Home tab. See Table 3-1 for a complete rundown on how to use each of these formatting buttons.

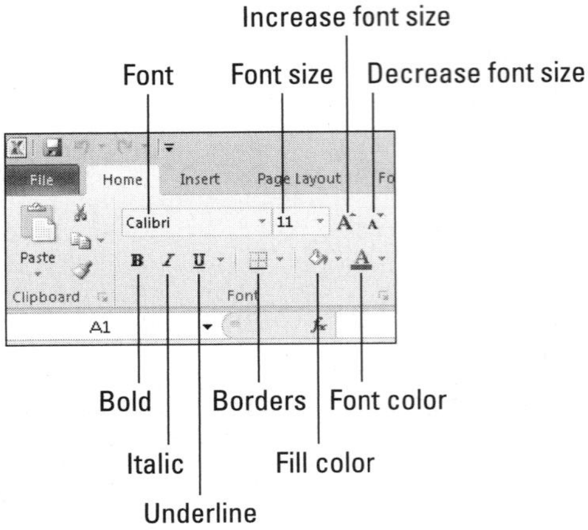

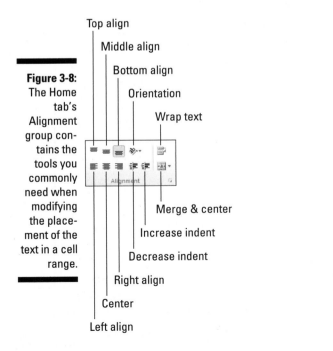

Figure 3-7: The Home tab's Font group contains the tools you commonly need when modifying the appearance of the text in a cell range.

Figure 3-8: The Home tab's Alignment group contains the tools you commonly need when modifying the placement of the text in a cell range.

Figure 3-9:
The Home tab's Number group contains the tools you commonly need when modifying the number format of the values in a cell range.

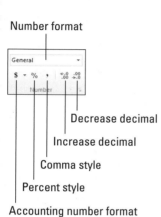

Number format

Decrease decimal

Increase decimal

Comma style

Percent style

Accounting number format

Table 3-1 **Formatting Command Buttons in the Font, Alignment, and Number Groups on the Home Tab**

Group	Button Name	Function
Font		
	Font	Displays a Font drop-down menu from which you can select a new font for your cell selection
	Font Size	Displays a Font Size drop-down menu from which you can select a new font size for your cell selection — click the Font Size text box and enter the desired point size if it doesn't appear on the drop-down menu
	Increase Font Size	Increases the size of the font in the cell selection by one point
	Decrease Font Size	Decreases the size of the font in the cell selection by one point
	Bold	Applies boldface to the entries in the cell selection
	Italic	Italicizes the entries in the cell selection
	Underline	Underlines the entries in the cell selection
	Borders	Displays a Borders drop-down menu from which you can select a border style for the cell selection

(continued)

Table 3-1 *(continued)*

Group	Button Name	Function
	Fill Color	Displays a Color drop-down palette from which you can select a new background color for the cell selection
	Font Color	Displays a Color drop-down palette from which you can select a new font color for the cell selection
Alignment		
	Align Left	Aligns all the entries in the cell selection with the left edge of their cells
	Center	Centers all the entries in the cell selection within their cells
	Align Right	Aligns all the entries in the cell selection with the right edge of their cells
	Decrease Indent	Decreases the margin between entries in the cell selection and their left cell borders by one tab stop
	Increase Indent	Increases the margin between the entries in the cell selection and their left cell borders by one tab stop
	Top Align	Aligns the entries in the cell selection with the top border of their cells
	Middle Align	Vertically centers the entries in the cell selection between the top and bottom borders of their cells
	Bottom Align	Aligns the entries in the cell selection with the bottom border of their cells
	Orientation	Displays a drop-down menu with options for changing the angle and direction of the entries in the cell selection
	Wrap Text	Wraps the entries in the cell selection that spill over their right borders onto multiple lines within the current column width
	Merge and Center	Merges the cell selection into a single cell and the centers the entry in the first cell between its new left and right border — click the Merge and Center drop-down button to display a menu of options that enable you to merge the cell selection into a single cell without centering the entries as well as to split up a merged cell back into its original individual cells

Group	Button Name	Function
Number		
	Number Format	Displays the number format applied to the active cell in the cell selection — click its drop-down button to display a menu showing the active cell in cell selection formatted with all of Excel's major number formats
	Accounting Number Format	Formats the cell selection using the Accounting number format that adds a dollar sign, uses commas to separate thousands, displays two decimal places, and encloses negative values in a closed pair of parentheses — click the Accounting Number Format's drop-down button to display a menu of other major Currency number formats from which you can choose
	Percent Style	Formats the cell selection using the Percentage number format that multiplies the values by 100 and adds a percent sign with no decimal places
	Comma Style	Formats the cell selection with the Comma Style number format that uses commas to separate thousands, displays two decimal places, and encloses negative values in a closed pair of parentheses
	Increase Decimal	Adds a decimal place to the values in the cell selection
	Decrease Decimal	Removes a decimal place from the values in the cell selection

Don't forget about these shortcut keys for quickly adding or removing attributes from the entries in the cell selection: Ctrl+B for toggling on and off bold in the cell selection, Ctrl+I for toggling on and off italic, and Ctrl+U for toggling on and off underlining.

Formatting Cells Close to the Source with the Mini-Toolbar

Excel 2010 makes it easy to apply common formatting changes to a cell selection right within the Worksheet area thanks to its new mini-toolbar feature, nicknamed the mini-bar (makes me thirsty just thinking about it!).

To display the mini-bar, select the cells that need formatting and then right-click somewhere in the cell selection. The mini-toolbar then appears immediately above the cell selection (see Figure 3-10).

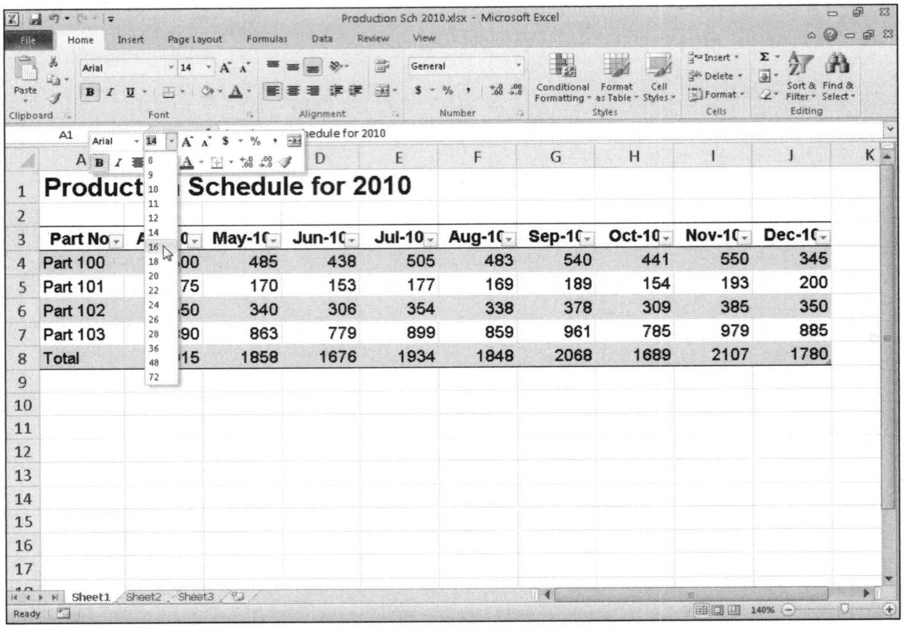

Figure 3-10:
Use the but-
tons on the
mini-toolbar
to apply
common
formatting
changes
to the cell
selection
within the
Worksheet
area.

As you can see in this figure, the mini-toolbar contains most of the buttons from the Font group of the Home tab (with the exception of the Underline button). It also contains the Center and Merge & Center buttons from the Alignment group (see "Altering the Alignment" later in this chapter) and the Accounting Number Format, Percent Style, Comma Style, Increase Decimal, and Decrease Decimal buttons from the Number group (see "Getting comfortable with the number formats" later in this chapter). Simply click these buttons to apply their formatting to the current cell selection.

Additionally, the mini-bar contains the Format Painter button from the Clipboard group of the Home tab that you can use to copy the formatting in the active cell to a cell selection you make (see "Fooling Around with the Format Painter" later in this chapter for details).

Using the Format Cells Dialog Box

Although the command buttons in the Font, Alignment, and Number groups on the Home tab give you immediate access to the most commonly used formatting commands, they do not represent all of Excel's formatting commands by any stretch of the imagination.

To have access to all the formatting commands, you need to open the Format Cells dialog box by doing any of the following:

- ✔ Click the More Number Formats option at the very bottom of the drop-down menu attached to the Number Format button
- ✔ Click the dialog box launcher in the lower right of the Number group
- ✔ Press Ctrl+1

The Format Cells dialog box that this command calls up contains six tabs: Number, Alignment, Font, Border, Fill, and Protection. In this chapter, I show you how to use them all except the Protection tab. For information on that tab, see Chapter 6.

The keystroke shortcut that opens the Format Cells dialog box — Ctrl+1 — is one worth knowing. Just press the Ctrl key plus the *number* 1 key, and not the *function key* F1.

Getting comfortable with the number formats

As I explain in Chapter 2, how you enter values into a worksheet determines the type of number format that they get. Here are some examples:

- ✔ If you enter a financial value complete with the dollar sign and two decimal places, Excel assigns a Currency number format to the cell along with the entry.
- ✔ If you enter a value representing a percentage as a whole number followed by the percent sign without any decimal places, Excel assigns the cell the Percentage number format that follows this pattern along with the entry.
- ✔ If you enter a date (dates are values, too) that follows one of the built-in Excel number formats, such as 11/06/02 or 06-Nov-02, the program assigns a Date number format that follows the pattern of the date along with a special value representing the date.

Although you can format values in this manner as you go along (which is necessary in the case of dates), you don't have to do it this way. You can always assign a number format to a group of values before or after you enter them.

Formatting numbers after you enter them is often the most efficient way to go because it's just a two-step procedure:

1. **Select all the cells containing the values that need dressing up.**

2. **Select the number format that you want to use from the formatting command buttons on the Home tab or the options available on the Number tab in the Format Cells dialog box.**

Even if you're a really, really good typist and prefer to enter each value exactly as you want it to appear in the worksheet, you still have to resort to using number formats to make the values that are calculated by formulas match the others you enter. This is because Excel applies a General number format (which the Format Cells dialog box defines: "General format cells have no specific number format.") to all the values it calculates as well as any you enter that don't exactly follow one of the other Excel number formats. The biggest problem with the General format is that it has the nasty habit of dropping all leading and trailing zeros from the entries. This makes it very hard to line up numbers in a column on their decimal points.

You can view this sad state of affairs in Figure 3-11, which is a sample worksheet with the first-quarter 2010 sales figures for Mother Goose Enterprises before any of the values have been formatted. Notice how the numbers in the monthly sales figures columns zig and zag because they don't align according to decimal place. This is the fault of Excel's General number format; the only cure is to format the values with a uniform number format.

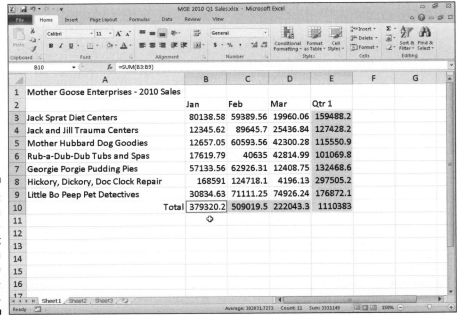

Figure 3-11: Numbers with decimals don't align when you choose General formatting.

Accenting your cells with the Accounting number format

Given the financial nature of most worksheets, you probably use the Accounting number format more than any other. Applying this format is easy because you can assign it to the cell selection simply by clicking the Accounting Number Format button on the Home tab.

The Accounting number format adds a dollar sign, commas between thousands of dollars, and two decimal places to any values in a selected range. If any of the values in the cell selection are negative, this number format displays them in parentheses (the way accountants like them). If you want a minus sign in front of your negative financial values rather than enclosing them in parentheses, select the Currency format on the Number Format drop-down menu or on the Number tab of the Format Cells dialog box.

You can see in Figure 3-12 only the cells containing totals are selected (cell ranges E3:E10 and B10:D10). This cell selection was then formatted with the Accounting number format by simply clicking its command button (the one with the $ icon, naturally) in the Number group on the Ribbon's Home tab.

Although you could put all the figures in the table into the Accounting number format to line up the decimal points, this would result in a superabundance of dollar signs in a fairly small table. In this example, I only formatted the monthly and quarterly totals with the Accounting number format.

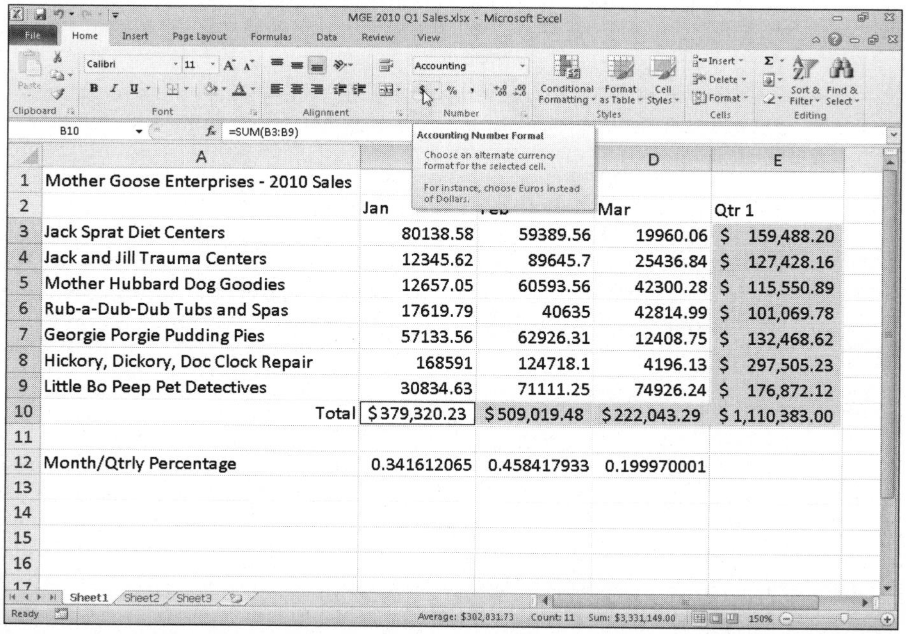

Figure 3-12:
The totals in the Mother Goose sales table after clicking the Accounting Number Format button on the Home tab.

	A	Jan	Feb	Mar	E
1	Mother Goose Enterprises - 2010 Sales				
2		Jan	Feb	Mar	Qtr 1
3	Jack Sprat Diet Centers	80138.58	59389.56	19960.06	$ 159,488.20
4	Jack and Jill Trauma Centers	12345.62	89645.7	25436.84	$ 127,428.16
5	Mother Hubbard Dog Goodies	12657.05	60593.56	42300.28	$ 115,550.89
6	Rub-a-Dub-Dub Tubs and Spas	17619.79	40635	42814.99	$ 101,069.78
7	Georgie Porgie Pudding Pies	57133.56	62926.31	12408.75	$ 132,468.62
8	Hickory, Dickory, Doc Clock Repair	168591	124718.1	4196.13	$ 297,505.23
9	Little Bo Peep Pet Detectives	30834.63	71111.25	74926.24	$ 176,872.12
10	Total	$379,320.23	$509,019.48	$222,043.29	$1,110,383.00
11					
12	Month/Qtrly Percentage	0.341612065	0.458417933	0.199970001	

"Look, Ma, no more format overflow!"

When I apply the Accounting number format to the selection in the cell ranges of E3:E10 and B10:D10 in the sales table shown in Figure 3-12, Excel adds dollar signs, commas between the thousands, a decimal point, and two decimal places to the highlighted values. At the same time, Excel automatically widens columns B, C, D, and E just enough to display all this new formatting. In versions of Excel earlier than Excel 2003, you had to widen these columns yourself, and instead of the perfectly aligned numbers, you were confronted with columns of #######s in cell ranges E3:E10 and B10:D10. Such pound signs (where nicely formatted dollar totals should be) serve as overflow indicators, declaring that whatever formatting you added to the value in that cell has added so much to the value's display that Excel can no longer display it within the current column width.

Fortunately, Excel eliminates the format overflow indicators when you're formatting the values in your cells by automatically widening the columns. The only time you'll ever run across these dreaded #######s in your cells is when you take it upon yourself to narrow a worksheet column manually (see the section "Calibrating Columns," later in this chapter) to the extent that Excel can no longer display all the characters in its cells with formatted values.

Currying your cells with the Comma Style

The Comma Style format offers a good alternative to the Currency format. Like Currency, the Comma Style format inserts commas in larger numbers to separate thousands, hundred thousands, millions, and . . . well, you get the idea.

This format also displays two decimal places and puts negative values in parentheses. What it doesn't display is dollar signs. This makes it perfect for formatting tables where it's obvious that you're dealing with dollars and cents or for larger values that have nothing to do with money.

The Comma Style format also works well for the bulk of the values in the sample first-quarter sales worksheet. Check out Figure 3-13 to see this table after I format the cells containing the monthly sales for all the Mother Goose Enterprises with the Comma Style format. To do this, select the cell range B3:D9 and click the Comma Style button — the one with the comma icon (,) — in the Number group on the Home tab.

Note how, in Figure 3-13, the Comma Style format takes care of the earlier decimal alignment problem in the quarterly sales figures. Moreover, Comma Style–formatted monthly sales figures align perfectly with the Currency format–styled monthly totals in row 10. If you look closely (you may need a magnifying glass for this one), you see that these formatted values no longer abut the right edges of their cells; they've moved slightly to the left. The gap on the right between the last digit and the cell border accommodates the right parenthesis in negative values, ensuring that they, too, align precisely on the decimal point.

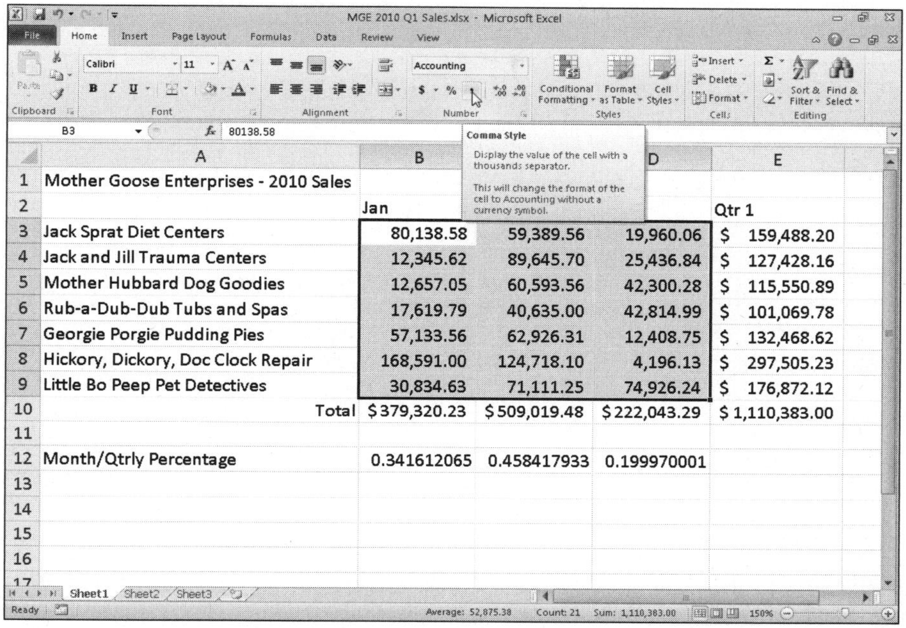

Figure 3-13:
Monthly
sales fig-
ures after
formatting
cells with
the Comma
Style num-
ber format.

Playing around with Percent Style

Many worksheets use percentages in the form of interest rates, growth
rates, inflation rates, and so on. To insert a percentage in a cell, type the
percent sign (%) after the number. To indicate an interest rate of 12 percent,
for example, you enter **12%** in the cell. When you do this, Excel assigns a
Percentage number format and, at the same time, divides the value by 100
(that's what makes it a percentage) and places the result in the cell (0.12 in
this example).

Not all percentages in a worksheet are entered by hand in this manner. Some
may be calculated by a formula and returned to their cells as raw decimal
values. In such cases, you should add a Percent format to convert the calculated decimal values to percentages (done by multiplying the decimal value
by 100 and adding a percent sign).

The sample first-quarter-sales worksheet just happens to have some percentages calculated by formulas in row 12 that need formatting (these formulas
indicate what percentage each monthly total is of the first-quarter total in cell
E10). In Figure 3-14, these values reflect Percent Style formatting. To accomplish this feat, you simply select the cells and click the Percent Style button
in the Number group on the Home tab. (Need I point out that it's the button
with the % symbol?)

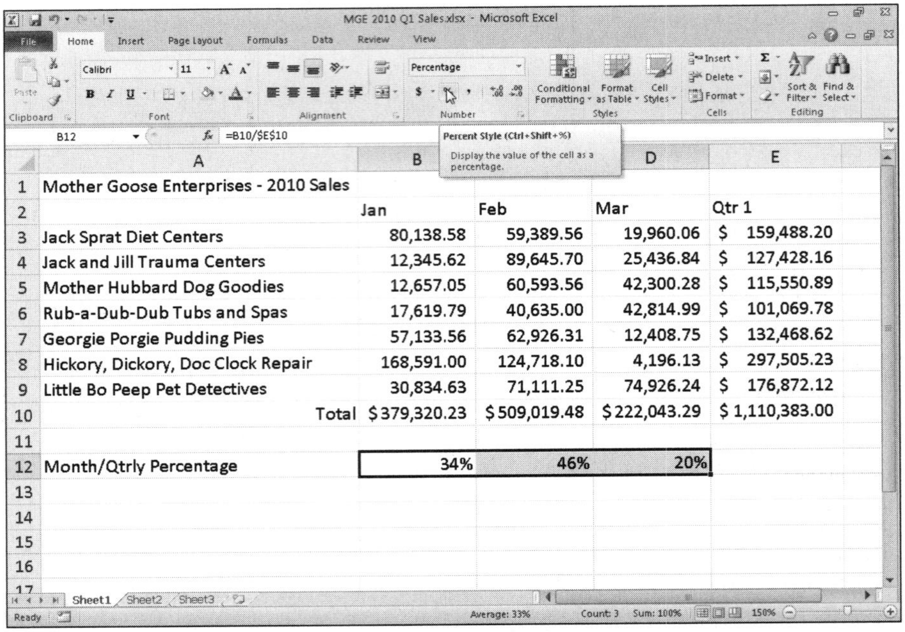

Figure 3-14:
Monthly-
to-quarterly
sales
percent-
ages with
Percentage
number
formatting.

Deciding how many decimal places

You can increase or decrease the number of decimal places used in a number entered by using the Accounting Number Format, Comma Style, or Percent Style button in the Number group of the Home tab simply by clicking the Increase Decimal button or the Decrease Decimal button in this group.

Each time you click the Increase Decimal button (the one with the arrow pointing left), Excel adds another decimal place to the number format you apply. Percentages appear in the cell range B12:D12 (see Figure 3-15) after I increase the number of decimal places in the Percent format from none to two. (Percent Style doesn't use any decimal places.) I accomplish this by clicking the Increase Decimal button twice.

The values behind the formatting

Make no mistake about it — all that these fancy number formats do is spiff up the presentation of the values in the worksheet. Like a good illusionist, a particular number format sometimes appears to transform some entries, but in reality, the entries are the same old numbers you started with. For example, suppose that a formula returns the following value:

```
25.6456
```

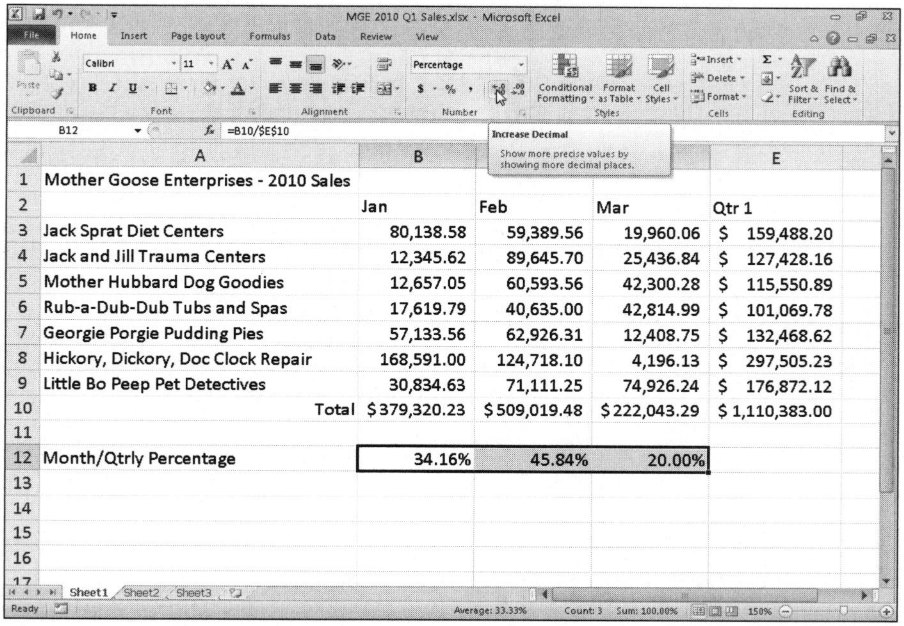

Figure 3-15:
Monthly-
to-quarterly
sales per-
centages
after adding
two deci-
mal places
to the
Percentage
number
format.

The following is the content shown in the Excel screenshot:

MGE 2010 Q1 Sales.xlsx - Microsoft Excel

B12 — =B10/$E$10

Increase Decimal
Show more precise values by
showing more decimal places.

	A	B			E
1	Mother Goose Enterprises - 2010 Sales				
2		Jan	Feb	Mar	Qtr 1
3	Jack Sprat Diet Centers	80,138.58	59,389.56	19,960.06	$ 159,488.20
4	Jack and Jill Trauma Centers	12,345.62	89,645.70	25,436.84	$ 127,428.16
5	Mother Hubbard Dog Goodies	12,657.05	60,593.56	42,300.28	$ 115,550.89
6	Rub-a-Dub-Dub Tubs and Spas	17,619.79	40,635.00	42,814.99	$ 101,069.78
7	Georgie Porgie Pudding Pies	57,133.56	62,926.31	12,408.75	$ 132,468.62
8	Hickory, Dickory, Doc Clock Repair	168,591.00	124,718.10	4,196.13	$ 297,505.23
9	Little Bo Peep Pet Detectives	30,834.63	71,111.25	74,926.24	$ 176,872.12
10	Total	$379,320.23	$509,019.48	$222,043.29	$1,110,383.00
11					
12	Month/Qtrly Percentage	34.16%	45.84%	20.00%	

Average: 33.33%   Count: 3   Sum: 100.00%   150%

Now suppose that you format the cell containing this value with the
Accounting Number Format button on the Home tab. The value now appears
as follows:

```
$25.65
```

This change may lead you to believe that Excel rounded the value up to two
decimal places. In fact, the program has rounded up only the *display* of the
calculated value — the cell still contains the same old value of 25.6456. If you
use this cell in another worksheet formula, Excel uses the behind-the-scenes
value in its calculation, not the spiffed-up one shown in the cell.

WARNING!

If you want the values to match their formatted appearance in the worksheet,
Excel can do that in a single step. Be forewarned, however, that this is a one-
way trip. You can convert all underlying values to the way they are displayed
by selecting a single check box, but you can't return them to their previous
state by deselecting this check box.

Well, because you insist on knowing this little trick anyway, here goes (just
don't write and try to tell me that you weren't warned):

1. **Make sure that you format all the values in your worksheet with the
   right number of decimal places.**

   You must do this step before you convert the precision of all values in
   the worksheet to their displayed form.

2. **Choose File⇨Options⇨Advanced or press Alt+FTA to open the Advanced tab of Excel Options dialog box.**

3. **In the When Calculating This Workbook section, click the Set Precision as Displayed check box (to fill it with a check mark).**

   Excel displays the Data Will Permanently Lose Accuracy alert dialog box.

4. **Go ahead (live dangerously) and click the OK button or press Enter to convert all values to match their display. Click OK again to close the Excel Options dialog box.**

Save the workbook with the calculated values. After converting all the values in a worksheet by selecting the Set Precision as Displayed check box, open the Save As dialog box (File⇨Save As or press Alt+FA). Edit the filename in the File Name text box (maybe by appending **as Displayed** to the current filename) before you click the Save button or press Enter. That way, you'll have two copies: the original workbook file with the values as entered and calculated by Excel and the new *as Displayed* version.

Make it a date!

In Chapter 2, I mention that you can easily create formulas that calculate the differences between the dates and times that you enter in your worksheets. The only problem is that when Excel subtracts one date from another date or one time from another time, the program automatically formats the calculated result in a corresponding date or time number format as well. For example, if you enter 8-15-10 in cell B4 and 4/15/10 in cell C4 and in cell D4 enter the following formula for finding the number of elapsed days between the two dates:

```
=B4-C4
```

Excel correctly returns the result of 122 (days) using the General number format. However, when dealing with formulas that calculate the difference between two times in a worksheet, you have to reformat the result that appears in a corresponding time format into the General format. For example, suppose that you enter 8:00 AM in cell B5 and 4:00 PM in cell C5 and then create in cell D5 the following formula for calculating the difference in hours between the two times:

```
=C5-B5
```

You then have to convert the result in cell D5 — that automatically appears as 8:00 AM — to the General format. When you do this, the fraction 0.333333 —

representing its fraction of the total 24-hour period — replaces 8:00 AM in cell D5. You can then convert this fraction of a total day into the corresponding number of hours by multiplying this cell by 24.

Ogling some of the other number formats

Excel supports more number formats than just the Accounting, Comma Style, and Percentage number formats. To use them, select the cell range (or ranges) you want to format and select Format Cells on the cell shortcut menu (right-click somewhere in the cell selection to activate this menu) or just press Ctrl+1 to open the Format Cells dialog box.

After the Format Cells dialog box opens with the Number tab displayed, you select the desired format from the Category list box. Some number formats — such as Date, Time, Fraction, and Special — give you further formatting choices in a Type list box. Other number formats, such as Number and Currency, have their own particular boxes that give you options for refining their formats. When you click the different formats in these list boxes, Excel shows what effect this would have on the first of the values in the current cell selection in the Sample area above. When the sample has the format that you want to apply to the current cell selection, you just click OK or press Enter to apply the new number format.

Excel contains a nifty category of number formats called Special. The Special category contains the following four number formats that may interest you:

- **Zip Code:** Retains any leading zeros in the value (important for zip codes and of absolutely no importance in arithmetic computations). Example: 00123.

- **Zip Code + 4:** Automatically separates the last four digits from the first five digits and retains any leading zeros. Example: 00123-5555.

- **Phone Number:** Automatically encloses the first three digits of the number in parentheses and separates the last four digits from the previous three with a dash. Example: (999) 555-1111.

- **Social Security Number:** Automatically puts dashes in the value to separate its digits into groups of three, two, and four. Example: 666-00-9999.

These Special number formats really come in handy when creating data lists in Excel that often deal with stuff like zip codes, telephone numbers, and sometimes even Social Security numbers (see Chapter 9 for more on creating and using data lists).

Calibrating Columns

For those times when Excel 2010 doesn't automatically adjust the width of your columns to your complete satisfaction, the program makes your changing the column widths a breeze. The easiest way to adjust a column is to do a *best-fit,* using the AutoFit feature. With this method, Excel automatically determines how much to widen or narrow the column to fit the longest entry currently in the column.

Here's how to use AutoFit to get the best fit for a column:

1. **Position the mouse pointer on the right border of the worksheet frame with the column letter at the top of the worksheet.**

   The mouse pointer changes to a double-headed arrow pointing left and right.

2. **Double-click the mouse button.**

   Excel widens or narrows the column width to suit the longest entry.

You can apply a best-fit to more than one column at a time. Simply select all the columns that need adjusting (if the columns neighbor one another, drag through their column letters on the frame; if they don't, hold down the Ctrl key while you click the individual column letters). After you select the columns, double-click any of the right borders on the frame.

Best-fit à la AutoFit doesn't always produce the expected results. A long title that spills into several columns to the right produces a very wide column when you use best-fit.

When AutoFit's best-fit won't do, drag the right border of the column (on the frame) until it's the size you need instead of double-clicking it. This manual technique for calibrating the column width also works when more than one column is selected. Just be aware that all selected columns assume whatever size you make the one that you're actually dragging.

You can also set the widths of columns from the Format button's drop-down list in the Cells group on the Home tab. When you click this drop-down button, the Cell Size section of this drop-down menu contains the following width options:

✔ **Column Width** to open the Column Width dialog box where you enter the number of characters that you want for the column width before you click OK

✔ **AutoFit Column Width** to have Excel apply best-fit to the columns based on the widest entries in the current cell selection

✔ **Default Width** to open the Standard Width dialog box containing the standard column width of 8.43 characters that you can apply to the columns in the cell selection

Rambling rows

The story with adjusting the heights of rows is pretty much the same as that with adjusting columns except that you do a lot less row adjusting than you do column adjusting. That's because Excel automatically changes the height of the rows to accommodate changes to their entries, such as selecting a larger font size or wrapping text in a cell. I discuss both of these techniques in the upcoming section "Altering the Alignment." Most row-height adjustments come about when you want to increase the amount of space between a table title and the table or between a row of column headings and the table of information without actually adding a blank row. (See the section "From top to bottom," later in this chapter, for details.)

To increase the height of a row, drag the bottom border of the row frame down until the row is high enough and then release the mouse button. To shorten a row, reverse this process and drag the bottom row-frame border up. To use AutoFit to best-fit the entries in a row, you double-click the bottom row-frame border.

As with columns, you can also adjust the height of selected rows using row options in the Cell Size section on the Format button's drop-down menu on the Home tab:

✔ **Row Height** to open the Row Height dialog box where you enter the number of points in the Row Height text box and then click OK

✔ **AutoFit Row Height** to return the height of selected rows to the best fit

Now you see it, now you don't

A funny thing about narrowing columns and rows: You can get carried away and make a column so narrow or a row so short that it actually disappears from the worksheet! This can come in handy for those times when you don't want part of the worksheet visible. For example, suppose you have a worksheet that contains a column listing employee salaries — you need these figures to calculate the departmental budget figures, but you would prefer to leave sensitive info off most printed reports. Rather than waste time moving the column of salary figures outside the area to be printed, you can just hide the column until after you print the report.

Hiding worksheet columns

Although you can hide worksheet columns and rows by just adjusting them out of existence, Excel does offer an easier method of hiding them, via the Hide & Unhide option on the Format button's drop-down menu (located in the Cells group of the Home tab). Suppose that you need to hide column B in the worksheet because it contains some irrelevant or sensitive information that you don't want printed. To hide this column, you could follow these steps:

1. **Click anywhere in column B to select the column.**

2. **Click the drop-down button attached to the Format button in the Cells group on the Home tab.**

    Excel opens the Format button's drop-down menu.

3. **Click Hide & Unhide⇨Hide Columns on the drop-down menu.**

That's all there is to it — column B goes *poof!* All the information in the column disappears from the worksheet. When you hide column B, notice that the row of column letters in the frame now reads A, C, D, E, F, and so forth.

You could just as well have hidden column B by right-clicking its column letter on the frame and then choosing the Hide command on the column's shortcut menu.

Now, suppose that you've printed the worksheet and need to make a change to one of the entries in column B. To unhide the column, follow these steps:

1. **Position the mouse pointer on column letter A in the frame and drag the pointer right to select both columns A and C.**

    You must drag from A to C to include hidden column B as part of the column selection — don't click while holding down the Ctrl key or you won't get B.

2. **Click the drop-down button attached to the Format button in the Cells group on the Home tab.**

3. **Click Hide & Unhide⇨Unhide Columns on the drop-down menu.**

Excel brings back the hidden B column, and all three columns (A, B, and C) are selected. You can then click the mouse pointer on any cell in the worksheet to deselect the columns.

You could also unhide column B by selecting columns A through C, right-clicking either one of them, and then choosing the Unhide command on the column shortcut menu.

Hiding worksheet rows

The procedure for hiding and unhiding rows of the worksheet is essentially the same as for hiding and unhiding columns. The only difference is that after selecting the rows to hide, you click Hide & Unhide➪Hide Rows on the Format button's drop-down menu and Hide & Unhide➪Unhide Rows to bring them back.

Don't forget that you can use the Hide and Unhide options on the rows' shortcut menu to make selected rows disappear and then reappear in the worksheet.

Futzing with the Fonts

When you start a new worksheet, Excel 2010 assigns a uniform font and type size to all the cell entries you make. The default font varies according to the version of Windows under which you're running Excel. When you run Excel on Windows 7 and Vista, Excel uses its new Calibri font (the so-called Body Font) in 11-point size, and when running Excel under Windows XP, it uses its standard Arial font in a 10-point size. Although these two fonts may be fine for normal entries, you may want to use something with a little more zing for titles and headings in the worksheet.

If you don't especially care for the standard font that Excel uses on your version of Windows, modify it from the General tab of the Excel Options dialog box (choose File➪Options or press Alt+FT). Look for the Use This Font drop-down list box (containing Body Font as the default choice) in the When Creating New Workbooks section and then click the name of new font you want to make standard from this drop-down list. If you want a different type size, choose the Font Size drop-down list box and click a new point size on its drop-down menu or enter the new point size for the standard font directly into the Font Size text box.

Using the buttons in the Font group on the Home tab, you can make most font changes (including selecting a new font style or new font size) without having to resort to changing the settings on the Font tab in the Format Cells dialog box (Ctrl+1):

> ✔ To select a new font for a cell selection, click the drop-down button next to the Font combo box and then select the name of the font you want to use from the list box. Excel displays the name of each font that appears

in this list box in the actual font named (so that the font name becomes an example of what the font looks like — onscreen anyway).

✔ To change the font size, click the drop-down button next to the Font Size combo box, select the new font size or click the Font Size text box, type the new size, and then press Enter.

You can also add **bold**, *italic*, underlining, or ~~strikethrough~~ to the font you use. The Font group of the Home tab contains the Bold, Italic, and Underline buttons, which not only add these attributes to a cell selection but remove them as well. After you click any of these attribute tools, notice that the tool becomes shaded whenever you position the cell cursor in the cell or cells that contain that attribute. When you click a selected format button to remove an attribute, Excel no longer shades the attribute button when you select the cell.

Although you'll probably make most font changes with the Home tab on the Ribbon, on rare occasions you may find it more convenient to make these changes from the Font tab in the Format Cells dialog box (Ctrl+1).

As you can see in Figure 3-16, this Font tab in the Format Cells dialog box brings together under one roof fonts, font styles (bold and italics), effects (strikethrough, superscript, and subscript), and color changes. When you want to make many font-related changes to a cell selection, working in the Font tab may be your best bet. One of the nice things about using this tab is that it contains a Preview box that shows you how your font changes appear (onscreen at least).

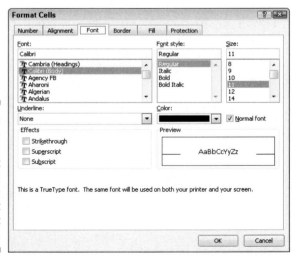

Figure 3-16: Use the Font tab on the Format Cells dialog box to make many font changes at one time.

To change the color of the entries in a cell selection, click the Font Color button's drop-down menu in the Font group on the Home tab and then select the color you want the text to appear in the drop-down palette. You can use Live Preview to see what the entries in the cell selection look like in a particular font color by moving the mouse pointer over the color swatches in the palette before you select one by clicking it (assuming, of course, that the palette doesn't cover the cells).

If you change font colors and then print the worksheet with a black-and-white printer, Excel renders the colors as shades of gray. The Automatic option at the top of the Font Color button's drop-down menu picks up the color assigned in Windows as the window text color. This color is black unless you change it in your display properties. (For help on this subject, please refer to *Microsoft Windows XP For Dummies, Microsoft Windows Vista For Dummies*, or *Microsoft Windows 7 For Dummies* all by Andy Rathbone — and be sure to tell Andy that Greg sent ya!)

Altering the Alignment

The horizontal alignment assigned to cell entries when you first make them is simply a function of the type of entry it is: All text entries are left-aligned, and all values are right-aligned with the borders of their cells. However, you can alter this standard arrangement anytime it suits you.

The Alignment group of the Home tab contains three normal horizontal alignment tools: the Align Left, Center, and Align Right buttons. These buttons align the current cell selection exactly as you expect them to. On the right side of the Alignment group, you usually find the special alignment button called Merge & Center.

Despite its rather strange name, you'll want to get to know this button. You can use it to center a worksheet title across the entire width of a table in seconds (or faster, depending upon your machine). I show you in Figures 3-17 and 3-18 how you can use this tool. In Figure 3-17, notice that the worksheet title Mother Goose Enterprises – 2010 Sales is in cell A1. To center this title over the table (which extends from column A through E), select the cell range A1:E1 (the width of the table) and then click the Merge & Center button in the Alignment group on the Ribbon's Home tab.

Figure showing Excel worksheet:

	A	B	C	D	E
1	Mother Goose Enterprises - 2010 Sales				
2		Jan	Feb	Mar	Qtr 1
3	Jack Sprat Diet Centers	80,138.58	59,389.56	19,960.06	$ 159,488.20
4	Jack and Jill Trauma Centers	12,345.62	89,645.70	25,436.84	$ 127,428.16
5	Mother Hubbard Dog Goodies	12,657.05	60,593.56	42,300.28	$ 115,550.89
6	Rub-a-Dub-Dub Tubs and Spas	17,619.79	40,635.00	42,814.99	$ 101,069.78
7	Georgie Porgie Pudding Pies	57,133.56	62,926.31	12,408.75	$ 132,468.62
8	Hickory, Dickory, Doc Clock Repair	168,591.00	124,718.10	4,196.13	$ 297,505.23
9	Little Bo Peep Pet Detectives	30,834.63	71,111.25	74,926.24	$ 176,872.12
10	Total	$379,320.23	$509,019.48	$222,043.29	$ 1,110,383.00
11					
12	Month/Qtrly Percentage	34.16%	45.84%	20.00%	

Figure 3-17: A worksheet title before merging and centering.

Look at Figure 3-18 to see the result: The cells in row 1 of columns A through E are merged into one cell, and now the title is properly centered in this "super" cell and consequently over the entire table.

TIP

If you ever need to split up a supercell that you've merged with Merge & Center back into its original, individual cells, select the cell and then simply click the Merge & Center button in the Alignment group on the Home tab again. You can also do this by clicking the drop-down button attached to the Merge & Center button on the Home tab and then clicking Unmerge Cells on this drop-down menu (a few more steps, I'd say!).

Intent on indents

In Excel 2010, you can indent the entries in a cell selection by clicking the Increase Indent button. The Increase Indent button in the Alignment group of the Home tab sports a picture of an arrow pushing the lines of text to the right. Each time you click this button, Excel indents the entries in the current cell selection to the right by three character widths of the standard font. (See the section "Futzing with the Fonts," earlier in this chapter, if you don't know what a standard font is or how to change it.)

You can remove an indent by clicking the Decrease Indent button (to the immediate left of the Increase Indent button) on the Home tab with the picture of the arrow pushing the lines of text to the left. Additionally, you can change how many characters an entry indents with the Increase Indent button (or outdents with the Decrease Indent button). Open the Format Cells dialog box (Ctrl+1). Select the Alignment tab, and then alter the value in the Indent text box (by typing a new value in this text box or by dialing up a new value with its spinner buttons).

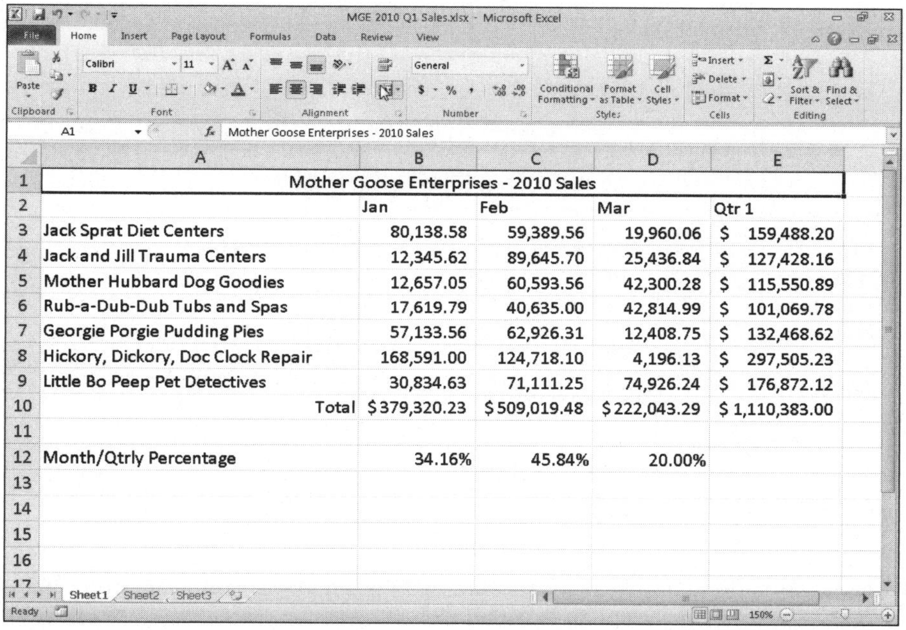

Figure 3-18:
A worksheet title after merging and centering it across columns A through E.

From top to bottom

Left, right, and *center* alignment all refer to the horizontal positioning of a text entry in relation to the left and right cell borders (that is, horizontally). You can also align entries in relation to the top and bottom borders of their cells (that is, vertically). Normally, all entries align vertically with the bottom of the cells (as though they were resting on the very bottom of the cell). You can also vertically center an entry in its cell or align it with the top of its cell.

To change the vertical alignment of a cell range that you've selected, click the appropriate button (Top Align, Middle Align, or Bottom Align) in the Alignment group on the Home tab.

Figure 3-19 shows the title for the 2010 Mother Goose Enterprises sales worksheet after centering it vertically in its cell by clicking the Middle Align button on the Home tab. (This text entry was previously centered across the cell range A1:E1; the height of row 1 is increased from the normal 15 points to 36 points.)

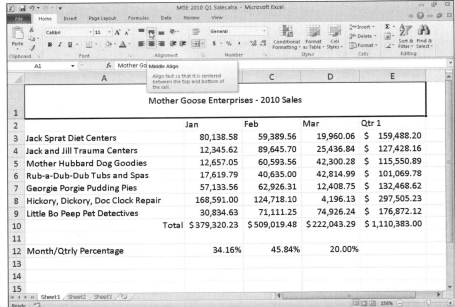

Figure 3-19:
The work-
sheet
title after
centering
it vertically
between the
top and bot-
tom edges
of row 1.

Tampering with how the text wraps

Traditionally, column headings in worksheet tables have been a problem — you had to keep them really short or abbreviate them if you wanted to avoid widening all the columns more than the data warranted. You can avoid this problem in Excel by using the Wrap Text button in the Alignment group on the Home tab (the one to the immediate right of the Orientation button). In Figure 3-20, I show a new worksheet in which the column headings containing the various companies within the vast Mother Goose Enterprises conglomerate use the Wrap Text feature to avoid widening the columns as much as these long company names would otherwise require.

To create the effect shown in Figure 3-20, select the cells with the column headings (the cell range B2:H2) and then click the Wrap Text button in the Alignment group on the Home tab.

Selecting Wrap Text breaks up the long text entries (that either spill over or cut off) in the selection into separate lines. To accommodate more than one line in a cell, the program automatically expands the row height so that the entire wrapped-text entry is visible.

When you select Wrap Text, Excel continues to use the horizontal and vertical alignment you specify for the cell. You can use any of the Horizontal alignment options found on the Alignment tab of the Format Cells dialog box (Ctrl+1), including Left (Indent), Center, Right (Indent), Justify, or Center Across Selection. However, you can't use the Fill option or Distributed (Indent) option. Select the Fill option on the Horizontal drop-down list box only when you want Excel to repeat the entry across the entire width of the cell.

If you want to wrap a text entry in its cell and have Excel justify the text with both the left and right borders of the cell, select the Justify option from the Horizontal drop-down list box in the Alignment tab in the Format Cells dialog box.

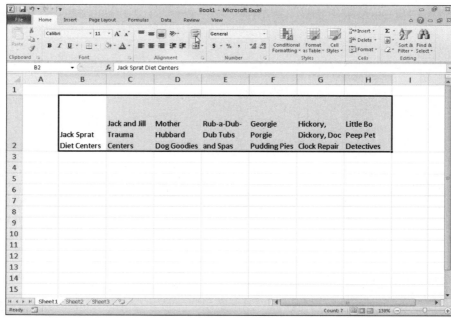

Figure 3-20: A new worksheet with the column headings formatted with the Wrap Text option.

TIP

You can break a long text entry into separate lines by positioning the insertion point in the cell entry (or on the Formula bar) at the place where you want the new line to start and pressing Alt+Enter. Excel expands the row containing the cell (and the Formula bar above) when it starts a new line. When you press Enter to complete the entry or edit, Excel automatically wraps the text in the cell, according to the cell's column width and the position of the line break.

Reorienting cell entries

Instead of wrapping text entries in cells, you may find it more beneficial to change the orientation of the text by rotating the text up (in a counterclockwise direction) or down (in a clockwise direction). Peruse Figure 3-21 for a situation where changing the orientation of the wrapped column headings works much better than just wrapping them in their normal orientation in the cells.

This example shows the same column headings for the sample order form I introduced in Figure 3-20 after rotating them 90 degrees counterclockwise. To make this switch, first select the cell range B2:H2. Next, click the Orientation button in the Alignment group on the Home tab and then click the Rotate Text Up option on the drop-down menu.

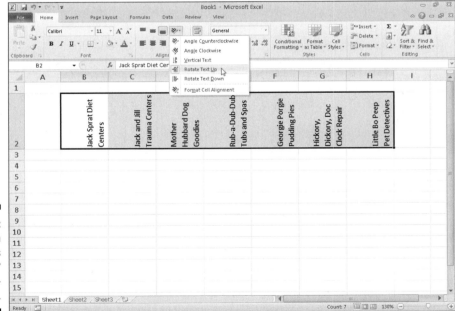

Figure 3-21:
Column headings rotated 90° counter-clockwise.

Figure 3-22 shows the same headings rotated up at a 45-degree angle. To create what you see in this figure, you click the Angle Counterclockwise option on the Orientation button's drop-down menu after making the same cell selection, B2:H2.

If you need to set the rotation of the entries in a spreadsheet at angles other than 45 and 90 degrees (up or down), you need to click the Format Cell Alignment option on the Orientation button's drop-down menu. Doing so opens the Alignment tab of the Format Cells dialog box (or press Ctrl+1 and click the Alignment tab) where you can then use the controls in the Orientation section to set the angle and number of degrees.

To set a new angle, enter the number of degrees in the Degrees text box, click the appropriate place on the semicircular diagram, or drag the line extending from the word *Text* in the diagram to the desired angle.

To angle text up using the Degrees text box, enter a positive number between 1 and 45 in the text box. To angle the text down, enter a negative number between −1 and −45.

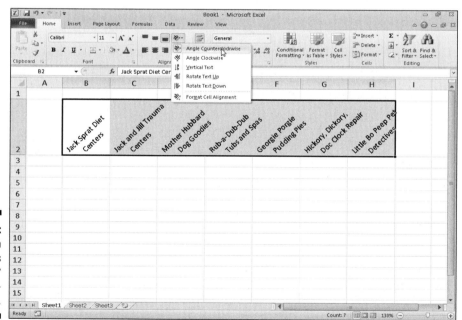

Figure 3-22: Column headings rotated 45° counter-clockwise.

To set the text vertically so that each letter is above the other in a single column, click the Vertical Text option on the Orientation button's drop-down menu on the Home tab.

Shrink to fit

For those times when you need to prevent Excel from widening the column to fit its cell entries (as might be the case when you need to display an entire table of data on a single screen or printed page), use the Shrink to Fit text control.

Click the Alignment tab of the Format Cells dialog box (Ctrl+1) and then click the Shrink to Fit check box in the Text Control section. Excel reduces the font size of the entries to the selected cells so that they don't require changing the current column width. Just be aware when using this Text Control option that, depending on the length of the entries and width of the column, you can end up with some text entries so small that they're completely illegible!

Bring on the borders!

The gridlines you normally see in the worksheet to separate the columns and rows are just guidelines to help you keep your place as you build your spreadsheet. You can choose to print them with your data or not (by checking or clearing the Print check box that appears in the Gridlines section of the Sheet Options group on the Page Layout tab).

To emphasize sections of the worksheet or parts of a particular table, you can add borderlines or shading to certain cells. Don't confuse the *borderlines* that you add to accent a particular cell selection with the *gridlines* used to define cell borders in the worksheet — borders that you add print regardless of whether you print the worksheet gridlines.

To see the borders that you add to the cells in a worksheet, remove the gridlines normally displayed in the worksheet by clearing the View check box in the Gridlines section of the Sheet Options group on the Page Layout tab.

To add borders to a cell selection, click the drop-down button attached to the Borders button in the Font group on the Home tab. This displays a drop-down menu with all the border options you can apply to the cell selection (see Figure 3-23) where you click the type of line you want to apply to all its cells.

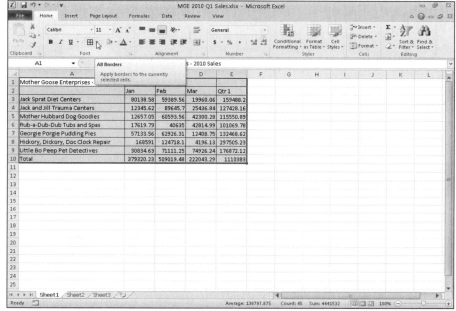

Figure 3-23:
Select
borders for
a cell selec-
tion with the
Borders but-
ton on the
Home tab.

When selecting options on this drop-down menu to determine where you want the borderlines drawn, keep these things in mind:

- ✔ To have Excel draw borders only around the outside edges of the entire cell selection (in other words, following the path of the expanded cell cursor), click the Outside Borders or the Thick Box Border options on this menu. To draw the outside borders yourself around an unselected cell range in the active worksheet, click the Draw Border option, drag the mouse (using the Pencil mouse pointer) through the range of cells, and then click the Borders button on the Home tab's Font group.

- ✔ If you want borderlines to appear around all four edges of each cell in the cell selection (like a paned window), select the All Borders option on this drop-down menu. If you want to draw the inside and outside borders yourself around an unselected cell range in the active worksheet, click the Draw Border Grid option, drag the mouse (using the Pencil mouse pointer) through the range of cells, and then click the Borders button on the Home tab.

To change the type of line, line thickness, or color of the borders you apply to a cell selection, you must open the Format Cells dialog box and use the options on its Border tab (click More Borders at the bottom of the Borders button's drop-down menu or press Ctrl+1 and then click the Border tab).

To select a new line thickness or line style for a border you're applying, click its example in the Style section. To change the color of the border you want to apply, click the color sample on the Color drop-down palette. After you select a new line style and/or color, apply the border to the cell selection by clicking the appropriate line in either the Presets or Border section of the Border tab before you click OK.

To get rid of existing borders in a worksheet, you must select the cell or cells that presently contain them and then click the No Border option at the top of the second section on the Borders button's drop-down menu.

Applying fill colors, patterns, and gradient effects to cells

You can also add emphasis to particular sections of the worksheet or one of its tables by changing the fill color of the cell selection and/or applying a pattern or gradient to it.

If you're using a black-and-white printer, you want to restrict your color choices to light gray in the color palette. Additionally, you want to restrict your use of pattern styles to the very open ones with few dots when enhancing a cell selection that contains any kind of entries (otherwise, the entries will be almost impossible to read when printed).

To choose a new fill color for the background of a cell selection, you can click the Fill Color button's drop-down menu in the Font group on the Home tab and then select the color you want to use in the drop-down palette. Remember that you can use Live Preview to see what the cell selection looks like in a particular fill color by moving the mouse pointer over the color swatches. Click one to select it.

To choose a new pattern for a cell selection, you must open the Format Cells dialog box (Ctrl+1), and then click the Fill tab. To change the pattern of the cell selection, click a pattern swatch from the Pattern Style button's pattern palette. To add a fill color to the pattern you select, click its color swatch in the Background Color section of the Fill tab.

If you want to add a gradient effect to the cell selection that goes from one color to another in a certain direction, click the Fill Effects button on the Fill tab to open the Fill Effects dialog box (see Figure 3-24). This dialog box contains a Gradient tab with controls that enable you to determine the two colors to use as well as shading style and variant.

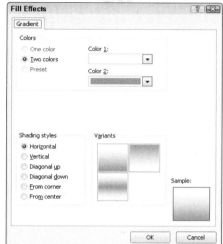

Figure 3-24:
Select a
new gradi-
ent for a cell
selection
in the Fill
Effects
dialog box.

After you select the colors and styles of the gradient, check the Sample swatch in the Fill Effects dialog box. When you have it the way you want it, click OK to close the Fill Effects dialog box and return to the Format Cells dialog box. The selected gradient effect then appears in its Sample area on the Fill tab in the Format Cells dialog box. Unfortunately, this is one area where Live Preview doesn't work, so you're just going to have to click its OK button to apply the gradient to the cell selection to see how it actually looks in the worksheet.

Although you can't select new patterns or gradients (only colors) with the Fill Color button on the Home tab, you can remove fill colors, patterns, and gradients assigned to a cell selection by clicking the No Fill option on the Fill Color button's drop-down menu.

Do It in Styles

In Excel 2010, cell styles really come alive in the form of the new Cell Styles gallery that you open by clicking the Cell Styles button in the Styles group on the Home tab. The Cell Styles gallery contains loads of readymade styles you can immediately apply to the current cell selection. Simply click the desired style sample in the gallery after using the Live Preview feature to determine which style looks best on your data.

Creating a new style for the gallery

To create a new style for the gallery by example, manually format a single cell with all the attributes you want (font, font size, font color, bold, italic, underlining, fill color, pattern, borders, orientation, and so on) and then click the Cell Styles button on the Home tab followed by the New Cell Style option at the bottom of the gallery. Excel then opens a Style dialog box where you replace the generic style name (Style 1, Style 2, and so on) with your own descriptive name before you click OK.

Excel then adds a sample of your new style — the style name formatted, with the new style's attributes — to a Custom section at the top of the Cell Styles gallery. To apply this custom style to a cell selection, you then only have to click its sample in the Custom section of the Cell Styles gallery.

The custom cell styles you create don't become part of the current workbook until the next time you save the workbook. Therefore, you need to remember to click the Save button on the Quick Access toolbar or press Ctrl+S to save your changes after creating a new cell style if you want that style to remain part of the workbook's Cell Styles gallery the next time you open the workbook in Excel.

Copying custom styles from one workbook into another

Excel makes it easy to copy custom cell styles that you've saved as part of one workbook into the workbook you're currently working on. To copy custom styles from one workbook to another, follow these steps:

1. **Open the workbook that needs the custom styles added to it from another existing workbook.**

   This can be a brand new workbook or one that you've opened for editing (see Chapter 4).

2. **Open the workbook that has the custom styles you want to copy saved as part of it.**

   See the previous section, "Creating a new style for the gallery" for tips on how to create and save cell styles.

3. **Switch back to the workbook into which you want to copy the saved custom styles.**

   You can do this by clicking the workbook's button on the Windows taskbar or using the Flip feature by pressing Alt+Tab until you select the workbook's thumbnail in the center of the display.

4. **Click the Cell Styles button on the Home tab followed by Merge Styles in the Cell Styles gallery or press Alt+HJM.**

   Excel opens the Merge Styles dialog box.

5. **Click the name of the open workbook file that contains the custom styles to copy in the Merge Styles From list box and then click OK.**

After you close the Merge Styles dialog box, Excel adds all the custom styles from the designated workbook into the current workbook adding it to the Custom section of its Cell Styles gallery. To retain the custom styles you just imported, save the current workbook (Save button on the Quick Access toolbar or Ctrl+S). Then, you can switch back to the workbook containing the original custom styles you just copied and close its file (Alt+FC).

Fooling Around with the Format Painter

Using cell styles to format ranges of worksheet cells is certainly the way to go when you have to apply the same formatting repeatedly in the workbooks you create. However, there may be times when you simply want to reuse a particular cell format and apply it to particular groups of cells in a single workbook without ever bothering to open the Cell Styles gallery.

For those occasions when you feel the urge to format on the fly (so to speak), use the Format Painter button (the paintbrush icon) in the Clipboard group on the Home tab. This wonderful little tool enables you to take the formatting from a particular cell that you fancy up and apply its formatting to other cells in the worksheet simply by selecting those cells.

To use the Format Painter to copy a cell's formatting to other worksheet cells, just follow these easy steps:

1. **Format an example cell or cell range in your workbook, selecting whatever fonts, alignment, borders, patterns, and color you want it to have.**

2. **With the cell cursor in one of the cells you just fancied up, click the Format Painter button in the Clipboard group on the Home tab.**

   The mouse pointer changes from the standard thick, white cross to a thick, white cross with an animated paintbrush by its side, and you see a marquee around the selected cell with the formatting to be used by the Format Painter.

3. **Drag the white-cross-plus-animated-paintbrush pointer (the Format Painter pointer) through all the cells you want to format.**

   As soon as you release the mouse button, Excel applies all the formatting used in the example cell to all the cells you just selected!

To keep the Format Painter selected so that you can format a bunch of different cell ranges with the Format Painter pointer, double-click the Format Painter button on the Home tab after you select the sample cell with the desired formatting. To stop formatting cells with the Format Painter pointer, you simply click the Format Painter button on the Home tab again (it remains selected when you double-click it) to restore the button to its unselected state and return the mouse pointer to its normal thick, white cross shape.

You can use the Format Painter to restore a cell range that you gussied all up back to its boring default (General) cell format. To do this, click an empty, previously unformatted cell in the worksheet before you click the Format Painter button and then use the Format Painter pointer to drag through the cells you want returned to the default General format.

Conditional Formatting

Before leaving behind the scintillating subject of cell formatting, there's one more formatting button in the Styles group of the Home tab of which you need to be aware. The Conditional Formatting button enables you to apply provisional formatting to a cell range based solely on the categories into which its current values fall. The cool thing about this kind of conditional formatting is that should you edit the numbers in the cell range so that their values fall into other categories, the program automatically changes their cell formatting to suit.

When you click the Conditional Formatting button in the Styles group of the Home tab, a drop-down menu appears with the following options:

- ✔ **Highlight Cells Rules** opens a continuation menu with various options for defining formatting rules that highlight the cells in the cell selection that contain certain values, text, or dates; that have values greater or less than a particular value; or that fall within a certain ranges of values.

- ✔ **Top/Bottom Rules** opens a continuation menu with various options for defining formatting rules that highlight the top and bottom values, percentages, and above and below average values in the cell selection.

- ✔ **Data Bars** opens a palette with different color data bars that you can apply to the cell selection to indicate their values relative to each other by clicking the data bar thumbnail.

- ✔ **Color Scales** opens a palette with different two- and three-colored scales that you can apply to the cell selection to indicate their values relative to each other by clicking the color scale thumbnail.

✔ **Icon Sets** opens a palette with different sets of icons that you can apply to the cell selection to indicate their values relative to each other by clicking the icon set.

✔ **New Rule** opens the New Formatting Rule dialog box where you define a custom conditional formatting rule to apply to the cell selection.

✔ **Clear Rules** opens a continuation menu where you can remove conditional formatting rules for the cell selection by clicking the Clear Rules from Selected Cells option, for the entire worksheet by clicking the Clear Rules from Entire Sheet option, or for just the current data table by clicking the Clear Rules from This Table option.

✔ **Manage Rules** opens the Conditional Formatting Rules Manager dialog box where you edit and delete particular rules as well as adjust their rule precedence by moving them up or down in the Rules list box.

Conditionally formatting values with sets of graphic scales and markers

The easiest conditional formatting that you can apply to a worksheet cell range is using the pop-up palettes of graphical scales and markers attached to the Data Bars, Color Scales, and Icon Sets options on the Conditional Formatting button's drop-down menu:

✔ **Data Bars** represents the relative values in the cell selection by the length of the color bar in each cell and are great for helping you quickly spot the lower and higher values within a large range of data.

✔ **Color Scales** classify the relative values in a cell selection with a color gradation using a one-, two-, or three-color scale and are great for identifying the distribution of values across a large range of data.

✔ **Icon Sets** classify the values in the cell selection into three to five categories and each icon within the set represents a range of values that go from high to low. Icon sets are great for quickly identifying the different ranges of values in a range of data.

Figure 3-25 shows you an example of cell ranges (containing identical values) using each of the three formatting types. The values in the first range (B2:B12) are conditionally formatted using blue Gradient Fill Data Bars. The values in the second range (D2:D12) are conditionally formatted using the Green, Yellow, Red Color Scale. The values in the third range (F2:F12) are conditionally formatted using the 3 Arrows Directional Icon set.

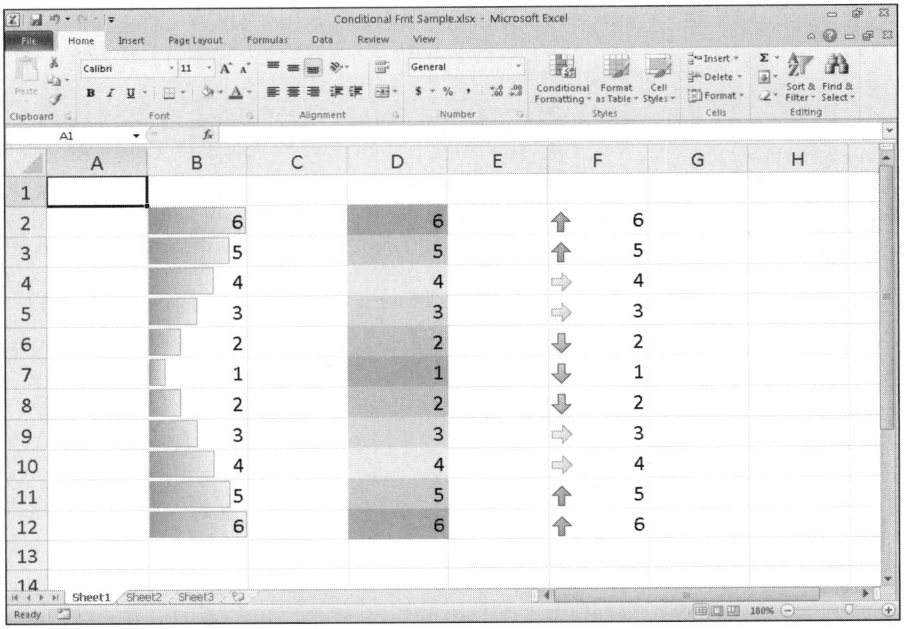

Figure 3-25:
Sample
worksheet
with three
identical
cell ranges
format-
ted with
Excel's Data
Bars, Color
Scales, and
Icon Sets
options.

In Figure 3-25, the particular conditional formatting types Excel assigned to each cell range can be interpreted as follows:

- **Data bars** added to the cells in the first cell range, B2:B12, represent the relative size of its values graphically, much like a standard bar chart.

- **Color scale** applied to the second range, D2:D12, represent the relative size of the values in the range by color and hue (red hues applied to the lower values, yellow to the middle values, and green to the higher values).

- **Directional icons** applied to the third cell range, F2:F12, represent the relative size of the values in the range with arrow icons pointing in different directions (arrows pointing straight down for the lower values, straight up for the higher values, and sideways for middling values).

Highlighting cells according to what ranges the values fall into

The Highlight Cells Rules and Top/Bottom Rules options on Excel's Conditional Formatting drop-down menu enable you to quickly identify cell entries of particular interest in various cell ranges in your worksheet.

The options on the Highlight Cells Rules continuation menu enable you to set formats that identify values that are greater than, less than, equal to, or even between particular values that you set. This menu also contains an option for setting special formats for identifying cells that contain particular text (such as Yes, No, or even Maybe answers in a data list) or certain dates (such as project milestones and deadlines).

Perhaps one of the most useful options on the Highlight Cells Rules continuation menu is the Duplicate Values option that enables you to flag duplicate entries in a cell range by assigning them a special formatting. Doing this not only makes it easy to visually identify duplicate entries in a data list or table but also to find them electronically by searching for their particular formatting characteristics. (See Chapter 6 for details on searching your worksheets.)

The options on the Top/Bottom Rules continuation menu enable you to specially format and, therefore, easily identify values in data tables and lists that are either above or below the norm. These options not only include those for automatically formatting all values in a range that are among the top 10 highest or lowest (either in value or percentage) but also above or below the average (as calculated by dividing the total by the number of values).

In addition to using the ready-made rules for conditional formatting located on the Highlight Cells Rules and Top/Bottom Rules continuation menus, you can also create your own custom rules. When you create a custom rule, you not only specify the rule type that identifies which values or text entries to format, but also you format the colors and other aspects included in the formatting. (For details on creating custom conditional formats, consult my *Excel 2010 All-in-One For Dummies*.)

Chapter 4

Going Through Changes

*P*icture this: You just finished creating, formatting, and printing a major project with Excel — a workbook with your department's budget for the next fiscal year. Because you finally understand a little bit about how the Excel thing works, you finish the job in crack time. You're actually ahead of schedule.

You turn the workbook over to your boss so that she can check the numbers. With plenty of time for making those inevitable last-minute corrections, you're feeling on top of this situation.

Then comes the reality check — your boss brings the document back, and she's plainly agitated. "We forgot to include the estimates for the temps and our overtime hours. They go right here. While you're adding them, can you move these rows of figures up and those columns over?"

As she continues to suggest improvements, your heart begins to sink. These modifications are in a different league than, "Let's change these column headings from bold to italic and add shading to that row of totals." Clearly, you're looking at a lot more work on this baby than you had contemplated. Even worse, you're looking at making structural changes that threaten to unravel the very fabric of your beautiful worksheet.

As the preceding fable points out, editing a worksheet in a workbook can occur on different levels:

- ✔ You can make changes that affect the contents of the cells, such as copying a row of column headings or moving a table to a new area in a particular worksheet.

- ✔ You can make changes that affect the structure of a worksheet itself, such as inserting new columns or rows (so that you can enter new data originally left out) or deleting unnecessary columns or rows from an existing table so that you don't leave any gaps.

- ✔ You can even make changes to the number of worksheets in a workbook (by either adding or deleting sheets).

In this chapter, you discover how to make these types of changes safely to a workbook. As you see, the mechanics of copying and moving data or inserting and deleting rows are simple to master. It's the impact that such actions have on the worksheet that takes a little more effort to understand. Not to worry! You always have the Undo feature to fall back on for those (hopefully rare) times when you make a little tiny change that throws an entire worksheet into complete and utter chaos.

In the final section of this chapter ("Stamping Out Errors with Text to Speech"), find out how to use the Text to Speech feature to check out and confirm the accuracy of the data entries you make in your worksheets. With Text to Speech, you can listen to your computer read back a series of cell entries while you visually corroborate their accuracy from the original source document. Text to Speech can make this sort of routine and otherwise labor-intensive editing much easier and greatly increase the accuracy of your spreadsheets.

Opening the Darned Thing Up for Editing

Before you can do any damage — I mean, make any changes — in a workbook, you have to open it up in Excel. To open a workbook, you can choose File⇨Open, press Alt+FO, or use the old standby keyboard shortcuts Ctrl+O or Ctrl+F12.

Operating the Open dialog box

If you're running Excel 2010 under Windows 7, an Open dialog box very much like the one in Figure 4-1 appears. This dialog box is divided into panes: the Navigation pane on the left where you can select a new folder to open and the main pane on the right showing the icons for all the subfolders in the current folder as well as the documents that Excel can open.

Change your view

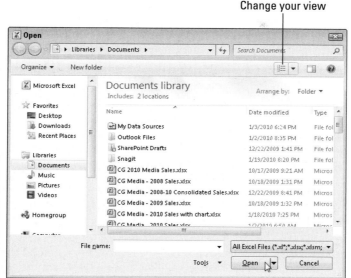

Figure 4-1:
Use the
Open dialog
box to find
and open a
workbook
for editing.

The folder with contents displayed in the Open dialog box is either the one designated as the Default File Location on the Save tab of the Excel Options dialog box or the folder you last opened during your current Excel work session. If you haven't changed the default folder location since installing Excel 2010 on your computer, this default folder is the Documents Library (simply referred to as Documents in Windows Vista).

If you're running Excel 2010 on Windows Vista, your Open dialog box is similar to the one shown in Figure 4-1 except that your Navigation pane contains a Folders item instead of Libraries under your list of Favorites. Additionally, the Views button appears between the Organize and New Folder buttons and not to their right above the Navigation and main panes.

To open a workbook in another folder, click its link in the Favorite Links section of the Navigation pane or click the Expand Folders button (the one with the triangle pointing upward) and click its folder in this list.

If you open a new folder and it appears empty of all files (and you know that it's not an empty folder), this just means the folder doesn't contain any of the types of files that Excel can open directly (such as workbooks, template files, and macro sheets). To display all the files whether or not Excel can open them directly (meaning without some sort of conversion), click the drop-down button that appears next to the drop-down list box that currently displays All Excel Files and then click All Files on its drop-down menu.

When the icon for the workbook file you want to work with appears in the Open dialog box, you can then open it either by clicking its file icon and then clicking the Open button or, if you're handy with the mouse, by just double-clicking the file icon.

You can use the slider attached to the Views drop-down list button in the Open dialog box to change the way folder and file icons appear in the dialog box. When you select Large Icons or Extra Large Icons on this slider (or anywhere in between), the Excel workbook icons actually show a preview of the data in the upper-left corner of the first worksheet when the file is saved with the preview picture option turned on:

✔ To enable the preview feature when saving workbooks in Excel 2010, select the Save Thumbnail check box in the Save As dialog box before saving the file for the first time.

✔ To enable the preview feature when saving workbooks in Excel 97 through 2003, click the Save Preview Picture check box on the Summary tab of the workbook's Properties dialog box (File⇨Properties) before saving the file for the first time.

This preview of part of the first sheet can help you quickly identify the workbook you want to open for editing or printing.

Opening more than one workbook at a time

If you know that you're going to edit more than one of the workbook files shown in the list box of the Open dialog box, you can select multiple files in the list box and Excel will then open all of them (in the order they're listed) when you click the Open button or press Enter.

Remember that in order to select multiple files that appear sequentially in the Open dialog box, you click the first filename and then hold down the Shift key while you click the last filename. To select files that aren't listed sequentially, you need to hold down the Ctrl key while you click the various filenames.

After the workbook files are open in Excel, you can then switch documents by selecting their filename buttons on the Windows taskbar or by using the Flip feature (Alt+Tab) to select the workbook's thumbnail. (See Chapter 7 for detailed information on working on more than one worksheet at a time.)

The Open dialog box in Excel 2010 running on Windows XP

The Open dialog box for Windows XP is arranged a bit differently from the one in Windows 7 and Windows Vista. This Open dialog box is divided into two sections: a My Places panel on the left and a folder and file list box on the right. If the folder open in the list box is not the one that has the workbook file you need to use, use the Up One Level button in the Open dialog box to change levels until you see the folder you want to open. Use the buttons displayed in the My Places panel on the left side of the Open dialog box (My Recent Documents, Desktop, My Documents, My Computer, and My Network Places) to open any folders associated with these buttons that contain workbook files.

When you locate the file that you want to use in the list box in the Open dialog box, open it by clicking its file icon and then clicking the Open button or pressing Enter (or by double-clicking the file icon).

Opening recently edited workbooks

If you know that the workbook you now need to edit is one of those that you opened recently, you don't even have to fool around with the Open dialog box. Just choose File⇨Recent to display a Recent Workbooks list to the right of the pull-down menu (or press Alt+FR) and then click the name of the workbook to open for editing.

When you open the Recent Workbooks list by pressing Alt+FR, Excel displays the number hot keys to each of the recently opened spreadsheet files in the list and you then can open the one you need to edit simply by typing its number.

Excel 2010 automatically keeps a running list of the last 20 files you opened in the Recent Workbooks list on the File tab. If you want, you can have Excel display more or fewer files in this list on the File tab.

To change the number of recently opened files that appear, follow these simple steps:

1. **Choose File⇨Options⇨Advanced or press Alt+FTA to open the Advanced tab of the Excel Options dialog box.**

2. **Type a new entry (between 1 and 50) in the Show This Number of Recent Documents text box or use the spinner buttons to increase or decrease this number.**

3. **Click OK or press Enter to close the Excel Options dialog box.**

If you don't want any files displayed in the Recent Workbooks list on the File tab, enter **0** in the Show This Number of Recent Documents text box or select it with the spinner buttons.

Select the Quickly Access This Number of Recent Workbooks check box on the Recent Workbooks panel in the Backstage View to have Excel display the four most recently opened workbooks as items on the File tab. That way, you can open any of them by clicking its button without having to open the Recent Workbooks panel. After selecting the Quickly Access This Number of Recent Workbooks check box, you change the number of recently opened workbooks added to the File tab by entering the new number in its text box or selecting the number with its spinner buttons.

When you don't know where to find them

The only problem you can encounter in opening a document from the Open dialog box is locating the filename. Everything's hunky-dory as long as you can see the workbook filename listed in the Open dialog box or know which folder to open in order to display it. But what about those times when a file seems to migrate mysteriously and can't be found on your computer?

When you run Excel 2010 under Windows 7 or Vista, the operating system adds a Search Documents text box (simply called Search in Vista) to the Open dialog box (see Figure 4-2). You can use this text box to search for missing workbooks from within the Open dialog box.

Figure 4-2:
Use the
Search
Documents
text box in
the Open
dialog box
to quickly
search for
any Excel
workbook
on your
computer.

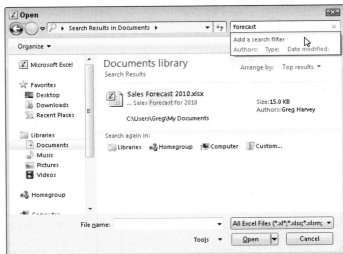

To find a missing workbook, click this search text box in the upper-right corner of the Open dialog box and then begin typing characters used in the workbook's filename or contained in the workbook itself.

As Windows finds any matches for the characters you type, the names of the workbook files (and other Excel files such as templates and macro sheets as well) appear in the Open dialog box. As soon as the workbook you want to open is listed, you can open it by clicking its icon and filename followed by the Open button or by double-clicking it.

The Open dialog box in Excel 2010 when running under Windows XP does not have a search feature built in to it. This means that to search for missing workbooks, you have to do it outside Excel by using Windows XP's search feature available on its Start menu.

Opening files with a twist

The drop-down button attached to the Open command button at the bottom of the Open dialog box enables you to open the selected workbook file(s) in a special way, including:

- **Open Read-Only:** This command opens the files you select in the Open dialog box's list box in a read-only state, which means that you can look but you can't touch. (Actually, you can touch; you just can't save your changes.) To save changes in a read-only file, you must use the Save As command (File➪Save As or Alt+FA) and give the workbook file a new filename. (Refer to Chapter 2.)

- **Open as Copy:** This command opens a copy of the files you select in the Open dialog box. Use this method of opening files as a safety net: If you mess up the copies, you always have the originals to fall back on.

- **Open in Browser:** This command opens workbook files you save as Web pages (which I describe in Chapter 12) in your favorite Web browser. This command isn't available unless the program identifies that the selected file or files were saved as Web pages rather than plain old Excel workbook files.

- **Open in Protected View:** This command opens the workbook file in Protected View mode that keeps you from making any changes to the contents of its worksheets until you click the Enable Editing button that appears in the orange Protected View panel at the top of the screen.

- **Open and Repair:** This command attempts to repair corrupted workbook files before opening them in Excel. When you select this command, a dialog box appears giving you a choice between attempting to repair the corrupted file or opening the recovered version, extracting data from the corrupted file, and placing it in a new workbook (which you can save with the Save command). Click the Repair button to attempt to recover and open the file. Click the Extract Data button if you tried unsuccessfully to have Excel repair the file.

Much Ado about Undo

Before you start tearing into the workbook that you just opened, get to know the Undo feature, including how it can put right many of the things that you could inadvertently mess up. The Undo command button on the Quick Access toolbar is a regular chameleon button. When you delete the cell selection by pressing the Delete key, the Undo button's ScreenTip reads Undo Clear (Ctrl+Z). If you move some entries to a new part of the worksheet by dragging it, the Undo command button ScreenTip changes to Undo Drag and Drop (Ctrl+Z).

In addition to clicking the Undo command button (in whatever guise it appears), you can also choose this command by pressing Ctrl+Z (perhaps for *unZap*).

The Undo command button on the Quick Access toolbar changes in response to whatever action you just took; that is, it changes after each action. If you forget to strike when the iron is hot, so to speak, and don't use the Undo feature to restore the worksheet to its previous state *before* you choose another command, you then need to consult the drop-down menu on the Undo button. Click its drop-down button that appears to the right of the Undo icon (the curved arrow pointing to the left). After the Undo drop-down menu appears, click the action on this menu that you want undone. Excel will then undo this action and all actions that precede it in the list (which are selected automatically).

Undo is Redo the second time around

After using the Undo command button on the Quick Access toolbar, Excel 2010 activates the Redo command button to its immediate right. If you delete an entry from a cell by pressing the Delete key and then click the Undo command button or press Ctrl+Z, the ScreenTip that appears when you position the mouse pointer over the Redo command button reads Redo Clear (Ctrl+Y).

When you click the Redo command button or press Ctrl+Y, Excel redoes the thing you just undid. Actually, this sounds more complicated than it is. It simply means that you use Undo to switch between the result of an action and the state of the worksheet just before that action until you decide how you want the worksheet (or until the cleaning crew turns off the lights and locks up the building).

What ya gonna do when you can't Undo?

Just when you think it is safe to begin gutting the company's most important workbook, I really feel that I have to tell you that (yikes!) Undo doesn't work all the time! Although you can undo your latest erroneous cell deletion, bad move, or unwise copy, you can't undo your latest rash save. (You know, like when you meant to choose Save As from the File tab to save the edited worksheet under a different document name but chose Save and ended up saving the changes as part of the current document.)

Unfortunately, Excel doesn't let you know when you are about to take a step from which there is no return — until it's too late. After you've gone and done the un-undoable and you click the Undo button where you expect its ScreenTip to say Undo *blah, blah*, it now reads Can't Undo.

One exception to this rule is when the program gives you advance warning (which you should heed). When you choose a command that is normally possible but because you're low on memory or the change will affect so much of the worksheet, or both, Excel knows that it can't undo the change if it goes through with it, the program displays an alert box telling you that there isn't enough memory to undo this action and asking whether you want to go ahead anyway. If you click the Yes button and complete the edit, just realize that you do so without any possibility of pardon. If you find out, too late, that you deleted a row of essential formulas (that you forgot about because you couldn't see them), you can't bring them back with Undo. In such a case, you would have to close the file (File➪Close) and *NOT save your changes.*

Doing the Old Drag-and-Drop Thing

The first editing technique you need to learn is *drag and drop.* As the name implies, you can use this mouse technique to pick up a cell selection and drop it into a new place on the worksheet. Although drag and drop is primarily a technique for moving cell entries around a worksheet, you can adapt it to copy a cell selection, as well.

To use drag and drop to move a range of cell entries (one cell range at a time), follow these steps:

1. **Select a cell range.**

2. **Position the mouse pointer on one edge of the extended cell cursor that now surrounds the entire cell range.**

   Your signal that you can start dragging the cell range to its new position in the worksheet is when the pointer changes to the arrowhead.

3. **Drag your selection to its destination.**

   Drag your selection by depressing and holding down the primary mouse button — usually the left one — while moving the mouse.

   While you drag your selection, you actually move only the outline of the cell range, and Excel keeps you informed of what the new cell range address would be (as a kind of drag-and-drop ScreenTip) if you were to release the mouse button at that location.

   Drag the outline until it's positioned where you want the entries to appear (as evidenced by the cell range in the drag-and-drop ScreenTip).

4. **Release the mouse button.**

   The cell entries within that range reappear in the new location as soon as you release the mouse button.

In Figures 4-3 and 4-4, I show how you can drag and drop a cell range. In Figure 4-3, I select the cell range A10:E10 (containing the quarterly totals) to move it to row 12 to make room for sales figures for two new companies (Simple Simon Pie Shoppes and Jack Be Nimble Candlesticks, which hadn't been acquired when this workbook was first created). In Figure 4-4, you see the Mother Goose Enterprises – 2010 Sales worksheet right after completing this move.

Figure 4-3:
Dragging the cell selection to its new position in a worksheet.

	A10	▼	*fx*	Total				
	A			B	C	D	E	F
1	Mother Goose Enterprises - 2010 Sales							
2				Jan	Feb	Mar	Qtr 1	
3	Jack Sprat Diet Centers			80,138.58	59,389.56	19,960.06	$ 159,488.20	
4	Jack and Jill Trauma Centers			12,345.62	89,645.70	25,436.84	$ 127,428.16	
5	Mother Hubbard Dog Goodies			12,657.05	60,593.56	42,300.28	$ 115,550.89	
6	Rub-a-Dub-Dub Tubs and Spas			17,619.79	40,635.00	42,814.99	$ 101,069.78	
7	Georgie Porgie Pudding Pies			57,133.56	62,926.31	12,408.75	$ 132,468.62	
8	Hickory, Dickory, Doc Clock Repair			168,591.00	124,718.10	4,196.13	$ 297,505.23	
9	Little Bo Peep Pet Detectives			30,834.63	71,111.25	74,926.24	$ 176,872.12	
10	Total			$379,320.23	$509,019.48	$222,043.29	$1,110,383.00	
11								
12								
13				A12:E12				
14								

The arguments for the SUM functions in cell range B13:E13 do not keep pace with the change — it continues to sum only the values in rows 3 through 9 after the move. However, when you enter the sales figures for these new enterprises in columns B through C in rows 10, 11, and 12, Excel shows off its smarts and updates the formulas in row 13 to include the new entries. For example, the SUM(B3:B9) formula in B13 magically becomes SUM(B3:B12).

	A12	▾	*fx*	Total				
	A			B	C	D	E	F
1	Mother Goose Enterprises - 2010 Sales							
2				Jan	Feb	Mar	Qtr 1	
3	Jack Sprat Diet Centers			80,138.58	59,389.56	19,960.06	$ 159,488.20	
4	Jack and Jill Trauma Centers			12,345.62	89,645.70	25,436.84	$ 127,428.16	
5	Mother Hubbard Dog Goodies			12,657.05	60,593.56	42,300.28	$ 115,550.89	
6	Rub-a-Dub-Dub Tubs and Spas			17,619.79	40,635.00	42,814.99	$ 101,069.78	
7	Georgie Porgie Pudding Pies			57,133.56	62,926.31	12,408.75	$ 132,468.62	
8	Hickory, Dickory, Doc Clock Repair			168,591.00	124,718.10	4,196.13	$ 297,505.23	
9	Little Bo Peep Pet Detectives			30,834.63	71,111.25	74,926.24	$ 176,872.12	
10								
11								
12	Total			$379,320.23	$509,019.48	$222,043.29	$1,110,383.00	
13								
14								
15								

Figure 4-4:
A worksheet after dropping the cell selection into its new place.

Copies, drag-and-drop style

What if you want to copy rather than drag and drop a cell range? Suppose that you need to start a new table in rows farther down the worksheet, and you want to copy the cell range with the formatted title and column headings for the new table. To copy the formatted title range in the sample worksheet, follow these steps:

1. **Select the cell range.**

   In the case of Figures 4-3 and 4-4, that's cell range A1:E2.

2. **Hold the Ctrl key down while you position the mouse pointer on an edge of the selection (that is, the expanded cell cursor).**

   The pointer changes from a thick, shaded cross to an arrowhead with a + (plus sign) to the right of it with the drag-and-drop ScreenTip beside it. The plus sign next to the pointer is your signal that drag and drop will *copy* the selection rather than *move* it.

3. **Drag the cell-selection outline to the place where you want the copy to appear and release the mouse button.**

If, when using drag and drop to move or copy cells, you position the outline of the selection so that it overlaps any part of cells that already contain entries, Excel displays an alert box that asks whether you want to replace the contents of the destination cells. To avoid replacing existing entries and to abort the entire drag-and-drop mission, click the Cancel button in this alert box. To go ahead and exterminate the little darlings, click OK or press Enter.

Insertions courtesy of drag and drop

Like the Klingons of *Star Trek* fame, spreadsheets, such as Excel, never take prisoners. When you place or move a new entry into an occupied cell, the new entry completely replaces the old as though the old entry never existed in that cell.

To insert the cell range you're moving or copying within a populated region of the worksheet without wiping out existing entries, hold down the Shift key while you drag the selection. (If you're copying, you have to get ambitious and hold down both the Shift and Ctrl keys at the same time!)

With the Shift key depressed while you drag, instead of a rectangular outline of the cell range, you get an I-beam shape that shows where the selection will be inserted if you release the mouse button along with the address of the cell range (as a kind of Insertion ScreenTip). When you move the I-beam shape, notice that it wants to attach itself to the column and row borders while you move it. After you position the I-beam at the column or row border where you want to insert the cell range, release the mouse button. Excel inserts the cell range, moving the existing entries to neighboring blank cells (out of harm's way).

When inserting cells with drag and drop, it may be helpful to think of the I-beam shape as a pry bar that pulls apart the columns or rows along the axis of the I. Also, sometimes after moving a range to a new place in the worksheet, instead of the data appearing, you see only #######s in the cells. (Excel 2010 doesn't automatically widen the new columns for the incoming data as it does when formatting the data.) Remember that the way to get rid of the #######s in the cells is by widening those troublesome columns enough to display all the data-plus-formatting; and the easiest way to do this kind of widening is by double-clicking the right border of the column.

I held down the Shift key just as you said . . .

Drag and drop in Insert mode is one of Excel's most finicky features. Sometimes you can do everything just right and still get the alert box warning you that Excel is about to replace existing entries instead of pushing them aside. When you see this alert box, always click the Cancel button! Fortunately, you can insert things with the Insert commands without worrying about which way the I-beam selection goes (see the "Staying In Step with Insert" section, later in this chapter).

Formulas on AutoFill

Copying with drag and drop (by holding down the Ctrl key) is useful when you need to copy a bunch of neighboring cells to a new part of the worksheet. Frequently, however, you just need to copy a single formula that you just created to a bunch of neighboring cells that need to perform the same type of calculation (such as totaling columns of figures). This type of formula copy, although quite common, can't be done with drag and drop. Instead, use the AutoFill feature (read about this in Chapter 2) or the Copy and Paste commands. (See the section "Cut and paste, digital style" later in this chapter.)

Here's how you can use AutoFill to copy one formula to a range of cells. In Figure 4-5, you can see the Mother Goose Enterprises – 2010 Sales worksheet with all the companies but this time with only one monthly total in row 12, which is in the process of being copied through cell E12.

Figure 4-5: Copying a formula to a cell range with AutoFill.

	B12	▾	*fx* =SUM(B3:B11)				
	A		B	C	D	E	F
1	Mother Goose Enterprises - 2010 Sales						
2			Jan	Feb	Mar	Qtr 1	
3	Jack Sprat Diet Centers		80,138.58	59,389.56	19,960.06	$ 159,488.20	
4	Jack and Jill Trauma Centers		12,345.62	89,645.70	25,436.84	$ 127,428.16	
5	Mother Hubbard Dog Goodies		12,657.05	60,593.56	42,300.28	$ 115,550.89	
6	Rub-a-Dub-Dub Tubs and Spas		17,619.79	40,635.00	42,814.99	$ 101,069.78	
7	Georgie Porgie Pudding Pies		57,133.56	62,926.31	12,408.75	$ 132,468.62	
8	Hickory, Dickory, Doc Clock Repair		168,591.00	124,718.10	4,196.13	$ 297,505.23	
9	Little Bo Peep Pet Detectives		30,834.63	71,111.25	74,926.24	$ 176,872.12	
10	Simple Simon Pie Shoppes		104,937.77	77,943.19	45,897.25	$ 228,778.21	
11	Jack-Be-Nimble Candlesticks		128,237.32	95,035.19	78,654.50	$ 301,927.01	
12	Total		$612,495.32				
13							
14							
15							

Figure 4-6 shows the worksheet after dragging the fill handle in cell B12 to select the cell range C12:E12 (where this formula should be copied).

Relatively speaking

Figure 4-6 shows the worksheet after the formula in a cell is copied to the cell range C12:E12 and cell B12 is active. Notice how Excel handles the copying of formulas. The original formula in cell B12 is as follows:

```
=SUM(B3:B11)
```

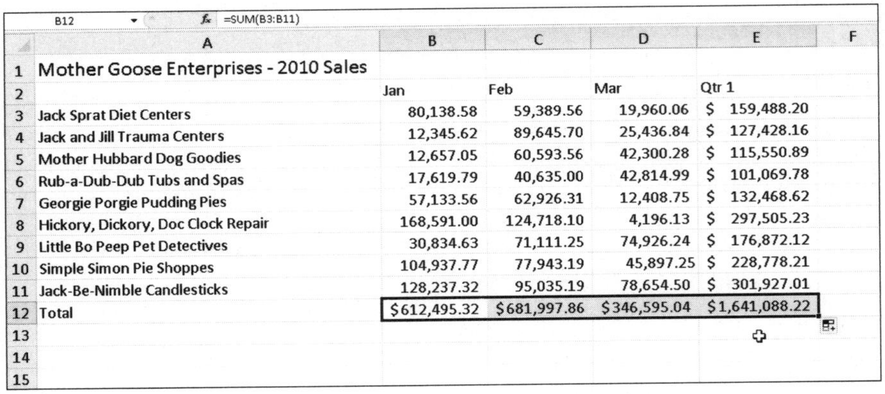

	B12	▾	*fx*	=SUM(B3:B11)		

	A	B	C	D	E	F
1	Mother Goose Enterprises - 2010 Sales					
2		Jan	Feb	Mar	Qtr 1	
3	Jack Sprat Diet Centers	80,138.58	59,389.56	19,960.06	$ 159,488.20	
4	Jack and Jill Trauma Centers	12,345.62	89,645.70	25,436.84	$ 127,428.16	
5	Mother Hubbard Dog Goodies	12,657.05	60,593.56	42,300.28	$ 115,550.89	
6	Rub-a-Dub-Dub Tubs and Spas	17,619.79	40,635.00	42,814.99	$ 101,069.78	
7	Georgie Porgie Pudding Pies	57,133.56	62,926.31	12,408.75	$ 132,468.62	
8	Hickory, Dickory, Doc Clock Repair	168,591.00	124,718.10	4,196.13	$ 297,505.23	
9	Little Bo Peep Pet Detectives	30,834.63	71,111.25	74,926.24	$ 176,872.12	
10	Simple Simon Pie Shoppes	104,937.77	77,943.19	45,897.25	$ 228,778.21	
11	Jack-Be-Nimble Candlesticks	128,237.32	95,035.19	78,654.50	$ 301,927.01	
12	Total	$612,495.32	$681,997.86	$346,595.04	$1,641,088.22	
13						
14						
15						

Figure 4-6:
The work-
sheet after
copying
the formula
totaling the
monthly
(and quar-
terly) sales.

When the original formula is copied to cell C12, Excel changes the formula slightly so that it looks like this:

```
=SUM(C3:C11)
```

Excel adjusts the column reference, changing it from B to C, because I copied from left to right across the rows.

When you copy a formula to a cell range that extends down the rows, Excel adjusts the row numbers in the copied formulas rather than the column letters to suit the position of each copy. For example, cell E3 in the Mother Goose Enterprises – 2010 Sales worksheet contains the following formula:

```
=SUM(B3:D3)
```

When you copy this formula to cell E4, Excel changes the copy of the formula to the following:

```
=SUM(B4:D4)
```

Excel adjusts the row reference to keep current with the new row 4 position. Because Excel adjusts the cell references in copies of a formula relative to the direction of the copying, the cell references are known as *relative cell references.*

Some things are absolutes!

All new formulas you create naturally contain relative cell references unless you say otherwise. Because most copies you make of formulas require adjustments of their cell references, you rarely have to give this arrangement a second thought. Then, every once in a while, you come across an exception that calls for limiting when and how cell references are adjusted in copies.

One of the most common of these exceptions is when you want to compare a range of different values with a single value. This happens most often when you want to compute what percentage each part is to the total. For example, in the Mother Goose Enterprises – 2010 Sales worksheet, you encounter this situation in creating and copying a formula that calculates what percentage each monthly total (in the cell range B14:D14) is of the quarterly total in cell E12.

Suppose that you want to enter these formulas in row 14 of the Mother Goose Enterprises – 2010 Sales worksheet, starting in cell B14. The formula in cell B14 for calculating the percentage of the January-sales-to-first-quarter-total is very straightforward:

```
=B12/E12
```

This formula divides the January sales total in cell B12 by the quarterly total in E12 (what could be easier?). Look, however, at what would happen if you dragged the fill handle one cell to the right to copy this formula to cell C14:

```
=C12/F12
```

The adjustment of the first cell reference from B12 to C12 is just what the doctor ordered. However, the adjustment of the second cell reference from E12 to F12 is a disaster. Not only do you not calculate what percentage the February sales in cell C12 are of the first quarter sales in E12, but you also end up with one of those horrible #DIV/0! error things in cell C14.

To stop Excel from adjusting a cell reference in a formula in any copies you make, convert the cell reference from relative to absolute. You do this by pressing the function key F4, after you put Excel in Edit mode (F2). Excel indicates that you make the cell reference absolute by placing dollar signs in front of the column letter and row number. For example, in Figure 4-7, cell B14 contains the correct formula to copy to the cell range C14:D14:

```
=B12/$E$12
```

Figure 4-7: Copying the formula for computing the ratio of monthly to quarterly sales with an absolute cell reference.

	A	B	C	D	E	F
1	Mother Goose Enterprises - 2010 Sales					
2		Jan	Feb	Mar	Qtr 1	
3	Jack Sprat Diet Centers	80,138.58	59,389.56	19,960.06	$ 159,488.20	
4	Jack and Jill Trauma Centers	12,345.62	89,645.70	25,436.84	$ 127,428.16	
5	Mother Hubbard Dog Goodies	12,657.05	60,593.56	42,300.28	$ 115,550.89	
6	Rub-a-Dub-Dub Tubs and Spas	17,619.79	40,635.00	42,814.99	$ 101,069.78	
7	Georgie Porgie Pudding Pies	57,133.56	62,926.31	12,408.75	$ 132,468.62	
8	Hickory, Dickory, Doc Clock Repair	168,591.00	124,718.10	4,196.13	$ 297,505.23	
9	Little Bo Peep Pet Detectives	30,834.63	71,111.25	74,926.24	$ 176,872.12	
10	Simple Simon Pie Shoppes	104,937.77	77,943.19	45,897.25	$ 228,778.21	
11	Jack-Be-Nimble Candlesticks	128,237.32	95,035.19	78,654.50	$ 301,927.01	
12	Total	$612,495.32	$681,997.86	$346,595.04	$1,641,088.22	
13						
14	Monthly/Qtrly Percentage	37%				
15						

Look at the worksheet after this formula is copied to the range C14:D14 with the fill handle and cell C14 is selected (see Figure 4-8). Notice that the Formula bar shows that this cell contains the following formula:

```
=C12/$E$12
```

	A	B	C	D	E	F
	C14		f_x =C12/$E$12			
1	Mother Goose Enterprises - 2010 Sales					
2		Jan	Feb	Mar	Qtr 1	
3	Jack Sprat Diet Centers	80,138.58	59,389.56	19,960.06	$ 159,488.20	
4	Jack and Jill Trauma Centers	12,345.62	89,645.70	25,436.84	$ 127,428.16	
5	Mother Hubbard Dog Goodies	12,657.05	60,593.56	42,300.28	$ 115,550.89	
6	Rub-a-Dub-Dub Tubs and Spas	17,619.79	40,635.00	42,814.99	$ 101,069.78	
7	Georgie Porgie Pudding Pies	57,133.56	62,926.31	12,408.75	$ 132,468.62	
8	Hickory, Dickory, Doc Clock Repair	168,591.00	124,718.10	4,196.13	$ 297,505.23	
9	Little Bo Peep Pet Detectives	30,834.63	71,111.25	74,926.24	$ 176,872.12	
10	Simple Simon Pie Shoppes	104,937.77	77,943.19	45,897.25	$ 228,778.21	
11	Jack-Be-Nimble Candlesticks	$128,237.32	95,035.19	$ 78,654.50	$ 301,927.01	
12	Total	$612,495.32	$681,997.86	$346,595.04	$1,641,088.22	
13						
14	Monthly/Qtrly Percentage	37%	42%	21%		
15						

Figure 4-8: The worksheet after copying the formula with the absolute cell reference.

Because E12 was changed to $E$12 in the original formula, all the copies have this same absolute (non-changing) reference.

If you goof up and copy a formula where one or more of the cell references should have been absolute but you left them all relative, edit the original formula as follows:

1. **Double-click the cell with the formula or press F2 to edit it.**

2. **Position the insertion point somewhere on the reference you want to convert to absolute.**

3. **Press F4.**

4. **When you finish editing, click the Enter button on the Formula bar and then copy the formula to the messed-up cell range with the fill handle.**

Be sure to press F4 only to change a cell reference to completely absolute as I describe earlier. If you press the F4 function key a second time, you end up with a so-called *mixed reference,* where only the row part is absolute and the column part is relative (as in E$12). If you then press F4 again, Excel comes up with another type of mixed reference, where the column part is absolute and the row part is relative (as in $E12). If you go on and press F4 yet again, Excel changes the cell reference back to completely relative (as in E12). After you're back where you started, you can continue to use F4 to cycle through this same set of cell reference changes all over again.

Cut and paste, digital style

Instead of using drag and drop or AutoFill, you can use the old standby Cut, Copy, and Paste commands to move or copy information in a worksheet. These commands use the Office Clipboard as a kind of electronic halfway house where the information you cut or copy remains until you decide to paste it somewhere. Because of this Clipboard arrangement, you can use these commands to move or copy information to any other workbook open in Excel or even to other programs running in Windows (such as a Word 2010 document).

To move a cell selection with Cut and Paste, follow these steps:

1. **Select the cells you want to move.**

2. **Click the Cut command button in the Clipboard group on the Home tab (the button with the scissors icon).**

   If you prefer, you can choose Cut by pressing Ctrl+X.

   Whenever you choose the Cut command in Excel, the program surrounds the cell selection with a *marquee* (a dotted line that travels around the cells' outline) and displays the following message on the Status bar:

   ```
   Select destination and press ENTER or choose Paste
   ```

3. **Move the cell cursor to the new range to which you want the information moved, or click the cell in the upper-left corner of the new range.**

4. **Press Enter to complete the move operation.**

   If you're feeling ambitious, click the Paste command button in the Clipboard group on the Home tab or press Ctrl+V.

Notice that when you indicate the destination range, you don't have to select a range of blank cells that matches the shape and size of the cell selection you're moving. Excel needs to know only the location of the cell in the upper-left corner of the destination range to figure out where to put the rest of the cells.

Copying a cell selection with the Copy and Paste commands follows an identical procedure to the one you use with the Cut and Paste commands. After selecting the range to copy, you can get the information into the Clipboard by clicking the Copy button on the Ribbon's Home tab, choosing Copy from the cell's shortcut menu, or pressing Ctrl+C.

Paste it again, Sam . . .

An advantage to copying a selection with the Copy and Paste commands and the Clipboard is that you can paste the information multiple times. Just make sure that, instead of pressing Enter to complete the first copy operation, you click the Paste button on the Home tab of the Ribbon or press Ctrl+V.

When you use the Paste command to complete a copy operation, Excel copies the selection to the range you designate without removing the marquee from the original selection. This is your signal that you can select another destination range (in either the same or a different document).

After you select the first cell of the next range where you want the selection copied, choose the Paste command again. You can continue in this manner, pasting the same selection to your heart's content. When you make the last copy, press Enter instead of choosing the Paste command button or pressing Ctrl+V. If you forget and choose Paste, get rid of the marquee around the original cell range by pressing the Esc key.

Keeping pace with Paste Options

Right after you click the Paste button on the Home tab of the Ribbon or press Ctrl+V to paste cell entries that you copy (not cut) to the Clipboard, Excel displays a Paste Options button with the label, (Ctrl), to its immediate right at the end of the pasted range. When you click this drop-down button or press the Ctrl key, a palette similar to the one shown in Figure 4-9 appears with three groups of buttons (Paste, Paste Values, and Other Paste Options).

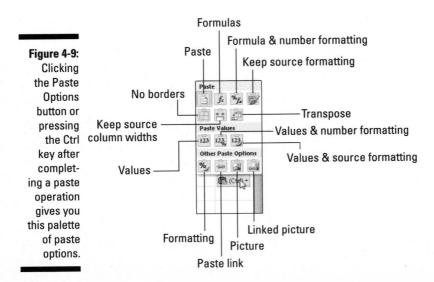

Figure 4-9: Clicking the Paste Options button or pressing the Ctrl key after completing a paste operation gives you this palette of paste options.

You can use these paste options to control or restrict the type of content and formatting that's included in the pasted cell range. The paste options (complete with the hot key sequences you can type to select them) on the Paste Options palette include:

- ✔ **Paste (P):** Excel pastes all the stuff in the cell selection (formulas, formatting, you name it).

- ✔ **Formulas (F):** Excel pastes all the text, numbers, and formulas in the current cell selection without their formatting.

- ✔ **Formulas & Number Formatting (O):** Excel pastes the number formats assigned to the copied values along with their formulas.

- ✔ **Keep Source Formatting (K):** Excel copies the formatting from the original cells and pastes this into the destination cells (along with the copied entries).

- ✔ **No Borders (B):** Excel pastes all the stuff in the cell selection without copying any borders applied to its cell range.

- ✔ **Keep Source Column Widths (W):** Excel makes the width of the columns in the destination range the same as those in the source range when it copies their cell entries.

- ✔ **Transpose (T):** Excel changes the orientation of the pasted entries. For example, if the original cells' entries run down the rows of a single column of the worksheet, the transposed pasted entries will run across the columns of a single row.

- ✔ **Values (V):** Excel pastes only the calculated results of any formulas in the source cell range.

- ✔ **Values & Number Formatting (A):** Excel pastes the calculated results of any formulas along with all the formatting assigned to the labels, values, and formulas in the source cell range into the destination range. This means that all the labels and values in the destination range appear formatted just like the source range even though all the original formulas are lost and only the calculated values are retained.

- ✔ **Values & Source Formatting (E):** Excel pastes the calculated results of any formulas along with all formatting assigned to the source cell range.

- ✔ **Formatting (R):** Excel pastes only the formatting (and not the entries) copied from the source cell range to the destination range.

- ✔ **Paste Link (N):** Excel creates linking formulas in the destination range so that any changes that you make to the entries in cells in the source range are immediately brought forward and reflected in the corresponding cells of the destination range.

- ✔ **Picture (U):** Excel pastes only the pictures in the copied cell selection.

- ✔ **Linked Picture (I):** Excel pastes a link to the pictures in the copied cell selection.

The options that appear on the Paste Options palette are context sensitive. This means that the particular paste options available on the palette depend directly upon the type of cell entries previously copied to the Office Clipboard. Additionally, you can access this same palette of paste options by clicking the drop-down button that appears directly beneath the Paste button on the Ribbon instead of clicking the Paste Options button that appears at the end of the pasted range in the worksheet or pressing the Ctrl key on your keyboard.

Paste it from the Clipboard task pane

The Clipboard can store multiple cuts and copies from any program running under Windows not just Excel. In Excel, this means that you can continue to paste stuff from the Clipboard into a workbook even after finishing a move or copy operation (even when you do so by pressing the Enter key rather than using the Paste command).

To open the Clipboard in its own task pane to the immediate left of the Worksheet area (see Figure 4-10), click the dialog box launcher in the lower-right corner of the Clipboard group on the Ribbon's Home tab.

To paste an item from the Office Clipboard into a worksheet other than the one with the data last cut or copied onto it, click the item in the Clipboard task pane to paste it into the worksheet starting at the current position of the cell cursor.

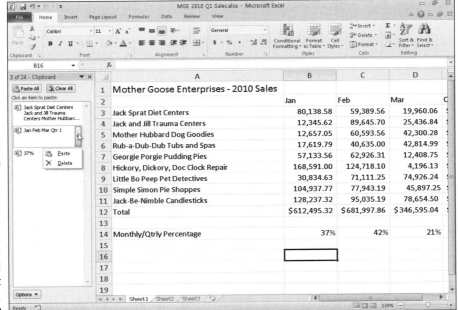

Figure 4-10:
The Clipboard task pane appears on the left side of the Excel Worksheet area.

You can paste all the items stored in the Office Clipboard into the current worksheet by clicking the Paste All button at the top of the Clipboard task pane. To clear the Office Clipboard of all the current items, click the Clear All button. To delete only a particular item from the Office Clipboard, position the mouse pointer over the item in the Clipboard task pane until its drop-down button appears. Click this drop-down button, and then choose Delete from the pop-up menu (refer to Figure 4-10).

To have the Clipboard task pane appear automatically after making two cuts or copies to the Clipboard in an Excel workbook, click the Show Office Clipboard Automatically option on the task pane's Options button menu. To open the Clipboard task pane in the Excel program window by pressing Ctrl+CC, click Show Office Clipboard When Ctrl+C Pressed Twice on the task pane's Options button. Pressing Ctrl+CC only opens the task pane. You still have to click the Close button on the Office Clipboard to close the task pane.

So what's so special about Paste Special?

Normally, unless you fool around with the Paste Options (see the section "Keeping pace with Paste Options" earlier in this chapter), Excel copies all the information in the range of cells you selected: formatting, as well the formulas, text, and other values you enter. You can use the Paste Special command to specify which entries and formatting to use in the current paste operation. Many of the Paste Special options are also available on the Paste Options palette.

To paste particular parts of a cell selection while discarding others, click the drop-down button that appears at the bottom of the Paste command button on the Ribbon's Home tab. Then, click Paste Special on its drop-down menu to open the Paste Special dialog box shown in Figure 4-11.

Figure 4-11:
Use the options in the Paste Special dialog box to control what part of the copied cell selection to include in the paste operation.

The options in the Paste Special dialog box include:

- ✔ **All** to paste all the stuff in the cell selection (formulas, formatting, you name it).

- ✔ **Formulas** to paste all the text, numbers, and formulas in the current cell selection without their formatting.

- ✔ **Values** to convert formulas in the current cell selection to their calculated values.

- ✔ **Formats** to paste only the formatting from the current cell selection, leaving the cell entries in the dust.

- ✔ **Comments** to paste only the notes that you attach to their cells (kind of like electronic self-stick notes — see Chapter 6 for details).

- ✔ **Validation** to paste only the data validation rules into the cell range that you set up with the Data Validation command (which enables you to set what value or range of values is allowed in a particular cell or cell range).

- ✔ **All Using Source Theme** to paste all the information plus the cell styles applied to the cells.

- ✔ **All Except Borders** to paste all the stuff in the cell selection without copying any borders you use there.

- ✔ **Column Widths** to apply the column widths of the cells copied to the Clipboard to the columns where the cells are pasted.

- ✔ **Formulas and Number Formats** to include the number formats assigned to the pasted values and formulas.

- ✔ **Values and Number Formats** to convert formulas to their calculated values and include the number formats you assign to all the pasted values.

- ✔ **All Merging Conditional Formats** to paste Conditional Formatting into the cell range.

- ✔ **None** to have Excel perform no mathematical operation between the data entries you cut or copy to the Clipboard and the data entries in the cell range where you paste.

- ✔ **Add** to add the data you cut or copy to the Clipboard and the data entries in the cell range where you paste.

- ✔ **Subtract** to subtract the data you cut or copy to the Clipboard from the data entries in the cell range where you paste.

- ✔ **Multiply** to multiply the data you cut or copy to the Clipboard by the data entries in the cell range where you paste.

- ✔ **Divide** to divide the data you cut or copy to the Clipboard by the data entries in the cell range where you paste.

✔ **Skip Blanks** check box when you want Excel to paste everywhere except for any empty cells in the incoming range. In other words, a blank cell cannot overwrite your current cell entries.

✔ **Transpose** check box when you want Excel to change the orientation of the pasted entries. For example, if the original cells' entries run down the rows of a single column of the worksheet, the transposed pasted entries will run across the columns of a single row.

✔ **Paste Link** button when you're copying cell entries and you want to establish a link between copies you're pasting and the original entries. That way, changes to the original cells automatically update in the pasted copies.

Let's Be Clear about Deleting Stuff

No discussion about editing in Excel would be complete without a section on getting rid of the stuff you put into cells. You can perform two kinds of deletions in a worksheet:

✔ **Clearing a cell:** Clearing just deletes or empties the cell's contents without removing the cell from the worksheet, which would alter the layout of the surrounding cells.

✔ **Deleting a cell:** Deleting gets rid of the whole kit and caboodle — cell structure along with all its contents and formatting. When you delete a cell, Excel has to shuffle the position of entries in the surrounding cells to plug up any gaps made by the action.

Sounding the all clear!

To get rid of just the contents of a cell selection rather than delete the cells and their contents, select the range of cells to clear and then simply press the Delete key.

If you want to get rid of more than just the contents of a cell selection, click the Clear button (the one with the eraser) in the Editing group on the Ribbon's Home tab and then click one of the following options on its drop-down menu:

✔ **Clear All:** Gets rid of all formatting and notes, as well as entries in the cell selection (Alt+HEA).

✔ **Clear Formats:** Deletes only the formatting from the cell selection without touching anything else (Alt+HEF).

- ✔ **Clear Contents:** Deletes only the entries in the cell selection just like pressing the Delete key (Alt+HEC).
- ✔ **Clear Comments:** Removes the notes in the cell selection but leaves everything else behind (Alt+HEM).
- ✔ **Clear Hyperlinks:** Removes the active hyperlinks (see Chapter 12) in the cell selection but leaves its descriptive text (Alt+HEL).

Get these cells outta here!

To delete the cell selection rather than just clear out its contents, select the cell range, click the drop-down button attached to the Delete command button in the Cells group of the Home tab, and then click Delete Cells on the drop-down menu (or press Alt+HDD). The Delete dialog box opens, showing options for filling in the gaps created when the cells currently selected are blotted out of existence:

- ✔ **Shift Cells Left:** This default option moves entries from neighboring columns on the right to the left to fill in gaps created when you delete the cell selection by clicking OK or pressing Enter.
- ✔ **Shift Cells Up:** Select this to move entries up from neighboring rows below.
- ✔ **Entire Row:** Select this to remove all the rows in the current cell selection.
- ✔ **Entire Columns:** Select this to delete all the columns in the current cell selection.

If you know that you want to shift the remaining cells to the left after deleting the cells in the current selection, you can simply click the Delete command button on the Home tab of the Ribbon. (This is the same thing as opening the Delete dialog box and then clicking OK when the default Shift Cells Left button is selected.

To delete an entire column or row from the worksheet, you can select the column or row on the workbook window frame, right-click the selection, and then click Delete from the column's or row's shortcut menu.

You can also delete entire columns and rows selected in the worksheet by clicking the drop-down button attached to the Delete command button on the Ribbon's Home tab and then clicking the Delete Sheet Columns (Alt+HDC) option or the Delete Sheet Rows option (Alt+HDR) on the drop-down menu.

Deleting entire columns and rows from a worksheet is risky business unless you are sure that the columns and rows in question contain nothing of value. Remember, when you delete an entire row from the worksheet, you delete *all information from column A through XFD* in that row (and you can see only a very few columns in this row). Likewise, when you delete an entire column from the worksheet, you delete *all information from row 1 through 1,048,576* in that column.

Staying in Step with Insert

For those inevitable times when you need to squeeze new entries into an already populated region of the worksheet, you can insert new cells in the area rather than go through all the trouble of moving and rearranging several individual cell ranges. To insert a new cell range, select the cells (many of which are already occupied) where you want the new cells to appear and then click the drop-down attached to the Insert command button in the Cells group of the Home tab and then click Insert Cells on the drop-down menu (or press Alt+HII). The Insert dialog box opens with the following option buttons:

  ✔ **Shift Cells Right:** Select this to shift existing cells to the right to make room for the ones you want to add before clicking OK or pressing Enter.

  ✔ **Shift Cells Down:** Use this default to instruct the program to shift existing entries down before clicking OK or pressing Enter.

  ✔ **Entire Row** or **Entire Column:** When you insert cells with the Insert dialog box, you can insert complete rows or columns in the cell range by selecting either of these radio buttons. You can also select the row number or column letter on the frame before you choose the Insert command.

If you know that you want to shift the existing cells to the right to make room for the newly inserted cells, you can simply click the Insert command button on the Ribbon's Home tab (this is the same thing as opening the Insert dialog box and then clicking OK when the Shift Cells Right button is selected).

Remember that you can also insert entire columns and rows in a worksheet by right-clicking the selection and then clicking Insert on the column's or row's shortcut menu.

As when you delete whole columns and rows, inserting entire columns and rows affects the entire worksheet, not just the part you see. If you don't know what's out in the hinterlands of the worksheet, you can't be sure how the insertion will affect — perhaps even sabotage — stuff (especially formulas) in the other unseen areas. I suggest that you scroll all the way out in both directions to make sure that nothing's out there.

Stamping Out Your Spelling Errors

If you're as good a speller as I am, you'll be relieved to know that Excel 2010 has a built-in spell checker that can catch and remove all those embarrassing little spelling errors. With this in mind, you no longer have any excuse for putting out worksheets with typos in the titles or headings.

To check the spelling in a worksheet, you have the following options:

✔ Click the Spelling command button on the Ribbon's Review tab

✔ Press Alt+RS

✔ Press F7

Any way you do it, Excel begins checking the spelling of all text entries in the worksheet. When the program comes across an unknown word, it displays the Spelling dialog box, similar to the one shown in Figure 4-12.

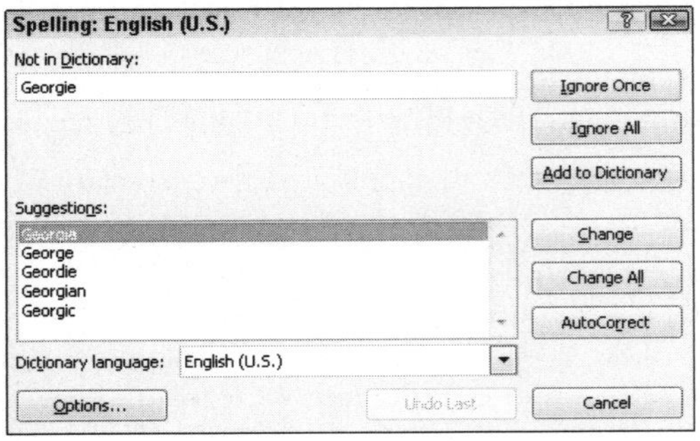

Figure 4-12:
Check your spelling from the Spelling dialog box.

Excel suggests replacements for the unknown word shown in the Not in Dictionary text box with a likely replacement in the Suggestions list box of the Spelling dialog box. If that replacement is incorrect, you can scroll through the Suggestions list and click the correct replacement. Use the Spelling dialog box options as follows:

✔ **Ignore Once** and **Ignore All:** When Excel's spell check comes across a word its dictionary finds suspicious but you know is viable, click the Ignore Once button. If you don't want the spell checker to bother querying you about this word again, click the Ignore All button.

✔ **Add to Dictionary:** Click this button to add the unknown (to Excel) word — such as your name — to a custom dictionary so that Excel won't flag it again when you check the spelling in the worksheet later on.

✔ **Change:** Click this button to replace the word listed in the Not in Dictionary text box with the word Excel offers in the Suggestions list box.

✔ **Change All:** Click this button to change all occurrences of this misspelled word in the worksheet to the word Excel displays in the Suggestions list box.

✔ **AutoCorrect:** Click this button to have Excel automatically correct this spelling error with the suggestion displayed in the Suggestions list box (by adding the misspelling and suggestion to the AutoCorrect dialog box; for more, read Chapter 2).

✔ **Dictionary Language:** To switch to another dictionary (such as a United Kingdom English dictionary, or a French dictionary when checking French terms in a multilingual worksheet), click this drop-down button and then select the name of the desired language in the list.

Notice that the Excel spell checker not only flags words not found in its built-in or custom dictionary but also flags occurrences of double words in a cell entry (such as *total total*) and words with unusual capitalization (such as *NEw York* instead of *New York*). By default, the spell checker ignores all words with numbers and all Internet addresses. If you want it to ignore all words in uppercase letters as well, click the Options button at the bottom of the Spelling dialog box, and then select the Ignore Words in UPPERCASE check box before clicking OK.

You can check the spelling of just a particular group of entries by selecting the cells before you click the Spelling command button on the Review tab of the Ribbon or press F7.

Stamping Out Errors with Text to Speech

The good news is that Excel 2010 still supports the Text to Speech feature introduced in Excel 2003. This feature enables your computer to read aloud any series of cell entries in the worksheet. By using Text to Speech, you can check your printed source while the computer reads aloud the values and labels that you've actually entered — a real nifty way to catch and correct errors that may otherwise escape unnoticed.

The Text to Speech translation feature requires no prior training or special microphones: All that's required is a pair of speakers or headphones connected to your computer.

Now for the bad news: Text to Speech is not available from any of the tabs on the Ribbon. The only way to access Text to Speech is by adding its Speak Cells command buttons as custom buttons on a custom tab on the Ribbon or as custom buttons on the Quick Access toolbar as follows:

1. **Click the Customize Quick Access Toolbar button at the very end of the Quick Access toolbar and then click More Commands on its menu.**

   The Quick Access Toolbar tab of the Excel Options dialog box opens.

2. **Click Commands Not in the Ribbon on the Choose Commands From drop-down menu and scroll down until you see the Speak Cells commands.**

   The Text to Speech command buttons include Speak Cells, Speak Cells – Stop Speaking Cells, Speak Cells by Columns, Speak Cells by Rows, and Speak Cells on Enter.

3. **Click the Speak Cells button in the Choose Commands From list box on the left and then click the Add button to add it to the bottom of the Customize Quick Access Toolbar list box on the right.**

4. **Repeat Step 3 until you've added the remaining Text to Speech buttons to the Quick Access toolbar: Speak Cells – Stop Speaking Cells, Speak Cells by Columns, Speak Cells by Rows, and Speak Cells on Enter.**

   If you want to reposition the Text to Speech buttons on the Quick Access toolbar, select each button in the Customize Quick Access Toolbar list and then move it left on the bar by clicking the Move Up button or right by clicking Move Down. If you want to set off the Text to Speech buttons as a separate group on the Quick Access toolbar, add a vertical separator ahead of the Speak Cells command button (and following the Speak Cells on Enter button if you have buttons not related to the Text to Speech function that follow on the Quick Access toolbar).

5. **Click the OK button to close the Excel Options dialog box.**

Figure 4-13 shows the Quick Access toolbar in my Excel 2010 program window after I moved the toolbar down so that it appears below the Ribbon and added athe Speak Cells command buttons to it.

After adding the Text to Speech commands as custom Speak Cells buttons on the Quick Access toolbar, you can use them to corroborate spreadsheet entries and catch those hard-to-spot errors as follows:

1. **Select the cells in the worksheet whose contents you want read aloud by Text to Speech.**

2. **Click the Speak Cells custom button on the Quick Access toolbar to have the computer read the entries in the selected cells.**

   By default, the Text to Speech feature reads the contents of each cell in the cell selection by reading down each column and then across the rows. If you want Text to Speech to read across the rows and then down the columns, click the Speak Cells by Rows button on the Quick Access toolbar (the button with the two opposing horizontal arrows).

3. **To have the Text to Speech feature read each cell entry while you press the Enter key (at which point the cell cursor moves down to the next cell in the selection), click the Speak Cells on Enter custom button (the button with the curved arrow Enter symbol) on the Quick Access toolbar.**

   As soon as you click the Speak Cells on Enter button, the computer tells you, "Cells will now be spoken on Enter." After selecting this option, you need to press Enter each time that you want to hear an entry read to you.

4. **To pause the Text to Speech feature when you're not using the Speak Cells on Enter option (Step 3) and you locate a discrepancy between what you're reading and what you're hearing, click the Stop Speaking button (the Speak Cells group button with the x).**

Figure 4-13: After adding the Speak Cells command buttons to the Quick Access toolbar, you can use them to check cell entries audibly.

	A	B	C	D	E	F
1	Mother Goose Enterprises - 2010 Sales					
2		Jan	Feb	Mar	Qtr 1	
3	Jack Sprat Diet Centers	80,138.58	59,389.56	19,960.06	$ 159,488.20	
4	Jack and Jill Trauma Centers	12,345.62	89,645.70	25,436.84	$ 127,428.16	
5	Mother Hubbard Dog Goodies	12,657.05	60,593.56	42,300.28	$ 115,550.89	
6	Rub-a-Dub-Dub Tubs and Spas	17,619.79	40,635.00	42,814.99	$ 101,069.78	
7	Georgie Porgie Pudding Pies	57,133.56	62,926.31	12,408.75	$ 132,468.62	
8	Hickory, Dickory, Doc Clock Repair	168,591.00	124,718.10	4,196.13	$ 297,505.23	
9	Little Bo Peep Pet Detectives	30,834.63	71,111.25	74,926.24	$ 176,872.12	
10	Simple Simon Pie Shoppes	104,937.77	77,943.19	45,897.25	$ 228,778.21	
11	Jack-Be-Nimble Candlesticks	$128,237.32	95,035.19	$ 78,654.50	$ 301,927.01	
12	Total	$612,495.32	$681,997.86	$346,595.04	$1,641,088.22	
13						
14	Monthly/Qtrly Percentage	37%	42%	21%		
15						

After you click the Speak Cells on Enter button on the Quick Access toolbar, the computer speaks *only* each new cell entry that you complete by pressing the Enter key (which moves the cell cursor down one row) rather than some other method, such as clicking the Enter button on the Formula bar or pressing the ↓ key.

You can also add any or all the Text to Speech buttons to a custom group on a custom tab on the Ribbon (for example, the Speak Cells group on the custom Misc tab in Figure 4-13 contains the Speak Cells and Stop Speaking buttons).

Chapter 5

Printing the Masterpiece

· ·

· ·

*F*or most people, getting data down on paper is what spreadsheets are all about (all the talk about a so-called paperless office to the contrary). Everything — all the data entry, all the formatting, all the formula checking, all the things you do to get a spreadsheet ready — is really just preparation for printing its information.

In this chapter, you find out just how easy it is to print reports with Excel 2010. Thanks to the program's new Print panel in Backstage View (Alt+FP), its Page Layout worksheet view, and its handy Page Layout tab on the Ribbon, you discover how to produce top-notch reports the first time you send the document to the printer (instead of the second or even the third time around).

The only trick to printing a worksheet is getting used to the paging scheme and learning how to control it. Many of the worksheets you create with Excel are not only longer than one printed page but also wider. Word processors, such as Word 2010, page the document only vertically; they won't let you create a document wider than the page size you're using. Spreadsheet programs like Excel 2010, however, often have to break up pages both vertically and horizontally to print a worksheet document (a kind of tiling of the print job, if you will).

When breaking a worksheet into pages, Excel first pages the document vertically down the rows in the first columns of the print area (just like a word processor). After paging the first columns, the program pages down the rows of the second set of columns in the print area. Excel pages down and then over until the entire document included in the current print area (which can include the entire worksheet or just sections) is paged.

When paging the worksheet, Excel doesn't break up the information within a row or column. If not all the information in a row will fit at the bottom of the page, the program moves the entire row to the following page. If not all the information in a column will fit at the right edge of the page, the program moves the entire column to a new page. (Because Excel pages down and then over, the column may not appear on the next page of the report.)

You can deal with such paging problems in several ways, and in this chapter, you see all of them! After you have these page problems under control, printing is a proverbial piece of cake.

Taking a Gander at the Pages in Page Layout View

Excel 2010's Page Layout View gives you instant access to the paging of the current worksheet. Activate this feature by clicking the Page Layout View button (the center one) to the immediate left of the Zoom slider on the Status bar or by clicking the Page Layout View command button on the Ribbon's View tab (Alt+WP). As you can see in Figure 5-1, when you switch to Page Layout View, Excel adds horizontal and vertical rulers to the column letter and row number headings. In the Worksheet area, this view shows the margins for each printed page, any headers and footers defined for the report, and the breaks between each page. (Often, you have to use the Zoom slider to reduce the screen magnification to display the page breaks on the screen.)

To see all the pages in the active worksheet, drag the slider button in the Zoom slider on the Status bar to the left until you decrease the screen magnification sufficiently to display all the pages of data.

Figure 5-1: Viewing a spreadsheet in Page Layout View.

Little Bo-Peep Pet Detectives - Client List

Case No	Last Name	First Name	Street	City	State	Zip	Status	Hours	Rate	Total
101-920	Harvey	Scott	12 Elm Street	Scholar	MN	58764	Active	250	75.00	$1
101-014	Andersen	Hans	341 The Shadow	Scholar	MN	58764	Closed	175	75.00	$1
103-023	Appleseed	Johnny	6789 Fruitree Tr	Along The Way	SD	66017	Active	321	125.00	$4
102-013	Baggins	Bingo	99 Hobbithole	Shire	ME	04047	Active	100	125.00	$1
103-007	Baum	L. Frank	447 Toto Too Rd	Oz	KS	65432	Closed	421	125.00	$5
104-026	Brown	Charles	59 Flat Plains	Saltewater	UT	84001	Active	575	125.00	$7
101-001	Bryant	Michael	326 Chef's Lane	Paris	TX	78705	Active	600	100.00	$6
101-028	Cassidy	Butch	Sundance Kidde	Hole In Wall	CO	80477	Closed	345.5	75.00	$2
102-006	Cinderella	Poore	8 Lucky Maiden Way	Oxford	TN	07557	Closed	800	75.00	$6
103-004	Cupid	Eros	97 Mount Olympus	Greece	CT	03331	Active	123.5	75.00	$
103-022	Dragon	Kai	2 Pleistocene Era	Ann's World	ID	00001	Active	450.2	75.00	$3
104-031	Eaters	Big	444 Big Pigs Court	Dogtown	AZ	85257	Closed	780	125.00	$5
106-022	Foliage	Red	49 Maple Syrup	Waffle	VT	05452	Active	205	125.00	$2
102-020	Franklin	Ben	1789 Constitution	Jefferson	WV	20178	Active	189.5	75.00	$1
104-019	Fudde	Elmer	8 Warner Way	Hollywood	CA	33461	Active	463.5	125.00	$5
102-002	Gearing	Shane	1 Gunfighter's End	LaLa Land	CA	90069	Active	902.5	125.00	$11

Client list

Page: 1 of 4

Excel displays rulers using the default units for your computer (inches on a U.S. computer and centimeters on a European machine). To change the units, open the Advanced tab of the Excel Options dialog box (File⇨Options⇨Advanced or Alt+FTA) and then select the appropriate unit (Inches, Centimeters, or Millimeters) on the Ruler Units drop-down menu in the Display section.

The Ruler check box on the View tab acts as a toggle switch so that the first time you click this button, Excel removes the rulers from the Page Layout View, and the second time you click this button, the program adds them again.

Checking and Printing a Report from the Print Panel

To save wasted paper and your sanity, print your worksheet directly from the Print panel in Backstage View by clicking File⇨Print (or simply pressing Ctrl+P or Ctrl+F2). As you see in Figure 5-2, the Print panel shows you at-a-glance your current print settings along with a preview of the first page of the printout.

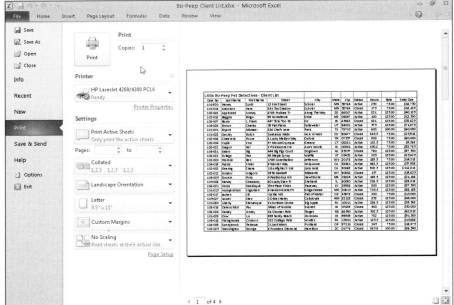

Figure 5-2:
The Print
panel in
Backstage
View shows
your current
print set-
tings plus a
preview of
the printout.

You can use the Print Preview feature in the Print panel before you print any worksheet, section of worksheet, or entire workbook. Because of the peculiarities in paging worksheet data, you often need to check the page breaks for any report that requires more than one page. The print preview area in the Print panel shows you exactly how the worksheet data will page when printed. If necessary, you can return to the worksheet where you can make changes to the page settings from the Page Layout tab on the Ribbon before sending the report to the printer when everything looks okay.

When Excel displays a full page in the print preview area, you can barely read its contents. To increase the view to actual size to verify some of the data, click the Zoom to Page button in the lower-right corner of the Print panel. Check out the difference in Figure 5-3 — you can see what the first page of the four-page report looks like after I zoom in by clicking this Zoom to Page button.

After you enlarge a page to actual size, use the scroll bars to bring new parts of the page into view in the print preview area. To return to the full-page view, click the Zoom to Page button a second time to deselect it.

Excel indicates the number of pages in a report at the bottom of the print preview area. If your report has more than one page, you can view pages that follow by clicking the Next Page button to the right of the final page number. To review a page you've already seen, back up a page by clicking the Previous Page button to the left of the first page number. (The Previous Page button is gray if you're on the first page.)

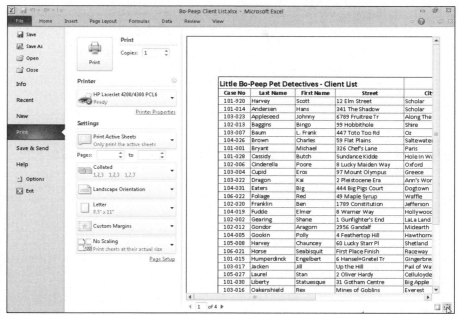

Figure 5-3:
Page 1 of a
four-page
report after
clicking the
Zoom to
Page button.

To display markers indicating the current left, right, top and bottom margins along with the column widths, select the Show Margins check box to the immediate left of the Zoom to Page button. You can then modify the column widths as well as the page margins by dragging the appropriate marker (see "Massaging the margins" later in this chapter for details).

When you finish previewing the report, the Print panel offers you the following options for changing certain print settings before you send it to the printer:

- ✔ **Print** button with the **Number of Copies** combo box: Use this button to print the spreadsheet report using the current print settings listed on the panel. Use the combo box to indicate the number of copies you want when you need multiple copies printed.

- ✔ **Printer** drop-down button: Use this button to select a new printer or fax to send the spreadsheet report to when more than one device is installed. (Excel automatically displays the name of the printer that's installed as the default printer in Windows.)

- ✔ **Settings** drop-down buttons: These include a **Print What** drop-down button with attendant **Pages** combo boxes: Use the Print What drop-down button to choose between printing only the active (selected) worksheets in the workbook (the default), the entire workbook, the current cell selection in the current worksheet, and the currently selected table in the current worksheet. Use the combo boxes to restrict what's printed to just the range of pages you enter in these boxes or select with their spinner buttons.

Beneath the combo boxes, you find drop-down list buttons to print on both sides of each page in the report, collate the pages of the report, and switch the page orientation from Portrait (aligned with the short side) to Landscape (aligned with the long side). Additionally, you can select a paper size other than the standard 8.5" x 11" letter, and customize the size of the report's margins (top, bottom, left, and right, as well as the margins for any header and footer on the page).

Printing Just the Current Worksheet

As long as you want to use Excel's default print settings to print all the cells in the current worksheet, printing in Excel 2010 is a breeze. Simply add the Quick Print button to the Quick Access toolbar (by clicking the Customize Quick Access Toolbar button and then clicking Quick Print on its drop-down menu).

After adding the Quick Print button to the Quick Access toolbar, you can use this button to print a single copy of all the information in the current worksheet, including any charts and graphics — but not including comments you add to cells. (See Chapter 6 for details about adding comments to your worksheet and Chapter 10 for details about charts and graphics.)

Understanding and using the print area

Excel includes a special printing feature called Print Area. Click Print Area⇨Set Print Area on the Ribbon's Page Layout tab or press Alt+PRS to define any cell selection on a worksheet as the print area. After you define the print area, Excel then prints this cell selection anytime you print the worksheet (by using either the Quick Print button, if you've added it to the Quick Access toolbar or by using the File⇨Print command or its Ctrl+P shortcut).

After you define the print area, its cell range is the only one you can print (regardless of what other Print What option you select in the Settings section of the Print panel). That is, unless you click the Ignore Print Area option at the very bottom of the Print What drop-down list or clear the print area. To clear the print area

(and return to the printing defaults that Excel establishes in the Print dialog box), click Print Area⇨Clear Print Area on the Page Layout tab or simply press Alt+PRC.

You can also define and clear the print area from the Sheet tab of the Page Setup dialog box by clicking the dialog box launcher in the Page Setup group on the Ribbon's Page Layout tab. To define the print area from this dialog box, click the Print Area text box on the Sheet tab to insert the cursor and then select the cell range or ranges in the worksheet (remembering that you can reduce the Page Setup dialog box to just this text box by clicking the Print Area Collapse/Expand button). To clear the print area from this dialog box, select the cell addresses in the Print Area text box and press the Delete key.

When you click the Quick Print button, Excel routes the print job to the Windows print queue, which acts like a middleman and sends the job to the printer. While Excel sends the print job to the print queue, Excel displays a Printing dialog box to inform you of its progress (displaying such updates as *Printing Page 2 of 3*). After this dialog box disappears, you are free to go back to work in Excel. To stop the printing while the job is still being sent to the print queue, click the Cancel button in the Printing dialog box.

If you don't realize that you want to cancel the print job until after Excel finishes shipping it to the print queue (that is, while the Printing dialog box appears onscreen), you must:

1. **Click the printer icon in the Notification area at the far right of the Windows taskbar (to the immediate left of the current time) with the secondary mouse button to open its shortcut menu.**

   This printer icon displays the ScreenTip *1 document(s) pending for so-and-so*. For example, when I'm printing, this message reads *1 document(s) pending for Greg* when I position the mouse pointer over the printer icon.

2. **Right-click the printer icon and then select the Open All Active Printers command from its shortcut menu.**

   This opens the dialog box for the printer with the Excel print job in its queue (as described under the Document Name heading in the list box).

3. **Select the Excel print job that you want to cancel in the list box of your printer's dialog box.**

4. **Choose Document⇨Cancel from the menu bar and then click Yes to confirm you want to cancel the print job.**

5. **Wait for the print job to disappear from the queue in the printer's dialog box and then click the Close button to return to Excel.**

My Page Was Set Up!

About the only thing the slightest bit complex in printing a worksheet is figuring out how to get the pages right. Fortunately, the command buttons in the Page Setup group on the Ribbon's Page Layout tab give you a great deal of control over what goes on which page.

Three groups of buttons on the Page Layout tab help you get your page settings exactly as you want them. The Page Setup group, the Scale to Fit group, and the Sheet Options group are described in the following sections.

To see the effect of changes you make in the Worksheet area, put the work-sheet into Page Layout View by clicking the Page Layout button on the Status bar while you work with the command buttons in the Page Setup, Scale to Fit, and Sheet Options groups on the Page Layout tab of the Ribbon.

Using the buttons in the Page Setup group

The Page Setup group of the Page Layout tab contains the following impor-tant command buttons:

- ✔ **Margins** button to select one of three preset margins for the report or to set custom margins on the Margins tab of the Page Setup dialog box. (See "Massaging the margins" that follows in this chapter.)

- ✔ **Orientation** button to switch between Portrait and Landscape mode for printing. (See the "Getting the lay of the landscape" section, later in this chapter.)

- ✔ **Size** button to select one of the preset paper sizes, set a custom size, or change the printing resolution or page number on the Page tab of the Page Setup dialog box.

- ✔ **Print Area** button to set and clear the print area. (See the nearby "Understanding and using the print area" sidebar.)

- ✔ **Breaks** button to insert or remove page breaks. (See "Solving Page Break Problems" later in this chapter.)

- ✔ **Background** button to open the Sheet Background dialog box where you can select a new graphic image or photo to use as a background for the current worksheet. (This button changes to Delete Background as soon as you select a background image.)

- ✔ **Print Titles** button to open the Sheet tab of the Page Setup dialog box where you can define rows of the worksheet to repeat at the top and col-umns of the worksheet to repeat at the left as print titles for the report. (See "Putting out the print titles" later in this chapter.)

Massaging the margins

The Normal margin settings that Excel applies to a new report uses standard top, bottom, left, and right margins of ¾ inch with just over a ¼ inch separat-ing the header and footer from the top and bottom margin, respectively.

In addition to the Normal margin settings, the program enables you to select two other standard margins from the Margins button's drop-down menu:

- ✔ **Wide** margins with 1-inch top, bottom, left, and right margins and ½ inch separating the header and footer from the top and bottom margin, respectively.

✔ **Narrow** margins with a top and bottom margin of ¾ inch and a left and right margin of ¼ inch with 0.3 inch separating the header and footer from the top and bottom margin, respectively.

Frequently, you find yourself with a report that takes up a full printed page and then just enough to spill over onto a second, mostly empty, page. To squeeze the last column or the last few rows of the worksheet data onto Page 1, try selecting Narrow on the Margins button's drop-down menu.

If that doesn't do it, you can try manually adjusting the margins for the report from the Margins tab of the Page Setup dialog box or by dragging the margin markers in the preview area of the Print panel in the Backstage View (Press Ctrl+P and click the Show Margins button). To get more columns on a page, try reducing the left and right margins. To get more rows on a page, try reducing the top and bottom margins.

To open the Margins tab of the Page Setup dialog box (shown in Figure 5-4), click Custom Margins on the Margins button's drop-down menu. There, enter the new settings in the Top, Bottom, Left, and Right text boxes — or select the new margin settings with their respective spinner buttons.

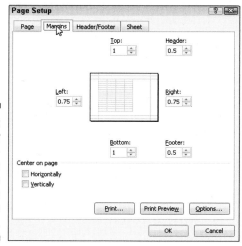

Figure 5-4:
Adjust your report margins from the Margins tab in the Page Setup dialog box.

Select one or both Center on Page options in the Margins tab of the Page Setup dialog box (refer to Figure 5-4) to center a selection of data (that takes up less than a full page) between the current margin settings. In the Center on Page section, select the Horizontally check box to center the data between the left and right margins. Select the Vertically check box to center the data between the top and bottom margins.

When you select the Show Margins button in the Print panel in the Backstage View (Ctrl+P) to modify the margin settings directly, you can also massage the column widths as well as the margins. (Refer to Figure 5-5.) To change one of the margins, position the mouse pointer on the desired margin marker (the pointer shape changes to a double-headed arrow) and drag the marker with your mouse in the appropriate direction. When you release the mouse button, Excel redraws the page, using the new margin setting. You may gain or lose columns or rows, depending on what kind of adjustment you make. Changing the column widths is the same story: Drag the column marker to the left or right to decrease or increase the width of a particular column.

Getting the lay of the landscape

The drop-down menu attached to the Orientation button in the Page Setup group of the Ribbon's Page Layout tab contains two options:

- **Portrait** (the default) where the printing runs parallel to the short edge of the paper

- **Landscape** where the printing runs parallel to the long edge of the paper

Figure 5-5:
Drag a marker to adjust its margin in the page preview area of the Print panel when the Show Margins button is selected.

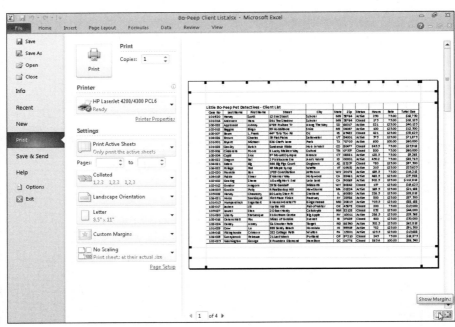

Because many worksheets are far wider than they are tall (such as budgets or sales tables that track expenditures over 12 months), you may find that wider worksheets page better if you switch the orientation from Portrait mode (which accommodates fewer columns on a page because the printing runs parallel to the short edge of the page) to Landscape mode.

In Figure 5-6, you can see the Print Preview window with the first page of a report in Landscape mode in the Page Layout View. For this report, Excel can fit three more columns of information on this page in Landscape mode than it can in Portrait mode. However, because this page orientation accommodates fewer rows, the total page count for this report increases from two pages in Portrait mode to four pages in Landscape mode.

Putting out the print titles

Excel's Print Titles feature enables you to print particular row and column headings on each page of the report. Print titles are important in multipage reports where the columns and rows of related data spill over to other pages that no longer show the row and column headings on the first page.

Don't confuse print titles with the header of a report (see "From Header to Footer" later in this chapter). Even though both are printed on each page, header information prints in the top margin of the report; print titles always appear in the body of the report — at the top, in the case of rows used as print titles, and on the left, in the case of columns.

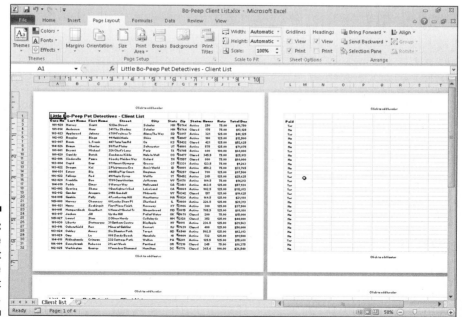

Figure 5-6: A Landscape mode report in Page Layout View.

To designate rows and/or columns as the print titles for a report, follow these steps:

1. **Click the Print Titles button on the Page Layout tab on the Ribbon or press Alt+PI.**

   The Page Setup dialog box appears with Sheet tab selected (refer to Figure 5-7).

   To designate worksheet rows as print titles, go to Step 2a. To designate worksheet columns as print titles, go to Step 2b.

2a. **Select the Rows to Repeat at Top text box and then drag through the rows with information you want to appear at the top of each page in the worksheet below. If necessary, reduce the Page Setup dialog box to just the Rows to Repeat at Top text box by clicking the text box's Collapse/Expand button.**

   For the example shown in Figure 5-7, I clicked the Collapse/Expand button associated with the Rows to Repeat at Top text box and then dragged through rows 1 and 2 in column A of the Little Bo Peep Pet Detectives – Client List worksheet. Excel entered the row range $1:$2 in the Rows to Repeat at Top text box.

   Excel indicates the print-title rows in the worksheet by placing a dotted line (that moves like a marquee) on the border between the titles and the information in the body of the report.

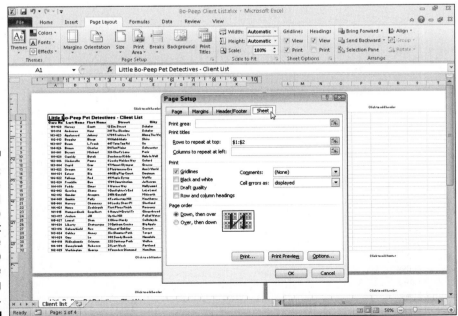

Figure 5-7:
Specify the rows and columns to use as print titles on the Sheet tab of the Page Setup dialog box.

2b. **Select the Columns to Repeat at Left text box and then drag through the range of columns with the information you want to appear at the left edge of each page of the printed report in the worksheet below. If necessary, reduce the Page Setup dialog box to just the Columns to Repeat at Left text box by clicking the text box's Collapse/Expand button.**

Excel indicates the print-title columns in the worksheet by placing a dotted line (that moves like a marquee) on the border between the titles and the information in the body of the report.

3. **Click OK or press Enter to close the Page Setup dialog box.**

The dotted line showing the border of the row and/or column titles disappears from the worksheet.

In Figure 5-7, rows 1 and 2 containing the worksheet title and column headings for the Little Bo Peep Pet Detectives client database are designated as the print titles for the report in the Page Setup dialog box. In Figure 5-8, you can see the Print Preview window with the second page of the report. Note how these print titles appear on all pages of the report.

To clear print titles from a report if you no longer need them, open the Sheet tab of the Page Setup dialog box and then delete the row and column ranges from the Rows to Repeat at Top and the Columns to Repeat at Left text boxes. Click OK or press Enter.

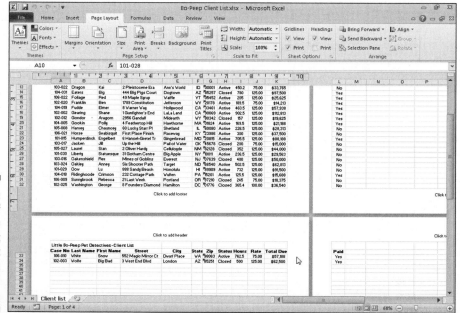

Figure 5-8:
Page 2 of a sample report in Print Preview with defined print titles.

Using the buttons in the Scale to Fit group

If your printer supports scaling options, you're in luck. You can always get a worksheet to fit on a single page simply by selecting the 1 Page option on the Width and Height drop-down menus attached to their command buttons in the Scale to Fit group on the Ribbon's Page Layout tab. When you select these options, Excel figures out how much to reduce the size of the information you're printing to fit it all on one page.

After clicking the Page Break Preview button on the Status bar, you might preview this page in the Print panel of the Backstage View (Ctrl+P) and find that the printing is just too small to read comfortably. Go back to the Normal worksheet view (Esc), select the Page Layout tab on the Ribbon, and try changing the number of pages in the Width and Height drop-down menus in the Scale to Fit group.

Instead of trying to stuff everything on one page, check out how your worksheet looks if you fit it on two pages across. Try this: Select 2 Pages on the Width button's drop-down menu on the Page Layout tab and leave 1 Page selected in the Height drop-down list button. Alternatively, see how the worksheet looks on two pages down: Select 1 Page on the Width button's drop-down menu and 2 Pages on the Height button's drop-down menu.

After using the Width and Height Scale to Fit options, you may find that you don't want to scale the printing. Cancel scaling by selecting Automatic on both the Width and Height drop-down menus and then entering **100** in the Scale text box (or select 100% with its spinner buttons).

Using the Print buttons in the Sheet Options group

The Sheet Options group contains two very useful Print check boxes (neither of which is selected automatically). The first is in the Gridlines column and the second is in the Headings column:

✔ Select the Print check box in the Gridlines column to print the column and row gridlines on each page of the report.

✔ Select the Print check box in the Headings column to print the row headings with the row numbers and the column headings with the column letters on each page of the report.

Select both check boxes (by clicking them to put check marks in them) when you want the printed version of your spreadsheet data to closely match its onscreen appearance. This is useful when you need to use the cell references on the printout to help you later locate the cells in the actual worksheet that need editing.

From Header to Footer

Headers and footers are simply standard text that appears on every page of the report. A header prints in the top margin of the page, and a footer prints — you guessed it — in the bottom margin. Both are centered vertically in the margins. Unless you specify otherwise, Excel does not automatically add either a header or footer to a new workbook.

Use headers and footers in a report to identify the document used to produce the report and display the page numbers and the date and time of printing.

The place to add a header or footer to a report is in Page Layout View. You can switch to this view by clicking the Page Layout View button on the Status bar or by clicking the Page Layout View button on the Ribbon's View tab, or by just pressing Alt+WP.

When the worksheet is in Page Layout View, position the mouse pointer over the section in the top margin of the first page marked Click to Add Header or in the bottom margin of the first page marked Click to Add Footer.

To create a centered header or footer, click the center section of this header/footer area to set the insertion point in the middle of the section. To add a left-aligned header or footer, click the left section to set the insertion point flush with the left edge. To add a right-aligned header or footer, click the right section to set the insertion point flush with the right edge.

Immediately after setting the insertion point in the left, center, or right section of the header/footer area, Excel adds a Header & Footer Tools contextual tab with its own Design tab (see Figure 5-9). The Design tab is divided into Header & Footer, Header & Footer Elements, Navigation, and Options groups.

Adding an Auto Header or Auto Footer

The Header and Footer command buttons on the Design tab of the Header & Footer Tools contextual tab enable you to add stock headers and footers in an instant. Simply click the appropriate command button and then click the header or footer example you want to use on the Header or Footer drop-down menu that appears.

To create the centered header and footer for the report shown in Figure 5-10, I selected Client List, Confidential, Page 1 on the Header command button's drop-down menu. Client List is the name of the worksheet; Confidential is stock text; and Page 1 is, of course, the current page number).

To set up the footer, I chose Page 1 of ? in the Footer command button's drop-down menu (which puts the current page number with the total number of pages, in the report). You can select this paging option on either the Header or Footer button's drop-down menu.

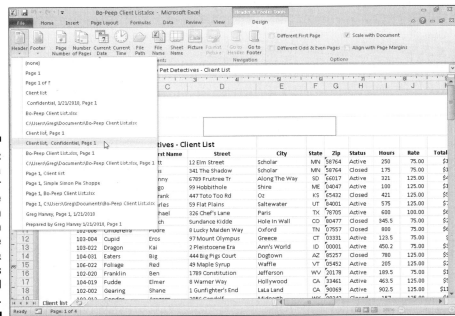

Figure 5-9:
Defining a new header using the buttons on the Design tab of the Header & Footer Tools contextual tab.

Check out the results in Figure 5-10, which is the first page of the report in Page Layout View. Here you can see the header and footer as they will print. You can also see how choosing Page 1 of ? works in the footer: On the first page, you see the centered footer Page 1 of 4; on the second page, the centered footer reads Page 2 of 4.

If, after selecting some stock header or footer info, you decide that you no longer need either the header or footer printed in your report, you can remove it. Simply click the (None) option at the top of the Header button's or Footer button's drop-down menu. (Remember that the Design tab with the Header and Footer command buttons under the Header & Footer Tools contextual tab is selected on the Ribbon the moment you click the header or footer in Page Layout View.)

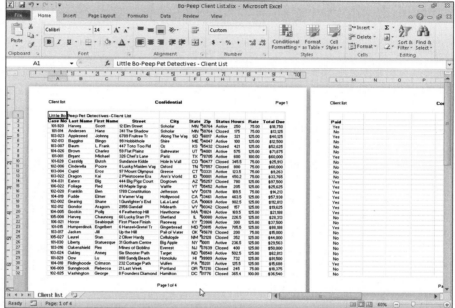

Creating a custom header or footer

Most of the time, the stock headers and footers available on the Header button's and Footer button's drop-down menus are sufficient for your report printing needs. Occasionally, however, you may want to insert information not available in these list boxes or in an arrangement that Excel doesn't offer in the readymade headers and footers.

For those times, you need to use the command buttons that appear in the Header & Footer Elements group of the Design tab on the Header & Footer Tools contextual tab. These command buttons enable you to blend your own information with that generated by Excel into different sections of the custom header or footer you're creating.

The command buttons in the Header & Footer Elements group include:

- **Page Number:** Click this button to insert the &[Page] code that puts in the current page number.

- **Number of Pages:** Click this button to insert the &[Pages] code that puts in the total number of pages.

- **Current Date:** Click this button to insert the &[Date] code that puts in the current date.

- **Current Time:** Click this button to insert the &[Time] code that puts in the current time.

- **File Path:** Click this button to insert the &[Path]&[File] codes that put in the directory path along with the name of the workbook file.

- **File Name:** Click this button to insert the &[File] code that puts in the name of the workbook file.

- **Sheet Name:** Click this button to insert the &[Tab] code that puts in the name of the worksheet as shown on the sheet tab.

- **Picture:** Click this button to insert the &[Picture] code that inserts the image that you select from the Insert Picture dialog box that shows the contents of the My Pictures folder on your computer by default.

- **Format Picture:** Click this button to apply the formatting that you choose from the Format Picture dialog box to the &[Picture] code that you enter with the Insert Picture button without adding any code of its own.

To use these command buttons in the Header & Footer Elements group to create a custom header or footer, follow these steps:

1. **Put your worksheet into Page Layout View by clicking the Page Layout View button on the Status bar or by clicking View⇨Page Layout View on the Ribbon or pressing Alt+WP.**

   In Page Layout View, the text, Click to Add Header, appears centered in the top margin of the first page and the text, Click to Add Footer, appears centered in the bottom margin.

2. **Position the mouse pointer in the top margin to create a custom header or the bottom margin to create a custom footer and then click the pointer in the left, center, or right section of the header or footer to set the insertion point and left-align, center, or right-align the text.**

   When Excel sets the insertion point, the text, Click to Add Header and Click to Add Footer, disappears and the Design tab on the Header & Footer Tools contextual tab becomes active on the Ribbon.

3. **To add program-generated information to your custom header or footer (such as the filename, worksheet name, current date, and so forth), click the information's corresponding command button in the Header & Footer Elements group.**

   Excel inserts the appropriate header/footer code preceded by an ampersand (&) into the header or footer. These codes are replaced by the actual information (filename, worksheet name, graphic image, and the like) as soon as you click another section of the header or footer or finish the header or footer by clicking the mouse pointer outside of it.

4. **(Optional) To add your own text to the custom header or footer, type it at the insertion point.**

   When joining program-generated information indicated by a header/footer code with your own text, be sure to insert the appropriate spaces and punctuation. For example, to have Excel display Page 1 of 4 in a custom header or footer, you do the following:

   a. *Type the word **Page** and press the spacebar.*

   b. *Click the Page Number command button and press the spacebar again.*

   c. *Type the word **of** and press the spacebar a third time.*

   d. *Click the Number of Pages command button.*

   This inserts *Page &[Page] of &[Pages]* in the custom header (or footer).

5. **(Optional) To modify the font, font size, or some other font attribute of your custom header or footer, drag through its codes and text, click the Home tab, and then click the appropriate command button in the Font group.**

   In addition to selecting a new font and font size for the custom header or footer, you can add bold, italic, underlining, and a new font color to its text with the Bold, Italic, Underline, and Font Color command buttons on the Home tab.

   After you finish defining and formatting the codes and text for your custom header or footer, click a cell in the Worksheet area to deselect the header or footer area.

   Excel replaces the header/footer codes in the custom header or footer with the actual information, while at the same time removing the Header & Footer Tools contextual tab from the Ribbon.

Figure 5-11 shows you a custom footer I added to a spreadsheet in Page Layout View. This custom footer blends my own text, Preliminary, with program-generated sheet name, date, and time information, and uses all three sections: left-aligned page information, centered Preliminary warning, and right-aligned current date and time.

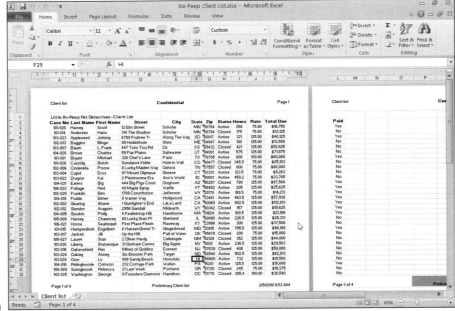

Figure 5-11:
Spread-
sheet
in Page
Layout View
showing
the custom
footer.

Creating unique first-page headers and footers

Excel 2010 enables you to define a header or footer for the first page that's
different from all the rest of the pages. Simply, click the Different First Page
check box to put a check mark in it. (This check box is part of the Options
group of the Design tab on the Header & Footer Tools contextual tab that
appears when you're defining or editing a header or footer in Page Layout
View.)

After selecting the Different First Page check box, go ahead and define the
unique header and/or footer for just the first page (now marked First Page
Header or First Page Footer). Then, on the second page of the report, define
the header and/or footer (marked simply Header or Footer) for the remaining pages of the report (see "Adding an Auto Header or Auto Footer" and
"Creating a custom header or footer" earlier in the chapter for details).

Use this feature when your spreadsheet report has a cover page that needs
no header or footer. For example, suppose that you have a report that needs
the current page number and total pages centered at the bottom of all pages
except the cover page. To do this, select the Different First Page check box
on the Design tab of the Header & Footer Tools contextual tab on the Ribbon.
Then define a centered Auto Footer that displays the current page number
and total pages (Page 1 of ?) on the second page of the report, leaving the
Click to Add Footer text intact on the first page.

Excel will correctly number both the total number of pages in the report and the current page number without printing this information on the first page. For example, if your report has six pages (including the cover page), the second page footer will read Page 2 of 6; the third page, Page 3 of 6; and so on, even if the first printed page has no footer.

Creating even and odd page headers and footers

If you plan to do two-sided printing or copying of your spreadsheet report, you may want to define one header or footer for the even pages and another for the odd pages of the report. That way, the header or footer information (such as the report name or current page) alternates between being right-aligned on the odd pages (printed on the front side of the page) and being left-aligned on the even pages (printed on the back of the page).

To create an alternating header or footer for a report, you click the Different Odd & Even Pages check box to put a check mark in it. (This check box is in the Options group of the Design tab on the Header & Footer Tools contextual tab that appears when you're defining or editing a header or footer in Page Layout View.)

After that, create a header or footer on the first page of the report (now marked Odd Page Header or Odd Page Footer) in the third, right-aligned section of the header or footer area and then re-create this header or footer on the second page (now marked Even Page Header or Even Page Footer), this time in the first, left-aligned section.

Solving Page Break Problems

The Page Break preview feature in Excel enables you to spot and fix page break problems in an instant, such as when the program wants to split information across different pages that you know should always be on the same page.

Figure 5-12 shows a worksheet in Page Break Preview with an example of a bad vertical page break that you can remedy by adjusting the location of the page break on Page 1 and Page 3. Given the page size, orientation, and margin settings for this report, Excel breaks the page between columns K and L. This break separates the Paid column (L) from all the others in the client list, effectively putting this information on its own Page 3 and Page 4 (not shown in Figure 5-12).

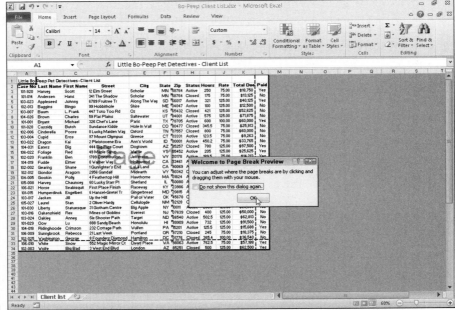

Figure 5-12:
Preview
page breaks
in a report
with Page
Break
Preview.

To prevent the data in the Paid column from printing on its own pages, you need to move the page break to a column on the left. In this case, I moved the page break to between columns G (with the zip code data) and H (containing the account status information) so that the name and address information stays together on Page 1 and Page 2 and the other client data is printed together on Page 3 and Page 4. Figure 5-13 shows vertical page breaks in the Page Break Preview worksheet view, which you can accomplish by following these steps:

1. **Click the Page Break Preview button (the third one in the cluster to the left of the Zoom slider) on the Status bar, or click View⇨Page Break Preview on the Ribbon or press Alt+WI.**

   This takes you into a Page Break Preview worksheet view that shows your worksheet data at a reduced magnification (60 percent of normal in Figure 5-13) with the page numbers displayed in large light type and the page breaks shown by heavy lines between the columns and rows of the worksheet.

   The first time you choose this command, Excel displays a Welcome to Page Break Preview dialog box (shown in Figure 5-13). To prevent this dialog box from reappearing each time you use Page Break Preview, click the Do Not Show This Dialog Again check box before you close the Welcome to Page Break Preview alert dialog box.

2. **Click OK or press Enter to get rid of the Welcome to Page Break Preview alert dialog box.**

3. **Position the mouse pointer somewhere on the page break indicator (one of the heavy lines surrounding the representation of the page) that you need to adjust; when the pointer changes to a double-headed arrow, drag the page indicator to the desired column or row and release the mouse button.**

   For the example shown in Figure 5-13, I dragged the page break indicator between Page 1 and Page 3 to the left so that it's between columns G and H. Excel placed the page break at this point, which puts all the name and address information together on Page 1 and Page 2. This new page break then causes all the other columns of client data to print together on Page 3 and Page 4.

4. **After you finish adjusting the page breaks in Page Break Preview (and, presumably, printing the report), click the Normal button (the first one in the cluster to the left of the Zoom slider) on the Status bar, or click View⇨Normal on the Ribbon or press Alt+WL to return the worksheet to its regular view of the data.**

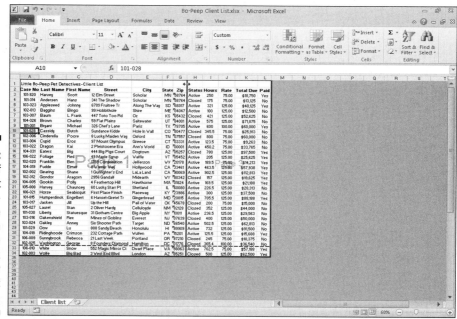

Figure 5-13:
Page 1 of the report after adjusting the page breaks in the Page Break Preview worksheet view.

You can also insert your own manual page breaks at the cell cursor's position by clicking Insert Page Break on the Breaks button's drop-down menu on the Page Layout tab (Alt+PBI) and remove them by clicking Remove Page Break on this menu (Alt+PBR). To remove all manual page breaks that you've inserted into a report, click Reset All Page Breaks on the Breaks button's drop-down menu (Alt+PBA).

Letting Your Formulas All Hang Out

A basic printing technique that you may need occasionally is printing the formulas in a worksheet instead of printing the calculated results of the formulas. You can check over a printout of the formulas in your worksheet to make sure that you haven't done anything stupid (like replace a formula with a number or use the wrong cell references in a formula) before you distribute the worksheet companywide.

Before you can print a worksheet's formulas, you have to display the formulas, rather than their results, in the cells by clicking the Show Formulas button (the one with the icon that looks like a page of a calendar with a tiny 15 above an *fx*) in the Formula Auditing group on the Ribbon's Formulas tab (Alt+MH).

Excel then displays the contents of each cell in the worksheet the way they appear in the Formula bar or when you're editing them in the cell. Notice that value entries lose their number formatting, formulas appear in their cells (Excel widens the columns with best-fit so that the formulas appear in their entirety), and long text entries no longer spill into neighboring blank cells.

Excel allows you to toggle between the normal cell display and the formula cell display by pressing Ctrl+`. (That is, press Ctrl and the key with the tilde on top.) This key — usually found in the upper-left corner of your keyboard — does double-duty as a tilde and a weird backward accent mark. (Don't confuse that backward accent mark with the apostrophe that appears on a key below the quotation mark!)

After Excel displays the formulas in the worksheet, you are ready to print it as you would any other report. You can include the worksheet column letters and row numbers as headings in the printout so that if you do spot an error, you can pinpoint the cell reference right away.

To include the row and column headings in the printout, put a check mark in the Print check box in the Headings column on the Sheet Options group of the Page Layout tab of the Ribbon before you send the report to the printer.

After you print the worksheet with the formulas, return the worksheet to normal by clicking the Show Formulas button on the Formulas tab of the Ribbon or by pressing Ctrl+`.

Part III
Getting Organized and Staying That Way

The 5th Wave   By Rich Tennant

At FEMA, employees often use Excel's custom format function to create formulas for disaster.

In this part . . .

In today's business world, we all know how vital it is to stay organized — as well as how difficult that can be. Keeping straight the spreadsheets that you create in Excel 2010 is no less important and, in some cases, no less arduous.

In this part, I help you tackle this conundrum by giving you the inside track on how to keep on top of all the stuff in every single worksheet that you create or edit. Not only do you discover how to keep track of the information in one worksheet, but you also find out how to juggle the information from one worksheet to another and even from one workbook to another.

Chapter 6

Maintaining the Worksheet

. . . .

In This Chapter

▶ Zooming in and out on a worksheet

▶ Splitting the workbook window into two or four panes

▶ Freezing columns and rows onscreen for worksheet titles

▶ Attaching comments to cells

▶ Naming your cells

▶ Finding and replacing stuff in your worksheet

▶ Looking up stuff using online resources in the Research task pane

▶ Controlling when you recalculate a worksheet

▶ Protecting your worksheets

. . . .

*E*ach worksheet in Excel 2010 offers an immense place in which to store information (and each workbook you open offers you three of these babies). But because your computer monitor lets you see only a tiny bit of any of the worksheets in a workbook at a time, the issue of keeping on top of information is not a small one (pun intended).

Although the Excel worksheet employs a coherent cell-coordinate system that you can use to get anywhere in the great big worksheet, you have to admit that this A1, B2 stuff — although highly logical — remains fairly alien to human thinking. (I mean, saying, "Go to cell IV88," just doesn't have anywhere near the same impact as saying, "Go to the corner of Hollywood and Vine.") Consider for a moment the difficulty of coming up with a meaningful association between the 2008 depreciation schedule and its location in the cell range AC50:AN75 so that you can remember where to find it.

In this chapter, I show you some of the more effective techniques for maintaining and keeping on top of information. You find out how to change the perspective on a worksheet by zooming in and out on the information, how to split the document window into separate panes so that you can display different sections of the worksheet at the same time, and how to keep particular rows and columns on the screen at all times.

And, as if that weren't enough, you also see how to add comments to cells, assign descriptive, English-type names to cell ranges (like Hollywood_and_ Vine!), and use the Find and Replace commands to locate and, if necessary, replace entries anywhere in the worksheet. Finally, you see how to control when Excel recalculates the worksheet and how to limit where changes can be made.

Zeroing In with Zoom

So what are you going to do now that the boss won't spring for that 21-inch monitor for your computer? All day long, it seems that you're straining your eyes to read all the information in those little, tiny cells or you're scrolling like mad trying to locate a table you can't seem to find. Never fear, the Zoom feature is here in the form of the Zoom slider on the Status bar. You can use the Zoom slider to quickly increase the magnification of part of the worksheet or shrink it down to the tiniest size.

You can use the Zoom slider on the Status bar of the Excel window in either of two ways:

✔ Drag the Zoom slider button to the left or the right on the slider to decrease or increase the magnification percentage (with 10% magnification the lowest percentage when you drag all the way to the left on the slider and 400% magnification the highest percentage when you drag all the way to the right).

✔ Click the Zoom Out (with the minus sign) or the Zoom In button (with the plus sign) at either end of the slider to decrease or increase the magnification percentage by 10 percent.

In Figure 6-1, you can see a blowup of the worksheet after increasing it to 200 percent magnification (twice the normal size). To blow up a worksheet like this, drag the Zoom slider button to the right until 200% appears on the Status bar to the left of the slider. (You can also do this by clicking View⇨Zoom and then clicking the 200% button in the Zoom dialog box, if you really want to go to all that trouble.) One thing's for sure: You don't have to go after your glasses to read the names in those enlarged cells! The only problem with 200 percent magnification is that you can see only a few cells at one time.

In Figure 6-2, check out the same worksheet, this time at 40 percent magnification. To reduce the display to this magnification, you drag the Zoom slider button to the left until 40% appears on the Status bar in front of the slider.

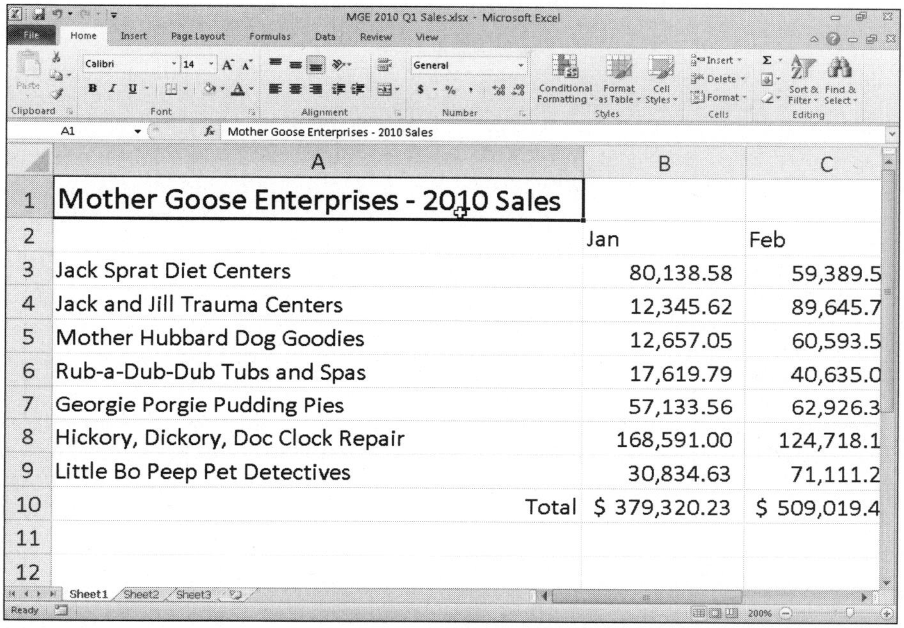

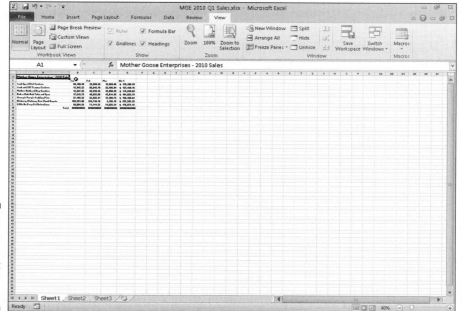

Figure 6-1:
Zooming a sample worksheet to 200% magnification.

Figure 6-2:
Zooming a sample worksheet to 40% magnification.

Whew! At 40 percent of normal screen size, the only thing you can be sure of is that you can't read a thing! However, notice that with this bird's-eye view, you can see at a glance how far over and down the data in this worksheet extends and how much empty space there is in the worksheet.

The Zoom dialog box (View⇨Zoom or Alt+WQ) offers five precise magnification settings — 200%, 100% (normal screen magnification), 75%, 50%, and 25%. To use other percentages besides those, you have the following options:

✔ If you want to use precise percentages other than the five preset percentages (such as 150% or 85%) or settings greater or less than the highest or lowest percentage (such as 400% or 10%), click within the Custom button's text box in the Zoom dialog box, type the new percentage, and press Enter.

✔ If you don't know what percentage to enter in order to display a particular cell range on the screen, select the range, click View⇨Zoom to Selection on the Ribbon or press Alt+WG. Excel figures out the percentage necessary to fill your screen with just the selected cell range.

To quickly return to 100% (normal) magnification in the worksheet after selecting any another percentage, all you have to do is click the bar in the center of the Zoom slider on the Status bar or click the 100% button on the View tab of the Ribbon.

You can use the Zoom feature to locate and move to a new cell range in the worksheet. First, select a small magnification, such as 50%. Then locate the cell range you want to move to and select one of its cells. Finally, use the Zoom feature to return the screen magnification to 100%. When Excel returns the display to normal size, the cell you select and its surrounding range appear onscreen.

Splitting the Difference

Although zooming in and out on the worksheet can help you get your bearings, it can't bring together two separate sections so that you can compare their data on the screen (at least not at a normal size where you can actually read the information). To manage this kind of trick, split the Worksheet area into separate panes and then scroll the worksheet in each pane so that they display the parts you want to compare.

Splitting the window is easy. Look at Figure 6-3 to see an Income Analysis worksheet after splitting its worksheet window horizontally into two panes and scrolling up rows 38 through 44 in the lower pane. Each pane has its own vertical scroll bar, which enables you to scroll different parts of the worksheet into view.

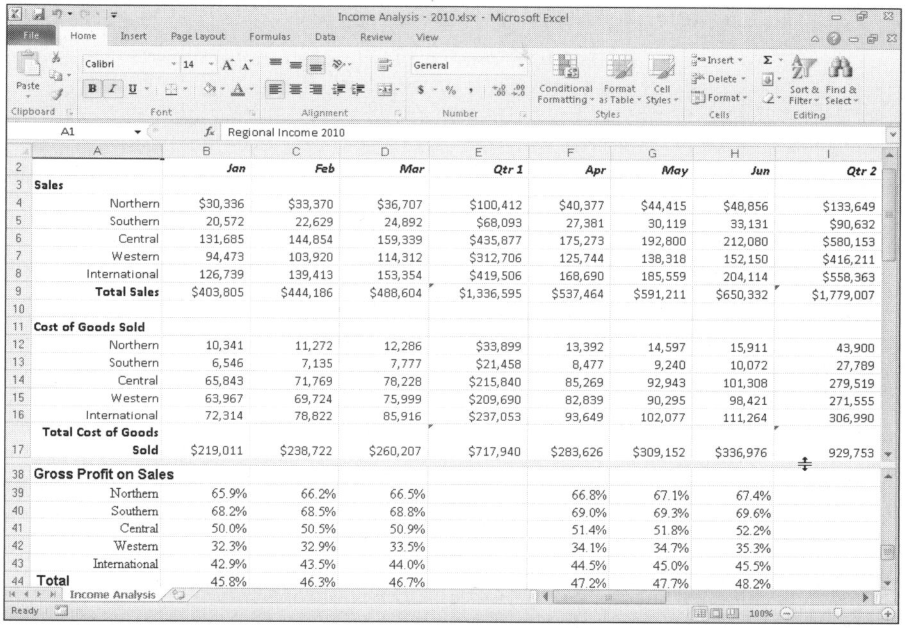

Figure 6-3: The worksheet in a split document window after scrolling up the bottom rows in the lower pane.

To split a worksheet into two (upper and lower) horizontal panes, you can drag the *split bar,* located right above the scroll arrow at the very top of the vertical scroll bar, down until the window divides as you want it. Use the following steps:

1. **Click the vertical split bar and hold down the primary mouse button.**

   The mouse pointer changes to a double-headed arrow with a split in its middle (like the one used to resize rows).

2. **Drag downward until you reach the row at which you want the document window divided.**

   A gray dividing line appears in the workbook window while you drag down, indicating where the window will be split.

3. **Release the mouse button.**

   Excel divides the window into horizontal panes at the pointer's location and adds a vertical scroll bar to the new pane.

You can also split the document window into two vertical (left and right) panes by following these steps:

1. **Click the split bar located at the right edge of the horizontal scroll bar.**

2. **Drag to the left until you reach the column at which you want the document window divided.**

3. Release the mouse button.

Excel splits the window at that column and adds a second horizontal scroll bar to the new pane.

Don't confuse the tab split bar to the left of the horizontal scroll bar with the horizontal split bar at its right. You drag the *tab split bar* to increase or decrease the number of sheet tabs displayed at the bottom of the workbook window; you use the *horizontal split bar* to divide the workbook window into two vertical panes.

You can make the panes in a workbook window disappear by double-clicking anywhere on the split bar that divides the window rather than having to drag the split bar all the way to one of the edges of the window to get rid of it.

Instead of dragging split bars, you can divide a document window by clicking the Split button on the Ribbon's View tab (Alt+WS). When you click this command button, Excel uses the position of the cell cursor to determine where to split the window into panes. The program splits the window vertically at the left edge of the pointer and horizontally along the top edge.

If you want the workbook window split into two horizontal panes, position the cell cursor in column A of the row in the worksheet where you want it divided. (Excel then splits the sheet into panes using the top edge of the cell cursor when you click the Split button.) If you want the workbook window split into two vertical windows, position the cell cursor in row 1 of the column in the worksheet where you want it divided. (Excel then divides the sheet into panes using the left edge of the cell cursor when you click the Split button.)

If you position the cell cursor somewhere in the midst of the cells displayed onscreen when you click View⇨Split or press Alt+WS, Excel splits the window into four panes along the top and left edge of the cell cursor. For example, if you position the cell cursor in cell B10 of the sample Income Analysis worksheet and then click View⇨Split, the window splits into four panes: A horizontal split occurs between rows 9 and 10, and a vertical split occurs between columns A and B (as shown in Figure 6-4).

Excel divides whatever portion of the worksheet is displayed onscreen given its current magnification into four equal panes when the cell cursor is in cell A1 at the time you click View⇨Split or press Alt+WS.

After you split the window into panes, you can move the cell cursor into a particular pane by clicking one of its cells. To remove the panes from a worksheet window, click View⇨Split on the Ribbon or press Alt+WS another time.

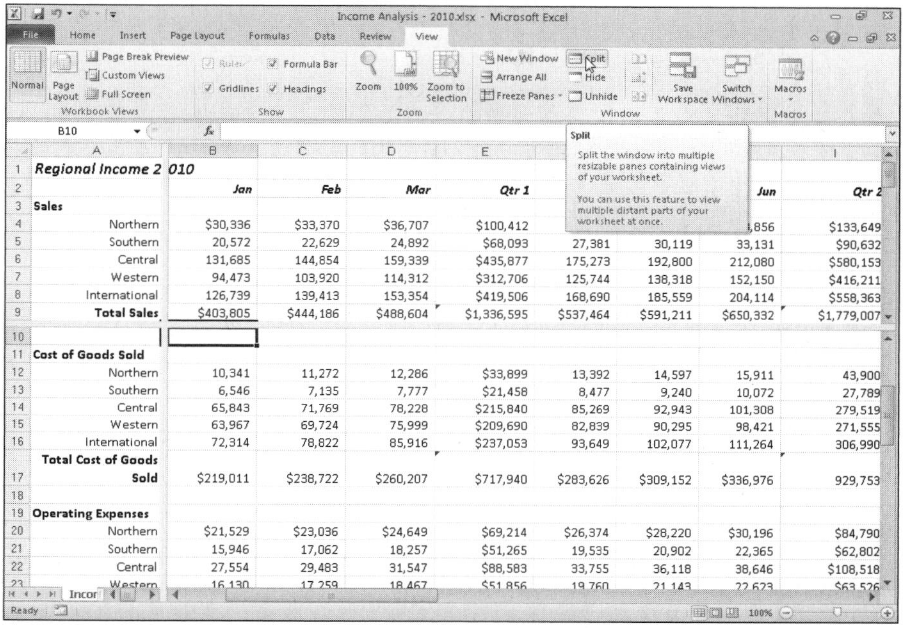

Figure 6-4:
The work-
sheet
window split
into four
panes after
placing the
cell cursor
in cell B10.

Fixed Headings Courtesy of Freeze Panes

Panes are great for viewing different parts of the same worksheet that normally can't be seen together. You can also use panes to freeze headings in
the top rows and first columns so that the headings stay in view at all times,
no matter how you scroll through the worksheet. Frozen headings are especially helpful when you work with a table that contains information that
extends beyond the rows and columns shown onscreen.

In Figure 6-5, you can see just such a table. The Income Analysis worksheet
contains more rows and columns than you can see at one time (unless you
decrease the magnification to about 40% with Zoom, which makes the data
too small to read). In fact, this worksheet continues down to row 52 and over
to column P.

By dividing the worksheet into four panes between rows 2 and 3 and columns
A and B and then freezing them on the screen, you can keep the column
headings in row 2 that identify each column of information on the screen
while you scroll the worksheet up and down to review information on income
and expenses. Additionally, you can keep the row headings in column A on
the screen while you scroll the worksheet to the right.

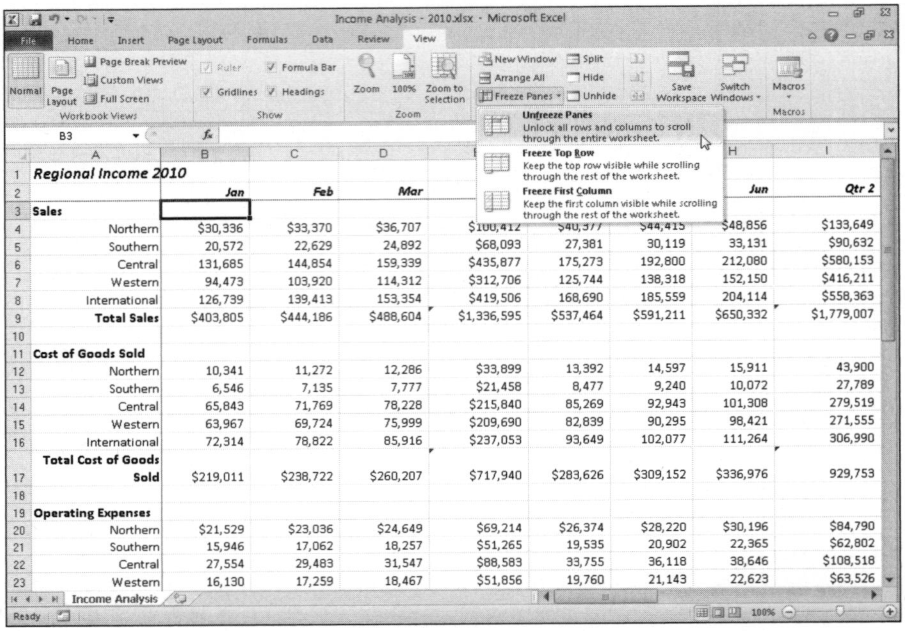

Figure 6-5:
Frozen
panes keep
the column
headings
and the row
headings on
the screen
at all times.

Refer to Figure 6-5 to see the worksheet right after splitting the window into four panes and freezing them. To create and freeze these panes, follow these steps:

1. **Position the cell cursor in cell B3.**

2. **Click View⇨Freeze Panes on the Ribbon and then click Freeze Panes on the drop-down menu or press Alt+WFF.**

   In this example, Excel freezes the top and left pane above row 3 and left of column B.

When Excel sets up the frozen panes, the borders of frozen panes are represented by a single line rather than a thin bar, as is the case when simply splitting the worksheet into panes.

See what happens when you scroll the worksheet up after freezing the panes (shown in Figure 6-6). In this figure, I scrolled the worksheet up so that rows 23 through 43 appear under rows 1 and 2. Because the vertical pane with the worksheet title and column headings is frozen, it remains onscreen. (Normally, rows 1 and 2 would have been the first to disappear when you scroll the worksheet up.)

Figure 6-6:
The Income
Analysis
worksheet
after scroll-
ing the rows
up to display
additional
income and
expense
data.

Income Analysis - 2010.xlsx - Microsoft Excel

B33   =SUM(B28:B32)

	A	B	C	D	E	F	G	H	I
1	**Regional Income 2010**								
2		*Jan*	*Feb*	*Mar*	*Qtr 1*	*Apr*	*May*	*Jun*	*Qtr 2*
23	Western	16,130	17,259	18,467	$51,856	19,760	21,143	22,623	$63,526
24	International	32,361	34,626	37,050	$104,037	39,644	42,419	45,388	$127,450
25	**Total Operating Expenses**	$113,520	$121,466	$129,969	$364,955	$139,067	$148,802	$159,218	$447,086
26									
27	**Net Income**								
28	Northern	($1,534)	($938)	($228)	($2,700)	$611	$1,598	$2,750	$4,959
29	Southern	(1,920)	(1,568)	(1,142)	($4,630)	(630)	(23)	694	$41
30	Central	38,289	43,602	49,564	$131,455	56,249	63,740	72,126	$192,115
31	Western	14,376	16,937	19,846	$51,159	23,144	26,880	31,105	$81,130
32	International	22,064	25,964	30,388	$78,416	35,397	41,063	47,462	$123,922
33	**Total Net Income**	$71,275	$83,997	$98,428	$253,700	$114,772	$133,257	$154,139	$402,168
34									
35									
36	**Regional Ratio Analysis**								
37		*Jan*	*Feb*	*Mar*		*Apr*	*May*	*Jun*	
38	**Gross Profit on Sales**								
39	Northern	65.9%	66.2%	66.5%		66.8%	67.1%	67.4%	
40	Southern	68.2%	68.5%	68.8%		69.0%	69.3%	69.6%	
41	Central	50.0%	50.5%	50.9%		51.4%	51.8%	52.2%	
42	Western	32.3%	32.9%	33.5%		34.1%	34.7%	35.3%	
43	International	42.9%	43.5%	44.0%		44.5%	45.0%	45.5%	

Income Analysis

Ready   100%

Look to Figure 6-7 to see what happens when you scroll the worksheet to
the right. In this figure, I scroll the worksheet so that the data in columns
M through P appear after the data in column A. Because the first column is
frozen, it remains onscreen, helping you identify the various categories of
income and expenses for each month.

Click Freeze Top Row or Freeze First Column on the Freeze Panes button's
drop-down menu to freeze the column headings in the top row of the worksheet or the row headings in the first column of the worksheet regardless of
where the cell cursor is located in the worksheet.

To unfreeze the panes in a worksheet, click View➪Freeze Panes on the
Ribbon and then click Unfreeze Panes on the Freeze Panes button's drop-
down menu or press Alt+WFF. Choosing this option removes the panes, indicating that Excel has unfrozen them.

Electronic Sticky Notes

You can add text comments to particular cells in an Excel worksheet.
Comments act kind of like electronic pop-up versions of sticky notes. For
example, you can add a comment to yourself to verify a particular figure

before printing the worksheet or to remind yourself that a particular value is only an estimate (or even to remind yourself that it's your anniversary and to pick up a little something special for your spouse on the way home!).

In addition to using notes to remind yourself of something you've done or that remains to be done, you can also use a comment to mark your current place in a large worksheet. You can then use the comment's location to quickly find your starting place the next time you work with that worksheet.

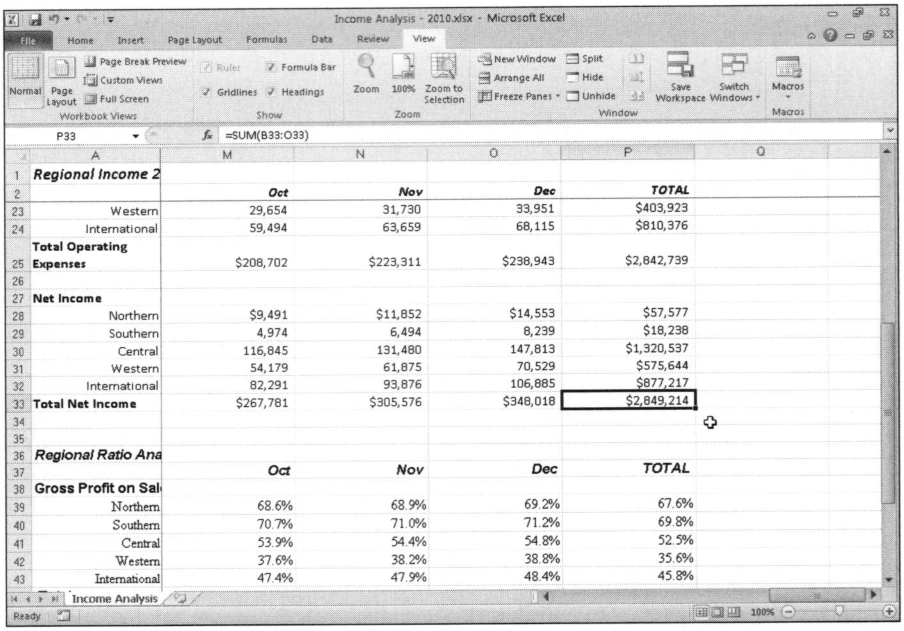

Figure 6-7:
The Income Analysis worksheet after scrolling the columns left to display the last group of columns in this table.

	Oct	Nov	Dec	TOTAL
Regional Income 2				
Western	29,654	31,730	33,951	$403,923
International	59,494	63,659	68,115	$810,376
Total Operating Expenses	$208,702	$223,311	$238,943	$2,842,739
Net Income				
Northern	$9,491	$11,852	$14,553	$57,577
Southern	4,974	6,494	8,239	$18,238
Central	116,845	131,480	147,813	$1,320,537
Western	54,179	61,875	70,529	$575,644
International	82,291	93,876	106,885	$877,217
Total Net Income	$267,781	$305,576	$348,018	$2,849,214
Regional Ratio Ana	Oct	Nov	Dec	TOTAL
Gross Profit on Sal				
Northern	68.6%	68.9%	69.2%	67.6%
Southern	70.7%	71.0%	71.2%	69.8%
Central	53.9%	54.4%	54.8%	52.5%
Western	37.6%	38.2%	38.8%	35.6%
International	47.4%	47.9%	48.4%	45.8%

Adding a comment to a cell

To add a comment to a cell, follow these steps:

1. **Move the cell cursor to or click the cell to which you want to add the comment.**

2. **Click the New Comment command button on the Ribbon's Review tab or press Alt+RC.**

    A new text box appears (similar to the one shown in Figure 6-8). This text box contains the name of the user as it appears in the User Name text box on the General tab in the Excel Options dialog box (Alt+FT) and the insertion point located at the beginning of a new line right below the user name.

3. **Type the text of your comment in the text box that appears.**

4. **When you finish entering the comment text, click somewhere on the worksheet outside of the text box.**

   Excel marks the location of a comment in a cell by adding a tiny triangle in the upper-right corner of the cell. (This triangular indicator appears in red on a color monitor.)

5. **To display the comment in a cell, position the thick white cross mouse pointer somewhere in the cell with the note indicator.**

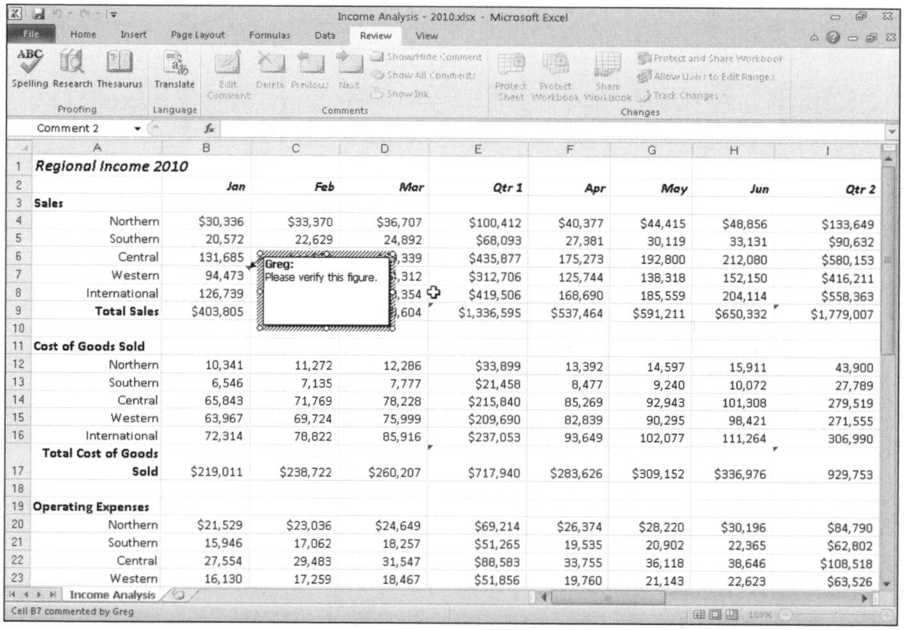

Figure 6-8:
Adding a comment to a cell in a new text box.

Comments in review

When you have a workbook with sheets that contain a bunch of comments, you probably won't want to take the time to position the mouse pointer over each of its cells in order to read each one. For those times, you need to click the Show All Comments command button on the Ribbon's Review tab (or press Alt+RA). When you click Show All Comments on the Review tab, Excels displays all the comments in the workbook (as shown in Figure 6-9).

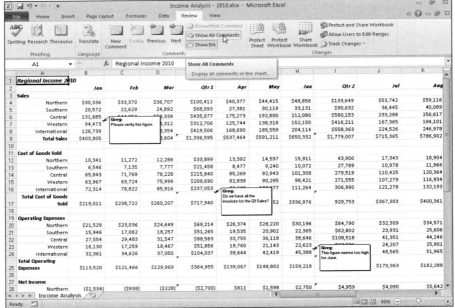

Figure 6-9:
Use the
Show All
Comments
button on
the Review
tab to
review the
comments
added to a
worksheet.

With the Review tab selected in the Ribbon, you can then move back and forth from comment to comment by clicking its Next and Previous command buttons in the Comments group (Alt+RN and Alt+RV, respectively). When you reach the last comment in the workbook, you receive an alert box asking you whether you want to continue reviewing the comments from the beginning (which you can do by simply clicking OK). After you finish reviewing the comments in your workbook, you can hide their display by clicking the Show All Comments command button on the Review tab of the Ribbon or pressing Alt+RA a second time.

Editing the comments in a worksheet

To edit the contents of a comment, select it by clicking the Next or Previous command button in the Comments group of the Review tab and then click the Edit Comment button (which replaces New Comment) or right-click the cell with the comment and select Edit Comment from the cell's shortcut menu.

To change the placement of a comment in relation to its cell, you select the comment by clicking somewhere on it and then position the mouse pointer on one of the edges of its text box. When a four-headed arrow appears at the tip of the mouse pointer, you can drag the text box to a new place in the worksheet. When you release the mouse button, Excel redraws the arrow connecting the comment's text box to the note indicator in the upper-right corner of the cell.

To change the size of a comment's text box, you select the comment, position the mouse pointer on one of its sizing handles, and then drag in the appropriate direction (away from the center of the box to increase its size or toward the center to decrease its size). When you release the mouse button, Excel redraws the comment's text box with the new shape and size. When you change the size and shape of a comment's text box, Excel automatically wraps the text to fit in the new shape and size.

To change the font of the comment text, select the text of the comment (by selecting the comment for editing and then dragging through the text), right-click the text box, and then click Format Comment on its shortcut menu (or you can press Ctrl+1 as I do). On the Font tab of the Format Cells dialog box that appears, you can then use the options to change the font, font style, font size, or color of the text displayed in the selected comment.

To delete a comment, select the cell with the comment in the worksheet or click the Next or Previous command buttons on the Review tab of the Ribbon until the comment is selected and then click the Delete command button in the Comments group (Alt+RD). Excel removes the comment along with the note indicator from the selected cell.

You can also delete all comments in the selected range by clicking Clear Comments from the Clear button's drop-down menu (the one with the eraser icon in the Editing group) on the Home tab of the Ribbon (Alt+HEM).

Getting your comments in print

When printing a worksheet, you can print comments along with worksheet data by selecting either At End of Sheet or As Displayed on Sheet on the Comments drop-down list on the Sheet tab of the Page Setup dialog box. Open this dialog box by clicking the dialog box launcher in the lower-right corner of the Page Setup group on the Ribbon's Page Layout tab (Alt+PSP).

The Cell Name Game

By assigning descriptive names to cells and cell ranges, you can go a long way toward keeping on top of the location of important information in a worksheet. Rather than try to associate random cell coordinates with specific information, you just have to remember a name. You can also use range names to designate the cell selection that you want to print or use in other Office 2010 programs, such as Microsoft Word or Access. Best of all, after you name a cell or cell range, you can use this name with the Go To feature.

If I only had a name . . .

When assigning range names to a cell or cell range, you need to follow a few guidelines:

- **Range names must begin with a letter of the alphabet, not a number.**

  For example, instead of 01Profit, use Profit01.

- **Range names cannot contain spaces.**

  Instead of a space, use the underscore (Shift+hyphen) to tie the parts of the name together. For example, instead of Profit 01, use Profit_01.

- **Range names cannot correspond to cell coordinates in the worksheet.**

  For example, you can't name a cell Q1 because this is a valid cell coordinate. Instead, use something like Q1_sales.

To name a cell or cell range in a worksheet, follow these steps:

1. **Select the cell or cell range that you want to name.**

2. **Click the cell address for the current cell that appears in the Name Box on the far left of the Formula bar.**

   Excel selects the cell address in the Name Box.

3. **Type the name for the selected cell or cell range in the Name Box.**

   When typing the range name, you must follow Excel's naming conventions: Refer to the bulleted list of cell-name do's and don'ts earlier in this section for details.

4. **Press Enter.**

To select a named cell or range in a worksheet, click the range name on the Name Box drop-down list. To open this list, click the drop-down arrow button that appears to the right of the cell address on the Formula bar.

You can also accomplish the same thing by clicking Home⇨Find & Select⇨Go To or by pressing F5, Ctrl+G, or Alt+HFDG to open the Go To dialog box (see Figure 6-10). Double-click the desired range name in the Go To list box (alternatively, select the name and click OK or press Enter). Excel moves the cell cursor directly to the named cell. If you select a cell range, all the cells in that range are selected.

Figure 6-10:
Select the
named cell
range to go
to in a
workbook.

Name that formula!

Cell names are not only a great way to identify and find cells and cell ranges in your spreadsheet, but they're also a great way to make out the purpose of your formulas. For example, suppose that you have a simple formula in cell K3 that calculates the total due to you by multiplying the hours you work for a client (in cell I3) by the client's hourly rate (in cell J3). Normally, you would enter this formula in cell K3 as

```
=I3*J3
```

However, if you assign the name Hours to cell I3 and the name Rate to cell J3, in cell K3 you could enter the formula

```
=Hours*Rate
```

I don't think there's anyone who would dispute that the formula =Hours*Rate is much easier to understand than =I3*J3.

To enter a formula using cell names rather than cell references, follow these steps (see Chapter 2 to brush up on how to create formulas):

1. **Assign range names to the individual cells as I describe earlier in this section.**

   For this example, give the name Hours to cell I3 and the name Rate to cell J3.

2. **Place the cell cursor in the cell where the formula is to appear.**

   For this example, put the cell cursor in cell K3.

3. **Type = (equal sign) to start the formula.**

4. **Select the first cell referenced in the formula by selecting its cell (either by clicking the cell or moving the cell cursor into it).**

   For this example, you select the Hours cell by selecting cell I3.

   5. **Type the arithmetic operator to use in the formula.**

   For this example, you would type * (asterisk) for multiplication. (Refer to Chapter 2 for a list of the other arithmetic operators.)

   6. **Select the second cell referenced in the formula by selecting its cell (either by clicking the cell or moving the cell cursor into it).**

   For this example, you select the Rate cell by selecting cell J3.

   7. **Click the Enter button or press Enter to complete the formula.**

   In this example, Excel enters the formula =Hours*Rate in cell K3.

You can't use the fill handle to copy a formula that uses cell names, rather than cell addresses, to other cells in a column or row that perform the same function (see Chapter 4). When you copy an original formula that uses names rather than addresses, Excel copies the original formula without adjusting the cell references to the new rows and columns. See the upcoming "Naming constants" section to find a way to use your column and row headings to identify the cell references in the copies, and include the original formula from which the copies are made.

Naming constants

Certain formulas use constant values, such as an 8.25% tax rate or a 10% discount rate. If you don't want to have to enter these constants into a cell of the worksheet in order to use the formulas, you create range names that hold their values and then use their range names in the formulas you create.

For example, to create a constant called *tax_rate* (of 8.25%), follow these steps:

   1. **Click the Define Name button on the Ribbon's Formulas tab or press Alt+MMD to open the New Name dialog box.**

   2. **In the New Name dialog box, type the range name (tax_rate in this example) into the Name text box.**

   Be sure to adhere to the cell range naming conventions when entering this new name.

   3. **(Optional) To have the range name defined for just the active worksheet instead of the entire workbook, click the name of the sheet on the Scope drop-down list.**

   Normally, you're safer sticking with the default selection of Workbook as the Scope option so that you can use your constant in a formula on any of its sheets. Only change the scope to a particular worksheet when you're sure that you'll use it only in formulas on that worksheet.

4. **Click in the Refers To text box after the equal to sign (=) and replace (enter) the current cell address with the constant value (8.25% in this example) or a formula that calculates the constant.**

5. **Click OK to close the New Name dialog box.**

After you assign a constant to a range name by using this method, you can apply it to the formulas that you create in the worksheet in one of two ways:

✔ Type the range name to which you assign the constant at the place in the formula where its value is required.

✔ Click the Use in Formula command button on the Formulas tab (or press Alt+MS) and then click the constant's range name on the drop-down menu that appears.

When you copy a formula that uses a range name containing a constant, its values remain unchanged in all copies of the formula that you create with the Fill handle. (In other words, range names in formulas act like absolute cell addresses in copied formulas — see Chapter 4 for more on copying formulas.)

Also, when you update the constant by changing its value in the Edit Name dialog box — opened by clicking the range name in the Name Manager dialog box (Alt+MN) and then clicking its Edit button — all the formulas that use that constant (by referring to the range name) are automatically updated (recalculated) to reflect this change.

Seek and Ye Shall Find . . .

When all else fails, you can use Excel's Find feature to locate specific information in the worksheet. Click Home➪Find & Select➪Find or press Ctrl+F, Shift+F5, or even Alt+HFDF to open the Find and Replace dialog box.

In the Find What drop-down box of this dialog box, enter the text or values you want to locate and then click the Find Next button or press Enter to start the search. Choose the Options button in the Find and Replace dialog box to expand the search options (as shown in Figure 6-11).

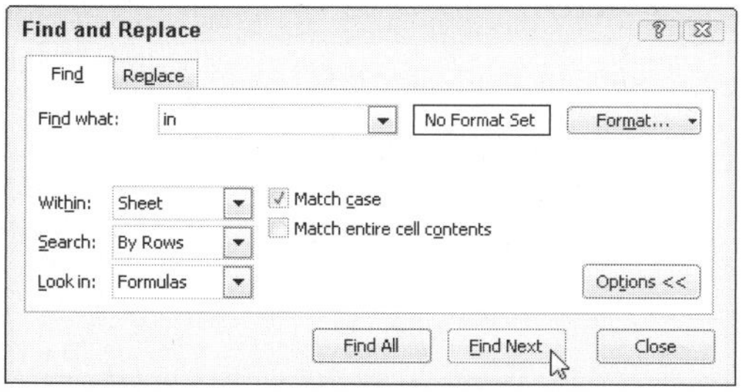

Figure 6-11:
Use options
in the Find
and Replace
dialog box
to locate
cell entries.

Find and Replace			
Find	Replace		
Find what:	in	No Format Set	Format...
Within:	Sheet	✓ Match case	
Search:	By Rows	☐ Match entire cell contents	
Look in:	Formulas		Options <<
	Find All	Find Next	Close

When you search for a text entry with the Find and Replace feature, be mindful of whether the text or number you enter in the Find What text box is separate in its cell or occurs as part of another word or value. For example, if you enter the characters **in** in the Find What text box and you don't select the Match Entire Cell Contents check box, Excel finds

- The *In* in Regional Income 2010 in cell A1
- The *In* in International in A8, A16, A24 and so on
- The *in* in Total Operating Expenses in cell A25

If you select the Match Entire Cell Contents check box in the Find and Replace dialog box before starting the search, Excel would not consider the *anything in the sheet to* be a match because all entries have other text surrounding the text you're searching for. If you had the state abbreviation for Indiana (IN) in a cell by itself and had chosen the Match Entire Cell Contents option, Excel would find that cell.

When you search for text, you can also specify whether you want Excel to match the case you use (uppercase or lowercase) when entering the search text in the Find What text box. By default, Excel ignores case differences between text in cells of your worksheet and the search text you enter in the Find What text box. To conduct a case-sensitive search, you need to select the Match Case check box (available when you click the Options button to expand the Find and Replace dialog box, shown in Figure 6-11).

If the text or values that you want to locate in the worksheet have special formatting, you can specify the formatting to match when conducting the search.

To have Excel match the formatting assigned to a particular cell in the worksheet, follow these steps:

1. **Click the drop-down button on the right of the Format button in the Find and Replace dialog box and choose the Choose Format from Cell option on the pop-up menu.**

   The Find and Replace dialog box temporarily disappears, and Excel adds an ink dropper icon to the normal white cross mouse pointer.

2. **Click this mouse pointer in the cell in the worksheet that contains the formatting you want to match.**

   The Find and Replace dialog box reappears, and the Find and Replace feature picks up the cell's formatting.

To select the formatting to match in the search from the options on the Find Format dialog box (which are identical to those of the Format Cells dialog box), follow these steps:

1. **Click the Format button or click its drop-down button and choose Format from its menu.**

2. **Then, select the formatting options to match from the various tabs (refer to Chapter 3 for help on selecting these options) and click OK.**

When you use either of these methods to select the kinds of formatting to match in your search, the No Format Set button (located between the Find What text box and the Format button) changes to a Preview button. The word *Preview* in this button appears in whatever font and attributes Excel picks up from the sample cell or through your selections in the Find Format dialog box. To reset the Find and Replace to search across all formats again, click Format⇨Clear Find Format, and No Form Set will appear again between the Find What and Format buttons.

When you search for values in the worksheet, be mindful of the difference between formulas and values. For example, say cell K24 of your worksheet contains the computed value $15,000 (from a formula that multiplies a value in cell I24 by that in cell J24). If you type **15000** in the Find What text box and press Enter to search for this value, instead of finding the value 15000 in cell K24, Excel displays an alert box with the following message:

```
Microsoft Excel cannot find the data you're searching for
```

This is because the value in this cell is calculated by the formula

```
=I24*J24
```

The value 15000 doesn't appear in that formula. To have Excel find any entry matching 15000 in the cells of the worksheet, you need to choose Values in the Look In drop-down menu of the Find and Replace dialog box in place of the normally used Formulas option.

To restrict the search to just the text or values in the text of the comments in the worksheet, choose the Comments option from the Look In drop-down menu.

If you don't know the exact spelling of the word or name or the precise value or formula you're searching for, you can use wildcards, which are symbols that stand for missing or unknown text. Use the question mark (?) to stand for a single unknown character; use the asterisk (*) to stand for any number of missing characters. Suppose that you enter the following in the Find What text box and choose the Values option in the Look In drop-down menu:

```
7*4
```

Excel stops at cells that contain the values 74, 704, and 75,234. Excel even finds the text entry 782 4th Street!

If you actually want to search for an asterisk in the worksheet rather than use the asterisk as a wildcard, precede it with a tilde (~), as follows:

```
~*4
```

This arrangement enables you to search the formulas in the worksheet for one that multiplies by the number 4. (Remember that Excel uses the asterisk as the multiplication sign.)

The following entry in the Find What text box finds cells that contain Jan, January, June, Janet, and so on.

```
J?n*
```

Normally, Excel searches only the current worksheet for the search text you enter. If you want the program to search all the worksheets in the workbook, you must select the Workbook option from the Within drop-down menu.

When Excel locates a cell in the worksheet that contains the text or values you're searching for, it selects that cell while leaving the Find and Replace dialog box open. (Remember that you can move the Find and Replace dialog box if it obscures your view of the cell.) To search for the next occurrence of the text or value, click the Find Next button or press Enter.

Excel normally searches down the worksheet by rows. To search across the columns first, choose the By Columns option in the Search drop-down menu. To reverse the search direction and revisit previous occurrences of matching cell entries, press the Shift key while you click the Find Next button in the Find and Replace dialog box.

You Can Be Replaced!

If your purpose for finding a cell with a particular entry is so that you can change it, you can automate this process by using the Replace tab on the Find and Replace dialog box. If you click Home⇨Find & Select⇨Replace or press Ctrl+H or Alt+HFDR, Excel opens the Find and Replace dialog box with

the Replace tab (rather than the Find tab) selected. On the Replace tab, enter
the text or value you want to replace in the Find What text box, and then
enter the replacement text or value in the Replace With text box.

When you enter replacement text, enter it exactly how you want it to appear
in the cell. In other words, if you want to replace all occurrences of Jan in the
worksheet with January, enter the following in the Replace With text box:

```
January
```

Make sure that you use a capital J in the Replace With text box, even though
you can enter the following in the Find What text box (providing you don't
check the Match Case check box that appears only when you choose the
Options button to expand the Find and Replace dialog box options):

```
jan
```

After specifying what to replace and what to replace it with (as shown in
Figure 6-12), you can have Excel replace occurrences in the worksheet on a
case-by-case basis or globally. To replace all occurrences in a single operation, click the Replace All button.

Figure 6-12:
Use Replace
options to
change par-
ticular cell
entries.

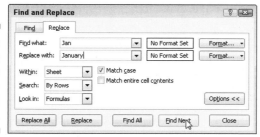

Be careful with global search-and-replace operations; they can really mess up
a worksheet in a hurry if you inadvertently replace values, parts of formulas,
or characters in titles and headings that you hadn't intended to change. With
this in mind, always follow one rule:

> Never undertake a global search-and-replace operation on an unsaved
> worksheet.

Also, verify whether the Match Entire Cell Contents check box (displayed
only when you click the Options>> button) is selected before you begin. You
can end up with many unwanted replacements if you leave this check box
unselected when you really only want to replace entire cell entries (rather
than matching parts in cell entries).

If you do make a mess, immediately click the Undo button on the Quick Access toolbar or press Ctrl+Z to restore the worksheet.

To see each occurrence before you replace it, click the Find Next button or press Enter. Excel selects the next cell with the text or value you enter in the Find What text box. To have the program replace the selected text, click the Replace button. To skip this occurrence, click the Find Next button to continue the search. When you finish replacing occurrences, click the Close button to close the Find and Replace dialog box.

Do Your Research

Excel 2010 includes the Research task pane that you can use to search for information using such online resources as Bing; Encarta Dictionary: English (North America); English, French, and Spanish Thesaurus; as well as MSN Money Stock Quotes. (Because these resources are online, to make use of the Research task pane, you must have Internet access available.)

To open the Research task pane (similar to the one shown in Figure 6-13), click the Research command button on the Ribbon's Review tab or press Alt+RR.

Figure 6-13: Looking up the stock quotes for Microsoft Corp (MSFT) in the Research task pane.

To look up something in the Research pane, enter the word or phrase you want to locate within the online resources using the Search For text box at the top of the Research pane. Then click the type of online reference to search on the Show Results From drop-down menu:

- ✔ **All Reference Books** to search for the word or phrase in any of the online reference books, such as the Encarta Dictionary: English (North America), Thesaurus: English (U.S.), and so on

- ✔ **All Research Sites** to look up the word or phrase in any online resource or any Web site such as Bing, Factiva iWorks, and HighBeam Research

- ✔ **All Business and Financial Sites** to look up the word or phrase in MSN Money Stock Quotes and Thomson Gale Company Profiles

To start the online search, click the Start Searching button to the immediate right of the Search For text box. Excel then connects you to the designated online resources and displays the search results in the list box below. Figure 6-13, for example, shows the various stock quotes for Microsoft Corporation for the day and time I did the search using MSN Money Stock Quotes.

When you include Web sites in your search, you can visit particular sites by clicking their links in the Research task pane. When you do, Windows then launches your default Web browser (such as Internet Explorer 8) and connects you to the linked page. To return to Excel after visiting a particular Web page, simply click the Close box in the upper-right corner of your Web browser's window.

You can modify which online services are available for use in a search by clicking the Research Options link that appears at the very bottom of the Research task pane. When you click this link, Excel opens a Research Options dialog box that enables you to add or remove particular reference books and sites by selecting their check boxes.

You Can Be So Calculating

Although extremely important, locating information in a worksheet is only part of keeping on top of the information in a worksheet. In really large workbooks that contain many completed worksheets, you may want to switch to manual recalculation so that you can control when the formulas in the worksheet are calculated. You need this kind of control when you find that Excel's recalculation of formulas each time you enter or change information in cells has slowed the program's response to a crawl. By holding off recalculations until you are ready to save or print the workbook, you find that you can work with Excel's worksheets without interminable delays.

To put the workbook into manual recalculation mode, click the Calculation Options button in the Calculation group on the Ribbon's Formulas tab and then click the Manual option on the drop-down menu or simply press Alt+MXM. After switching to manual recalculation, Excel displays Calculate on the status bar whenever you make a change to the worksheet that somehow affects the current values of its formulas. Whenever you see Calculate on the Status bar, you need to bring the formulas up-to-date before saving the workbook (as you would before you print its worksheets).

To recalculate the formulas in a workbook when calculation is manual, press F9 or Ctrl+= (equal sign) or click the Calculate Now button (the one with a picture of a calculator in the upper-right corner of the Calculation group) on the Formulas tab (Alt+MB).

Excel then recalculates the formulas in all the worksheets of your workbook. If you made changes to only the current worksheet and you don't want to wait around for Excel to recalculate every other worksheet in the workbook, you can restrict the recalculation to the current worksheet. Press Shift+F9 or click the Calculate Sheet button (the one with picture of a calculator under the worksheet in the lower-right corner of the Calculation group) on the Formulas tab (Alt+MJ).

If your worksheet contains data tables that perform different what-if scenarios (see Chapter 8 for details), you can have Excel automatically recalculate all parts of the worksheet except for those data tables by clicking Automatic Except Data Tables on the Calculation Options button's drop-down menu on the Formulas tab (Alt+MXE).

To return a workbook to fully automatic recalculation mode, click the Automatic option on the Calculation Options button's drop-down menu on the Formulas tab (Alt+MXA).

Putting on the Protection

After you more or less finalize a worksheet by checking out its formulas and proofing its text, you often want to guard against any unplanned changes by protecting the document.

Each cell in the worksheet can be locked or unlocked. By default, Excel locks all the cells in a worksheet so that, when you follow these steps, Excel locks the whole thing up tighter than a drum.

1. **Click the Protect Sheet command button in the Changes group on the Ribbon's Review tab or press Alt+RPS.**

Excel opens the Protect Sheet dialog box (see Figure 6-14) in which you select the check box options you want to be available when the protection is turned on in the worksheet. By default, Excel selects the Protect Worksheet and Contents of Locked Cells check box at the top of the Protect Sheet dialog box. Additionally, the program selects both the Select Locked Cells and Select Unlocked Cells check boxes in the Allow All Users of This Worksheet To list box below.

Figure 6-14:
Protection
options in
the Protect
Sheet dialog
box.

2. **(Optional) Click any of the check box options in the Allow All Users of This Worksheet To list box (such as Format Cells or Insert Columns) that you still want to be functional when the worksheet protection is operational.**

3. **If you want to assign a password that must be supplied before you can remove the protection from the worksheet, type the password in the Password to Unprotect Sheet text box.**

4. **Click OK or press Enter.**

   If you type a password in the Password to Unprotect Sheet text box, Excel opens the Confirm Password dialog box. Re-enter the password in the Reenter Password to Proceed text box exactly as you typed it in the Password to Unprotect Sheet text box in the Protect Sheet dialog box and then click OK or press Enter.

If you want to go a step further and protect the layout of the worksheets in the workbook, you protect the entire workbook as follows:

1. **Click the Protect Workbook command button in the Changes group on the Ribbon's Review tab or press Alt+RPW.**

   Excel opens the Protect Structure and Windows dialog box, where the Structure check box is selected and the Windows check box is not selected. With the Structure check box selected, Excel won't let you mess around with the sheets in the workbook (by deleting them or rearranging them). If you want to protect any windows that you set up (as I describe in Chapter 7), you need to select the Windows check box as well.

2. **To assign a password that must be supplied before you can remove the protection from the worksheet, type the password in the Password (Optional) text box.**

3. **Click OK or press Enter.**

   If you type a password in the Password (Optional) text box, Excel opens the Confirm Password dialog box. Re-enter the password in the Reenter Password to Proceed text box exactly as you typed it into the Password (Optional) text box in the Protect Structure and Windows dialog box and then click OK or press Enter.

Selecting the Protect Sheet command makes it impossible to make further changes to the contents of any of the locked cells in that worksheet except for those options that you specifically exempt in the Allow All Users of This Worksheet To list box. (See Step 2 in the first set of steps in this section.) Selecting the Protect Workbook command makes it impossible to make further changes to the layout of the worksheets in that workbook.

Excel displays an alert dialog box with the following message when you try to edit or replace an entry in a locked cell:

```
The cell or chart you are trying to change is protected
and therefore read-only.

To modify a protected cell or chart, first remove
protection using the Unprotect Sheet command (Review
tab, Changes group). You may be prompted for a
password.
```

Usually, your intention in protecting a worksheet or an entire workbook is not to prevent all changes but to prevent changes in certain areas of the worksheet. For example, in a budget worksheet, you may want to protect all the cells that contain headings and formulas but allow changes in all the cells where you enter the budgeted amounts. That way, you can't inadvertently wipe out a title or formula in the worksheet simply by entering a value in the wrong column or row (a common occurrence).

To leave certain cells unlocked so that you can still change them after protecting the worksheet or workbook, select all the cells as the cell selection, open the Format Cells dialog box (Ctrl+1), and then click the Locked check box on the Protection tab to remove its check mark. Then, after unlocking the cells that you still want to be able to change, protect the worksheet as described earlier.

To remove protection from the current worksheet or workbook document so that you can again make changes to its cells (whether locked or unlocked), click the Unprotect Sheet or the Unprotect Workbook command button in the Changes group on the Ribbon's Review tab (or press Alt+RPS and Alt+RPW, respectively). If you assign a password when protecting the worksheet or workbook, you must then reproduce the password exactly as you assigned it (including any case differences) in the Password text box of the Unprotect Sheet or Unprotect Workbook dialog box.

To protect and share . . .

If you create a workbook with contents updated by several users on your network, you can use the Protect and Share Workbook command button in the Changes group of the Ribbon's Review tab (Alt+RO) to ensure that Excel tracks all the changes made and that no user can intentionally or inadvertently remove Excel's tracking of the changes made. To do this, simply select the Sharing with Track Changes check box in the Protect Shared Workbook dialog box that appears after you choose the command button. After you select this check box, you can add a password in the Password (Optional) text box below that each user must supply before he or she can open the workbook to make any changes. Then click OK or press Enter.

Chapter 7

Maintaining Multiple Worksheets

In This Chapter

▶ Moving from sheet to sheet in your workbook

▶ Adding and deleting sheets in a workbook

▶ Selecting sheets for group editing

▶ Naming sheet tabs descriptively

▶ Rearranging sheets in a workbook

▶ Displaying parts of different sheets

▶ Comparing two worksheets side by side

▶ Copying or moving sheets from one workbook to another

▶ Creating formulas that span different worksheets

*W*hen you're brand new to spreadsheets, you have enough trouble keeping track of a single worksheet — let alone three worksheets — and the very thought of working with more than one may be a little more than you can take. However, after you get a little experience under your belt, you'll find that working with more than one worksheet in a workbook is no more taxing than working with just a single worksheet.

Don't confuse the term *workbook* with *worksheet*. The workbook forms the document (file) that you open and save while you work. Each workbook (file) normally contains three blank worksheets. These worksheets are like the loose-leaf pages in a notebook binder; you can delete or add what you need. To help you keep track of the worksheets in your workbook and navigate between them, Excel provides sheet tabs (Sheet1, Sheet 2, and Sheet3) that are like the tab dividers in a loose-leaf notebook.

Juggling Worksheets

You need to see *how* to work with more than one worksheet in a workbook, but it's also important to know *why* you'd want to do such a crazy thing in the first place. The most common situation is, of course, when you have a bunch of worksheets that are related to each other and, therefore, naturally belong together in the same workbook. For example, consider the case of Mother Goose Enterprises with its different companies: Jack Sprat Diet Centers, Jack and Jill Trauma Centers, Mother Hubbard Dog Goodies; Rub-a-Dub-Dub Hot Tubs and Spas; Georgie Porgie Pudding Pies; Hickory, Dickory, Dock Clock Repair; Little Bo Peep Pet Detectives; Simple Simon Pie Shoppes; and Jack Be Nimble Candlesticks. To keep track of the annual sales for all these companies, you could create a workbook containing a worksheet for each of the nine different companies.

By keeping the sales figures for each company in a different sheet of the same workbook, you gain all the following benefits:

- You can enter the stuff that's needed in all the sales worksheets (if you select those sheet tabs) just by typing it once into the first worksheet (see the section "Editing en masse," later in this chapter).

- In order to help you build the worksheet for the first company's sales, you can attach macros to the current workbook so that they are readily available when you create the worksheets for the other companies. (A *macro* is a sequence of frequently performed, repetitive tasks and calculations that you record for easy playback — see Chapter 12 for details.)

- You can quickly compare the sales of one company with the sales of another (see the section "Opening Windows on Your Worksheets," later in this chapter).

- You can print all the sales information for each company as a single report in one printing operation. (Read Chapter 5 for specifics on printing an entire workbook or particular worksheets in a workbook.)

- You can easily create charts that compare certain sales data from different worksheets (see Chapter 10 for details).

- You can easily set up a summary worksheet with formulas that total the quarterly and annual sales for all nine companies (see the upcoming "To Sum Up . . ." section).

Sliding between the sheets

Each workbook that you create contains three worksheets, rather predictably named Sheet1, Sheet 2, and Sheet3. In typical Excel fashion, these names appear on tabs at the bottom of the workbook window. To go from one worksheet to another, you simply click the tab that contains the name of the sheet you want to see. Excel then brings that worksheet to the top of the stack, displaying its information in the current workbook window. You can always tell which worksheet is current because its name is in bold type on the tab and its tab appears as an extension of the current worksheet without any dividing line.

The only problem with moving to a new sheet by clicking its sheet tab occurs when you add so many worksheets to a workbook (as I describe in the upcoming section "Don't Short-Sheet Me!") that not all the sheet tabs are visible at any one time, and the sheet tab you want to click is not visible in the workbook. To deal with this problem, Excel provides Tab scrolling buttons (shown in the lower-left corner of Figure 7-1) that you can use to bring new sheet tabs into view.

- ✔ Click the Next tab scroll button (with the triangle pointing right) to bring the next unseen tab of the sheet on the right into view. Hold down the Shift key while you click this button to scroll several tabs at a time.

- ✔ Click the Previous tab scroll button (with the triangle pointing left) to bring the next unseen tab of the sheet on the left into view. Hold down the Shift key while you click this button to scroll several tabs at a time.

- ✔ Click the Last tab scroll button (with the triangle pointing right to the vertical bar) to bring the last group of sheet tabs, including the very last tab, into view.

- ✔ Click the First tab scroll button (with the triangle pointing left to the vertical bar) to bring the first group of sheet tabs, including the very first tab, into view.

Figure 7-1:
Use Tab scrolling buttons to bring new sheet tabs into view.

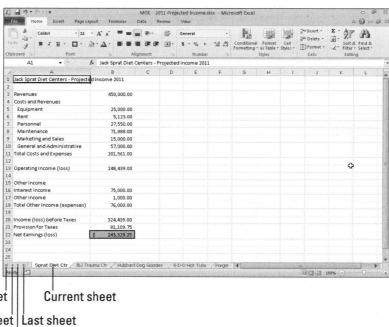

First sheet   Current sheet

Previous sheet   Last sheet

Next sheet

Going sheet to sheet via the keyboard

You can forget all about the darned Tab scrolling buttons and sheet tabs and just go back and forth through the sheets in a workbook with your keyboard. To move to the next worksheet in a workbook, press Ctrl+PgDn. To move to the previous worksheet in a workbook, press Ctrl+PgUp. The nice thing about using the keyboard shortcuts Ctrl+PgDn and Ctrl+PgUp is that they work whether or not the next or previous sheet tab is displayed in the workbook window!

Just don't forget that scrolling the sheet tab into view is not the same thing as selecting it: You still need to click the tab for the desired sheet to bring it to the front of the stack. You can also display a pop-up list of all the sheets in the current workbook and then select a particular sheet by right-clicking the Tab scroll buttons and then clicking the name of the sheet to select from the list.

To make it easier to find the sheet tab you want to select without having to do an inordinate amount of tab scrolling, drag the Tab split bar (see Figure 7-2) to the right to reveal more sheet tabs (consequently making the horizontal scroll bar shorter). If you don't care at all about using the horizontal scroll bar, you can maximize the number of sheet tabs in view by actually getting rid of this scroll bar. To do this, drag the Tab split bar to the right until it's smack up against the vertical split bar.

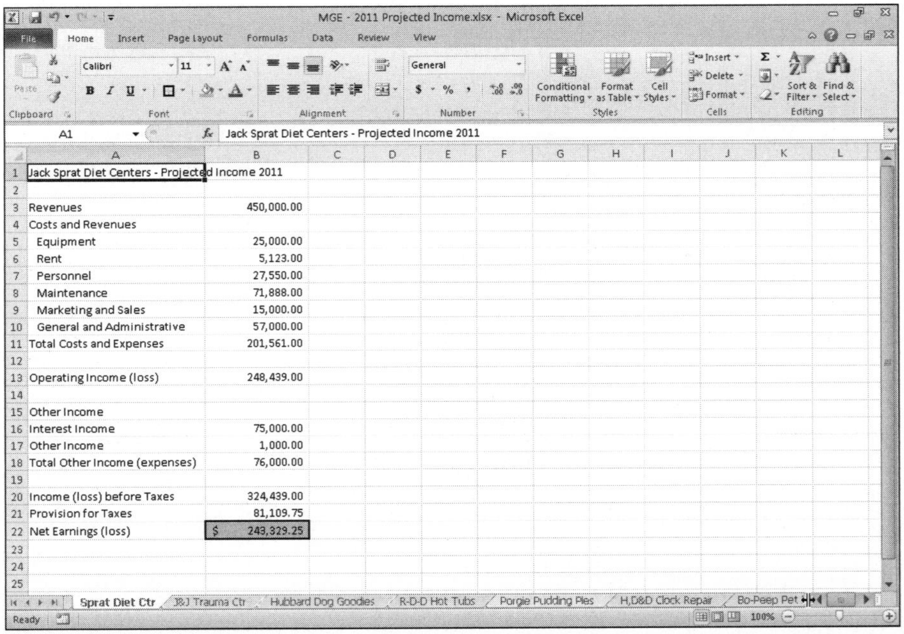

Figure 7-2:
Drag the
Tab split bar
to the right
to display
more sheet
tabs as you
make the
horizontal
scroll bar
shorter.

When you want to restore the horizontal scroll bar to its normal length, you can either manually drag the Tab split bar to the left or simply double-click it.

Editing en masse

Each time you click a sheet tab, you select that worksheet and make it active, enabling you to make whatever changes are necessary to its cells. You may encounter times, however, when you want to select bunches of worksheets so that you can make the same editing changes to all of them simultaneously. When you select multiple worksheets, any editing change that you make to the current worksheet — such as entering information in cells or deleting stuff from them — affects the same cells in all the selected sheets in exactly the same way.

Suppose you need to set up a new workbook with three worksheets that contain the names of the months across row 3 beginning in column B. Prior to entering January in cell B3 and using the AutoFill handle (as described in Chapter 2) to fill in the 11 months across row 3, you select all three worksheets (Sheet1, Sheet2, and Sheet3, for argument's sake). When you enter the names of the months in the third row of the first sheet, Excel will insert the names of the months in row 3 of all three selected worksheets. (Pretty slick, huh?)

Likewise, suppose you have another workbook in which you need to get rid of Sheet2 and Sheet3. Instead of clicking Sheet2, clicking Home➪Delete➪Delete Sheet on the Ribbon or pressing Alt+HDS, and then clicking Sheet3 and repeating the Delete Sheet command, select both worksheets and then zap them out of existence in one fell swoop by clicking Home➪Delete➪Delete Sheet on the Ribbon or pressing Alt+HDS.

To select a bunch of worksheets in a workbook, you have the following choices:

- ✔ To select a group of neighboring worksheets, click the first sheet tab and then scroll the sheet tabs until you see the tab of the last worksheet you want to select. Hold the Shift key while you click the last sheet tab to select all the tabs in between — the old Shift-click method applied to worksheet tabs.

- ✔ To select a group of non-neighboring worksheets, click the first sheet tab and then hold down the Ctrl key while you click the tabs of the other sheets you want to select.

✔ To select all the sheets in the workbook, right-click the tab of the worksheet that you want active and choose Select All Sheets from its shortcut menu that appears.

Excel shows you worksheets that you select by turning their sheet tabs white (although only the active sheet's tab name appears in bold) and displaying [Group] after the filename of the workbook on the Excel window's title bar.

To deselect the group of worksheets when you finish your group editing, you simply click a nonselected (that is, grayed out) worksheet tab. You can also deselect all the selected worksheets other than the one you want active by right-clicking the tab of the sheet you want displayed in the workbook window and then clicking Ungroup Sheets on its shortcut menu.

Don't Short-Sheet Me!

For some of you, the three worksheets automatically put into each new workbook that you start are as many as you would ever, ever need (or want) to use. For others of you, a measly three worksheets might seldom, if ever, be sufficient for the workbooks you create (for example, suppose that your company operates in 10 locations, or you routinely create budgets for 20 different departments or track expenses for 40 account representatives).

Excel 2010 makes it a snap to insert additional worksheets in a workbook (up to 255 total) — simply click the Insert Worksheet button that appears to the immediate right of the last sheet tab.

To insert a bunch of new worksheets in a row in the workbook, select a group with the same number of tabs as the number of new worksheets you want to add, starting with the tab where you want to insert the new worksheets. Next, click Home⇨Insert⇨Insert Sheet on the Ribbon or press Alt+HIS.

To delete a worksheet from the workbook, follow these steps:

1. **Click the tab of the worksheet that you want to delete.**

2. **Click Home⇨Delete⇨Delete Sheet on the Ribbon or press Alt+HDS or right-click the tab and choose Delete from its shortcut menu.**

   If the sheet you're deleting contains any data, Excel displays a scary message in an alert box about how you're going to delete the selected sheets permanently.

3. **Go ahead and click the Delete button or press Enter if you're sure that you won't be losing any data you need when Excel zaps the entire sheet.**

    This is one of those situations where Undo is powerless to put things right by restoring the deleted sheet to the workbook.

To delete a bunch of worksheets from the workbook, select all the worksheets you want to delete and then click Home➪Delete➪Delete Sheet, press Alt+HDS, or choose Delete from the tab's shortcut menu. Then, when you're sure that none of the worksheets will be missed, click the Delete button or press Enter when the alert dialog box appears.

If you find yourself constantly monkeying around with the number of worksheets in a workbook, either by adding a bunch of new worksheets or deleting all but one, you may want to think about changing the default number of worksheets so that the next time you open a new workbook, you have a more realistic number of sheets on hand. To change the default number, choose File➪Options or press Alt+FT to open the General tab of the Excel Options dialog box. Enter a new number between 1 and 255 in the Include This Many Sheets text box in the When Creating New Workbooks section or select a new number with the spinner buttons before you click OK.

A worksheet by any other name . . .

The sheet names that Excel comes up with for the tabs in a workbook (Sheet1, Sheet2, Sheet3) are, to put it mildly, not very original — and are certainly not descriptive of their function in life! Luckily, you can easily rename a worksheet tab to whatever helps you remember what you put on the worksheet (provided this descriptive name is no longer than 31 characters).

To rename a worksheet tab, just follow these steps:

1. **Double-click the sheet tab or right-click the sheet tab and then click Rename on its shortcut menu.**

    The current name on the sheet tab appears selected.

2. **Replace the current name on the sheet tab by typing the new sheet name.**

3. **Press Enter.**

    Excel displays the new sheet name on its tab at the bottom of the workbook window.

Short and sweet (sheet names)

Although Excel allows up to 31 characters (including spaces) for a sheet name, you want to keep your sheet names much briefer for two reasons:

✔ The longer the name, the longer the sheet tab. The longer the sheet tab, the fewer the tabs that can display and the more tab scrolling you have to do to select the sheets you want to work with.

✔ Should you start creating formulas that use cells in different worksheets (see the upcoming section "To Sum Up . . ." for an example), Excel uses the sheet name as part of the cell reference in the formula. (How else could Excel keep straight the value in cell C1 on Sheet1 from the value in cell C1 on Sheet2?) Therefore, if your sheet names are long, you end up with unwieldy formulas in the cells and on the Formula bar even when you're dealing with simple formulas that only refer to cells in a couple of different worksheets.

Generally, the fewer characters in a sheet name, the better. Also, remember that each name must be unique — no duplicates allowed.

A sheet tab by any other color . . .

In Excel 2010, you can assign colors to the different worksheet tabs. This feature enables you to color-code different worksheets. For example, you could assign red to the tabs of those worksheets that need immediate checking and blue to the tabs of those sheets that you've already checked.

To assign a color to a worksheet tab, right-click the tab and highlight Tab Color on its shortcut menu to open a submenu containing the Tab Color pop-up palette. Then, click the new color for the tab by clicking its color square on the color palette. After you select a new color for a sheet tab, the name of the active sheet tab appears underlined in the color you just selected. When you make another sheet tab active, the entire tab takes on the assigned color (and the text of the tab name changes to white if the selected color is sufficiently dark enough that black lettering is impossible to read).

To remove a color from a tab, right-click the sheet tab and highlight the Tab Color option to open the Tab Color pop-up palette. Then, click No Color at the bottom of the Tab Color palette.

Getting your sheets in order

Sometimes, you may find that you need to change the order in which the sheets appear in the workbook. Excel makes this possible by letting you drag the tab of the sheet you want to arrange in the workbook to the place where you want to insert it. While you drag the tab, the pointer changes to a sheet icon with an arrowhead on it, and the program marks your progress among the sheet tabs (see Figures 7-3 and 7-4 for examples). When you release the mouse button, Excel reorders the worksheets in the workbook by inserting the sheet at the place where you dropped the tab off.

If you hold down the Ctrl key while you drag the sheet tab icon, Excel inserts a copy of the worksheet at the place where you release the mouse button. You can tell that Excel is copying the sheet rather than just moving it in the workbook because the pointer shows a plus sign (+) on the sheet tab icon containing the arrowhead. When you release the mouse button, Excel inserts the copy in the workbook, which is designated by the addition of (2) after the tab name.

For example, if you copy Sheet5 to another place in the workbook, the sheet tab of the copy is named Sheet5 (2). You can then rename the tab to something civilized (see the earlier section "A worksheet by any other name . . ." for details).

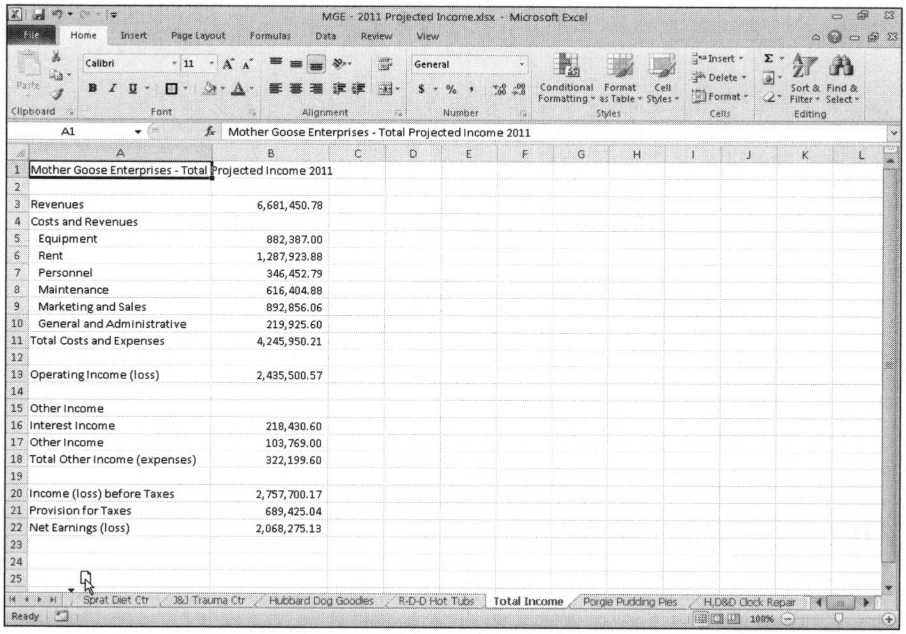

Figure 7-3:
Drag the
Total
Income tab
to the front
to reorder
the sheets
in this
worksheet.

	A	B	C
1	Mother Goose Enterprises - Total Projected Income 2011		
2			
3	Revenues	6,681,450.78	
4	Costs and Revenues		
5	Equipment	882,387.00	
6	Rent	1,287,923.88	
7	Personnel	346,452.79	
8	Maintenance	616,404.88	
9	Marketing and Sales	892,856.06	
10	General and Administrative	219,925.60	
11	Total Costs and Expenses	4,245,950.21	
12			
13	Operating Income (loss)	2,435,500.57	
14			
15	Other Income		
16	Interest Income	218,430.60	
17	Other Income	103,769.00	
18	Total Other Income (expenses)	322,199.60	
19			
20	Income (loss) before Taxes	2,757,700.17	
21	Provision for Taxes	689,425.04	
22	Net Earnings (loss)	2,068,275.13	
23			
24			
25			

Cell A1: Mother Goose Enterprises - Total Projected Income 2011

MGE - 2011 Projected Income.xlsx - Microsoft Excel

Sheet tabs: Sprat Diet Ctr / J&J Trauma Ctr / Hubbard Dog Goodies / R-D-D Hot Tubs / **Total Income** / Porgie Pudding Pies / H,D&D Clock Repair

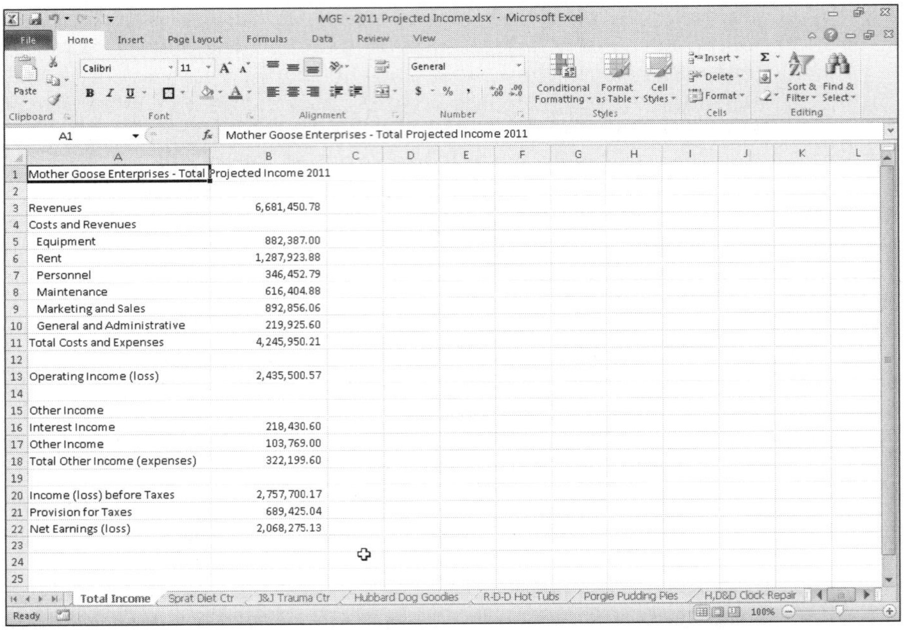

Figure 7-4:
The relo-
cated Total
Income
sheet is now
at the front
of the
workbook.

You can also move or copy worksheets from one part of a workbook to another by activating the sheet that you want to move or copy and then choosing Move or Copy on its shortcut menu. In the Before Sheet list box in the Move or Copy dialog box, click the name of the worksheet in front of which you want the active sheet moved or copied.

To move the active sheet immediately ahead of the sheet you select in the Before Sheet list box, simply click OK. To copy the active sheet, be sure to select the Create a Copy check box before you click OK. If you copy a work-sheet instead of just moving it, Excel adds a number to the sheet name. For example, if you copy a sheet named Total Income, Excel automatically names the copy of the worksheet Total Income (2), which appears on its sheet tab.

Opening Windows on Your Worksheets

Just as you can split a single worksheet into panes so that you can view and compare different parts of that same sheet on the screen (see Chapter 6), you can split a single workbook into worksheet windows and then arrange the windows so that you can view different parts of each worksheet on the screen.

To open the worksheets that you want to compare in different windows, you simply insert new workbook windows (in addition to the one that Excel automatically opens when you open the workbook file itself) and then select the worksheet that you want to display in the new window. You can accomplish this with the following steps:

1. **Click the New Window command button on the Ribbon's View tab or press Alt+WN to create a second worksheet window; then click the tab of the worksheet that you want to display in this second window (indicated by the :2 that Excel adds to the end of the filename in the title bar).**

2. **Click the New Window command button or press Alt+WN again to create a third worksheet window; then click the tab of the worksheet that you want to display in this third window (indicated by the :3 that Excel adds to the end of the filename in the title bar).**

3. **Continue clicking the New Window command button or pressing Alt+WN to create a new window and then selecting the tab of the worksheet you want to display in that window for each worksheet you want to compare.**

4. **Click the Arrange All command button on the View tab or press Alt+WA and select one of the Arrange options in the Arrange Windows dialog box (as I describe next); then click OK or press Enter.**

When you open the Arrange Windows dialog box, you're presented with the following options:

- ✔ **Tiled:** Select this button to have Excel arrange and size the windows so that they all fit side by side on the screen. (Check out Figure 7-5 to see the screen that appears after you choose the Tiled button to organize four worksheet windows.)

- ✔ **Horizontal:** Select this button to have Excel size the windows equally and place them one above the other. (In Figure 7-6, you can see the screen that appears after you choose the Horizontal button to organize four worksheet windows.)

- ✔ **Vertical:** Select this button to have Excel size the windows equally and place them next to each other. (Look at Figure 7-7 to see the screen that appears after you choose the Vertical option to arrange four worksheet windows.)

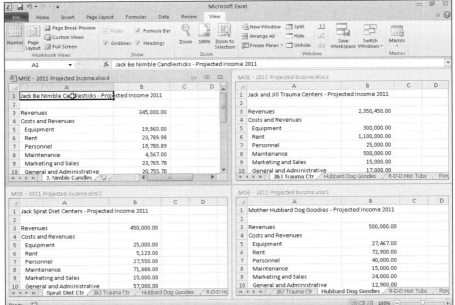

Figure 7-5:
Arrange
four work-
sheet
windows
with the
Tiled option.

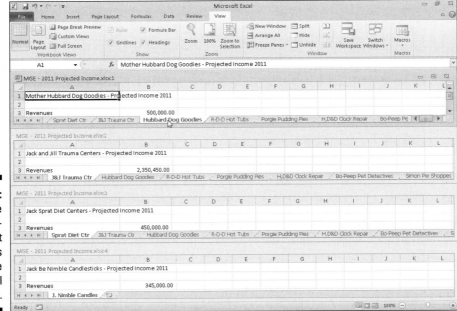

Figure 7-6:
Arrange
four work-
sheet
windows
with the
Horizontal
option.

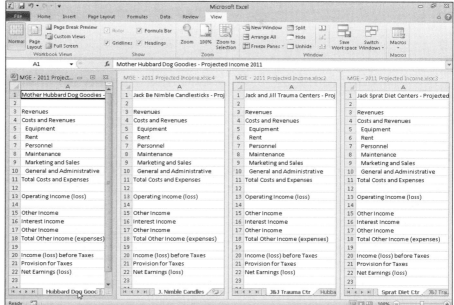

Figure 7-7:
Arrange
four work-
sheet
windows
with the
Vertical
option.

- **Cascade:** Select this button to have Excel arrange and size the windows so that they overlap one another with only their title bars showing. (See Figure 7-8 for the screen that appears after you select the Cascade option to arrange four worksheet windows.)

- **Windows of Active Workbook:** Select this check box to have Excel show only the windows that you have open in the current workbook. Otherwise, Excel also displays all the windows in any other workbooks you have open. Yes, it is possible to open more than one workbook — as well as more than one window within each open workbook — provided your computer has enough memory and you have enough stamina to keep track of all that information.

After you place windows in one arrangement or another, activate the one you want to use (if it isn't selected already) by clicking it. In the case of the cascade arrangement, you need to click the worksheet window's title bar, or you can click its button on the Windows Vista or XP taskbar. Use the button's ScreenTip to determine the number of the window when the buttons are too short to display this information. In Windows 7, you can click the Excel button in the taskbar, and then click the pop-up thumbnail for the worksheet you want.

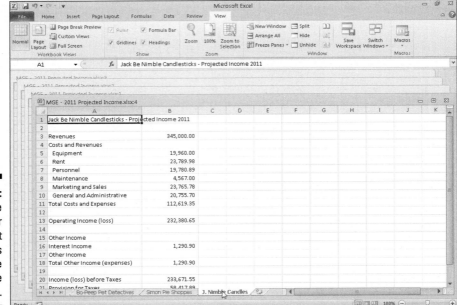

Figure 7-8:
Arrange
four
worksheet
windows
with the
Cascade
option.

When you click a worksheet window that has been tiled or placed in the horizontal or vertical arrangement, Excel indicates that the window is selected by highlighting its title bar and adding scroll bars to the window. When you click the title bar of a worksheet window you place in the cascade arrangement, the program displays the window on the top of the stack, highlights its title bar, and adds scroll bars.

You can temporarily zoom the window to full size by clicking the Maximize button on the window's title bar. When you finish your work in the full-size worksheet window, return it to its previous arrangement by clicking the window's Restore button.

To select the next tiled, horizontal, or vertical window on the screen or display the next window in a cascade arrangement with the keyboard, press Ctrl+F6. To select the previous tiled, horizontal, or vertical window or to display the previous window in a cascade arrangement, press Ctrl+Shift+F6. These keystrokes work to select the next and previous worksheet window even when the windows are maximized in the Excel program window.

If you close one of the windows by clicking Close (the X in the upper-right corner) or by pressing Ctrl+W, Excel doesn't automatically resize the other open windows to fill in the gap. Likewise, if you create another window by clicking the New Window command button on the View tab, Excel doesn't automatically arrange it in with the others. (In fact, the new window just sits on top of the other open windows.)

To fill in the gap created by closing a window or to integrate a newly opened window into the current arrangement, click the Arrange command button to open the Arrange Windows dialog box and click OK or press Enter. (The button you selected last time is still selected; if you want to choose a new arrangement, select a new button before you click OK.)

Don't try to close a particular worksheet window by choosing File⟹Close or by pressing Alt+FC because you'll only succeed in closing the entire workbook file, getting rid of all the worksheet windows you created.

When you save your workbook, Excel saves the current window arrangement as part of the file along with all the rest of the changes. If you don't want to save the current window arrangement, close all but one of the windows (by clicking their Close buttons or selecting their windows and then pressing Ctrl+W). Then click that last window's Maximize button and select the tab of the worksheet that you want to display the next time you open the workbook before saving the file.

Comparing Two Worksheets Side by Side

You can use the View Side by Side command button (the one with the picture of two sheets side by side like tiny tablets of the Ten Commandments) on the Ribbon's View tab to quickly and easily do a side-by-side comparison of any two worksheet windows that you have open. When you click this button (or press Alt+WB after opening two windows), Excel automatically tiles them horizontally (as though you had selected the Horizontal option in the Arrange Windows dialog box), as shown in Figure 7-9.

If you have more than two windows open at the time you click the View Side by Side command button (Alt+WB), Excel opens the Compare Side by Side dialog box where you click the name of the window that you want to compare with the one that's active at the time you choose the command. As soon as you click OK in the Compare Side by Side dialog box, Excel horizontally tiles the active window above the one you just selected.

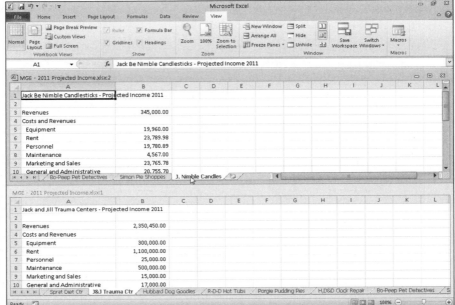

Figure 7-9: Comparing two worksheet windows side by side.

Immediately below the View Side by Side command button in the Window group of the View tab on the Ribbon, you find these following two command buttons useful when comparing windows side by side:

- ✔ **Synchronous Scrolling:** When this command button is selected (as it is by default), any scrolling that you do in the worksheet in the active window is mirrored and synchronized in the worksheet in the inactive window beneath it. To be able to scroll the worksheet in the active window independently of the inactive window, click the Synchronous Scrolling button to deselect it.

- ✔ **Reset Window Position:** Click this command button after you manually resize the active window (by dragging its size box or an edge of the window) to restore the two windows to their previous side-by-side arrangement.

Moving and Copying Sheets to Other Workbooks

In some situations, you need to move a particular worksheet or copy it from one workbook to another. To move or copy worksheets between workbooks, follow these steps:

1. **Open both the workbook with the worksheet(s) that you want to move or copy and the workbook that is to contain the moved or copied worksheet(s).**

   Choose File⇨Open or press Ctrl+O to open both the workbooks.

2. **Select the workbook that contains the worksheet(s) that you want to move or copy.**

   To select the workbook with the sheet(s) to move or copy, click its button on the Windows taskbar.

3. **Select the worksheet(s) that you want to move or copy.**

   To select a single worksheet, click its sheet tab. To select a group of neighboring sheets, click the first tab and then hold down Shift while you click the last tab. To select various nonadjacent sheets, click the first tab and then hold down Ctrl while you click each of the other sheet tabs.

4. **Right-click its sheet tab and then click Move or Copy on its shortcut menu.**

   Excel opens up the Move or Copy dialog box (similar to the one shown in Figure 7-10) in which you indicate whether you want to move or copy the selected sheet(s) and where to move or copy them.

5. **In the To Book drop-down list box, select the name of the workbook to which you want to copy or move the worksheets.**

   If you want to move or copy the selected worksheet(s) to a new workbook rather than to an existing one that you have open, select the (new book) option that appears at the very top of the To Book drop-down list.

6. **In the Before Sheet list box, select the name of the sheet that the worksheet(s) you're about to move or copy should precede. If you want the sheet(s) that you're moving or copying to appear at the end of the workbook, choose the (Move to End) option.**

7. **Select the Create a Copy check box to copy the selected worksheet(s) to the designated workbook (rather than move them).**

8. **Click OK or press Enter to complete the move or copy operation.**

If you prefer a more direct approach, you can move or copy sheets between open workbooks by dragging the sheet tabs from one workbook window to another. This method works with several sheets or a single sheet; just be sure that you select all the sheet tabs before you begin the drag-and-drop procedure.

To drag a worksheet from one workbook to another, you must open both workbooks. Click the Arrange All command button on the View tab or press Alt+WA and then select an arrangement (such as Horizontal or Vertical to put the workbook windows either on top of each other or side by side). Before you close the Arrange Windows dialog box, be sure that the Windows of Active Workbook check box is not selected; that is, does *not* contain a check mark.

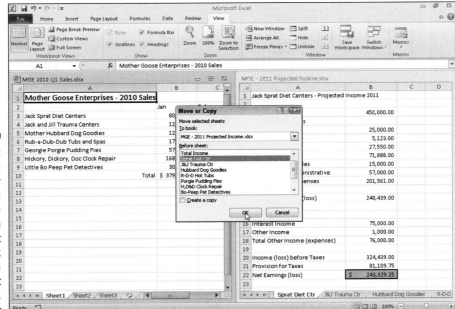

Figure 7-10:
Use the
Move or
Copy dialog
box to move
or copy from
the current
workbook
into a
different
workbook.

After arranging the workbook windows, drag the worksheet tab from one workbook to another. If you want to copy rather than move the worksheet, hold down the Ctrl key while you drag the sheet icon(s). To locate the worksheet in the new workbook, position the downward-pointing triangle that moves with the sheet icon in front of the worksheet tab where you want to insert it; then release the mouse button.

This drag-and-drop operation is one of those that you can't reverse by using Excel's Undo feature (see Chapter 4). This means that if you drop the sheet in the wrong workbook, you'll have to go get the wayward sheet yourself and then drag and drop it into the place where it once belonged!

In Figures 7-11 and 7-12, I show how easy it is to move or copy a worksheet from one workbook to another using this drag-and-drop method.

In Figure 7-11, you see two workbook windows: the MGE 2010 Q1 Sales workbook (left pane) and the MGE – 2011 Projected Income workbook (right pane). I arranged these workbook windows with the View Side by Side command button on the View tab. To move the Sprat Diet Ctr sheet from the MGE – 2011 Projected Income workbook to the MGE 2010 Q1 Sales workbook, I simply select the Sprat Diet Ctr sheet tab and drag the sheet icon to its new position before Sheet2 of the MGE 2010 Q1 Sales workbook.

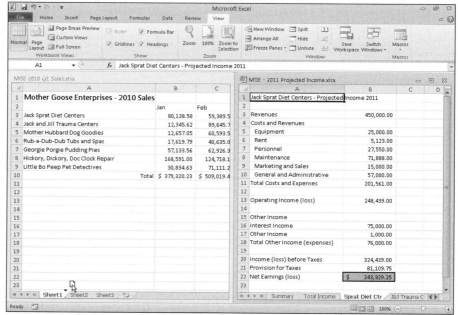

Figure 7-11:
Moving the worksheet to the MGE 2010 Q1 Sales workbook via drag and drop.

Now look at Figure 7-12 to see the workbooks after I release the mouse button. As you can see, Excel inserts the copy of the Sprat Diet Ctr worksheet into the MGE 2010 Q1 Sales workbook at the place indicated by the triangle that accompanies the sheet icon (between Sheet1 and Sheet2 in this example).

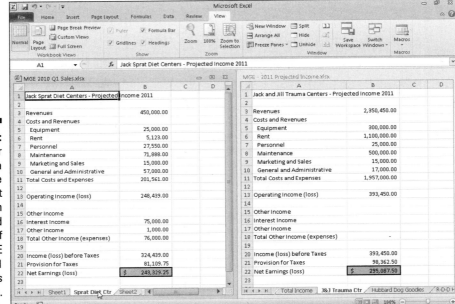

Figure 7-12: After inserting a copy of the worksheet between Sheet1 and Sheet2 of the MGE 2010 Q1 Sales workbook.

To Sum Up . . .

I'd be remiss if I didn't introduce you to the fascinating subject of creating a *summary worksheet* that recaps or totals the values stored in a bunch of other worksheets in the workbook.

The best way that I can show you how to create a summary worksheet is to walk you through the procedure of making one (entitled Total Projected Income) for the MGE – 2011 Projected Income workbook. This summary worksheet totals the projected revenue and expenses for all the companies that Mother Goose Enterprises owns.

Because the MGE – 2011 Projected Income workbook already contains nine worksheets, each with the 2011 projected revenue and expenses for one of these companies, and because these worksheets are all laid out in the same arrangement, creating this summary worksheet will be a breeze:

1. I insert a new worksheet in front of the other worksheets in the MGE – 2011 Projected Income workbook and rename its sheet tab from Sheet1 to Total Income.

   To find out how to insert a new worksheet, refer to this chapter's "Don't Short-Sheet Me!" section. To find out how to rename a sheet tab, read the earlier "A worksheet by any other name . . ." section.

2. Next, I enter the worksheet title **Mother Goose Enterprises – Total Projected Income 2011** in cell A1.

   Do this by selecting cell A1 and then typing the text.

3. Finally, I copy the rest of the row headings for column A (containing the revenue and expense descriptions) from the Sprat Diet Ctr worksheet to the Total Income worksheet.

   To do this, select cell A3 in the Total Income sheet and then click the Sprat Diet Ctr tab. Select the cell range A3:A22 in this sheet; then press Ctrl+C, click the Total Income tab again, and press Enter.

I am now ready to create the master SUM formula that totals the revenues of all nine companies in cell B3 of the Total Income sheet:

1. I start by clicking cell B3 and then clicking the AutoSum button in the Editing group on the Ribbon's Home tab.

   Excel then puts =SUM( ) in the cell with the insertion point placed between the two parentheses.

2. I click the Sprat Diet Ctr sheet tab, and then click its cell B3 to select the projected revenues for the Jack Sprat Diet Centers.

   The Formula bar reads =SUM('Sprat Diet Ctr'!B3) after selecting this cell.

3. Next, I type a comma (,) — the comma starts a new argument. I click the J&J Trauma Ctr sheet tab and then click its cell B3 to select projected revenues for the Jack and Jill Trauma Centers.

   The Formula bar now reads =SUM('Sprat Diet Ctr'!B3,'J&J Trauma Ctr'!B3) after I select this cell.

4. I continue in this manner, typing a comma (to start a new argument) and then selecting cell B3 with the projected revenues for all the other companies in the following seven sheets.

   At the end of this procedure, the Formula bar now appears with the whopping SUM formula shown on the Formula bar in Figure 7-13.

5. To complete the SUM formula in cell B3 of the Total Income worksheet, I then click the Enter box in the Formula bar (I could press Enter on my keyboard, as well).

   In Figure 7-13, note the result in cell B3. As you can see in the Formula bar, the master SUM formula that returns 6,681,450.78 to cell B3 of the Total Income worksheet gets its result by summing the values in B3 in all nine of the supporting worksheets.

If you want to select the same cell across multiple worksheets, you can press and hold the Shift key, and then select the last worksheet. All worksheets in between the first and last will be included in the selection, or in the case above, the calculation.

All that's left to do now is to use AutoFill to copy the master formula in cell B3 down to row 22 as follows:

1. With cell B3 still selected, I drag the AutoFill handle in the lower-right corner of cell B3 down to cell B22 to copy the formula for summing the values for the nine companies down this column.

2. Then I delete the SUM formulas from cells B4, B12, B14, B15, and B19 (all of which contain zeros because these cells have no income or expenses to total).

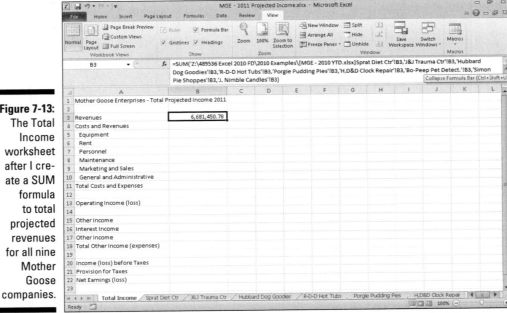

Figure 7-13:
The Total Income worksheet after I create a SUM formula to total projected revenues for all nine Mother Goose companies.

In Figure 7-14, you see the first section of the summary Total Income worksheet after I copy the formula created in cell B3 and after I delete the formulas from the cells that should be blank (all those that came up 0 in column B).

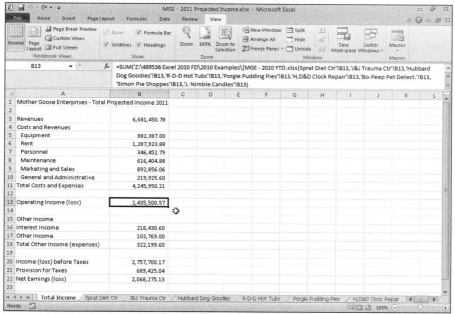

Figure 7-14:
The Total
Income
worksheet
after I copy
the SUM
formula and
delete
formulas
that return
zero values.

Part IV
Digging Data Analysis

The 5th Wave   By Rich Tennant

© RICHTENNANT

"Unless there's a corrupt cell in our spreadsheet analysis concerning the importance of trunk space, this should be a big seller next year."

In this part . . .

In this part, you find out how to use basic what-if analysis tools in your spreadsheets so that you can better predict the changes you must make to achieve desired goals and avoid unwanted results. You're introduced to Excel's most versatile summary tool — the pivot table and its associated pivot chart. You find out how to use these extraordinary tools to obtain varied perspectives on the data you work with — perspectives that can enable you to quickly uncover and easily spot trends with both potentially disastrous consequences and golden opportunities.

Chapter 8

Doing What-If Analysis

*I*t would be a big mistake to regard Excel 2010 merely as a fancy calculator that shines at performing static computations, for the program excels (if you don't mind the pun) at performing various types of more dynamic *what-if* analysis as well. What-if analysis enables you to explore the possibilities in a worksheet by inputting a variety of promising or probable values into the same equation and letting you see the possible outcomes in black and white (or, at least, in the cells of the spreadsheet).

In Excel 2010, what-if analysis comes in a wide variety of flavors (some of which are more involved than others). In this chapter, I introduce you to these three simple and straightforward methods:

✔ **Data tables** enable you to see how changing one or two variables affect the bottom line (for example, you may want to know what happens to the net profit if you fall into a 25 percent tax bracket, a 35 percent tax bracket, and so on).

✔ **Goal seeking** enables you to find out what it takes to reach a predetermined objective, such as how much you have to sell to make a $15 million profit this year.

✔ **Scenarios** let you set up and test a wide variety of cases, all the way from the best-case scenario (profits grow by 8.5 percent) to the worst-case scenario (you don't make any profit and actually lose money).

Playing What-If with Data Tables

Data tables enable you to enter a series of possible values that Excel then plugs into a single formula. Excel supports two types of data tables: a one-variable data table that substitutes a series of possible values for a single input value in a formula and a two-variable data table that substitutes series of possible values for two input values in a single formula.

Both types of data tables use the very same Data Table dialog box that you open by clicking Data➪What-If Analysis➪Data Table on the Ribbon or pressing Alt+AWT. The Data Table dialog box contains two text boxes: Row Input Cell and Column Input Cell.

When creating a one-variable data table, you designate one cell in the worksheet that serves either as the Row Input Cell (if you've entered the series of possible values across columns of a single row) *or* as the Column Input Cell (if you've entered the series of possible values down the rows of a single column).

When creating a two-variable data table, you designate two cells in the worksheet and, therefore, use both text boxes. One cell serves as the Row Input Cell that substitutes the series of possible values you've entered across columns of a single row, and the other cell serves as the Column Input Cell that substitutes the series of possible values you've entered down the rows of a single column.

Creating a one-variable data table

Figure 8-1 shows a 2011 Sales Projections spreadsheet for which a one-variable data table is to be created. In this worksheet, the projected sales amount in cell B5 is calculated by adding last year's sales total in cell B2 to the amount that we expect it to grow in 2011 (calculated by multiplying last year's total in cell B2 by the growth percentage in cell B3), giving you the formula:

```
=B2+(B2*B3)
```

Because I clicked the Create From Selection command button on the Ribbon's Formulas tab after making A2:B5 the selection and accepted the Left Column check box default, the formula uses the row headings in column A and reads:

```
=Sales_2010+(Sales_2010*Growth_2011)
```

As you can see, I entered a column of possible growth rates ranging from 1% all the way to 5.5% down column B in the range B8:B17. To create the one-variable data table shown in Figure 8-2 that plugs each of these values into the sales growth formula, I follow these simple steps:

1. **Copy the original formula entered in cell B5 into cell C7 by typing = (equal to) and then clicking cell B5 to create the formula `=Projected_Sales_2011`.**

   The copy of the original formula (to substitute the series of different growth rates in B8:B17 into) is now the column heading for the one-variable data table.

2. **Select the cell range B7:C17.**

   The range of the data table includes the formula along with the various growth rates.

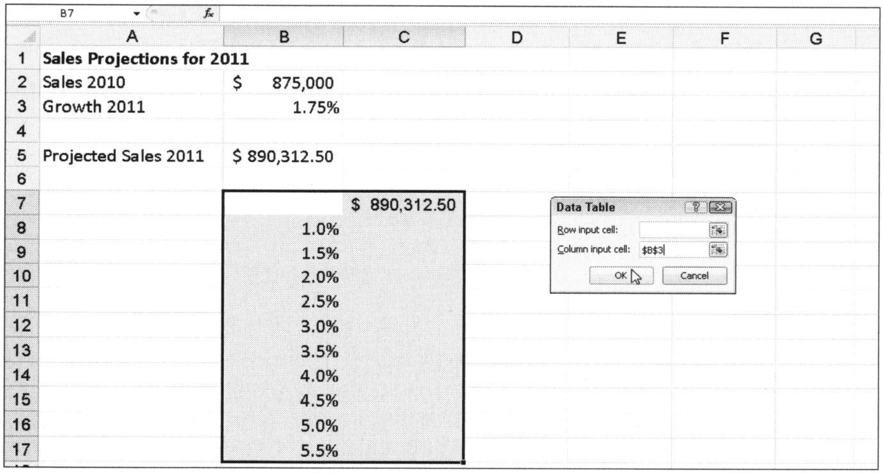

	A	B	C
1	**Sales Projections for 2011**		
2	Sales 2010	$ 875,000	
3	Growth 2011	1.75%	
4			
5	Projected Sales 2011	$ 890,312.50	
6			
7			$ 890,312.50
8		1.0%	
9		1.5%	
10		2.0%	
11		2.5%	
12		3.0%	
13		3.5%	
14		4.0%	
15		4.5%	
16		5.0%	
17		5.5%	

Figure 8-1: Sales projection spreadsheet with a column of possible growth percentages to plug into a one-variable data table.

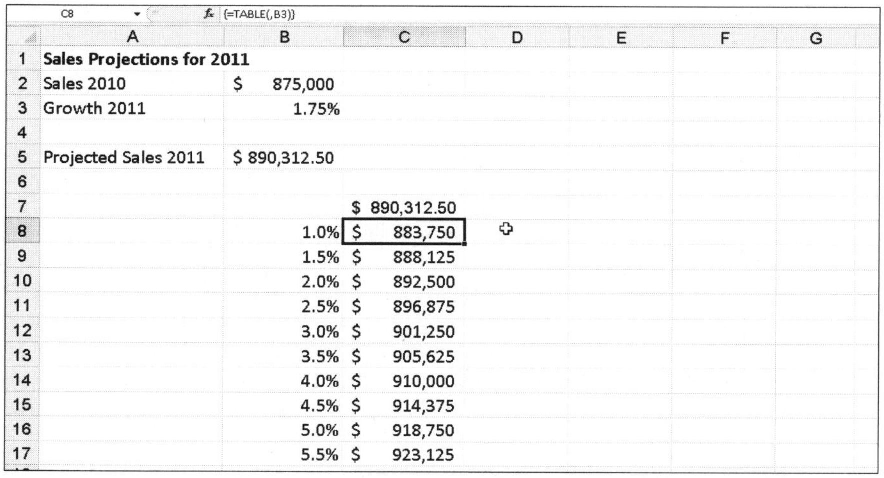

	A	B	C
1	**Sales Projections for 2011**		
2	Sales 2010	$ 875,000	
3	Growth 2011	1.75%	
4			
5	Projected Sales 2011	$ 890,312.50	
6			
7			$ 890,312.50
8		1.0%	$ 883,750
9		1.5%	$ 888,125
10		2.0%	$ 892,500
11		2.5%	$ 896,875
12		3.0%	$ 901,250
13		3.5%	$ 905,625
14		4.0%	$ 910,000
15		4.5%	$ 914,375
16		5.0%	$ 918,750
17		5.5%	$ 923,125

Figure 8-2: Sales projection spreadsheet after creating the one-variable data table in the range C8:C17.

3. **Click Data⇨What-If Analysis⇨Data Table on the Ribbon.**

   Excel opens the Data Table dialog box.

4. **Click the Column Input Cell text box in the Data Table dialog box and then click cell B3, the Growth_2011 cell with the original percentage, in the worksheet.**

   Excel inserts the absolute cell address, $B$3, into the Column Input Cell text box.

5. **Click OK to close the Data Table dialog box.**

   As soon as you click OK, Excel creates the data table in the range C8:C17 by entering a formula using its TABLE function into this range. Each copy of this formula in the data table uses the growth rate percentage in the same row in column B to determine the possible outcome.

6. **Click cell C7, then click the Format Painter command button in the Clipboard group on the Home tab and drag through the cell range C8:C17.**

   Excel copies the Accounting number format to the range of possible outcomes calculated by this data table.

A couple of important things to note about the one-variable data table created in this spreadsheet:

✔ If you modify any growth rate percentages in the cell range B8:B17, Excel immediately updates the associated projected sales result in the data table. To prevent Excel from updating the data table until you click the Calculate Now (F9) or Calculate Sheet command button (Shift+F9) on the Formulas Tab, click the Calculation Options button on the Formulas tab and then click the Automatic Except for Data Tables option (Alt+MXE).

✔ If you try to delete any single TABLE formula in the cell range C8:C17, Excel displays a Cannot Change Part of a Data Table alert. You must select the entire range of formulas (C8:C17 in this case) before you press Delete or click the Clear or Delete button on the Home tab.

Array formulas and the TABLE function in data tables

Excel's Data Table feature works by creating a special kind of formula called an array formula in the blank cells of the table. An array formula (enclosed in a pair of curly brackets) is unique in that Excel creates copies of the formula into each blank cell of the selection at the time you enter the original formula. (You don't make the formula copies yourself.) As a result, editing changes, such as moving or deleting, are restricted to the entire cell range containing the array formula — it's always all or nothing when editing these babies!

Creating a two-variable data table

To create a two-variable data table, you enter two ranges of possible input values for the same formula in the Data Table dialog box: a range of values for the Row Input Cell across the first row of the table and a range of values for the Column Input Cell down the first column of the table. You then enter the formula (or a copy of it) in the cell located at the intersection of this row and column of input values.

Figure 8-3 illustrates this type of situation. This version of the projected sales spreadsheet uses two variables to calculate the projected sales for year 2011: a growth rate as a percentage of increase over last year's sales (in cell B3 named Growth_2011) and expenses calculated as a percentage of last year's sales (in cell B4 named Expenses_2011). In this example, the original formula created in cell B5 is a bit more complex:

```
=Sales_2010+(Sales_2010*Growth_2011) -
          (Sales_2010*Expenses_2011)
```

To set up the two-variable data table, I added a row of possible Expenses_2011 percentages in the range C7:F7 to a column of possible Growth_2011 percentages in the range B8:B17. I then copied the original formula named Projected_Sales_2011 from cell B5 to cell B7, the cell at the intersection of this row of Expenses_2011 percentages and column of Growth_2011 percentages with the formula:

```
=Projected_Sales_2011
```

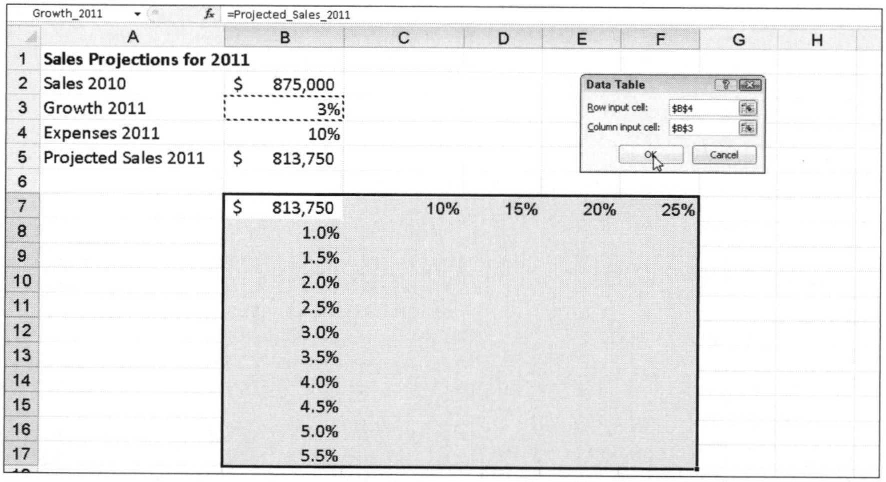

Figure 8-3: Sales projection spreadsheet with a series of possible growth and expense percentages to plug in to a two-variable data table.

With these few steps, I created the two-variable data table you see in Figure 8-4:

1. **Select the cell range B7:F17.**

   This cell incorporates the copy of the original formula along with the row of possible expenses and growth rate percentages.

2. **Click Data➪What-If Analysis➪Data Table on the Ribbon.**

   Excel opens the Data Table dialog box with the insertion point in the Row Input Cell text box.

3. **Click cell B4 to enter the absolute cell address, $B$4, in the Row Input Cell text box.**

4. **Click the Column Input Cell text box and then click cell B3 to enter the absolute cell address, $B$3, in this text box.**

5. **Click OK to close the Data Table dialog box.**

   Excel fills the blank cells of the data table with a TABLE formula using B4 as the Row Input Cell and B3 as the Column Input Cell.

6. **Click cell B7, then click the Format Painter command button in the Clipboard group on the Home tab and drag through the cell range C8:F17 to copy the Accounting number format with no decimal places to this range.**

   This Accounting number format is too long to display given the current width of columns C through F — indicated by the ###### symbols. With the range C8:F17 still selected from using the Format Painter, Step 7 fixes this problem.

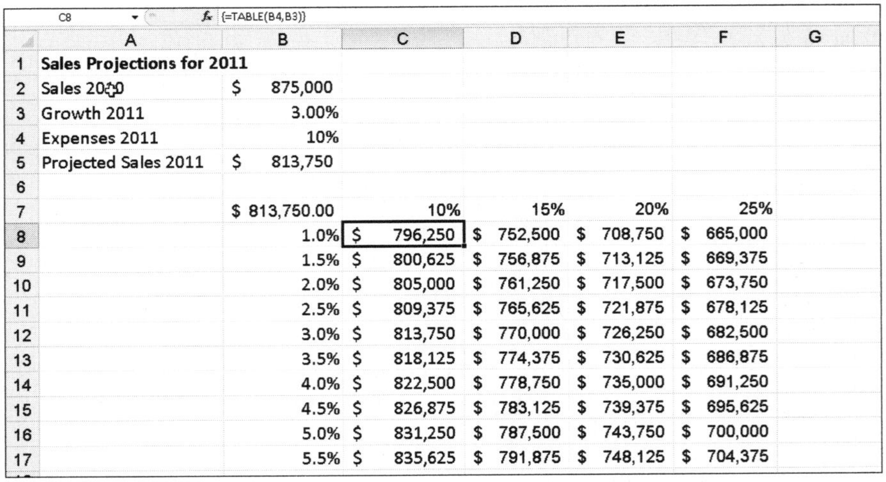

Figure 8-4: Sales projection spreadsheet after creating the two-variable data table in the range C8:F17.

	A	B	C	D	E	F	G
	C8 ▾	fx {=TABLE(B4,B3)}					
1	Sales Projections for 2011						
2	Sales 2010	$ 875,000					
3	Growth 2011	3.00%					
4	Expenses 2011	10%					
5	Projected Sales 2011	$ 813,750					
6							
7		$ 813,750.00	10%	15%	20%	25%	
8		1.0%	$ 796,250	$ 752,500	$ 708,750	$ 665,000	
9		1.5%	$ 800,625	$ 756,875	$ 713,125	$ 669,375	
10		2.0%	$ 805,000	$ 761,250	$ 717,500	$ 673,750	
11		2.5%	$ 809,375	$ 765,625	$ 721,875	$ 678,125	
12		3.0%	$ 813,750	$ 770,000	$ 726,250	$ 682,500	
13		3.5%	$ 818,125	$ 774,375	$ 730,625	$ 686,875	
14		4.0%	$ 822,500	$ 778,750	$ 735,000	$ 691,250	
15		4.5%	$ 826,875	$ 783,125	$ 739,375	$ 695,625	
16		5.0%	$ 831,250	$ 787,500	$ 743,750	$ 700,000	
17		5.5%	$ 835,625	$ 791,875	$ 748,125	$ 704,375	

7. **Click the Format command button in the Cells group of the Home tab and then click AutoFit Column Width on its drop-down menu.**

The array formula {=TABLE(B4,B3)} that Excel creates for the two-variable data table in this example specifies both a Row Input Cell argument (B4) and a Column Input Cell argument (B3). (See the nearby "Array formulas and the TABLE function in data tables" sidebar.) Because this single array formula is entered into the entire data table range of C8:F17, any editing (in terms of moving or deleting) is restricted to this range.

Playing What-If with Goal Seeking

Sometimes when doing what-if analysis, you have a particular outcome in mind, such as a target sales amount or growth percentage. When you need to do this type of analysis, you use Excel's Goal Seek feature to find the input values needed to achieve the desired goal.

To use the Goal Seek feature located on the What-If Analysis button's drop-down menu, you need to select the cell containing the formula that will return the result you're seeking (referred to as the *set cell* in the Goal Seek dialog box). Then indicate the target value you want the formula to return as well as the location of the input value that Excel can change to reach this target.

Figures 8-5 and 8-6 illustrate how you can use the Goal Seek feature to find out how much sales must increase to realize first quarter income of $300,000 (given certain growth, cost of goods sold, and expense assumptions) in a Sales Forecast table.

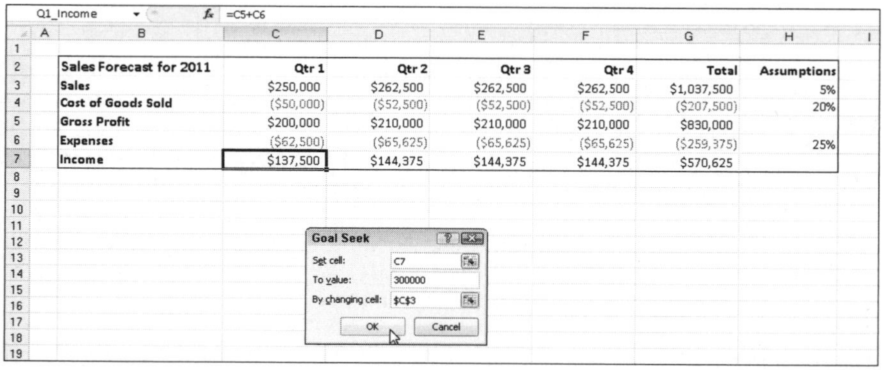

Figure 8-5:
Using goal seeking to find out how much sales must increase to reach a target income.

	Q1_Income	fx =C5+C6						
	A	B	C	D	E	F	G	H	I
2		Sales Forecast for 2011	Qtr 1	Qtr 2	Qtr 3	Qtr 4	Total	Assumptions
3		Sales	$250,000	$262,500	$262,500	$262,500	$1,037,500	5%
4		Cost of Goods Sold	($50,000)	($52,500)	($52,500)	($52,500)	($207,500)	20%
5		Gross Profit	$200,000	$210,000	$210,000	$210,000	$830,000	
6		Expenses	($62,500)	($65,625)	($65,625)	($65,625)	($259,375)	25%
7		Income	$137,500	$144,375	$144,375	$144,375	$570,625	

Goal Seek

Set cell: C7

To value: 300000

By changing cell: $C$3

OK   Cancel

C7	▼	fx	=C5+C6				

	A	B	C	D	E	F	G	H	I
1									
2		Sales Forecast for 2011	Qtr 1	Qtr 2	Qtr 3	Qtr 4	Total	Assumptions	
3		Sales	$545,455	$572,727	$572,727	$572,727	$2,263,636	5%	
4		Cost of Goods Sold	($109,091)	($114,545)	($114,545)	($114,545)	($452,727)	20%	
5		Gross Profit	$436,364	$458,182	$458,182	$458,182	$1,810,909		
6		Expenses	($136,364)	($143,182)	($143,182)	($143,182)	($565,909)	25%	
7		Income	$300,000	$315,000	$315,000	$315,000	$1,245,000		
8									

Goal Seek Status

Goal Seeking with Cell C7 found a solution.

Target value: 300000
Current value: $300,000

Step | Pause | OK | Cancel

Figure 8-6:
Forecast
spreadsheet
showing
goal seeking
solution.

To find out how much sales must increase to return a net income of $300,000 in the first quarter, select cell C7, which contains the formula that calculates the forecast for the first quarter of 2011 before you click Data➪What-If Analysis➪Goal Seek on the Ribbon or press Alt+AWG.

This action opens the Goal Seek dialog box, similar to the one shown in Figure 8-5. Because cell C7 is the active cell when you open this dialog box, the Set Cell text box already contains the cell reference C7. You then select the To Value text box and enter **300000** as the goal. Then, you click the By Changing Cell text box and click cell C3 in the worksheet (the cell that contains the first quarter sales) to enter the absolute cell address, $C$3, in this text box.

Figure 8-6 shows you the Goal Seek Status dialog box that appears when you click OK in the Goal Seek dialog box to have Excel go ahead and adjust the sales figure to reach your desired income figure. As this figure shows, Excel increases the sales in cell B3 from $250,000 to $545,455, which, in turn, returns $300,000 as the income in cell C7.

The Goal Seek Status dialog box informs you that goal seeking has found a solution and that the current value and target value are now the same. When this is not the case, the Step and Pause buttons in the dialog box become active, and you can have Excel perform further iterations to try to narrow and ultimately eliminate the gap between the target and current value.

If you want to keep the values entered in the worksheet as a result of goal seeking, click OK to close the Goal Seek Status dialog box. If you want to return to the original values, click the Cancel button instead.

To flip between the "after" and "before" values when you've closed the Goal Seek Status dialog box, click the Undo button or press Ctrl+Z to display the original values before goal seeking and click the Redo button or press Ctrl+Y to display the values engendered by the goal seeking solution.

Examining Different Cases with Scenario Manager

Excel's Scenario Manager option on the What-If Analysis button's drop-down menu on the Data tab of the Ribbon enables you to create and save sets of different input values that produce different calculated results, named *scenarios* (such as Best Case, Worst Case, and Most Likely Case). Because these scenarios are saved as part of the workbook, you can use their values to play what-if simply by opening the Scenario Manager and having Excel show the scenario in the worksheet.

After setting up the various scenarios for a spreadsheet, you can also have Excel create a summary report that shows both the input values used in each scenario as well as the results they produce in your formula.

Setting up the various scenarios

The key to creating the various scenarios for a table is to identify the various cells in the data whose values can vary in each scenario. You then select these cells (known as changing cells) in the worksheet before you open the Scenario Manager dialog box by clicking Data⇨What-If Analysis⇨Scenario Manager on the Ribbon or by pressing Alt+AWS.

Figure 8-7 shows the Sales Forecast table for 2011 after selecting the three changing cells in the worksheet — H3 named Sales_Growth, H4 named COGS (Cost of Goods Sold), and H6 named Expenses — and then opening the Scenario Manager dialog box (Alt+AWS).

I want to create three scenarios using the following sets of values for the three changing cells:

- ✔ **Most Likely Case** where the Sales_Growth percentage is 5%, COGS is 20%, and Expenses is 25%

- ✔ **Best Case** where the Sales_Growth percentage is 8%, COGS is 18%, and Expenses is 20%

- ✔ **Worst Case** where the Sales_Growth percentage is 2%, COGS is 25%, and Expenses is 35%

To create the first scenario, I click the Add button in the Scenario Manager dialog box to open the Add Scenario dialog box, enter **Most Likely Case** in the Scenario Name box, and then click OK. (Remember that the three cells currently selected in the worksheet, H3, H4, and H6, are already listed in the Changing Cells text box of this dialog box.)

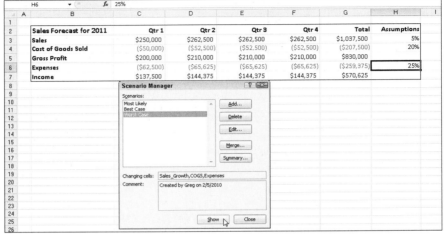

Figure 8-7:
Adding
various
scenarios
to the Sales
Forecast for
2011 table.

Excel then displays the Scenario Values dialog box where I accept the following values already entered in each of the three text boxes (from the Sales Forecast for 2011 table), Sales_Growth, COGS, and Expenses, before clicking its Add button:

- **0.05** in the Sales_Growth text box
- **0.20** in COGS text box
- **0.25** in the Expenses text box

Always assign range names as described in Chapter 6 to your changing cells before you begin creating the various scenarios that use them. That way, Excel always displays the cell's range names rather than their addresses in the Scenario Values dialog box.

After clicking the Add button, Excel redisplays the Add Scenario dialog box where I enter **Best Case** in the Scenario Name box and the following values in the Scenario Values dialog box:

- **0.08** in the Sales_Growth text box
- **0.18** in the COGS text box
- **0.20** in the Expenses text box

After making these changes, I click the Add button again. Doing this opens the Add Scenario dialog box where I enter **Worst Case** as the scenario name and the following scenario values:

- ✔ **0.02** in the Sales_Growth text box
- ✔ **0.25** in the COGS text box
- ✔ **0.35** in the Expenses text box

Because this is the last scenario that I want to add, I then click the OK button instead of Add. Doing this opens the Scenario Manager dialog box again, this time displaying the names of all three scenarios, Most Likely Case, Best Case, and Worst Case in its Scenarios list box. To have Excel plug the changing values assigned to any of these three scenarios into the Sales Forecast table, I click the scenario name in this list box followed by the Show button.

After adding the various scenarios for a table in your spreadsheet, don't forget to save the workbook after closing the Scenario Manager dialog box. That way, you'll have access to the various scenarios each time you open the workbook in Excel simply by opening the Scenario Manager, selecting the scenario name, and clicking the Show button.

Producing a summary report

After adding your scenarios to a table in a spreadsheet, you can have Excel produce a summary report like the one shown in Figure 8-8. This report displays the changing and resulting values for not only all the scenarios you've defined but also the current values that are entered into the changing cells in the worksheet table at the time you generate the report.

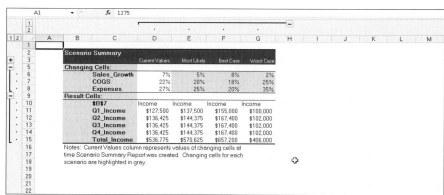

Figure 8-8:
Scenario
Summary
report
showing
the various
scenarios
added to
the Sales
Forecast for
2011 table.

To produce a summary report, open the Scenario Manager dialog box (Data⇨What-If Analysis⇨Scenario Manager or Alt+AWS) and then click the Summary button to open the Scenario Summary dialog box.

This dialog box gives you a choice between creating a (static) Scenario Summary (the default) and a (dynamic) Scenario PivotTable Report (see Chapter 9). You can also modify the range of cells in the table that is included in the Result Cells section of the summary report by adjusting the cell range in the Result Cells text box before you click OK to generate the report.

After you click OK, Excel creates the summary report for the changing values in all the scenarios (and the current worksheet) along with the calculated values in the Result Cells on a new worksheet (named Scenario Summary). You can then rename and reposition the Scenario Summary worksheet before you save it as part of the workbook file.

Performing what-if analysis with the Solver add-in

In addition to the straightforward what-if analysis offered by the Scenario Manager, Goal Seek, and Data Table options on the What-If Analysis button's drop-down menu on the Data tab of the Ribbon, Excel 2010 supports a more complex what-if analysis in the form of the Solver add-in program (see Chapter 12 for information on add-ins). With the Solver, you can create models that not only involve changes to multiple input values but also impose constraints on these inputs or on the results themselves. For details on using the Solver in Excel 2010, see my *Microsoft Office Excel 2010 All-in-One For Dummies.*

Chapter 9

Playing with Pivot Tables

· ·

In This Chapter

▶ Understanding what makes a pivot table tick

▶ Creating a new pivot table

▶ Formatting a new pivot table

▶ Sorting and filtering the pivot table data

▶ Modifying the structure and layout of a pivot table

▶ Creating a pivot chart

· ·

*P*ivot table is a name given to a special type of summary table that's unique to Microsoft Excel. Pivot tables are great for summarizing particular values in a data list or database because they do their magic without making you create formulas to perform the calculations. They also enable you to quickly and easily examine and analyze relationships inherent in their data sources (either data lists you maintain in Excel or external database tables you maintain with a standalone program, such as Microsoft Office Access).

Pivot tables also let you play around with the arrangement of the summarized data — even after you generate the table. This capability of changing the arrangement of the summarized data on the fly simply by rotating row and column headings gives the pivot table its name. And, if you're the type who relates better to data represented in pictorial form, Excel enables you to summarize your data list graphically as a pivot chart using any of the many, many chart types now supported by the program.

Pivot Tables: The Ultimate Data Summary

Pivot tables are so very versatile because they enable you to summarize data by using a variety of summary functions (although totals created with the SUM function will probably remain your old standby). When setting up the original pivot table (as described in the following section) you make several decisions: what summary function to use, which columns (fields) the summary function is applied to, and which columns (fields) these computations are tabulated with.

Pivot tables are perfect for cross-tabulating one set of data in your data list with another. For example, you can create a pivot table from an employee database table that totals the salaries for each job category cross-tabulated (arranged) by department or job site.

Producing a Pivot Table

Creating a pivot table has never been as easy as it is in Excel 2010. You simply open the worksheet that contains the data list (see Chapter 11) you want to summarize with the pivot table, position the cell cursor somewhere in the cells of this list, and then click the PivotTable command button on the Ribbon's Insert tab or press Alt+NVT.

Excel then opens the Create PivotTable dialog box and selects all the data in the list containing the cell cursor (indicated by a marquee around the cell range). You can then adjust the cell range in the Table/Range text box under the Select a Table or Range button if the marquee does not include all the data to summarize in the pivot table. By default, Excel builds the new pivot table on a new worksheet it adds to the workbook. If, however, you want the pivot table to appear on the same worksheet, click the Existing Worksheet button and then indicate the location of the first cell of the new table in the Location text box, as shown in Figure 9-1. (Just be sure that this new pivot table isn't going to overlap any existing tables of data).

If the data source for your pivot table is an external database table created with a separate database management program, such as Access, you need to click the Use an External Data Source button, click the Choose Connection button, and then click the name of the connection in the Existing Connections dialog box. (See Chapter 11 for information on establishing a connection with an external file and importing its data through a query.)

After you indicate the source and location for the new pivot table in the Create PivotTable dialog box and click its OK button, the program adds a blank grid for the new table and displays a PivotTable Field List task pane on the right side of the Worksheet area (see Figure 9-2). The PivotTable Field List task pane is divided into two areas: the Choose Fields to Add to Report list box with the names of all the fields in the data list you can select as the source of the table preceded by empty check boxes and a Drag Fields between Areas Below section divided into four drop zones (Report Filter, Column Labels, Row Labels, and Values).

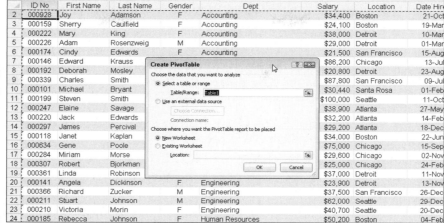

Figure 9-1:
Indicate
the data
source and
pivot table
location in
the Create
PivotTable
dialog box.

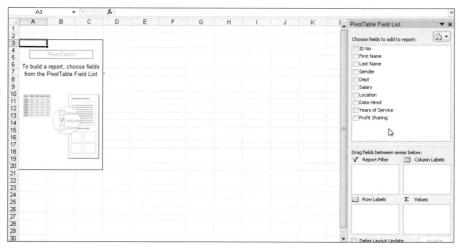

Figure 9-2:
New pivot
table dis-
playing the
blank table
grid and the
PivotTable
Field List
task pane.

To complete the new pivot table, all you have to do is assign the fields in the PivotTable Field List task pane to the various parts of the table. You do this by dragging a field name from the Choose Fields to Add to Report list box and dropping it in one of the four areas below called drop zones:

 ✓ **Report Filter:** This area contains the fields that enable you to page through the data summaries shown in the actual pivot table by filtering out sets of data — they act as the filters for the report. For example, if you designate the Year field from a data list as a report filter, you can display data summaries in the pivot table for individual years or for all years represented in the data list.

> ✔ **Column Labels:** This area contains the fields that determine the arrangement of data shown in the columns of the pivot table.
>
> ✔ **Row Labels:** This area contains the fields that determine the arrangement of data shown in the rows of the pivot table.
>
> ✔ **Values:** This area contains the fields that determine which data are presented in the cells of the pivot table — they are the values that are summarized in its last column (totaled by default).

To understand how these various zones relate to a pivot table, look at the completed pivot table in Figure 9-3.

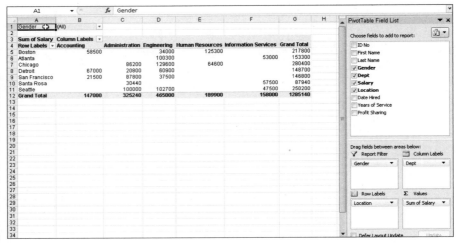

Figure 9-3: Completed pivot table after adding the fields from the employee data list to the various drop zones.

For this pivot table, I assigned the Gender field from the data list (a field that contains F (for female) or M (for male) to indicate the employee's gender in the Report Filter drop zone. I also assigned the Dept field (that contains the names of the various departments in the company) to the Column Labels drop zone, the Location field (that contains the names of the various cities with corporate offices) to the Row Labels drop zone, and the Salary field to the Values drop zone. As a result, this pivot table now displays the sum of the salaries for both the male and female employees in each department (across the columns) and then presents these sums by their corporate location (in each row).

As soon as you create a new pivot table (or select the cell of an existing table in a worksheet), Excel selects the Options tab of the PivotTable Tools contextual tab that automatically appears in the Ribbon. Among the many groups on this tab, you find the Show group that contains the following useful command buttons:

- ✔ **Field List** to hide and redisplay the PivotTable Field List task pane on the right side of the Worksheet area

- ✔ +/- **Buttons** to hide and redisplay the expand (+) and collapse (-) buttons in front of particular column fields or row fields that enable you to temporarily remove and then redisplay their particular summarized values in the pivot table

- ✔ **Field Headers** to hide and redisplay the fields assigned to the Column Labels and Row Labels in the pivot table

Formatting a Pivot Table

Excel 2010 makes formatting a new pivot table you've added to a worksheet as quick and easy as formatting any other table of data or list of data. All you need to do is click a cell of the pivot table to add the PivotTable Tools contextual tab to the Ribbon and then click its Design tab to display its command buttons.

The Design tab on the PivotTable Tools contextual tab is divided into three groups:

- ✔ **Layout** group that enables you to add subtotals and grand totals to the pivot table and modify its basic layout

- ✔ **PivotTable Style Options** group that enables you to refine the pivot table style you select for the table using the PivotTable Styles gallery to the immediate right

- ✔ **PivotTable Styles** group that contains the gallery of styles you can apply to the active pivot table by clicking the desired style thumbnail

Figure 9-4 shows the pivot table created for the Employee Data List in Figure 9-3 after applying Pivot Style Medium 10 in the PivotTable Styles gallery to it. This style applies a light version of the background color (rose) to the Gender Report Filter field and a darker version to the Values Label (Sum of Salary), Dept Column Labels, and Location Row Labels (so dark in fact, that Excel automatically reverses the label text to white).

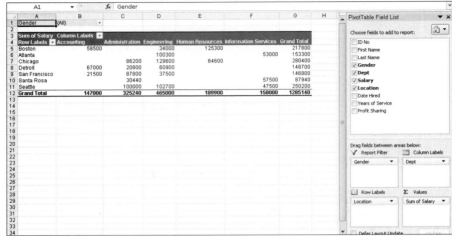

Figure 9-4:
New pivot table formatted with Pivot Style Medium 10 selected from the PivotTable Styles gallery.

Refining the Pivot Table style

After applying any style from the Light, Medium, or Dark group in the PivotTable Styles gallery, you can then use Live Preview to see how the pivot table would look in any style that you mouse over in the gallery.

After selecting a style from the gallery in the PivotTable Styles group on the Design tab, you can then refine the style using the check box command buttons in the PivotTable Style Options group. For example, you can add banding to the columns or rows of a style that doesn't already use alternate shading to add more contrast to the table data by putting a check mark in the Banded Rows or Banded Columns check box or remove this banding by clearing these check boxes of their check marks.

Formatting the values in the pivot table

To format the summed values entered as the data items of the pivot table with an Excel number format, you follow these steps:

1. **Click the field in the table that contains the words "Sum of" and the name of the field whose values are summarized there, click the Active Field command button on the Options tab under the PivotTable Tools contextual tab, and then click the Fields Settings option on its pop-up menu.**

   Excel opens the Value Field Settings dialog box.

2. **Click the Number Format button in the Value Field Settings dialog box to open the Number tab of the Format Cells dialog box.**

3. **Click the type of number format you want to assign to the values in the pivot table on the Category list box of the Number tab.**

4. **(Optional) Modify any other options for the selected number format, such as Decimal Places, Symbol, and Negative Numbers that are available for that format.**

5. **Click OK twice, the first time to close the Format Cells dialog box and the second to close the Value Field Settings dialog box.**

Sorting and Filtering the Pivot Table Data

When you create a new pivot table, you'll notice that Excel automatically adds drop-down buttons to the Report Filter field as well as the labels for the column and row fields. These drop-down buttons, known officially as *filter buttons* (see Chapter 11 for details), enable you to filter all but certain entries in any of these fields, and in the case of the column and row fields, to sort their entries in the table.

If you've added more than one column or row field to your pivot table, Excel adds collapse buttons (-) that you can use to temporarily hide subtotal values for a particular secondary field. After clicking a collapse button in the table, it immediately becomes an expand button (+) that you can click to redisplay the subtotals for that one secondary field.

Filtering the report

Perhaps the most important filter buttons in a pivot table are the ones added to the Report Filter field(s). By selecting a particular option on the drop-down lists attached to one of these filter buttons, only the summary data for that subset you select displays in the pivot table.

For example, in the example pivot table (refer to Figure 9-4) that uses the Gender field from the Employee Data list as the Report Filter field, you can display the sum of just the men's or women's salaries by department and location in the body of the pivot table doing either of the following:

✔ Click the Gender field's filter button and then click M on the drop-down list before you click OK to see only the totals of the men's salaries by department.

✔ Click the Gender field's filter button and then click F on the drop-down list before you click OK to see only the totals of the women's salaries by department.

When you later want to redisplay the summary of the salaries for all the employees, you then re-select the (All) option on the Gender field's drop-down filter list before you click OK.

When you filter the Gender Report Filter field in this manner, Excel then displays M or F in the Gender Report Filter field instead of the default (All). The program also replaces the standard drop-down button with a cone-shaped filter icon, indicating that the field is filtered and showing only some of the values in the data source.

Filtering individual column and row fields

The filter buttons on the column and row fields attached to their labels enable you to filter out entries for particular groups and, in some cases, individual entries in the data source. To filter the summary data in the columns or rows of a pivot table, click the column or row field's filter button and start by clicking the check box for the (Select All) option at the top of the drop-down list to clear this box of its check mark. Then, click the check boxes for all the groups or individual entries whose summed values you still want displayed in the pivot table to put back check marks in each of their check boxes. Then click OK.

As with filtering a Report Filter field, Excel replaces the standard drop-down button for that column or row field with a cone-shaped filter icon, indicating that the field is filtered and displaying only some of its summary values in the pivot table. To redisplay all the values for a filtered column or row field, you need to click its filter button and then click (Select All) at the top of its drop-down list. Then click OK.

Figure 9-5 shows the sample pivot table after filtering its Gender Report Filter field to women and its Dept Column field to Accounting, Administration, and Human Resources.

Notice in Figure 9-5 that after filtering the pivot table by selecting F in the Gender Report Filter field and selecting Accounting, Administration, and Human Resources departments as the only column fields, the filtered pivot table no longer displays salary summaries for all the company's locations (Santa Rosa, Seattle, and Atlanta locations are missing). You can tell that the table is missing these locations because there are no women employees in the three selected departments. That isn't a result of filtering the row field because the Location drop-down button still uses the standard icon and not the cone-shaped filter icon now shown on the right of the Gender Report Filter and Dept column fields.

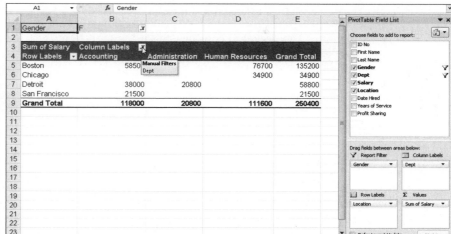

Figure 9-5:
Pivot table
after filter-
ing the
Gender
Report Filter
field and
the Dept
Column
field.

Filtering with slicers

Slicers are a brand new graphic object in Excel 2010 that you can use to filter your pivot tables. Slicers are easy to create and to use, and they make it a snap to filter the contents of your pivot table on more than one field. (They even allow you to connect with fields of other pivot tables that you've created in the workbook.)

To add slicers to your pivot table, you follow just two steps:

1. **Click one of the cells in your pivot table to select it and then click the Insert Slicer option on the Insert Slicer button located in the Sort & Filter group of the PivotTable Options contextual tab.**

   Excel opens the Insert Slicers dialog box with a list of all the fields in the active pivot table.

2. **Select the check boxes for all the fields that you want to use in filtering the pivot table and for which you want slicers created and then click OK.**

   Excel then adds slicers (as graphic objects — see Chapter 10 for details) for each pivot table field you select.

After you create slicers for the pivot table, you can use them to filter its data simply by selecting the items you want displayed in each slicer. You select items in a slicer by clicking them just as you do cells in a worksheet — hold down Ctrl as you click nonconsecutive items and Shift to select a series of sequential items.

Figure 9-6 shows you the sample pivot table after using slicers created for the Gender, Dept, and Location fields to filter the data so that only salaries for the men in the Human Resources and Administration departments in the Boston, Chicago, and San Francisco offices display.

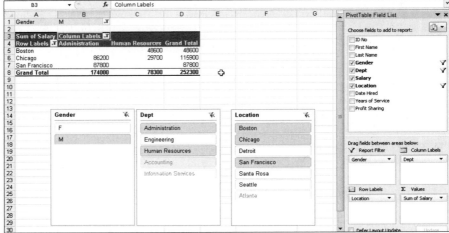

Figure 9-6: Pivot table filtered with slicers created for the Gender, Dept, and Location fields.

Because slicers are Excel graphic objects (albeit some pretty fancy ones), you can move, resize, and delete them just as you would any other Excel graphic; see Chapter 10 for details.

Sorting the pivot table

You can instantly reorder the summary values in a pivot table by sorting the table on one or more of its column or row fields. To re-sort a pivot table, click the filter button for the column or row field you want to use in the sorting and then click the Sort A to Z option or the Sort Z to A option at the top of the field's drop-down list.

Click the Sort A to Z option when you want the table reordered by sorting the labels in the selected field alphabetically or, in the case of values, from the smallest to largest value or, in the case of dates, from the oldest to newest date. Click the Sort Z to A option when you want the table reordered by sorting the labels in reverse alphabetical order, values from the highest to smallest, and dates from the newest to oldest.

Modifying a Pivot Table

Pivot tables are much more dynamic than standard Excel data tables because they remain so easy to manipulate and modify. Excel makes it just as easy to change which fields from the original data source display in the table as it did adding them when the table was created. Additionally, you can instantly restructure the pivot table by dragging its existing fields to new positions on the table. Add the ability to select a new summary function using any of Excel's basic Statistical functions, and you have yourself the very model of a flexible data table!

Modifying the pivot table fields

To modify the fields used in your pivot table, first you display the PivotTable Field List by following these steps:

1. **Click any of the pivot table's cells.**

   Excel adds the PivotTable Tools contextual tab with the Options and Design tabs to the Ribbon.

2. **Click the Options tab under the PivotTable Tools contextual tab to display its buttons on the Ribbon.**

3. **Click the Field List button in the Show group.**

   Excel displays the PivotTable Field List task pane, showing the fields that are currently in the pivot table as well as to which areas they're currently assigned. This task pane is usually displayed automatically when creating or selecting a Pivot Table, but if you do not see the task pane, click the Field List button.

After displaying the PivotTable Field List task pane, you can make any of the following modifications to the table's fields:

✔ To remove a field, drag its field name out of any of its drop zones (Report Filter, Column Labels, Row Labels, and Values) and, when the mouse pointer changes to an x, release the mouse button or click its check box in the Choose Fields to Add to Report list to remove its check mark.

✔ To move an existing field to a new place in the table, drag its field name from its current drop zone to a new zone (Report Filter, Column Labels, Row Labels, or Values) at the bottom of the task pane.

✔ To add a field to the table, drag its field name from the Choose Fields to Add to Report list and drop the field in the desired drop zone (Report Filter, Column Labels, Row Labels, or Values). If all you want to do is add a field to the pivot table as an additional Row Labels field, you can do this by selecting the field's check box in the Choose Fields to Add to Report list to add a check mark.

Pivoting the table's fields

As *pivot* implies, the fun of pivot tables is being able to restructure the table simply by rotating the column and row fields. For example, suppose that after making the Dept field the column field and the Location field the row field in the example pivot table, I now decide I want to see what the table looks like with the Location field as the column field and the Dept field as the row field.

No problem at all: In the PivotTable Field List task pane, I simply drag the Dept field label from the Column Labels drop zone to the Row Labels drop zone and the Location field from the Row Labels drop zone to the Column Labels drop zone.

Voilà — Excel rearranges the totaled salaries so that the rows of the pivot table show the departmental grand totals and the columns now show the location grand totals.

You can switch column and row fields by dragging their labels to their new locations directly in the pivot table itself. Before you can do that, however, you must select the Classic PivotTable Layout (Enables Dragging of Fields in the Grid) check box on the Display tab of the PivotTable Options dialog box (opened by clicking the Options button on the Options tab beneath the PivotTable Tools contextual tab).

Modifying the table's summary function

By default, Excel uses the good old SUM function to create subtotals and grand totals for the numeric field(s) that you assign as the Data Items in the pivot table.

Some pivot tables, however, require the use of another summary function, such as AVERAGE or COUNT. To change the summary function that Excel uses, simply click the Sum Of field label that's located at the cell intersection of the first column field and row field in a pivot table. Next, click the Active Field command button on the Options tab followed by Field Settings. Doing this opens the Value Field Settings dialog box for that field, similar to the one shown in Figure 9-7.

Figure 9-7:
Selecting
a new
summary
function in
the Value
Field
Settings
dialog box.

After you open the Value Field Settings dialog box, you can change its summary function from the default Sum to any of the following functions by selecting it in the Summarize Value Field By list box:

- ✔ **Count** to show the count of the records for a particular category (Count is the default setting for any text fields that you use as Data Items in a pivot table)

- ✔ **Average** to calculate the average (that is, the arithmetic mean) for the values in the field for the current category and page filter

- ✔ **Max** to display the largest numeric value in that field for the current category and page filter

- ✔ **Min** to display the smallest numeric value in that field for the current category and page filter

- ✔ **Product** to display the product of the numeric values in that field for the current category and page filter (all non-numeric entries are ignored)

- ✔ **Count Numbers** to display the number of numeric values in that field for the current category and page filter (all non-numeric entries are ignored)

- ✔ **StdDev** to display the standard deviation for the sample in that field for the current category and page filter

- ✔ **StdDevp** to display the standard deviation for the population in that field for the current category and page filter

- ✔ **Var** to display the variance for the sample in that field for the current category and page filter

- ✔ **Varp** to display the variance for the population in that field for the current category and page filter

After you select the new summary function to use in the Summarize Value Field By list box on the Summarize Values By tab of the Value Field Settings dialog box, click the OK button to have Excel apply the new function to the data present in the body of the pivot table.

Get Smart with a Pivot Chart

After creating a pivot table, you can create a pivot chart to display its summary values graphically in two simple steps:

1. **Click the PivotChart command button in the Tools group on the Options tab under the PivotTable Tools contextual tab to open the Insert Chart dialog box.**

   Remember that the PivotTable Tools contextual tab with its two tabs — Options and Design — automatically appears whenever you click any cell in an existing pivot table.

2. **Click the thumbnail of the type of chart you want to create in the Insert Chart dialog box and then click OK.**

As soon you click OK after selecting the chart type, Excel displays two things in the same worksheet as the pivot table:

✔ **Pivot chart** using the type of chart you selected that you can move and resize as needed (officially known as an *embedded chart* — see Chapter 10 for details)

✔ **PivotChart Tools contextual tab** divided into four tabs — Design, Layout, Format, and Analyze — each with its own set of buttons for customizing and refining the pivot chart

Moving a pivot chart to its own sheet

Although Excel automatically creates all new pivot charts on the same worksheet as the pivot table, you may find it easier to customize and work with it if you move the chart to its own chart sheet in the workbook. To move a new pivot chart to its own chart sheet in the workbook, you follow these steps:

1. **Click the Design tab under the PivotChart Tools contextual tab to bring its tools to the Ribbon.**

   If the PivotChart Tools contextual tab doesn't appear at the end of your Ribbon, click anywhere on the new pivot chart to make this tab reappear.

2. **Click the Move Chart button, the sole selection in the Location group at the far right of the Design tab.**

   Excel opens a Move Chart dialog box.

3. **Click the New Sheet button in the Move Chart dialog box.**

4. **(Optional) Rename the generic Chart1 sheet name in the accompanying text box by entering a more descriptive name there.**

5. **Click OK to close the Move Chart dialog box and open the new chart sheet with your pivot chart.**

Figure 9-8 shows a clustered column pivot chart after moving the chart to its own chart sheet in the workbook.

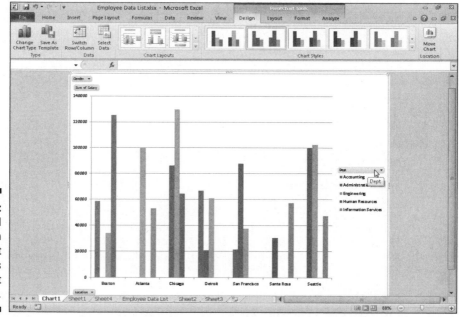

Figure 9-8:
Clustered
column
pivot chart
moved to its
own chart
sheet.

Filtering a pivot chart

When you graph the data in a pivot table using a typical chart type, such as column, bar, or line, that uses both an x- and y-axis, the Row Labels in the pivot table appear along the x- (or category) axis at the bottom of the chart and the Column Labels in the pivot table become the data series that are delineated in the chart's legend. The numbers in the Values field are represented on the y- (or value) axis that goes up the left side of the chart.

You can use the drop-down buttons that appear after the Report Filter, Legend fields, Axis fields, and Values field in the PivotChart to filter the charted data represented in this fashion like you do the values in the pivot table. As with the pivot table, remove the check mark from the (Select All) or (All) option and then add a check mark to each of the fields you still want represented in the filtered pivot chart.

Click the following drop-down buttons to filter a different part of the pivot chart:

✔ **Axis Fields (Categories)** to filter the categories that are charted along the x-axis at the bottom of the chart

✔ **Legend Fields (Series)** to filter the data series shown in columns, bars, or lines in the chart body and identified by the chart legend

✔ **Report Filter** to filter the data charted along the y-axis on the left side of the chart

✔ **Values** to filter the values represented in the PivotChart

Formatting a pivot chart

The command buttons on the Design, Layout, and Format tabs attached to the PivotChart Tools contextual tab make it easy to further format and customize your pivot chart. Use the Design tab buttons to select a new chart style for your pivot chart or even a brand new chart type. Use the Layout tab buttons to refine your pivot chart by adding chart titles, text boxes, and gridlines. Use the Format tab buttons to refine the look of any graphics you've added to the chart as well as select a new background color for your chart.

To get specific information on using the buttons on these tabs, see Chapter 10, which covers creating charts from regular worksheet data. The Chart Tools contextual tab that appears when you select a chart you've created contains the same Design, Layout, and Format tabs with comparable command buttons.

Part V
Life beyond the Spreadsheet

The 5th Wave   By Rich Tennant

"I assume everyone on your team is on board with the proposed changes to the office layout."

In this part . . .

1 created this part in case you need to stray beyond the confines of the spreadsheet into such exotic areas as creating charts and adding graphics; creating, sorting, and filtering data lists; loading and using add-in programs; linking sheets with hyperlinks; and recording command sequences as macros. The entertaining information about making charts, the fact-filled information on working with Excel data lists, and the coverage of recording and running macros will more than prepare you should you ever have to go beyond the pale of the good old Excel spreadsheet.

Chapter 10

Charming Charts and Gorgeous Graphics

*A*s Confucius was reported to have once said, "A picture is worth a thousand words" (or, in our case, numbers). By adding charts to worksheets, you not only heighten interest in the otherwise boring numbers but also illustrate trends and anomalies that may not be apparent from just looking at the values alone. Because Excel 2010 makes it so easy to chart the numbers in a worksheet, you can also experiment with different types of charts until you find the one that best represents the data — in other words, the picture that best tells the particular story.

Making Professional-Looking Charts

I just want to say a few words about charts in general before taking you through the steps for making them in Excel 2010. Remember your high-school algebra teacher valiantly trying to teach you how to graph equations by plotting different values on an x-axis and a y-axis on graph paper? Of course, you were probably too busy with more important things like cool cars and rock 'n' roll to pay too much attention to an old algebra teacher. Besides, you probably told yourself, "I'll never need this junk when I'm out on my own and get a job!"

Well, see, you just never know. It turns out that even though Excel automates almost the entire process of charting worksheet data, you may need to be able to tell the x-axis from the y-axis, just in case Excel doesn't draw the chart the way you had in mind. To refresh your memory and make your algebra teacher proud, the x-axis is the horizontal axis, usually located along the bottom of the chart; the y-axis is the vertical one, usually located on the left side of the chart.

In most charts that use these two axes, Excel plots the categories along the x-axis at the bottom and their relative values along the y-axis on the left. The x-axis is referred to as the *Category* axis, while the y-axis is referred to as the *Value* axis. Often the x-axis can be thought of as the *time axis* because the chart often depicts values along this axis in time periods, such as months, quarters, years, and so on.

Worksheet values represented graphically in the chart remain dynamically linked to the chart so that, should you make a change to one or more of the charted values in the worksheet, Excel automatically updates the affected part of the chart to suit.

Creating a new chart

Excel makes the process of creating a new chart in a worksheet as painless as possible:

1. **Click a cell in the table of data you want graphed, or, when you only want to graph a part of the data in a table, select the cell range, including headings and data.**

   If you find that Excel selects too much or too little table data completing these steps and creating the new chart, click the Select Data button on the Design tab (see "Customizing the chart type and style from the Design tab" later in this chapter) and correct the Chart Data Range in the Edit Source Data dialog box.

2. **On the Insert tab of the Ribbon, click the button in the Charts group for the type of chart you want to create: Column, Line, Pie, Bar, Area, Scatter, or Other Charts.**

   Excel then displays a drop-down gallery with thumbnails showing all the different styles you can choose for the type of chart you select.

3. **Click the thumbnail with the style of chart you want to create.**

   Style options within a chart type include 2-D, 3-D, Cylinder, Cone, Pyramid, Surface, Doughnut, Bubble, or Radar style to name a few.

As soon as you click one of the styles in the drop-down gallery, Excel immediately creates a free-floating chart (called an embedded chart) on the same worksheet as the table of data the chart represents graphically.

Instant charts

If you just don't have time to fool with the Chart buttons on the Insert tab of the Ribbon, position the cell cursor in the table of data or select the portion to chart and then just press F11. Excel then creates a clustered column chart using the table's data or cell selection on its own chart sheet (Chart1) that precedes all the other sheets in the workbook, which you can then customize as described later in this chapter.

Figure 10-1 shows an embedded two-dimensional clustered column chart created immediately after clicking the Clustered Column chart style thumbnail, the first one on the Column chart style gallery. Because this chart graphs only the first quarter sales in 2010 (without the totals), I selected the range A2:D11 in the table, clicked the Column button on the Insert tab and then clicked the Clustered Column chart style thumbnail on the drop-down Column gallery.

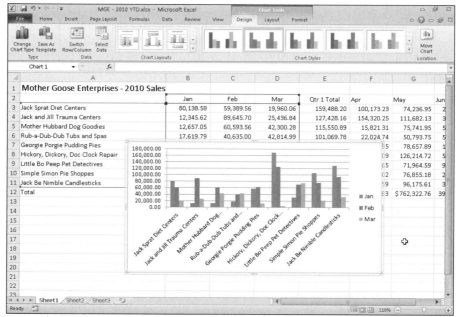

Figure 10-1:
Embedded clustered column chart right after creating it.

Moving and resizing an embedded chart in a worksheet

Right after you create a new chart in a worksheet, you can easily move or resize the embedded chart because the chart is still selected. (You can always tell when a graphic object, such as a chart, is selected because you see *selection handles* — those tiny dots — around the edges of the object.)

Whenever an embedded chart is selected (as it is automatically immediately after creating it or after clicking any part of it), the Chart Tools contextual tab with its Design, Layout, and Format tabs appears on the Ribbon, and Excel outlines each group of cells represented in the selected chart in a different color in the worksheet.

When an embedded chart is selected in a worksheet, you can move or resize it as follows:

✔ To move the chart, position the mouse pointer in a blank area inside the chart and drag the chart to a new location.

✔ To resize the chart (you may want to make it bigger if it seems distorted in any way), position the mouse pointer on one of the selection handles. When the pointer changes from the arrowhead to a double-headed arrow, drag the side or corner (depending on which handle you select) to enlarge or reduce the chart.

When the chart is properly sized and positioned in the worksheet, set the chart in place by deselecting it (simply click the mouse pointer in any cell outside the chart). As soon as you deselect the chart, the selection handles disappear, as does the Chart Tools contextual tab from the Ribbon.

To re-select the chart later to edit, size, or move it again, just click anywhere on the chart with the mouse pointer. The moment you do, the sizing handles return to the embedded chart and the Chart Tools contextual tab appears on the Ribbon.

Moving an embedded chart onto its own chart sheet

Although Excel automatically embeds all new charts on the same worksheet as the data they graph (unless you create the chart by using the F11 trick), you may find it easier to customize and work with it if you move the chart to its own chart sheet in the workbook. To move an embedded chart to its own chart sheet in the workbook, follow these steps:

1. **Click the Move Chart button on the Design tab under the Chart Tools contextual tab to open the Move Chart dialog box.**

   If the Chart Tools contextual tab doesn't appear at the end of your Ribbon, click anywhere on the new chart to select the chart and make this tab appear.

2. **Click the New Sheet button in the Move Chart dialog box.**

3. **(Optional) Rename the generic Chart1 sheet name in the accompanying text box by entering a more descriptive name.**

4. **Click OK to close the Move Chart dialog box and open the new chart sheet with your chart.**

If, after customizing the chart on its own sheet, you decide you want the finished chart to appear on the same worksheet as the data it represents, click the Move Chart button on the Design tab again. This time, click the Object In button and then select the name of the worksheet in its associated drop-down list box before you click OK.

Customizing the chart type and style from the Design tab

You can use the command buttons on the Design tab of the Chart Tools contextual tab to make all kinds of changes to your new chart. The Design tab contains the following groups of buttons to use:

- ✔ **Type:** Click the Change Chart Type button to change the type of chart and then click the thumbnail of the new chart type in the Change Chart Type dialog box that shows all the kinds of charts in Excel. Click the Save As Template button to open the Save Chart Template dialog box where you save the current chart's formatting and layout (usually after thoroughly customizing) as a template to use in creating future charts.

- ✔ **Data:** Click the Switch Row/Column button to interchange the worksheet data used for the Legend Entries (series) with that used for the Axis Labels (Categories) in the selected chart. Click the Select Data button to open the Select Data Source dialog box where you can not only interchange the Legend Entries (series) with the Axis Labels (Categories) but also edit out or add particular entries to either category.

✔ **Chart Layouts:** Click the More button (the last one with the horizontal bar and triangle pointing downward) to display all the thumbnails on the Chart Layouts drop-down gallery and then click the thumbnail of the new layout style you want applied to the selected chart.

✔ **Chart Styles:** Click the More button (the last one with the horizontal bar and triangle pointing downward) to display all the thumbnails on the Chart Styles drop-down gallery and then click the thumbnail of the new chart style you want applied to the selected chart.

✔ **Location:** Click the Move Chart button to move the chart to a new chart sheet or another worksheet.

✔ **Mode:** Click the button to select Draft or Normal mode for the chart to control how the chart looks onscreen and when you print it.

The Chart Layout and the Chart Styles galleries do not utilize the Live Preview feature. You have to click a thumbnail in the gallery and actually apply it to the selected chart in order to see how its style looks.

Figure 10-2 shows the original clustered column chart (created in Figure 10-1) after clicking the Layout 9 thumbnail on the Chart Layouts drop-down gallery and the Style 42 thumbnail on the Chart Styles drop-down gallery. Selecting Style 42 gives the clustered column chart its high contrast, whereas selecting Layout 9 adds the generic chart titles and positions.

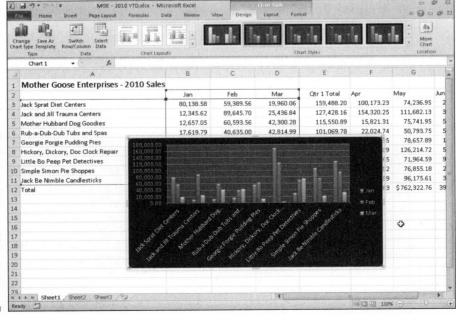

Figure 10-2: Embedded clustered column chart after selecting a new chart layout and chart style from the Design tab.

Customizing chart elements from the Layout tab

The command buttons on the Layout tab under the Chart Tools contextual tab make it easy to customize particular parts of your chart. This customization can include:

- ✔ Repositioning discrete chart elements, including the legend and x- and y-axis as well as the display of data labels and data tables in the chart

- ✔ Adding, removing, and repositioning the titles in the chart, including the chart and x- and y-axis titles

- ✔ Modifying the display of the chart's background, including the plot area for 2-D charts and the chart wall, floor, and view for 3-D charts

To make a change to a particular chart element from the Layout tab, click its command button and then click the option you want to use from the drop-down menu (some options have continuation drop-down menus attached to them). If none of the preset options fits your needs, click the More option at the bottom of the drop-down list to open a format dialog box for the selected chart element normally containing Fill, Border Color, Border Styles, Shadow, Glow and Soft Edges, 3-D Format, and Alignment tabs with oodles of options that you can use to customize the chart element.

For example, to add a title to a chart (when you've selected a chart style that doesn't automatically add one) and reposition or customize an existing title, you click the Chart Title button on the Layout tab to display the following options on its drop-down list:

- ✔ **None** to remove an existing chart title from the chart

- ✔ **Centered Overlay Title** to add or reposition the chart title so that it appears centered at the top of the plot area

- ✔ **Above Chart** to add or reposition the chart title so that it appears centered above the plot area

- ✔ **More Title Options** to open the Format Chart Title dialog box where you can use the options on its Fill, Border Color, Border Styles, Shadow, Glow and Soft Edges, 3-D Format, and Alignment tabs to customize the appearance of the chart title

 The Properties group at the end of the Layout tab contains a sole Chart Name text box that you can use to modify the generic chart name (Chart 1, Chart 2, and so forth) to something more descriptive. If your worksheet contains more than one chart, you may find it advantageous to give it a more descriptive name so that it's easy to identify in the Selection Pane.

Adding data labels to the series in a chart

Data labels display values from the worksheet represented in the chart at each of its data points. To add data labels to your selected chart and position them, click the Data Labels button on the Layout tab and then click one of the following options on its drop-down menu:

- ✔ **Center** to position the data labels in the middle of each data point

- ✔ **Inside End** to position the data labels inside each data point near the end

- ✔ **Inside Base** to position the data labels at the base of each data point

- ✔ **Outside End** to position the data labels outside of the end of each data point

- ✔ **More Data Label Options** to open the Format Data Labels dialog box where you can use the options on Label Options, Number, Fill, Border Color, Border Styles, Shadow, Glow and Soft Edges, 3-D Format, and Alignment tabs to custom the appearance and position of the data labels

To remove all data labels from the data points in a selected chart, click the None option at the top of the Data Labels button's drop-down menu on the Layout tab of the Chart Tools contextual tab.

Adding a data table to a chart

Sometimes, instead of data labels that can easily obscure the data points in the chart, you'll want Excel to draw a data table beneath the chart showing the worksheet data it represents in graphic form. To add the worksheet data to your selected chart, click the Data Table button on the Layout tab and then click one of these options:

- ✔ **Show Data Table** to have Excel draw the table at the bottom of the chart

- ✔ **Show Data Table with Legend Keys** to have Excel draw the table at the bottom of the chart, including the color keys used in the legend to differentiate the data series in the first column

- ✔ **More Data Table Options** to open the Format Data Table dialog box where you can use the options on the Data Table Options, Fill, Border Color, Border Styles, Shadow, Glow and Soft Edges, and 3-D Format tabs to customize the appearance and position of the data table

Figure 10-3 illustrates how the sample clustered column chart looks with a data table added to it. This data table includes the legend keys as its first column.

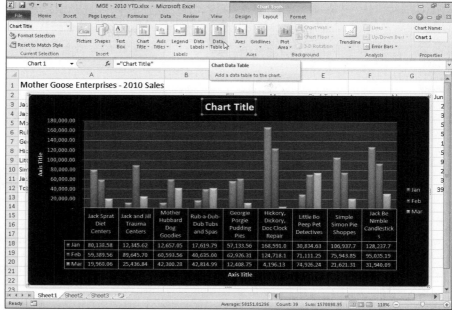

Figure 10-3:
Embedded
clustered
column
chart with
data table
with legend
keys.

If you decide that displaying the worksheet data in a table at the bottom of the chart is no longer necessary, simply click the None option on the Data Table button's drop-down menu on the Layout tab of the Chart Tools contextual tab.

Editing the titles in a chart

When Excel first adds titles to a new chart, it gives them generic names, such as Chart Title and Axis Title (for both the x- and y-axis title). To replace these generic titles with the actual chart titles, click the title in the chart or click the name of the title on the Chart Elements drop-down list. (Chart Elements is the first drop-down button in the Current Selection group on the Layout or Format tab under Chart Tools. Its text box displays the name of the element currently selected in the chart). Excel lets you know that a particular chart title is selected by placing selection handles around its perimeter.

After you select a title, you can click the insertion point in the text and then edit as you would any worksheet text or you can click to select the title, type the new title, and press Enter to completely replace it with the text you type. To force part of the title onto a new line, click the insertion point at the place in the text where the line break is to occur. After the insertion point is positioned in the title, press Enter to start a new line.

After you finish editing the title, click somewhere else on the chart area to deselect it (or a worksheet cell if you've finished formatting and editing the chart).

Formatting chart elements from the Format tab

The Format tab under the Chart Tools contextual tab contains command buttons that make it easy to format particular chart elements after you select them.

Excel gives you a choice of methods for selecting individual chart elements:

✔ Click the element directly in the chart to select it — use the ScreenTip that appears at the mouse pointer to identify the chart object before you click to select it.

✔ Click the name of the chart element on the Chart Elements drop-down list in the Current Selection group on the Format tab — Excel shows you which element is currently selected by displaying its name inside the Chart Elements combo box.

After you select an element in the chart by clicking it, you can cycle through and select the other elements in succession by pressing the ↑ and ↓ keys. Pressing the → key selects the next object; pressing the ← key selects the previous object.

You can tell when an element is selected in the chart because selection handles appear around it and its name appears in the Chart Elements combo box on the Format tab.

After you select a chart element, you can then make any of the following changes to it:

✔ Format the element by selecting the appropriate command button in the Shape Styles group or by clicking the Format Selection button in the Current Selection group to open the Format dialog box for that element and use its options to make the desired changes.

✔ Move the element within the chart by positioning the arrowhead pointer in their midst and then dragging their boundary — with some elements, you can use the selection handles to resize or reorient the object.

✔ Remove the element from the chart by pressing the Delete key.

All chart elements have shortcut menus attached to them. If you know that you want to choose a command from the shortcut menu while you select a part of the chart, you can select the object and open the shortcut menu by right-clicking the chart object. (You don't have to click the object with the left button to select it and then click again with the right button to open the menu.)

Formatting the chart titles

When you add titles to your chart, Excel uses the Calibri (Body) font for the chart title (in 18-point size) and the x- and y-axis (in 10-point size). To change the font used in a title or any of its attributes, select the title and then use the appropriate command buttons in the Font group on the Home tab.

Use Live Preview to see how a particular font or font size for the selected chart title looks in the chart before you select it. Simply click the Font or Font Size drop-down buttons and then highlight different font names or sizes to have the selected chart title appear in them.

If you need to change other formatting options for the titles in the chart, you can do so using the command buttons on the Format tab of the Chart Tools contextual tab. To format the entire text box that contains the title, click one of the following buttons in the Shape Styles group:

✔ **Shape Styles** thumbnail in its drop-down gallery to format both the text and text box for the selected chart title

✔ **Shape Fill** button to select a new color for the text box containing the selected chart title from its drop-down palette

✔ **Shape Outline** button to select a new color for the outline of the text box for the selected chart text from its drop-down palette

✔ **Shape Effects** button to apply a new effect (Shadow, Reflection, Glow, Soft Edges, and so on) to the text box containing the selected chart title from its drop-down list

To format just the text in chart titles, click one of the buttons in the WordArt Styles group:

✔ **WordArt Styles** thumbnail in its drop-down gallery to apply a new WordArt style to the text of the selected chart title

✔ **Text Fill** button to select a new fill color for the text in the selected chart title from its gallery

✔ **Text Outline** button (immediately below the Text Fill button) to select a new outline color for the text in the selected chart title from its drop-down palette

✔ **Text Effects** button (immediately below the Text Outline button) to apply a text effect (Shadow, Reflection, Glow, Bevel, and so on) to the text of the selected chart title from its drop-down list

Figure 10-4 shows the example clustered column chart after formatting the chart titles using the Black, Text 1, Lighter 15% option on the Shape Fill button's gallery.

Formatting the Category x-axis and Value y-axis

When charting a bunch of values, Excel isn't too careful how it formats the values that appear on the y-axis (or the x-axis when using some chart types, such as the 3-D Column chart or an XY Scatter chart).

If you're not happy with the way the values appear on either the x-axis or y-axis, you can easily change the formatting as follows:

1. **Click the x-axis or y-axis directly in the chart or click the Chart Elements button (the first button in the Current Selection group of the Layout or Format tab) and then click Horizontal (Category) Axis (for the x-axis) or Vertical (Value) Axis (for the y-axis) on its drop-down list.**

   Excel surrounds the axis you select with selection handles.

2. **Click the Format Selection button in the Current Selection group of the Layout or Format tab or press Ctrl+1.**

   Excel opens the Format Axis dialog box containing the following tabs: Axis Options, Number, Fill, Line Color, Line Style, Shadow, Glow and Soft Edges, 3-D Format, and Alignment.

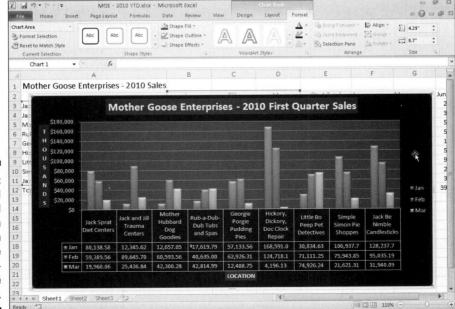

Figure 10-4:
Embedded clustered column chart with data table after formatting the chart titles.

3. **To change the scale of the axis, the appearance of its tick marks, and where it crosses the other axis, change the appropriate options on the Axis Options tab (automatically selected when you first open the Format Axis dialog box) as needed.**

   These options include those that fix the maximum and minimum amount for the first and last tick mark on the axis, display the values in reverse order (highest to lowest), and apply a logarithmic scale. You can display units on the axis (hundreds, thousands, millions, and so forth) and divide the values by those units, reposition the tick marks on the axis, and modify the value at which the other axis (y-axis when modifying the x-axis and x-axis when modifying the y-axis) crosses.

4. **To change the number formatting for all values on the selected axis, click the Number tab and then click the number format you want to apply in the Category list box followed by the appropriate options associated with that format.**

   For example, to select the number format with the comma as the thousands separator and no decimal places, you select Number in the Category list box; then leave the Use 1000 Separator (,) check box selected and enter **0** in the Decimal Places text box.

5. **To change the alignment and orientation of the labels on the selected axis, click the Alignment tab and then indicate the new orientation by clicking the desired vertical alignment in the Vertical Alignment drop-down list box and desired text direction in the Text Direction drop-down list.**

6. **Click Close to close the Format Axis dialog box.**

As you choose new options for the selected axis, Excel 2010 shows you the change in the chart. However, these changes are set in the chart only when you click Close in the Format Axis dialog box.

To change the default font, font size, or other text attributes for entries along the selected x- or y-axis, click the appropriate command buttons in the Font group on the Home tab (see Chapter 3 for details).

Adding Great Looking Graphics

Charts are not the only kind of graphic objects you can add to a worksheet. Indeed, Excel lets you spruce up a worksheet with a whole bevy of graphics, including sparklines (new tiny charts that fit right inside worksheet cells), text boxes, clip art drawings supplied by Microsoft, as well as graphic images imported from other sources, such as digital photos, scanned images, and pictures downloaded from the Internet.

In addition to these graphics, Excel 2010 supports the creation of fancy graphic text called WordArt as well as a whole bevy of organizational and process diagrams known collectively as SmartArt graphics.

Sparking up the data with sparklines

Excel 2010 introduces a new type of information graphic called a *sparkline* that represents trends or variations in collected data. Sparklines are tiny graphs generally about the size of the text that surrounds them. In Excel 2010, sparklines are the height of the worksheet cells whose data they represent and can be any of the following chart types:

- ✔ **Line** that represents the relative value of the selected worksheet data
- ✔ **Column** where the selected worksheet data is represented by tiny columns
- ✔ **Win/Loss** where the selected worksheet data appears as a win/loss chart; wins are represented by blue squares that appear above red squares (representing the losses)

To add sparklines to the cells of your worksheet:

1. **Select the cells in the worksheet with the data you want to represent with a sparkline.**

2. **Click the chart type you want for your sparkline (Line, Column, or Win/Loss) in the Sparklines group of the Insert tab or press Alt+NSL for Line, Alt+NSO for Column, or Alt+NSW for Win/Loss.**

   Excel opens the Create Sparklines dialog box containing two text boxes:

   - *Data Range:* Shows the cells you select with the data you want to graph.

   - *Location Range:* Lets you designate the cell or cell range where you want the sparkline to appear.

3. **Select the cell or cell range where you want your sparkline to appear in the Location Range text box and then click OK.**

   When creating a sparkline that spans more than a single cell, the amount of rows and columns in the location range must match the amount of rows and columns in the data range. (That is, the arrays need to be of equal size and shape.)

TIP

Because sparklines are so small, you can easily add them to the cells in the final column of a table. That way, the sparklines (shown in this figure) can depict the data visually and enhance meaning while being an integral part of the table.

Mother Goose Enterprises - 2010 Sales	Jan	Feb	Mar	Qtr 1 Trend	Qtr 1 Total
Jack Sprat Diet Centers	80,138.58	59,389.56	19,960.06		159,488.20
Jack and Jill Trauma Centers	12,345.62	89,645.70	25,436.84		127,428.16
Mother Hubbard Dog Goodies	12,657.05	60,593.56	42,300.28		115,550.89
Rub-a-Dub-Dub Tubs and Spas	17,619.79	40,635.00	42,814.99		101,069.78
Georgie Porgie Pudding Pies	57,133.56	62,926.31	12,408.75		132,468.62
Hickory, Dickory, Doc Clock Repair	168,591.00	124,718.10	4,196.13		297,505.23
Little Bo Peep Pet Detectives	30,834.63	71,111.25	74,926.24		176,872.12
Simple Simon Pie Shoppes	106,937.77	75,943.85	21,621.31		204,502.93
Jack Be Nimble Candlesticks	128,237.74	95,035.19	31,940.09		255,213.02
Total	$ 614,495.74	$ 679,998.52	$ 275,604.69		$ 1,570,098.95

After you add sparklines to your worksheet, Excel 2010 adds a Sparkline Tools Design tab to the Ribbon that appears when the cell or range with the sparkline is selected. This Design tab contains buttons that you can use to edit the type, style, and format of the sparklines. The final group (called Group) on this Design tab enables you to band a range of sparklines into a single group that can share the same axis and/or minimum or maximum values (selected using the options on the Axis drop-down button). This is very useful when you want a collection of sparklines to share the same charting parameters so that they represent the trends in the data equally.

Telling all with a text box

Text boxes, as their name implies, are boxes in which you can add commentary or explanatory text to the charts you create in Excel. They're like Excel comments (see Chapter 6) that you add to worksheet cells except that you have to add the arrow if you want the text box to point to something in the chart.

In Figure 10-5, you see a clustered column chart for the MGE (Mother Goose Enterprises) 2010 First Quarter Sales. I added a text box with an arrow that points out how extraordinary the sales were for the Hickory, Dickory, Doc Clock Repair shops in this quarter and formatted the values on the y-axis with the Currency number format with zero decimal places.

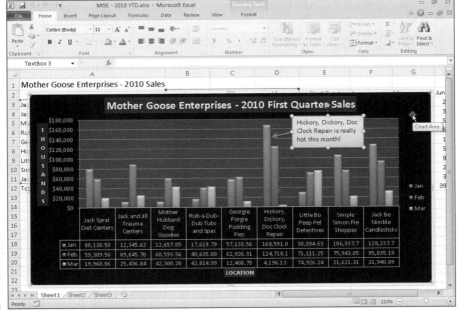

Figure 10-5:
Clustered
column
chart, with
added text
box and
formatted
y-axis
values.

Adding and formatting a text box

To add a text box like the one shown in Figure 10-5 to the chart when a chart is selected, click the Text Box command button in the Insert group on the Layout tab under the Chart Tools contextual tab. If the chart is not selected, you can click the Text Box command button on the Ribbon's Insert tab.

Excel then changes the mouse pointer to a narrow vertical line with a short cross near the bottom. Click the location where you want to draw the text box and then draw the box by dragging its outline. When you release the mouse button after dragging this mouse pointer, Excel draws a text box in the shape and size of the outline.

After creating a horizontal text box, the program positions the insertion point at the top left, and you can then type the text you want to appear within it. The text you type appears in the text box and will wrap to a new line should you reach the right edge of the text box. You can press Enter when you want to force text to appear on a new line. When you finish entering the message for your text box, click anywhere outside the box to deselect it.

After adding a text box to a chart or worksheet while it's still selected, you can edit it as follows:

- ✔ Move the text box to a new location in the chart by dragging it.
- ✔ Resize the text box by dragging the appropriate selection handle.
- ✔ Rotate the text box by dragging its rotation handle (the green circle at the top) in a clockwise or counterclockwise direction.
- ✔ Modify the formatting and appearance of the text box using the various command buttons in the Shape Styles group on the Format tab under the Drawing Tools contextual tab.
- ✔ Delete the text box by clicking its perimeter so that the dotted lines connecting the selection handles become solid and then pressing the Delete key.

Adding an arrow to a text box

When creating a text box, you may want to add an arrow to point directly to the object or part of the chart you're referencing. To add an arrow, follow these steps:

1. **Click the text box to which you want to attach the arrow in the chart or worksheet.**

   Selection handles appear around the text box and the Format tab under the Drawing Tools contextual tab is selected on the Ribbon.

2. **Click the Arrow command button in the Insert Shapes drop-down gallery on the Format tab.**

   The Arrow command button is the third from the left in the first row of shapes (with the picture of an arrow). When you click this button, it's selected in the palette (indicated by the new color) and the mouse pointer assumes the crosshair shape.

3. **Drag the crosshair mouse pointer from the place on the text box where the end of the arrow (the one *without* the arrowhead) is to appear to the place where the arrow starts (and the arrowhead will appear) and release the mouse button.**

   As soon as you release the mouse button, Excel draws two points, one at the base of the arrow (attached to the text box) and another at the arrowhead. At the same time, the contents of the Shape Styles drop-down gallery changes to line styles.

4. **Click the More button in the lower-right corner of the Shape Styles drop-down gallery to display the thumbnails of all its line styles and then mouse over the thumbnails to see how the arrow would look in each.**

As you mouse through the different line styles in this gallery, Excel draws the arrow between the two selected points in the text box using the highlighted style.

5. Click the thumbnail of the line style you want the new arrow to use in the Shape Styles gallery.

Excel then draws a new arrow using the selected shape style, which remains selected (with selection handles at the beginning and end of the arrow). You can then edit the arrow as follows:

- ✔ Move the arrow by dragging its outline into position.

- ✔ Change the length of the arrow by dragging the selection handle at the arrowhead.

- ✔ Change the direction of the arrow by pivoting the mouse pointer around a stationary selection handle.

- ✔ Change the shape of the arrowhead or the thickness of the arrow's shaft by clicking a thumbnail on the Shape Styles drop-down gallery. Click a new option on the Shape Outline and Shape Effects buttons on the Format tab of the Drawing Tools contextual tab or open the Format Shape dialog box (Ctrl+1) and then select the appropriate options on its Line Color, Line Style, Shadow, Reflection, Glow and Soft Edges, 3-D Format, 3-D Rotation, Size, and Text Box tabs.

- ✔ Delete the arrow by pressing the Delete key.

The wonderful world of clip art

Clip art is the name given to the over 150,000 ready-made illustrations offered by Microsoft for use in its various Microsoft Office programs, including Excel 2010. Clip art drawings are now so numerous that the images are classified into a bunch of different categories ranging from Abstract to Web Elements.

To bring in a piece of clip art included with Office 2010, you click the Clip Art button on the Ribbon's Insert tab or press Alt+NF. When you do this, Excel 2010 displays the Clip Art task pane (similar to the one shown in Figure 10-6) from which you search for the type of art you want to use. To locate the clip(s) you want to insert into the current worksheet in the Clip Art task pane, follow these steps:

1. Click the Search For text box at the top, and then enter the keyword(s) for the type of clip art you want to find.

When you enter keywords for finding particular types of clip art, try general, descriptive terms such as *trees, flowers, people, flying,* and the like.

2. **(Optional) Click the Results Should Be drop-down button and remove (deselect) check marks from any clip art collections that you don't want to search.**

   By default, Excel searches all the collections of clip art (including the Office.com collection on the Web). To limit your search, you need to make sure that only the clip art collections you want to include in the search have check marks before their names, and if you don't want to search the online content, uncheck the Include Office.com Content option below the drop-down button.

3. **(Optional) To limit the search to clip art only, click the Results Should Be drop-down button and remove check marks from the All Media Types, Photographs, Videos, and Audio categories.**

4. **Click the Go button to the immediate right of the Search For text box to initiate the search.**

To insert one of the thumbnails displayed in the Clip Art task pane into the current worksheet (see Figure 10-7), click the thumbnail. You can also insert an image by positioning the mouse over it to display its drop-down button, clicking the drop-down button, and then choosing Insert at the top of its drop-down menu.

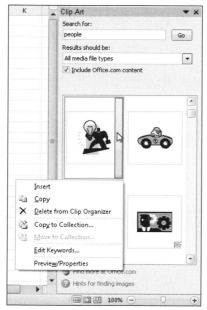

Figure 10-6:
Use the Clip Art task pane to search for clip art.

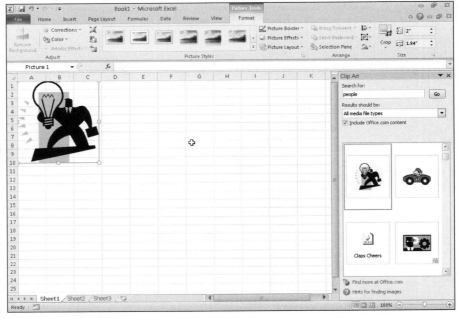

Figure 10-7:
Click the thumbnail in your search results in the Clip Art task pane to insert its image in the worksheet.

Click the Find More at Office.com link at the bottom of the Clip Art pane if you want to include thousands of additional clip art images and photos from Microsoft Office in your search. When you click this link, Windows launches your Web browser and displays the Images tab of the Office.com Web site. There, you can search for, select, and download clip art images for use in Excel.

When you insert a clip art image into the worksheet, it's selected automatically (indicated by the selection handles around its perimeter and its rotation handle at the top). To deselect the clip art image and set it in the worksheet, click anywhere in the worksheet outside of the image.

Inserting pictures from graphics files

If you want to bring in an image such as a digital photo or a scanned image saved in its own graphics file, click the Picture button on the Insert tab of the Ribbon or press Alt+NP. This opens the Insert Picture dialog box (which works just like opening an Excel workbook file in the Open dialog box) where you select the graphics file and then import it into the worksheet by clicking the Insert button.

If you want to bring in a graphic image created in another graphics program that isn't saved in its own file, select the graphic in that program and then copy it to the Clipboard (press Ctrl+C). When you get back to your worksheet, place the cursor where you want the picture to appear and then paste the image (press Ctrl+V or click the Paste command button at the beginning of the Home tab).

When you insert a picture from a graphics file into the worksheet, it's selected automatically (indicated by the selection handles around its perimeter and its rotation handle at the top). To deselect the graphic image and set it in the worksheet, click anywhere in the worksheet outside of the image.

Editing clip art and imported pictures

While a clip art image or a picture that you've inserted into your worksheet is selected (indicated by the appearance of the selection handles around its perimeter and a rotation handle at the top), you can make any of the following changes:

- ✔ Move the clip art image or imported picture to a new location in the chart by dragging it.

- ✔ Resize the clip art image or imported picture by dragging the appropriate selection handle.

- ✔ Rotate the clip art image or imported picture by dragging its rotation handle (the green circle at the top) in a clockwise or counterclockwise direction.

- ✔ Delete the clip art image or imported picture by pressing the Delete key.

Formatting clip art and imported pictures

Additionally, when a clip art image or imported picture is selected, Excel adds the Picture Tools Contextual tab to the Ribbon and automatically selects the sole Format tab under it.

The Format tab is divided into four groups: Adjust, Picture Styles, Arrange, and Size. The Adjust group contains the following important command buttons:

- ✔ **Remove Background** opens the Background Removal tab and makes a best guess about what parts of the picture to remove. You have the option to mark areas of the picture to keep or further remove, and the shaded areas automatically update as you isolate what areas of the picture you want to keep. Click Keep Changes when you are finished or Discard All Changes to revert back to the original picture.

✔ **Corrections** to open a drop-down menu with a palette of presets you can choose for sharpening or softening the image and/or increasing or decreasing its brightness. Or select the Picture Corrections Options item to open the Format Picture dialog box with the Picture Corrections tab selected. There you can sharpen or soften the image or modify its brightness or contrast by selecting a new preset thumbnail on the appropriate Presets palette or by entering a new positive percentage (to increase) or negative percentage (to decrease) where 0% is normal in the appropriate combo box or dragging its slider.

✔ **Color** to open a drop-down menu with a palette of Color Saturation, Color Tone, or Recolor presets you can apply to the image, set a transparent color (usually the background color you want to remove from the image), or select the Picture Color Options item to open the Picture Color tab of the Format Picture dialog box. There you can adjust the image's colors using Color Saturation, Color Tone, or Recolor presets or by setting a new saturation level or color tone temperature by entering a new percentage in the appropriate combo box or selecting it with a slider.

✔ **Artistic Effects** to open a drop-down menu with special effect presets you can apply to the image or select the Artistic Effects Options item to open the Artistic Effects tab of the Format Picture dialog box where you can apply a special effect by selecting its preset thumbnail from the palette that appears when you click the Artistic Effect drop-down button.

✔ **Compress Pictures** to open the Compress Pictures dialog box to compress all images in the worksheet or just the selected graphic image to make them more compact and thus make the Excel workbook somewhat smaller when you save the images as part of its file.

✔ **Change Picture** to open the Insert Picture dialog box where you can select an image in a new graphics file to replace the picture.

✔ **Reset Picture** button to remove all formatting changes made and return the picture to the state it was in when you originally inserted it into the worksheet.

You can also format a selected clip art image or imported picture by opening the Format Shape dialog box (Ctrl+1) and then selecting the appropriate tab. Options include Fill, Line Color, Line Style, Shadow, Reflection, Glow and Soft Edges, 3-D Format, 3-D Rotation, Picture Corrections, Picture Color, Artistic Effects, Crop, Size, Properties, and Alt Text.

In addition to the command buttons in the Picture Tools group, you can use the command buttons in the Picture Styles group. Click a thumbnail on the Picture Styles drop-down gallery to select a new orientation and style for the selected picture. You can also modify any of the following:

✔ Border shape and color on the Picture Border button's drop-down palette

✔ Shadow or 3-D rotation effect on the Picture Effects button's drop-down menus

✔ Layout on the Picture Layout button's drop-down palette to format a picture with SmartArt-styles.

Figure 10-8 shows the imported clip art image formatted in Live Preview with the Relaxed Perspective, White style selected on the Picture Styles drop-down gallery. In this style, Excel applies perspective to the image so that it appears to be laying on the worksheet and adds a thick white border to it.

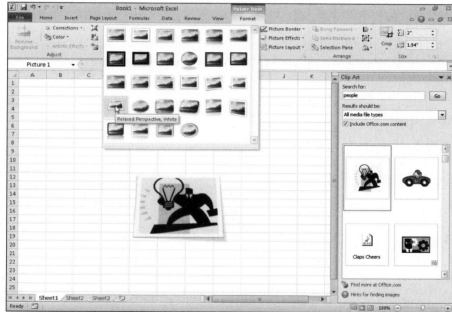

Figure 10-8: Live Preview in the Picture Styles gallery enables you to see how a style affects your picture before you apply it.

Adding preset graphic shapes

In addition to clip art images and pictures imported from graphics files, you can insert preset graphic shapes in your chart or worksheet by selecting their thumbnails on the Shapes drop-down gallery on the Insert tab of the Ribbon (see Figure 10-9).

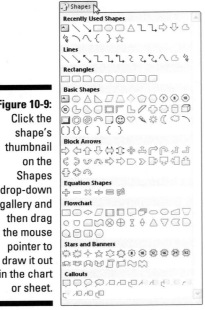

Figure 10-9:
Click the
shape's
thumbnail
on the
Shapes
drop-down
gallery and
then drag
the mouse
pointer to
draw it out
in the chart
or sheet.

When you open the Shapes gallery by clicking the Shapes button in the Illustrations group on the Insert tab of the Ribbon, you see that it's divided into nine sections: Recently Used Shapes, Lines, Rectangles, Basic Shapes, Block Arrows, Equation Shapes, Flowchart, Stars and Banners, and Callouts.

After you click the thumbnail of a preset shape in this drop-down gallery, the mouse pointer becomes a crosshair you use to draw the graphic by dragging it to the size you want.

After you release the mouse button, the shape you've drawn in the worksheet is still selected. This is indicated by the selection handles around its perimeter and the rotation handle at the top, which you can use to reposition, resize, and rotate the shape, if need be. Additionally, the program activates the Format tab on the Drawing Tools contextual tab and you can use the Shape Styles gallery or other command buttons to further format the shape to the way you want it. To set the shape and remove the selection and rotation handles, click anywhere in the worksheet outside of the shape.

Working with WordArt

If selecting gazillions of preset shapes available from the Shapes gallery doesn't provide enough variety for jazzing up your worksheet, you may want to try adding some fancy text using the WordArt gallery, opened by clicking the WordArt command button in the Text group of the Insert tab.

You can add this type of "graphic" text to your worksheet by following these steps:

1. **Click the WordArt command button on the Ribbon's Insert tab or press Alt+NW.**

   Excel displays the WordArt drop-down gallery, as shown in Figure 10-10.

Figure 10-10: Select the type of text from the WordArt Gallery.

2. **Click the A thumbnail in the WordArt style you want to use in the WordArt drop-down gallery.**

   Excel inserts a selected text box containing Your Text Here in the center of the worksheet in the WordArt style you selected in the gallery.

3. **Type the text you want to display in the worksheet in the Your Text Here text box.**

   As soon as you start typing, Excel replaces Your Text Here with the characters you enter.

4. **(Optional) To format the background of the text box, use Live Preview in the Shape Styles drop-down gallery on the Format tab to find the style to use and then set it by clicking its thumbnail.**

   The Format tab under the Drawing Tools contextual tab is added and activated automatically when WordArt text is selected in the worksheet.

5. **After making any final adjustments to the size, shape, or orientation of the WordArt text with the selection and rotation handles, click a cell somewhere outside of the text to deselect the graphic.**

When you click outside of the WordArt text, Excel deselects the graphic, and the Drawing Tools contextual tab disappears from the Ribbon. (If you ever want this tab to reappear, all you have to do is click somewhere on the WordArt text to select the graphic.)

Figure 10-11 shows the name of my company, Mind over Media after creating the text in the Fill – Red, Accent 2, Matte Bevel style.

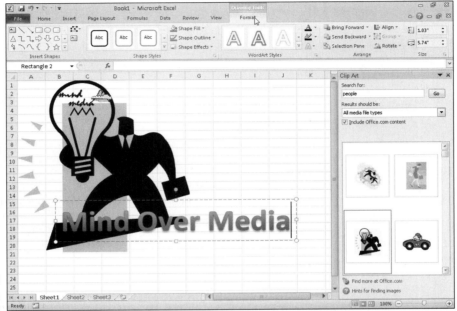

Figure 10-11:
The Mind over Media company name entered into a worksheet as a WordArt graphic.

You can change the size of WordArt text and the font it uses after creating it by dragging through the WordArt text to select it and then using the Font and Font Size command buttons on the Home tab to make your desired changes.

Make mine SmartArt

Excel 2010 SmartArt is a special type of graphic object that gives you the ability to construct fancy graphical lists and diagrams in your worksheet quickly and easily. SmartArt lists and diagrams come in a wide array of configurations (including a bunch of organizational charts and various process and flow diagrams) that enable you to combine your own text with the predefined graphic shapes.

To insert a SmartArt list or diagram into the worksheet, click the SmartArt button on the Insert tab or press Alt+NM to open the Choose a SmartArt Graphic dialog box (shown in Figure 10-12). Then click a category in the navigation pane on the left followed by the list's or diagram's thumbnail in the center section before you click OK.

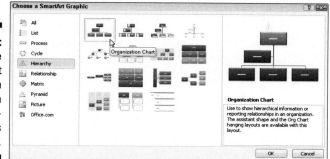

Figure 10-12:
Select the
SmartArt list
or diagram
to insert in
the work-
sheet in this
dialog box.

Excel then inserts the basic structure of the list or diagram into your worksheet along with a text pane (displaying Type Your Text Here on its title bar)
to its immediate left and [Text] in the shapes in the diagram where you can
enter the text for the various parts of the list or diagram (as shown in Figure
10-13). At the same time, the Design tab of the SmartArt Tools contextual tab
with Layouts and SmartArt Styles galleries for the particular type of SmartArt
list or diagram you originally selected appears on the Ribbon.

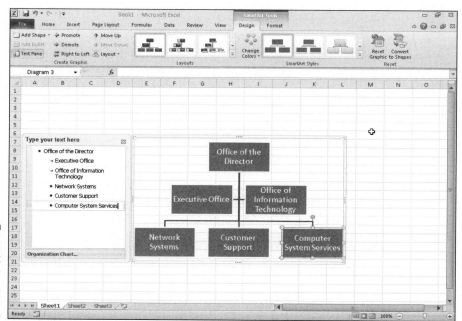

Figure 10-13:
Adding text
to a new
organiza-
tional chart.

Filling in the text for a new SmartArt graphic

To fill in the text for the first section of the new list or diagram in the outline text box that already contains the insertion point, simply type the text. Then press the ↓ key or click the next list or diagram section to set the insertion point there.

Don't press the Tab key or the Enter key to complete a text entry in the list or diagram as you naturally do in the regular worksheet. In a SmartArt list or diagram, pressing the Enter key inserts a new section of the list or diagram (at the same level in hierarchical diagrams, such as an org chart). Pressing Tab indents the level of the current section on the outline (in hierarchical diagrams) or does nothing.

When you finish entering the text for your new diagram, click the Close button (with an X) on the text pane in the upper-right corner opposite the title, Type Your Text Here. (You can always reopen this box if you need to edit any of the text by clicking the button that appears in the middle of the left side of the selected list or diagram after you close the text pane.)

If the style of the SmartArt list or diagram you select comes with more sections than you need, you can delete the unused graphics by clicking them to select them (indicated by the selection and rotation handles around it) and then pressing the Delete key.

Formatting a SmartArt graphic

After you close the text pane attached to your SmartArt list or diagram, you can still format its text and graphics. To format the text, select all the graphic objects in the SmartArt list or diagram that need the same type of text formatting. (Remember you can select several objects in the list or diagram by holding down Ctrl as you click them.) Then click the appropriate command buttons in the Font group on the Home tab of the Ribbon.

To refine or change the default formatting of the graphics in a SmartArt list or diagram, you can use the Layouts, Change Colors, and SmartArt Styles drop-down galleries available on the Design tab of the SmartArt Tools contextual tab:

✔ Click the More button in the Layouts group and then click a thumbnail on the Layouts drop-down gallery to select an entirely new layout for your SmartArt list or diagram.

✔ Click the Change Colors button in the SmartArt Styles group and then click a thumbnail in the drop-down gallery to change the colors for the current layout.

✔ Click the More button in the SmartArt Styles group and then click a thumbnail on the SmartArt Styles drop-down gallery to select a new style for the current layout using the selected colors.

Figure 10-14 shows my fully formatted organizational chart after selecting Table Hierarchy in the Layouts gallery, Colorful – Accent Colors in the
Change Colors gallery, and 3-D Inset in the SmartArt Styles gallery.

Figure 10-14:
Worksheet
with com-
pleted and
formatted
organiza-
tional chart.

Screenshots anyone?

For the first time ever, Excel 2010 supports the creation of screenshot graphics of objects on your Windows desktop that you can automatically insert
into your worksheet. To take a picture of a window open on the desktop
or any other object on it, click the Screenshot drop-down button in the
Illustrations group of the Ribbon's Insert tab (Alt+NSC).

Excel then opens a drop-down menu that displays a thumbnail of available
screen shots (ones currently available) followed by the Screen Clipping item.
To take a picture of any portion of your Windows desktop, click the Screen
Clipping option. Excel then automatically minimizes the Excel program
window on the Windows taskbar and then brightens the screen and changes
the mouse pointer to a thick black cross. You can then use this pointer to
drag an outline around the objects on the Windows desktop you want to
include in the screenshot graphic.

The moment you release the mouse button, Excel 2010 then automatically reopens the program window to its previous size displaying the selected graphic containing the Windows screenshot. You can then resize, move, and adjust this screenshot graphic as you would any other that you add to the worksheet.

Excel automatically saves the screenshot graphic that you add to a worksheet when you save its workbook. However, the program does not provide you with a means by which to save the screenshot graphic in a separate graphics file for use in other programs. If you need to do this, you should select the screenshot graphic in the Excel worksheet, copy it to the Windows Clipboard, and then paste it into another open graphics program where you can use its Save command to store it in a favorite graphics file format for use in other documents.

Theme for a day

Through its themes, Excel 2010 supports a way to format uniformly all the text and graphics you add to a worksheet. You can do this by simply clicking the thumbnail of the new theme you want to use in the Themes drop-down gallery opened by clicking the Themes button on the Page Layout tab of the Ribbon or by pressing Alt+PTH.

Use Live Preview to see how the text and graphics you've added to your worksheet appear in the new theme before you click its thumbnail.

Excel Themes combine three default elements: the color scheme applied to the graphics, the font (body and heading) used in the text and graphics, and the graphic effects applied. If you prefer, you can change any or all of these elements in the worksheet by clicking their command buttons in the Themes group at the start of the Page Layout tab:

 ✔ **Colors** to select a new color scheme by clicking its thumbnail on the drop-down palette. Click Create New Theme Colors at the bottom of this palette to open the Create New Theme Colors dialog box where you can customize each element of the color scheme and save it with a new descriptive name.

 ✔ **Fonts** to select a new font by clicking its thumbnail on the drop-down list. Click Create New Theme Fonts at the bottom of this list to open the Create New Theme Fonts dialog box where you can customize the body and heading fonts and save it with a new descriptive name.

 ✔ **Effects** to select a new set of graphic effects by clicking its thumbnail in the drop-down gallery.

To save your newly selected color scheme, font, and graphic effects as a custom theme that you can reuse in other workbooks, click the Themes command button and then click Save Current Theme at the bottom of the gallery to open the Save Current Theme dialog box. Edit the generic Theme1 filename in the File Name text box (without deleting the `.thmx` filename extension) and then click the Save button. Excel then adds the custom theme to a Custom Themes section in the Themes drop-down gallery and you can apply it to any active worksheet simply by clicking its thumbnail.

Controlling How Graphic Objects Overlap

In case you haven't noticed, graphic objects float on top of the cells of the worksheet. Most of the objects (including charts) are opaque, meaning that they hide (*without* replacing) information in the cells beneath. If you move one opaque graphic so that it overlaps part of another, the one on top hides the one below, just as putting one sheet of paper partially on top of another hides some of the information on the one below. Most of the time, you should make sure that graphic objects don't overlap one another or overlap cells with worksheet information that you want to display.

Reordering the layering of graphic objects

When graphic objects (including charts, text boxes, clip art, imported pictures, drawn shapes, and SmartArt graphics) overlap each other, you can change how they overlay each other by sending the objects back or forward so that they reside on different (invisible) layers.

Excel 2010 enables you to move a selected graphic object to a new layer in one of two ways:

- ✔ For a clip art image, picture, SmartArt diagram, or graphic shape, click the Bring Forward button's arrow and select Bring to Front or click the Send Backward button's arrow and select Send to Back on the Format tab under the Drawing Tools, Picture Tools, or SmartArt tools contextual tab to bring the selected object to the topmost or bottommost layer of the stack, respectively.

- ✔ Click the Selection Pane command button in the Arrange group on the Format tab under the Drawing Tools, Picture Tools, or SmartArt Tools contextual tab to display the Selection and Visibility task pane. Then, click the Bring Forward or Send Backward buttons at the bottom of this task pane in the Re-order section until the selected graphic object appears on the desired layer.

Grouping graphic objects

Sometimes you may find that you need to group several graphic objects so that they act as one unit (like a text box with its arrow). That way, you can move these objects or size them in one operation.

To group objects, Ctrl+click each object you want to group to select them all. Next, click the Group button (the second in the right column of the Arrange group with the picture of two entwined squares) on the Format tab under the Drawing Tools or Picture Tools contextual tab and then click Group on its drop-down menu.

After grouping several graphic objects, whenever you click any part of the mega-object, every part is selected (and selection handles appear only around the perimeter of the combined object).

If you need to independently move or size grouped objects, you can ungroup them by right-clicking an object and then choosing Group⇨Ungroup on the object's shortcut menu or by clicking Group⇨Ungroup on the Format tab under the Drawing Tools or Picture Tools contextual tabs.

Hiding graphic objects

The Selection and Visibility task pane enables you not only to change the layering of various graphic objects in the worksheet but also to control whether they are hidden or displayed.

The way you open the Selection and Visibility task pane depends on the type of graphic object you've selected in the worksheet:

- ✔ **Charts:** Click the Selection Pane button on the Format tab of the Chart Tools contextual tab or press Alt+JOAP.

- ✔ **Text boxes and shapes:** Click the Selection Pane button on the Format tab under the Drawing Tools contextual tab or press Alt+JDAP.

- ✔ **Clip art and pictures:** Click the Selection Pane button on the Format tab under the Picture Tools contextual tab or press Alt+JPAP.

- ✔ **SmartArt:** Click the Selection Pane on the Arrange button's drop-down palette on the Format tab of the SmartArt Tools contextual tab or press Alt+JOAP.

After you open the Selection and Visibility task pane, you can temporarily hide any of the graphic objects listed by clicking its eye check box (to remove the eye icon). To remove the display of all the charts and graphics in the worksheet, click the Hide All button at the bottom of the Selection and Visibility task pane instead.

To redisplay a hidden graphic object, simply click its empty eye check box to put the eye icon back into it. To redisplay all graphic objects after hiding them all, click the Show All button at the bottom of the task pane.

If you hide all the charts and graphics in a worksheet by clicking the Hide All button and then close the Selection and Visibility task pane by clicking its Close button, you'll have no way of redisplaying this task pane so that you can bring back their display by clicking the Show All button. That's because you have no graphic objects left to select in the worksheet and, therefore, no way to get the contextual tabs with their Selection Pane buttons to appear on the Ribbon.

In this dire case, the only way I know to get the Selection and Visibility task pane to appear so that you can click the Show All button is to create a dummy (pardon my French) graphic object in the worksheet (such as an arrow or oval in the Illustrations group on the Insert tab). Then click the Selection Pane button on the Format tab of its Drawing Tools contextual tab. With the Selection and Visibility task pane open, click the Show All button to bring back the display of all the charts and graphics you want to keep. Get rid of the still-selected dummy graphic object by pressing the Delete key. (Whew, that was a close one!)

Printing Just the Charts

Sometimes, you may want to print only a particular chart embedded in the worksheet (independent of the worksheet data it represents or any of the other stuff you've added). To do this, open the Selection and Visibility task pane (as described in the preceding section) and make sure that any hidden charts are displayed in the worksheet by putting the eye icon back in their check boxes.

Next, click the chart to select it in the worksheet and then choose File⇨Print or press Ctrl+P to open the Print Settings panel in Backstage View, where you see the chart now displayed in the print preview area.

If you need to change the printed chart size or the orientation of the printing (or both), click the File tab and then click the Page Setup dialog box launcher on the Page Layout tab of the Ribbon to open the Page Setup dialog box. To change the orientation of the printing (or the paper size), change the appropriate options on the Page tab in the Page Setup dialog box. To change the print quality or print a color chart in black and white, click the Chart tab and change these options. You can then return to the print preview area in the Print Settings panel in Backstage View by clicking the Print Preview button at the bottom of the Page Setup dialog box. If everything looks good in the print preview area, start printing the chart by clicking the Print button.

Chapter 11

Getting on the Data List

• •

In This Chapter

▶ Setting up a data list in Excel

▶ Entering and editing records in the data list

▶ Sorting records in the data list

▶ Filtering records in the data list

▶ Importing external data into the worksheet

• •

*T*he purpose of all the worksheet tables that I discuss elsewhere in this book has been to perform essential calculations (such as to sum monthly or quarterly sales figures) and then present the information in an understandable form. However, you can create another kind of worksheet table in Excel: a *data list* (less accurately and more colloquially known as a *database*). The purpose of a data list is not so much to calculate new values but rather to store lots and lots of information in a consistent manner. For example, you can create a data list that contains the names and addresses of all your clients, or you can create a list that contains all the essential facts about your employees.

Creating a Data List

Creating a new data list in a worksheet is much like creating a worksheet table except that it has only column headings and no row headings. To set up a new data list, follow these steps:

1. **Click the blank cell where you want to start the new data list and then enter the column headings (technically known as *field names* in database parlance) that identify the different kinds of items you need to keep track of (such as First Name, Last Name, Street, City, State, and so on) in the columns to the right.**

   After creating the fields of the data list by entering their headings, you're ready to enter the first row of data.

2. **Make the first entries in the appropriate columns of the row immediately following the one containing the field names.**

   These entries in the first row beneath the one with the field names constitute the first *record* of the data list.

3. **Click the Format as Table button in the Styles group of the Ribbon's Home tab and then click a thumbnail of one of the table styles in the drop-down gallery.**

   Excel puts a marquee around all the cells in the new data list, including the top row of field names. As soon as you click a table style in the drop-down gallery, the Format As Table dialog box appears listing the address of the cell range enclosed in the marquee in the Where Is the Data for Your Table text box.

4. **Click the My Table Has Headers check box to select it, if necessary.**

5. **Click the OK button to close the Format As Table dialog box.**

Excel formats your new data list in the selected table format and adds filters (drop-down buttons) to each of the field names in the top row (see Figure 11-1).

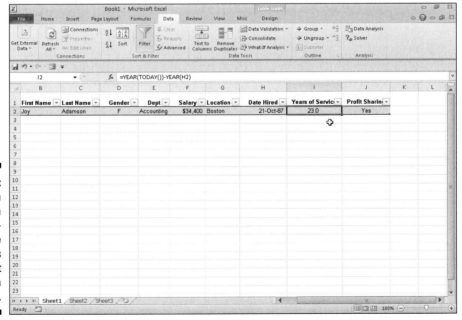

Figure 11-1:
Creating a new data list by formatting the field names and the first record as a table.

Calculated field entries

When you want Excel to calculate the entries for a particular field by formula, you need to enter that formula in the correct field in the first record of the data list. In the sample Employee Data list, for example, the Years of Service field in cell I2 of the first record shown in Figure 11-1 is calculated by the formula =YEAR(TODAY())-YEAR(H2). Cell H2 contains the date of hire that this formula uses to compute the number of years that an employee has worked at the company. Excel then inserts the result of this calculation into the cell as the field entry.

Adding records to a data list

After creating the field names and one record of the data list and formatting them as a table, you're ready to start entering the rest of its data as records in subsequent rows of the list. The most direct way to do this is to press the Tab key when the cell cursor is in the last cell of the first record. Doing this causes Excel to add an extra row to the data list where you can enter the appropriate information for the next record.

When doing data entry directly in a data list table, press the Tab key to proceed to the next field in the new record rather than the ← key. That way, when you complete the entry in the last field of the record, you automatically extend the data list, add a new record, and position the cell cursor in the first field of that record. If you press ← to complete the entry, Excel simply moves the cell cursor to the next cell outside the data list table.

Adding the Form button to the Quick Access toolbar

Instead of entering the records of a data list directly in the table, you can use Excel's data form to make the entries. The only problem with using the data form is that the command to display the form in a worksheet with a data list is not part of the Ribbon commands. You can access the data form only by adding its command button to the Quick Access toolbar. To do this, you must follow these steps:

1. **Click the Customize Quick Access Toolbar button at the end of the Quick Access toolbar and then click the More Commands item at the bottom of its drop-down menu.**

   Excel opens the Excel Options dialog box with the Quick Access Toolbar tab selected.

   The Form command button you want to add to the Quick Access toolbar is only available when you click the Commands Not in the Ribbon option on the Choose Commands From drop-down list.

2. **Click the Commands Not in the Ribbon option near the top of the Choose Commands From drop-down list.**

3. **Click Form in the Choose Commands From list box and then click the Add button.**

   Excel adds the Form button to the very end of the Quick Access toolbar. If you so desire, you can click the Move Up and Move Down buttons to reposition the Form button on this toolbar.

4. **Click OK to close the Excel Options dialog box and return to the worksheet with the data list.**

You can also add the Form button to a custom group on a custom tab. For example, in Figure 11-2, you see that I've added the Form button to a Data List group on a custom Misc tab on the Ribbon as well as to the Quick Access toolbar (shown below the Ribbon).

Adding records to a data list using the data form

The first time you click the custom Form button you added to the Quick Access toolbar, Excel analyzes the row of field names and entries for the first record and creates a data form. This data form lists the field names down the left side of the form with the entries for the first record in the appropriate text boxes next to them. In Figure 11-2, you can see the data form for the new Employee Data database; it looks kind of like a customized dialog box.

The data form Excel creates includes the entries you made in the first record. The data form also contains a series of buttons (on the right side) that you use to add, delete, or find specific records in the database. Right above the first button (New), the data form lists the number of the record you're looking at followed by the total number of records (1 of 1 when you first create the data form). When creating new entries it will display New Record above this button instead of the record number.

All the formatting that you assign to the particular entries in the first record is applied automatically to those fields in subsequent records you enter and is used in the data form. For example, if your data list contains a telephone field, you need to enter only the ten digits of the phone number in the Telephone field of the data form if the initial telephone number entry is formatted in the first record with the Special Phone Number format. (See Chapter 3 for details on sorting number formats.) That way, Excel takes a new entry in the Telephone file, such as 3075550045, for example, and automatically formats it so that it appears as (307) 555-0045 in the appropriate cell of the data list.

The process for adding records to a data list with the data form is simple. When you click the New button, Excel displays a blank data form (marked New Record at the right side of the data form), which you get to fill in.

Form buttons

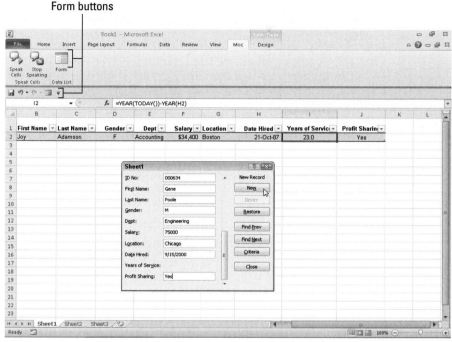

Figure 11-2:
Enter the
second
record of
the data list
in its data
form.

After you enter the information for the first field, press the Tab key to advance to the next field in the record.

Whoa! Don't press the Enter key to advance to the next field in a record. If you do, you'll insert the new, incomplete record into the database.

Continue entering information for each field and pressing Tab to go to the next field in the database.

- ✔ If you notice that you've made an error and want to edit an entry in a field you already passed, press Shift+Tab to return to that field.
- ✔ To replace the entry, just start typing.
- ✔ To edit some of the characters in the field, press → or click the I-beam pointer in the entry to locate the insertion point; then edit the entry from there.

When entering information in a particular field, you can copy the entry made in that field from the previous record by pressing Ctrl+' (apostrophe). Press Ctrl+', for example, to carry forward the same entry in the State field of each new record when entering a series of records for people who all live in the same state.

When entering dates in a date field, use a consistent date format that Excel knows. (For example, enter something like **7/21/98.**) When entering zip codes that sometimes use leading zeros that you don't want to disappear from the entry (such as zip code 00102), format the first field entry with the Special Zip Code number format (refer to Chapter 3 for details on sorting number formats). In the case of other numbers that use leading zeros, you can format it by using the Text format or put an ' (apostrophe) before the first 0. The apostrophe tells Excel to treat the number like a text label but doesn't show up in the database itself. (The only place you can see the apostrophe is on the Formula bar when the cell cursor is in the cell with the numeric entry.)

Press the ↓ key when you've entered all the information for the new record. Or, instead of the ↓ key, you can press Enter or click the New button (refer to Figure 11-2). Excel inserts the new record as the last record in the database in the worksheet and displays a new blank data form in which you can enter the next record (see Figure 11-3).

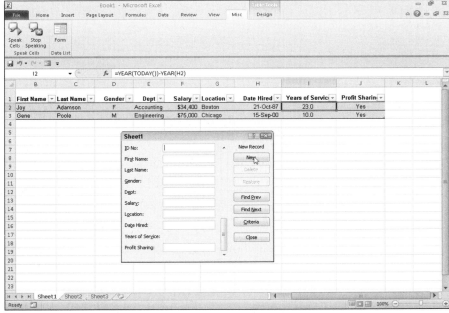

Figure 11-3: When you advance to a new record in the data form, Excel inserts the record just completed as the last row of the list.

When you finish adding records to the database, press the Esc key or click the Close button at the bottom of the dialog box to close the data form.

Editing records with the data form

After the database is under way and you're caught up with entering new records, you can start using the data form to perform routine maintenance on the database. For example, you can use the data form to locate a record you want to change and then make the edits to the particular fields. You can also use the data form to find a specific record you want to remove and then delete it from the database.

✔ Locate the record you want to edit in the database by bringing up its data form. See the following two sections ("Moving through the records in the data form" and "Finding records with the data form") and Table 11-1 for hints on locating records.

✔ To edit the fields of the current record, move to that field by pressing Tab or Shift+Tab and replace the entry by typing a new one.

 Alternatively, press ← or → or click the I-beam cursor to reposition the insertion point, and then make your edits.

✔ To clear a field entirely, select it and then press the Delete key.

To delete the entire record from the database, click the Delete button in the data form. Excel displays an alert box with the following dire warning:

```
Displayed record will be permanently deleted
```

To delete the record displayed in the data form, click OK. To play it safe and keep the record intact, click the Cancel button.

You cannot use the Undo feature to bring back a record you removed with the Delete button! Excel is definitely not kidding when it warns *permanently deleted*. As a precaution, always save a back-up version of the worksheet with the database before you start removing old records.

Moving through the records in the data form

In the data form, you can use the scroll bar to the right of the list of field names or various keystrokes (both summarized in Table 11-1) to move through the records in the database until you find the one you want to edit or delete.

✔ **To move to the data form for the next record in the data list:** Press ↓, press Enter, or click the down scroll arrow at the bottom of the scroll bar.

✔ **To move to the data form for the previous record in the data list:** Press ↑, press Shift+Enter, or click the up scroll arrow at the top of the scroll bar.

✔ **To move to the data form for the first record in the data list:** Press Ctrl+↑, press Ctrl+PgUp, or drag the scroll box to the very top of the scroll bar.

✔ **To move to a new data form immediately following the last record in the database:** Press Ctrl+↓, press Ctrl+PgDn, or drag the scroll box to the very bottom of the scroll bar.

Table 11-1	Ways to Get to a Particular Record
Keystrokes or Scroll Bar Technique	*Result*
Press ↓ or Enter or click the down scroll arrow or the Find Next button	Moves to the next record in the data list and leaves the same field selected
Press ↑ or Shift+Enter or click the up scroll arrow or the Find Prev button	Moves to the previous record in the data list and leaves the same field selected
Press PgDn	Moves forward ten records in the data list
Press PgUp	Moves backward ten records in the data list
Press Ctrl+↑ or Ctrl+PgUp or drag the scroll box to the top of the scroll bar	Moves to the first record in the data list
Drag the scroll box to almost the bottom of the scroll bar	Moves to the last record in the data list

Finding records with the data form

In a large data list, trying to find a particular record by moving from record to record — or even moving ten records at a time with the scroll bar — can take all day. Rather than waste time trying to manually search for a record, you can use the Criteria button in the data form to look it up.

When you click the Criteria button, Excel clears all the field entries in the data form (and replaces the record number with the word *Criteria*) so that you can enter the criteria to search for in the blank text boxes.

For example, suppose that you need to edit Sherry Caulfield's profit sharing status. Unfortunately, her paperwork doesn't include her ID number. All you know is that she works in the Boston office and spells her last name with a *C* instead of a *K*.

To find her record, you can use the information you have to narrow the search to all the records where the last name begins with the letter *C* and the Location field contains Boston. To limit your search in this way, open the data form for the Employee Data database, click the Criteria button, and then type **C*** in the text box for the Last Name field. Also enter **Boston** in the text box for the Location field (see Figure 11-4).

When you enter search criteria for records in the blank text boxes of the data form, you can use the ? (for single) and * (for multiple) wildcard characters.

Now click the Find Next button. Excel displays in the data form the first record in the database where the last name begins with the letter *C* and the Location field contains Boston. As shown in Figure 11-5, the first record in this database that meets these criteria is for William Cobb. To find Sherry's record, click the Find Next button again. Sherry Caulfield's record shows up in Figure 11-6. Having located Caulfield's record, you can then edit her profit sharing status from No to Yes in the text box for the Profit Sharing field. When you click the Close button, Excel records her new profit sharing status in the data list.

Figure 11-6:
Eureka!
Caulfield's
long lost
record is
found in the
database.

When you use the Criteria button in the data form to find records, you can include the following operators in the search criteria you enter to locate a specific record in the database:

Operator	*Meaning*
=	Equal to
>	Greater than
>=	Greater than or equal to
<	Less than
<=	Less than or equal to
<>	Not equal to

For example, to display only those records where an employee's salary is greater than or equal to $50,000, enter **>=50000** in the text box for the Salary field and then click the Find Next button.

When specifying search criteria that fit a number of records, you may have to click the Find Next or Find Prev button several times to locate the record you want. If no record fits the search criteria you enter, the computer beeps at you when you click these buttons.

To change the search criteria, first clear the data form by clicking the Criteria button again and then clicking the Clear button.

To switch back to the current record without using the search criteria you enter, click the Form button. (This button replaces the Criteria button as soon as you click the Criteria button.)

Sorting Records in a Data List

Every data list you put together in Excel will have some kind of preferred order for maintaining and viewing the records. Depending on the list, you may want to see the records in alphabetical order by last name. In the case of a database of clients, you may want to see the records arranged alphabetically by company name. In the case of the Employee Data list, the preferred order is in numerical order by the ID number assigned to each employee when he or she is hired.

When you initially enter records for a new data list, you no doubt enter them in either the preferred order or the order in which you retrieve their records. However you start out, as you will soon discover, you don't have the option of adding subsequent records in that preferred order. Whenever you add a new record, Excel tacks that record onto the bottom of the database by adding a new row.

Suppose you originally enter all the records in a Client data list in alphabetical order by company (from Acme Pet Supplies to Zastrow and Sons), and then you add the record for a new client: Pammy's Pasta Palace. Excel puts the new record at the bottom of the barrel — in the last row right after Zastrow and Sons — instead of inserting it in its proper position, which is somewhere after Acme Pet Supplies but definitely well ahead of Zastrow and his wonderful boys!

This isn't the only problem you can have with the original record order. Even if the records in the data list remain stable, the preferred order merely represents the order you use *most* of the time. What about those times when you need to see the records in another, special order?

For example, if you usually work with a client data list in numerical order by case number, you might instead need to see the records in alphabetical order by the client's last name to quickly locate a client and look up his or her balance due in a printout. When using records to generate mailing labels for a mass mailing, you want the records in zip code order. When generating a report for your account representatives showing which clients are in whose territory, you need the records in alphabetical order by state and maybe even by city.

Up and down the ascending and descending sort orders

When you use the ascending sort order on a field in the data list that contains many different kinds of entries, Excel places numbers (from smallest to largest) before text entries (in alphabetical order), followed by any logical values (FALSE and TRUE), error values, and finally, blank cells. When you use the descending sort order, Excel arranges the different entries in reverse: numbers are still first, arranged from largest to smallest; text entries go from Z to A; and the TRUE logical value precedes the FALSE logical value.

To have Excel correctly sort the records in a data list, you must specify which field's values determine the new order of the records. (Such fields are technically known as the *sorting keys* in the parlance of the database enthusiast.) Further, you must specify what type of order you want to create using the information in these fields. Choose from two possible orders:

- **Ascending order:** Text entries are placed in alphabetical order from A to Z, values are placed in numerical order from smallest to largest, and dates are placed in order from oldest to newest.

- **Descending order:** This is the reverse of alphabetical order from Z to A, numerical order from largest to smallest, and dates from newest to oldest.

Sorting records on a single field

When you need to sort the data list on only one particular field (such as the Record Number, Last Name, or Company field), you simply click that field's AutoFilter button and then click the appropriate sort option on its drop-down list:

- **Sort A to Z** or **Sort Z to A** in a text field

- **Sort Smallest to Largest** or **Sort Largest to Smallest** in a number field

- **Sort Oldest to Newest** or **Sort Newest to Oldest** in a date field

Excel then reorders all the records in the data list in accordance with the new ascending or descending order in the selected field. If you find that you've sorted the list in error, simply click the Undo button on the Quick

Access toolbar or press Ctrl+Z right away to return the list to its order before you selected one of these sort options.

 Excel shows when a field has been used to sort the data list by adding an up or down arrow to its AutoFilter button. An arrow pointing up indicates that the ascending sort order was used and an arrow pointing down indicates that the descending sort order was used.

Sorting records on multiple fields

You need to use more than one field in sorting when the first field you use contains duplicate values and you want a say in how the records with duplicates are arranged. (If you don't specify another field to sort on, Excel just puts the records in the order in which you entered them.)

The best and most common example of when you need more than one field is when sorting a large database alphabetically by last name. Suppose that you have a database that contains several people with the last name Smith, Jones, or Zastrow (as is the case when you work at Zastrow and Sons). If you specify the Last Name field as the only field to sort on (using the default ascending order), all the duplicate Smiths, Joneses, and Zastrows are placed in the order in which their records were originally entered. To better sort these duplicates, you can specify the First Name field as the second field to sort on (again using the default ascending order), making the second field the tie-breaker, so that Ian Smith's record precedes that of Sandra Smith, and Vladimir Zastrow's record comes after that of Mikhail Zastrow.

To sort records in a data list on multiple fields, follow these steps:

1. **Position the cell cursor in one of the cells in the data list table.**

2. **If the Home tab on the Ribbon is selected, click Custom Sort on the Sort & Filter button's drop-down list (Alt+HSU). If the Data tab is selected, click the Sort command button.**

   Excel selects all the records of the database (without including the first row of field names) and opens the Sort dialog box, shown in Figure 11-7.

3. **Click the name of the field you first want the records sorted by in the Sort By drop-down list.**

   If you want the records arranged in descending order, remember also to click the descending sort option (Z to A, Largest to Smallest, or Newest to Oldest) Order drop-down list to the right.

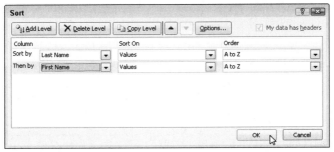

Figure 11-7:
Set up to
sort records
alphabeti-
cally by last
name and
then first
name.

4. **(Optional) If the first field contains duplicates and you want to specify how the records in this field are sorted, click the Add Level button to insert another sort level. Select a second field to sort on in the Then By drop-down list and select either the ascending or descending option in its Order drop-down list to its right.**

5. **(Optional) If necessary, repeat Step 4, adding as many additional sort levels as required.**

6. **Click OK or press Enter.**

   Excel closes the Sort dialog box and sorts the records in the data list using the sorting fields in the order of their levels in this dialog box. If you see that you sorted the database on the wrong fields or in the wrong order, click the Undo button on the Quick Access toolbar or press Ctrl+Z to restore the database records to their previous order.

Check out how I set up my search in the Sort dialog box in Figure 11-7. In the Employee Data List, I chose the Last Name field as the first field to sort on (Sort By) and the First Name field as the second field (Then By) — the second field sorts records with duplicate entries in the first field. I also chose to sort the records in the Employee Data List in alphabetical (A to Z) order by last name and then first name. See the Employee Data List right after sorting (in Figure 11-8). Note how the Edwards — Cindy and Jack — are now arranged in the proper first name/last name alphabetical order.

Sorting something besides a data list

The Sort command is not just for sorting records in the data list. You can use it to sort financial data or text headings in the spreadsheet tables you build as well. When sorting regular worksheet tables, just be sure to select all the cells with the data to be sorted (and only those with the data to be sorted) before you open the Sort dialog box by clicking Custom Sort on the Sort & Filter button's drop-down list on the Ribbon's Home tab or the Sort button on the Data tab.

Excel automatically excludes the first row of the cell selection from the sort (on the assumption that this row is a header row containing field names that shouldn't be included). To include the first row of the cell selection in the sort, be sure to deselect the My Data Has Headers check box before you click OK to begin sorting.

If you want to sort worksheet data by columns, click the Options button in the Sort dialog box. Click the Sort Left to Right button in the Sort Options dialog box and then click OK. Now you can designate the number of the row (or rows) to sort the data on in the Sort dialog box.

Figure 11-8:
The Employee Data List sorted in alphabetical order by last name and then by first name.

	A	B	C	D	E	F	G	H	I	J
1	ID No	First Name	Last Name	Gende	Dept	Salary	Location	Date Hire	Years of Servic	Profit Shar
2	000928	Joy	Adamson	F	Accounting	$34,400	Boston	21-Oct-87	23.0	Yes
3	000262	Lance	Bird	M	Human Resources	$21,100	Boston	13-Aug-97	13.0	Yes
4	000307	Robert	Bjorkman	M	Engineering	$25,000	Chicago	24-Feb-98	12.0	Yes
5	000101	Michael	Bryant	M	Administration	$30,440	Santa Rosa	01-Feb-91	19.0	Yes
6	000159	Sherry	Caulfield	F	Accounting	$24,100	Boston	19-Mar-94	16.0	Yes
7	000139	William	Cobb	M	Human Resources	$27,500	Boston	28-May-01	9.0	Yes
8	000141	Angela	Dickinson	F	Engineering	$23,900	Detroit	13-Nov-96	14.0	No
9	000174	Cindy	Edwards	F	Accounting	$21,500	San Francisco	15-Aug-85	25.0	No
10	000220	Jack	Edwards	M	Engineering	$32,200	Atlanta	14-Feb-97	13.0	Yes
11	000367	Amanda	Fletcher	F	Human Resources	$26,500	Boston	03-Jan-99	11.0	No
12	000315	Dave	Grogan	M	Information Services	$47,500	Seattle	03-Apr-98	12.0	No
13	000185	Rebecca	Johnson	F	Human Resources	$50,200	Boston	04-Feb-96	14.0	No
14	000211	Stuart	Johnson	M	Engineering	$62,000	Seattle	29-Dec-00	10.0	No
15	000118	Janet	Kaplan	F	Engineering	$34,000	Boston	22-Jun-91	19.0	Yes
16	000222	Mary	King	F	Accounting	$38,000	Detroit	10-Mar-97	13.0	No
17	000146	Edward	Krauss	M	Administration	$86,200	Chicago	13-Jul-99	11.0	Yes
18	000162	Kimberly	Lerner	F	Human Resources	$34,900	Chicago	28-Jun-99	11.0	No
19	000603	Sarah	Michaels	F	Information Services	$57,500	Santa Rosa	23-Mar-02	8.0	No
20	000210	Victoria	Morin	F	Engineering	$40,700	Seattle	20-Dec-96	14.0	No
21	000284	Miriam	Morse	F	Engineering	$29,600	Chicago	02-Nov-97	13.0	No
22	000192	Deborah	Mosley	F	Administration	$20,800	Detroit	23-Aug-01	9.0	No
23	000297	James	Percival	M	Engineering	$29,200	Atlanta	18-Dec-97	13.0	Yes
24	000634	Gene	Poole	M	Engineering	$75,000	Chicago	15-Sep-00	10.0	No
25	000348	Carl	Reese	M	Information Services	$25,800	Atlanta	13-Sep-88	22.0	No
26	000361	Linda	Robinson	F	Engineering	$37,000	Detroit	11-Nov-98	12.0	No
27	000226	Adam	Rosenzweig	M	Accounting	$29,000	Detroit	01-Mar-01	9.0	No
28	000190	Elizabeth	Santos	F	Information Services	$27,200	Atlanta	17-Jul-96	14.0	Yes

Filtering the Records in a Data List

Excel's Filter feature makes it a breeze to hide everything in a data list except the records you want to see. To filter the data list to just those records that contain a particular value, you then click the appropriate field's AutoFilter button to display a drop-down list containing all the entries made in that field and select the one you want to use as a filter. Excel then displays only those records that contain the value you selected in that field. (All other records are hidden temporarily.)

If for any reason, the column headings of your data list table don't have filter drop-down buttons displayed in their cells after the field names, you can get them back simply by clicking Home➪Sort & Filter➪Filter or pressing Alt+HSF.

For example, in Figure 11-9, I filtered the Employee Data List to display only those records in which the Location is either Boston or San Francisco by clicking the Location field's AutoFilter button and then clicking the (Select All) check box to remove its check mark. I then clicked the Boston and San Francisco check boxes to add check marks to them before clicking OK. (It's as simple as that.)

Figure 11-9:
The Employee Data List after filtering out all records except those with Boston or San Francisco in the Location field.

	A	B	C	D	E	F	G	H	I	J
1	ID Nc	First Name	Last Name	Gende	Dept	Salary	Location	Date Hire	Years of Servic	Profit Shar
2	000928	Joy	Adamson	F	Accounting	$34,400	Boston	21-Oct-87	23.0	Yes
3	000262	Lance	Bird	M	Human Resources	$21,100	Boston	13-Aug-97	13.0	Yes
6	000159	Sherry	Caulfield	F	Accounting	$24,100	Boston	19-Mar-94	16.0	Yes
7	000139	William	Cobb	M	Human Resources	$27,500	Boston	28-May-01	9.0	Yes
9	000174	Cindy	Edwards	F	Accounting	$21,500	San Francisco	15-Aug-85	25.0	No
11	000367	Amanda	Fletcher	F	Human Resources	$26,500	Boston	03-Jan-99	11.0	No
13	000185	Rebecca	Johnson	F	Human Resources	$50,200	Boston	04-Feb-96	14.0	No
15	000118	Janet	Kaplan	F	Engineering	$34,000	Boston	22-Jun-91	19.0	Yes
30	000339	Charles	Smith	M	Administration	$87,800	San Francisco	09-Jul-98	12.0	No
33	000366	Richard	Zucker	M	Engineering	$37,500	San Francisco	26-Dec-00	10.0	No

After you filter a data list so that only the records you want to work with are displayed, you can copy those records to another part of the worksheet to the right of the database (or better yet, another worksheet in the workbook). Simply select the cells, then click the Copy button on the Home tab or press Ctrl+C, move the cell cursor to the first cell where the copied records are to appear, and then press Enter. After copying the filtered records, you can then redisplay all the records in the database or apply a slightly different filter.

If you find that filtering the data list by selecting a single value in a field drop-down list box gives you more records than you really want to contend with, you can further filter the database by selecting another value in a second field's drop-down list. For example, suppose that you select Boston as the filter value in the Location field's drop-down list and end up with hundreds of Boston records displayed in the worksheet. To reduce the number of Boston records to a more manageable number, you could then select a value (such as Human Resources) in the Dept field's drop-down list to further filter the database and reduce the records you have to work with onscreen. When you finish working with the Boston Human Resources employee records, you can display another set by displaying the Dept field's drop-down list again and changing the filter value from Human Resources to some other department, such as Accounting.

When you're ready to display all the records in the database again, click the filtered field's AutoFilter button (indicated by the appearance of a cone filter on its drop-down button) and then click the (Select All) option near the middle of the drop-down list before you click OK.

You can temporarily remove the AutoFilter buttons from the cells in the top row of the data list containing the field names and later redisplay them by clicking the Filter button on the Data tab or by pressing Alt+AT.

Using ready-made number filters

Excel contains a number filter option called Top 10. You can use this option on a number field to show only a certain number of records (like the ones with the ten highest or lowest values in that field or those in the ten highest or lowest percent in that field). To use the Top 10 option to filter a database, follow these steps:

1. **Click the AutoFilter button on the numeric field you want to filter with the Top 10 option. Then highlight Number Filters in the drop-down list and click Top 10 on its submenu.**

   Excel opens the Top 10 AutoFilter dialog box. By default, the Top 10 AutoFilter chooses to show the top ten items in the selected field. However, you can change these default settings before filtering the database.

2. **To show only the bottom ten records, change Top to Bottom in the leftmost drop-down list box.**

3. **To show more or fewer than the top or bottom ten records, enter the new value in the middle text box (that currently holds 10) or select a new value by using the spinner buttons.**

4. **To show those records that fall into the Top 10 or Bottom 10 (or whatever) percent, change Items to Percent in the rightmost drop-down list box.**

5. **Click OK or press Enter to filter the database by using your Top 10 settings.**

In Figure 11-10, you can see the Employee Data List after using the Top 10 option (with all its default settings) to show only those records with salaries that are in the top ten. David Letterman would be proud!

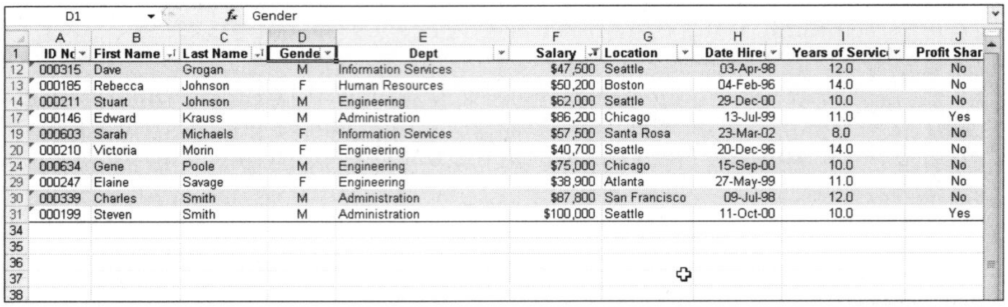

	A	B	C	D	E	F	G	H	I	J
1	ID Nc	First Name	Last Name	Gende	Dept	Salary	Location	Date Hire	Years of Servic	Profit Shar
12	000315	Dave	Grogan	M	Information Services	$47,500	Seattle	03-Apr-98	12.0	No
13	000185	Rebecca	Johnson	F	Human Resources	$50,200	Boston	04-Feb-96	14.0	No
14	000211	Stuart	Johnson	M	Engineering	$62,000	Seattle	29-Dec-00	10.0	No
17	000146	Edward	Krauss	M	Administration	$86,200	Chicago	13-Jul-99	11.0	Yes
19	000603	Sarah	Michaels	F	Information Services	$57,500	Santa Rosa	23-Mar-02	8.0	No
20	000210	Victoria	Morin	F	Engineering	$40,700	Seattle	20-Dec-96	14.0	No
24	000634	Gene	Poole	M	Engineering	$75,000	Chicago	15-Sep-00	10.0	No
29	000247	Elaine	Savage	F	Engineering	$38,900	Atlanta	27-May-99	11.0	No
30	000339	Charles	Smith	M	Administration	$87,800	San Francisco	09-Jul-98	12.0	No
31	000199	Steven	Smith	M	Administration	$100,000	Seattle	11-Oct-00	10.0	Yes
34										
35										
36										
37										
38										

Figure 11-10: The Employee Data List after using the Top 10 AutoFilter to filter out all records except for those with the ten highest salaries.

Using ready-made date filters

When filtering a data list by the entries in a date field, Excel makes available a variety of date filters that you can apply to the list. These ready-made filters include Tomorrow, Today, Yesterday, as well as Next, This, and Last for the Week, Month, Quarter, and Year. Additionally, Excel offers Year to Date and All Dates in the Period filters. When you select the All Dates in the Period filter, Excel enables you to choose between Quarter 1 through 4 or any of the twelve months, January through December, as the period to use in filtering the records.

To select any of these date filters, you click the date field's AutoFilter button, then highlight Date Filters on the drop-down list and click the appropriate date filter option on the continuation menu(s).

Getting creative with custom filtering

In addition to filtering a data list to records that contain a particular field entry (such as Newark as the City or CA as the State), you can create custom AutoFilters that enable you to filter the list to records that meet less-exacting criteria (such as last names starting with the letter M) or ranges of values (such as salaries between $25,000 and $75,000 a year).

To create a custom filter for a field, you click the field's AutoFilter button and then highlight Text Filters, Number Filters, or Date Filters (depending on the type of field) on the drop-down list and then click the Custom Filter option at the bottom of the continuation list. When you select the Custom Filter option, Excel displays a Custom AutoFilter dialog box, similar to the one shown in Figure 11-11.

You can also open the Custom AutoFilter dialog box by clicking the initial operator (Equals, Does Not Equal, Greater Than, and so on) on the field's Text Filters, Number Filters, or Date Filters submenus.

Figure 11-11:
Use a
custom
AutoFilter
to display
records
with entries
in the
Salary field
between
$25,000 and
$75,000.

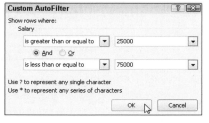

In this dialog box, you select the operator that you want to use in the first drop-down list box. (See Table 11-2 for operator names and what they locate.) Then enter the value (text or numbers) that should be met, exceeded, fallen below, or not found in the records of the database in the text box to the right.

Table 11-2	Operators Used in Custom AutoFilters	
Operator	**Example**	**What It Locates in the Database**
Equals	Salary equals 35000	Records where the value in the Salary field is equal to $35,000
Does not equal	State does not equal NY	Records where the entry in the State field is not NY (New York)
Is greater than	Zip is greater than 42500	Records where the number in the Zip field comes after 42500

(continued)

Table 11-2 *(continued)*

Operator	Example	What It Locates in the Database
Is greater than or equal to	Zip is greater than or equal to 42500	Records where the number in the Zip field is equal to 42500 or comes after it
Is less than	Salary is less than 25000	Records where the value in the Salary field is less than $25,000 a year
Is less than or equal to	Salary is less than or equal to 25000	Records where the value in the Salary field is equal to $25,000 or less than $25,000
Begins with	Begins with d	Records with specified fields have entries that start with the letter *d*
Does not begin with	Does not begin with d	Records with specified fields have entries that do not start with the letter *d*
Ends with	Ends with ey	Records whose specified fields have entries that end with the letters *ey*
Does not end with	Does not end with ey	Records with specified fields have entries that do not end with the letters *ey*
Contains	Contains Harvey	Records with specified fields have entries that contain the name Harvey
Does not contain	Does not contain Harvey	Records with specified fields have entries that don't contain the name Harvey

If you want to filter records in which only a particular field entry matches, exceeds, falls below, or simply is not the same as the one you enter in the text box, you then click OK or press Enter to apply this filter to the database. However, you can use the Custom AutoFilter dialog box to filter the database to records with field entries that fall within a range of values or meet either one of two criteria.

To set up a range of values, you select the "is greater than" or "is greater than or equal to" operator for the top operator and then enter or select the lowest (or first) value in the range. Then, make sure that the And option is selected, select "is less than" or "is less than or equal to" as the bottom operator, and enter the highest (or last) value in the range.

Check out Figures 11-11 and 11-12 to see how I filter the records in the Employee Data List so that only those records where Salary amounts are between $25,000 and $75,000 are displayed. As shown in Figure 11-11, you set up this range of values as the filter by selecting "is greater than or equal to" as the operator and 25,000 as the lower value of the range. Then, with the And option selected, you select "is less than or equal to" as the operator and 75,000 as the upper value of the range. The results of applying this filter to the Employee Data List are shown in Figure 11-12.

Figure 11-12: The Employee Data List after applying the custom AutoFilter.

ID No	First Name	Last Name	Gender	Dept	Salary	Location	Date Hire	Years of Servic	Profit Shar
000928	Joy	Adamson	F	Accounting	$34,400	Boston	21-Oct-87	23.0	Yes
000307	Robert	Bjorkman	M	Engineering	$25,000	Chicago	24-Feb-98	12.0	Yes
000101	Michael	Bryant	M	Administration	$30,440	Santa Rosa	01-Feb-91	19.0	Yes
000139	William	Cobb	M	Human Resources	$27,500	Boston	28-May-01	9.0	Yes
000220	Jack	Edwards	M	Engineering	$32,200	Atlanta	14-Feb-97	13.0	Yes
000367	Amanda	Fletcher	F	Human Resources	$26,500	Boston	03-Jan-99	11.0	No
000315	Dave	Grogan	M	Information Services	$47,500	Seattle	03-Apr-98	12.0	No
000185	Rebecca	Johnson	F	Human Resources	$50,200	Seattle	04-Feb-96	14.0	No
000211	Stuart	Johnson	M	Engineering	$62,000	Seattle	29-Dec-00	10.0	No
000118	Janet	Kaplan	F	Engineering	$34,000	Boston	22-Jun-91	19.0	Yes
000222	Mary	King	F	Accounting	$38,000	Detroit	10-Mar-97	13.0	No
000162	Kimberly	Lerner	F	Human Resources	$34,900	Chicago	28-Jun-99	11.0	No
000603	Sarah	Michaels	F	Information Services	$57,500	Santa Rosa	23-Mar-02	8.0	No
000210	Victoria	Morin	F	Engineering	$40,700	Seattle	20-Dec-96	14.0	No
000284	Miriam	Morse	F	Engineering	$29,600	Chicago	02-Nov-97	13.0	No
000297	James	Percival	M	Engineering	$29,200	Atlanta	18-Dec-97	13.0	Yes
000634	Gene	Poole	M	Engineering	$75,000	Chicago	15-Sep-00	10.0	No
000348	Carl	Reese	M	Information Services	$25,800	Atlanta	13-Sep-88	22.0	No
000361	Linda	Robinson	F	Engineering	$37,000	Detroit	11-Nov-98	12.0	No
000226	Adam	Rosenzweig	M	Accounting	$29,000	Detroit	01-Mar-01	9.0	No
000190	Elizabeth	Santos	F	Information Services	$27,200	Atlanta	17-Jul-96	14.0	Yes
000247	Elaine	Savage	F	Engineering	$38,900	Atlanta	27-May-99	11.0	No
000324	George	Tallan	M	Human Resources	$29,700	Chicago	20-May-99	11.0	No
000366	Richard	Zucker	M	Engineering	$37,500	San Francisco	26-Dec-00	10.0	No

To set up an either/or condition in the Custom AutoFilter dialog box, you normally choose between the "equals" and "does not equal" operators (whichever is appropriate) and then enter or select the first value that must be met or must not be equaled. Then you select the Or option and select whichever operator is appropriate and enter or select the second value that must be met or must not be equaled.

For example, if you want to filter the data list so that only records for the Accounting or Human Resources departments in the Employee Data List appear, you select "equals" as the first operator and then select or enter Accounting as the first entry. Next, you click the Or option, select "equals" as the second operator, and then select or enter Human Resources as the second entry. When you then filter the database by clicking OK or pressing Enter, Excel displays only those records with either Accounting or Human Resources as the entry in the Dept field.

Importing External Data

Excel 2010 makes it easy to import data into a worksheet from other database tables created with standalone database management systems (such as Microsoft Office Access), a process known as making an *external data query*.

You can also use Web queries to import data directly from various Web pages containing financial and other types of statistical data that you need to work with in the Excel worksheet.

Querying an Access database table

To make an external data query to an Access database table, you click the From Access command button on the Ribbon's Data tab or press Alt+AFA. Excel opens the Select Data Source dialog box where you select the name of the Access database (using an * . accb file extension) and then click Open. The Select Table dialog box appears from which you can select the data table that you want to import into the worksheet. After you select the data table and click OK in this dialog box, the Import Data dialog box appears.

The Import Data dialog box contains the following options:

- ✔ **Table** to have the data in the Access data table imported into an Excel table in either the current or new worksheet — see Existing Worksheet and New Worksheet entries that follow

- ✔ **PivotTable Report** to have the data in the Access data table imported into a new pivot table (see Chapter 9) that you can construct with the Access data

✔ **PivotChart and PivotTable Report** to have the data in the Access data table imported into a new pivot table (see Chapter 9) with an embedded pivot chart that you can construct with the Access data

✔ **Only Create Connection** to link to the data in the selected Access data table without bringing its data into the Excel worksheet

✔ **Existing Worksheet** (default) to have the data in the Access data table imported into the current worksheet starting at the current cell address listed in the text box below

✔ **New Worksheet** to have the data in the Access data table imported into a new sheet that's added to the beginning of the workbook

Figure 11-13 shows you an Excel worksheet after importing the Invoices data table from the sample Northwind Access database as a new data table in Excel. After importing the data, you can then use the AutoFilter buttons attached to the various fields to sort and filter the data (as described earlier in this chapter).

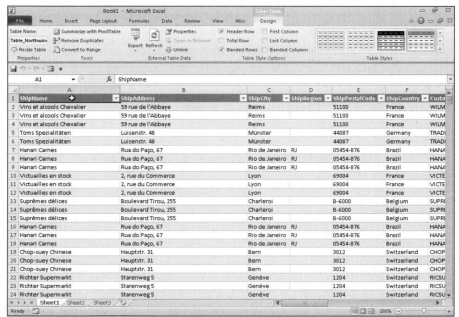

Figure 11-13:
Worksheet after importing Access data table.

Excel keeps a list of all the external data queries you make so that you can reuse them to import updated data from another database or Web page. To reuse a query, click the Existing Connections button on the Data tab (Alt+AX) to open the Existing Connections dialog box to access this list and then click the name of the query to repeat.

Databases created and maintained with Microsoft Office Access are not, of course, the only external data sources on which you can perform external data queries. To import data from other sources, you click the From Other Sources button on the Data tab or press Alt+AFO to open a drop-down menu with the following options:

- ✔ **From SQL Server** to import data from an SQL Server table

- ✔ **From Analysis Services** to import data from an SQL Server Analysis cube

- ✔ **From XML Data Import** to import data from an XML file that you open and map

- ✔ **From Data Connection Wizard** to import data from a database table using the Data Connection Wizard and OLEDB (Object Linking and Embedding Database)

- ✔ **From Microsoft Query** to import data from a database table using Microsoft Query and ODBC (Open Database Connectivity)

For specific help with importing data using these various sources, see my *Excel 2010 All-In-One Desk Reference For Dummies*.

Performing a New Web query

To make a Web page query, you click the From Web command button on the Data tab of the Ribbon or press Alt+AFW. Excel then opens the New Web Query dialog box containing the Home page for your computer's default Web browser (Internet Explorer 8 in most cases). To select the Web page containing the data you want to import into Excel, you can:

- ✔ Type the URL Web address in the Address text box at the top of the Home page in the New Web Query dialog box.

- ✔ Use the Search feature offered on the Home page or its links to find the Web page containing the data you wish to import.

When you have the Web page containing the data you want to import displayed in the New Web Query dialog box, Excel indicates which tables of information you can import from the Web page into the worksheet by adding a yellow box with an arrowhead pointing right. To import these tables, you simply click this box to add a check mark to it (see Figure 11-14).

After you finish checking all the tables you want to import on the page, click the Import button to close the New Web Query dialog box. Excel then opens a version of the Import Data dialog box with only the Table option available where you can indicate where the table data is to be imported by selecting one of these options:

- ✔ **Existing Worksheet** (default) to have the data in the Access data table imported into the current worksheet starting at the current cell address listed in the text box
- ✔ **New Worksheet** to have the data in the Access data table imported into a new sheet that's added to the beginning of the workbook

After you click OK in the Import Data dialog box, Excel closes the dialog box and then imports all the tables of data you selected on the Web page into a new worksheet starting at cell A1 or in the existing worksheet starting at the cell whose address was entered in the text box in the Import Data dialog box.

Figure 11-15 shows the results of the Web query initiated in the New Web Query dialog box shown in Figure 11-14.

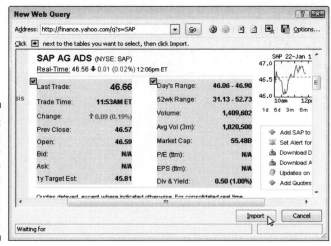

Figure 11-14: Selecting the table of data to import on the Yahoo! Finance Web page.

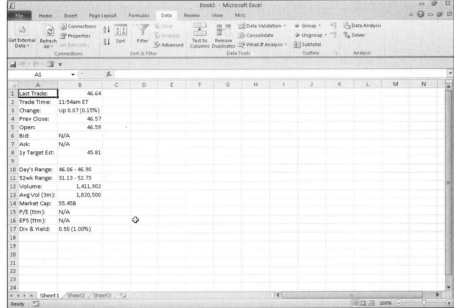

Figure 11-15:
New work-
sheet after
importing
the then
current
data in the
Volume
Leaders
table on
the Yahoo!
Finance
Web page.

Excel brings this data from the Volume Leaders table on the Yahoo! Finance Web page into the worksheet as cell ranges rather than as an Excel Table. If you then want to be able to sort or filter this imported financial data, you need to select one of its cells and then select the Format as Table button on the Home tab to format them and add the requisite AutoFilter buttons (see Chapter 3 for details). When formatting data as a table, you remove all external connections to the data on the Web site.

You can make Web queries only when your computer has Internet access. Therefore, if you're using Excel on a laptop computer and can't connect to the Web, you won't be able to perform a new Web query until you're in a place where you can connect.

Chapter 12

Linking, Automating, and Sharing Spreadsheets

● ●

In This Chapter

▶ Using add-ins to automate and enhance Excel 2010

▶ Adding hyperlinks to other workbooks, worksheets, Office documents, Web pages, or e-mail

▶ Creating and using macros to automate common spreadsheet tasks

▶ Sharing your worksheets on the Web

▶ Editing your worksheets with Excel Web applications

● ●

*A*t your first reading of the chapter title, you might have the impression that this is just a catch-all, potpourri chapter, containing the last bits of program information that don't fit anywhere else in the book. Actually, however, this is not the case as this chapter has a very definite theme, and that theme is how you go about extending the power of Excel.

It just so happens that add-ins, hyperlinks, and macros are three major ways to make Excel more vigorous and versatile: add-ins through the extra features they give Excel 2010; hyperlinks through links to other worksheets and Office documents; and Web pages and macros through complex automated command sequences that you can play back whenever needed. And sharing your worksheets by attaching them to e-mail messages or publishing them to the Web as well as being able to edit them anywhere in the world using the new online Excel Web application are all part of the new collaboration features that enable you to both communicate and collaborate more quickly and effectively.

Using Add-Ins in Excel 2010

Add-in programs are small modules that extend the power of Excel by giving you access to a wide array of features and calculating functions not otherwise offered in the program. There are three types of add-ins:

- ✔ Built-in add-ins available when you install Excel 2010
- ✔ Add-ins that you can download for Excel 2010 from Microsoft's Office Online Web site (http://www.office.microsoft.com)
- ✔ Add-ins developed by third-party vendors for Excel 2010 that often must be purchased

When you first install Excel 2010, the built-in add-in programs included with Excel are fully loaded and ready to use. To load any other add-in programs, you follow these steps:

1. **Choose File⇨Options or press Alt+FT to open the Excel Options dialog box and then click the Add-Ins tab.**

   The Add-Ins tab lists the name, location, and type of add-ins you have access to.

2. **Click the Go button while Excel Add-Ins is selected in the Manage drop-down list box.**

   Excel opens the Add-Ins dialog box (similar to the one shown in Figure 12-1) showing all the names of the built-in add-in programs you can load.

3. **Click the check boxes for each add-in program that you want loaded in the Add-Ins Available list box.**

   Click the name of the add-in in the Add-Ins Available list box to display a brief description of its function at the bottom of this dialog box.

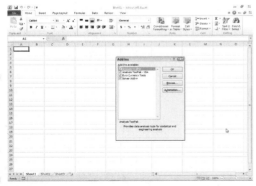

Figure 12-1: Activating built-in add-ins in the Add-Ins dialog box.

4. **Click the OK button to close the Add-Ins dialog box.**

   An alert dialog box may appear, asking whether you want to install each selected add-in.

5. **Click the OK button in each alert dialog box to install its add-in.**

Excel automatically places command buttons for the activated add-ins in either an Analysis group on the Ribbon's Data tab or in a Solutions group on the Formulas tab, depending upon the type of add-in. For example, Excel places the command buttons for the Analysis ToolPak or Solver add-in in the Analysis group on the Data tab. For the Euro Currency Tools, Excel places its command buttons in the Solutions group on the Formulas tab.

 If you end up never using a particular add-in you've loaded, you can unload it (and thereby free up some computer memory) by following the previously outlined procedure to open the Add-Ins dialog box and then clicking the name of the add-in to remove the check mark from its check box. Then click OK.

Adding Hyperlinks to a Worksheet

Hyperlinks automate Excel worksheets by making the opening of other Office documents and Excel workbooks and worksheets just a mouse click away. It doesn't matter whether these documents are located on your hard drive, a server on your LAN (Local Area Network), or Web pages on the Internet or a company's intranet. You can also set up e-mail hyperlinks that automatically address messages to co-workers with whom you routinely correspond, and you can attach Excel workbooks or other types of Office files to these messages.

The hyperlinks that you add to your Excel worksheets can be of the following types:

- ✔ Text entries in cells (known as hypertext, normally formatted as underlined blue text)

- ✔ Clip art and imported graphics from files you've inserted into the worksheet (see Chapter 10)

- ✔ Graphics you've created from the Shapes drop-down gallery on the Insert tab (see also Chapter 10) — in effect, turning the graphic images into buttons

When creating a text or graphic hyperlink, you can make a link to another Excel workbook or other type of Office file, a Web site address (using the URL address — you know, that monstrosity that begins with http://), a named location in the same workbook, or even a person's e-mail address. The named location can be a cell reference or named cell range (see Chapter 6 for details on naming cell ranges) in a particular worksheet.

To add the hyperlink to the text entry made in the current cell or a selected graphic object (see Chapter 10) in your worksheet, follow these steps:

1. **Click the Hyperlink button on the Ribbon's Insert tab or press Alt+NI, or simply press Ctrl+K.**

   Excel opens the Insert Hyperlink dialog box (similar to the one shown in Figure 12-2) in which you indicate the file, the Web address (URL), or the named location in the workbook.

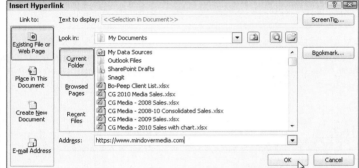

Figure 12-2:
Linking to a
Web page
in the Insert
Hyperlink
dialog box.

2a. **To have the hyperlink open another document, a Web page on a company's intranet, or a Web site on the Internet, click the Existing File or Web Page button if it isn't already selected and then enter the file's directory path or Web page's URL in the Address text box.**

   If the document you want to link to is located on your hard drive or a hard drive that is mapped on your computer, click the Look In drop-down button, select the folder, and then select the file in the list box. If you've recently opened the document you want to link to, you can click the Recent Files button and then select it from the list box.

   If the document you want to link to is located on a Web site and you know its Web address (the www.dummies.com–like thing), you can type it into the Address text box. If you recently browsed the Web page you want to link to, you can click the Browsed Pages button and then select the address of the page from the list box.

2b. **To have the hyperlink move the cell cursor to another cell or cell range in the same workbook, click the Place in This Document button. Next, type the address of the cell or cell range in the Type the Cell Reference text box or select the desired sheet name or range name from the Or Select a Place in This Document list box (shown in Figure 12-3).**

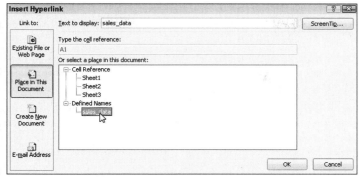

Figure 12-3:
Linking to a
worksheet
range name
or cell ref-
erence in
the Insert
Hyperlink
dialog box.

2c. **To open a new e-mail message addressed to a particular recipient, click the E-mail Address button and then enter the recipient's e-mail address in the E-mail Address text box (as shown in Figure 12-4).**

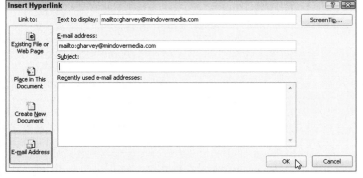

Figure 12-4:
Linking to
an e-mail
address
page in
the Insert
Hyperlink
dialog box.

In most cases, your e-mail program is Windows Live Mail on Windows 7, Windows Mail on Vista, or Outlook Express on Windows XP or Microsoft Outlook 2010 if you purchased a version of Microsoft Office 2010 that includes this personal information manager plus e-mail program.

As soon as you begin typing the e-mail address in the E-mail Address text box, Excel inserts the text `mailto:` in front of whatever you've typed. (`mailto:` is the HTML tag that tells Excel to open your e-mail program when you click the hyperlink.)

If you want the hyperlink to add the subject of the e-mail message when it opens a new message in your e-mail program, enter this text in the Subject text box.

If the recipient's address is displayed in the Recently Used E-mail Addresses list box, you can enter it into the E-mail Address text box simply by clicking the address.

3. **(Optional) To change the hyperlink text that appears in the cell of the worksheet (underlined and in blue) or add text if the cell is blank, type the desired label in the Text to Display text box.**

4. **(Optional) To add a ScreenTip to the hyperlink that appears when you position the mouse pointer over the hyperlink, click the ScreenTip button, type the text that you want to appear next to the mouse pointer in the ScreenTip box, and then click OK.**

5. **Click OK to close the Insert Hyperlink dialog box.**

After you create a hyperlink in a worksheet, you can follow it to whatever destination you associated with the hyperlink. To follow a hyperlink, position the mouse pointer over the underlined blue text (if you assigned the hyperlink to text in a cell) or over the graphic image (if you assigned the hyperlink to a graphic inserted in the worksheet). When the mouse pointer changes to a hand with the index finger pointing upward, click the hypertext or graphic image, and Excel makes the jump to the designated external document, Web page, cell within the workbook, or e-mail message.

After you follow a hypertext link to its destination, the color of its text changes from the traditional blue to a dark shade of purple (without affecting its underlining). This color change indicates that the hyperlink has been used. (Note, however, that graphic hyperlinks do not show any change in color after you follow them.) Additionally, Excel restores this underlined text to its original (unfollowed) blue color the next time that you open the workbook file.

If you need to edit a hyperlink attached to a worksheet cell or graphic object, you must be careful that, when getting Excel into Edit mode so that you can change the text, you don't inadvertently follow the link. When dealing with hypertext in a cell, you need to click and hold down the mouse button a few seconds to select the cell (if you click and release immediately, you follow the link) or click Hyperlink on the Insert tab. When dealing with a graphic object you're best off right-clicking the image and then clicking the appropriate editing command (Edit Hyperlink or Remove Hyperlink) on its shortcut menu.

Automating Commands with Macros

Macros automate the Excel worksheet by enabling you to record complex command sequences. By using macros that perform routine tasks, you not only speed up the procedure considerably (because Excel can play back your keystrokes and mouse actions much faster than you can perform them manually), but you are also assured that each step in the task is carried out the same way every time you perform the task.

Excel 2010's macro recorder records all the commands and keystrokes that you make in a language called Visual Basic for Applications (VBA), which is a special version of the BASIC programming language developed and refined by the good folks at Microsoft for use with all their Office application programs. You can then later learn how to use Excel's Visual Basic Editor to display and make changes to the macro's VBA code.

Recording new macros

Excel 2010 enables you to add an optional Developer tab to the Ribbon that contains its own Record Macro command button (among other command buttons that are very useful when doing more advanced work with macros). To add the Developer tab to the Excel 2010 Ribbon, follow these two steps:

1. **Choose File⇨Options or press Alt+FT to open the Excel Options dialog box.**

2. **Click the Customize Ribbon tab, select the Developer check box under Main Tabs in the Customize the Ribbon list box on the right side of the dialog box, and then click OK.**

Even if you don't add the Developer tab to the Ribbon, the Excel Status bar at the bottom of the Excel 2010 program window contains a Record Macro button (the button with the worksheet with a red dot to the immediate right of the Ready status indicator). You click this button to turn on the macro recorder. Also, the View tab contains a Macros command button with a drop-down menu containing a Record Macro option.

When you turn on the macro recorder either by clicking the Record Macro button on the Status bar, clicking the Record Macro option on the Macros button's drop-down menu (Alt+WMR), or clicking the Record Macro button on the Developer tab (Alt+LR), the macro recorder records all your actions in the active worksheet or chart sheet when you make them.

The macro recorder doesn't record the keystrokes or mouse actions that you take to accomplish an action — only the VBA code required to perform the action itself. This means that mistakes that you make while taking an action that you rectify won't be recorded as part of the macro; for example, if you make a typing error and then edit it while the macro recorder is on, only the corrected entry shows up in the macro without the original mistakes and steps taken to remedy them.

The macros that you create with the macro recorder can be stored as part of the current workbook, in a new workbook, or in a special, globally available Personal Macro Workbook named PERSONAL.XLSB that's stored in a folder called XLSTART on your hard drive. When you record a macro as part of your Personal Macro Workbook, you can run that macro from any workbook that you have open. (This is because the PERSONAL.XLSB workbook is secretly opened whenever you launch Excel, and although it remains hidden, its macros are always available.) When you record macros as part of the current workbook or a new workbook, you can run those macros only when the workbook in which they were recorded is open in Excel.

When you create a macro with the macro recorder, you decide not only the workbook in which to store the macro but also what name and shortcut keystrokes to assign to the macro that you are creating. When assigning a name for your macro, use the same guidelines that you use when you assign a standard range name to a cell range in your worksheet. When assigning a shortcut keystroke to run the macro, you can assign

- The Ctrl key plus a letter from A to Z, as in Ctrl+Q
- Ctrl+Shift and a letter from A to Z, as in Ctrl+Shift+Q

You can't, however, assign the Ctrl key plus a punctuation or number key (such as Ctrl+1 or Ctrl+/) to your macro.

To see how easy it is to create a macro with the macro recorder, follow these steps for creating a macro that enters the Company Name in 12-point, bold type and centers the company name across rows A through E with the Merge and Center feature:

1. **Open the Excel workbook that contains the worksheet data or chart you want your macro to work with.**

   If you're building a macro that adds new data to a worksheet (as in this example), open a worksheet with plenty of blank cells in which to add the data. If you're building a macro that needs to be in a particular cell when its steps are played back, put the cell pointer in that cell.

2. **Click the Record Macro button on the Status bar.**

   The Record Macro dialog box opens, similar to the one shown in Figure 12-5, where you enter the macro name, define any keystroke shortcut, select the workbook in which to store the macro, and enter a description of the macro's function.

3. **Replace the Macro1 temporary macro name by entering your name for the macro in the Macro Name text box.**

   Remember that when naming a macro, you must not use spaces in the macro name and it must begin with a letter and not some number or punctuation symbol. For this example macro, you replace Macro1 in the Macro Name text box with the name Company_Name.

Next, you can enter a letter between A and Z that acts like a shortcut key for running the macro when you press Ctrl followed by that letter key. Just remember that Excel has already assigned a number of Ctrl+letter keystroke shortcuts for doing common tasks, such as Ctrl+C for copying an item to the Clipboard and Ctrl+V for pasting an item from the Clipboard into the worksheet (see the Cheat Sheet online at www. dummies.com/cheatsheet/excel2010 for a complete list). If you assign the same keystrokes to the macro you're building, your macro's shortcut keys override and, therefore, disable Excel's ready-made shortcut keystrokes.

Figure 12-5:
Defining the new macro to record in the Record Macro dialog box.

4. **(Optional) Click the Shortcut key text box and then enter the letter of the alphabet that you want to assign to the macro.**

    For this example macro, press Shift+C to assign Ctrl+Shift+C as the shortcut keystroke (so as not to disable the ready-made Ctrl+C shortcut).

    Next, you need to decide where to save the new macro that you're building. Select Personal Macro Workbook on the Store Macro In drop-down list box to be able to run the macro anytime you like. Select This Workbook (the default) when you need to run the macro only when the current workbook is open. Select New Workbook if you want to open a new workbook in which to record and save the new macro.

5. **Click the Personal Macro Workbook, New Workbook, or This Workbook option on the Store Macro In drop-down list to indicate where to store the new macro.**

    For this example macro, select the Personal Macro Workbook so that you can use it to enter the company name in any Excel workbook that you create or edit.

    Next, you should document the purpose and function of your macro in the Description list box. Although this step is purely optional, it is a good idea to get in the habit of recording this information every time you build a new macro so that you and your co-workers can always know what to expect from the macro it's run.

6. **(Optional) Click the Description list box and then insert a brief description of the macro's purpose in front of the information indicating the date and who recorded the macro.**

   Now you're ready to close the Record Macro dialog box and start recording your macro.

7. **Click OK to close the Record Macro dialog box.**

   The Record Macro dialog box closes and the circular red Record Macro button on the Status bar and the Developer tab becomes a square blue Stop Recording button.

   On the Macros button's drop-down menu on the Ribbon's View tab and Code group on the Developer tab, you find a Use Relative References option. You click this drop-down menu item or command button when you want the macro recorder to record the macro relative to the position of the current cell. For this example macro, which enters the company name and formats it in the worksheet, you definitely need to click the Use Relative References button before you start recording commands. Otherwise, you can use the macro only to enter the company name starting in cell A1 of a worksheet.

8. **(Optional) Click the Use Relative References option on the Macros button's drop-down menu on the View tab or click the Use Relative References button on the Developer tab if you want to be able to play back the macro anywhere in the worksheet.**

9. **Select the cells, enter the data, and choose the Excel commands required to perform the tasks that you want recorded just as you normally would in creating or editing the current worksheet, using the keyboard, the mouse, or a combination of the two.**

   For the example macro, you type the company name and click the Enter button on the Formula bar to complete the entry in the current cell. Next, click the Bold button and then click 12 on the Font Size drop-down list in the Font group on the Home tab. Finally, drag through cells A1:E1 to select this range and then click the Merge and Center command button, again on the Home tab.

   After you finish taking all the actions in Excel that you want recorded, you're ready to shut off the macro recorder.

10. **Click the Stop Recording button on the Status bar or Developer tab on the Ribbon.**

    The square blue Stop Recording button on the Status bar and the Developer tab change back into circular red Record Macro buttons, letting you know that the macro recorder is now turned off and no further actions will be recorded.

Running macros

After you record a macro, you can run it by clicking the View Macros option on the Macros button's drop-down menu on the View tab, the Macros button on the Developer tab of the Ribbon, or by pressing Alt+F8 to open the Macro dialog box (see Figure 12-6). As this figure shows, Excel lists the names of all the macros in the current workbook and in your Personal Macro Workbook (provided you've created one) in the Macro Name list box. Simply click the name of the macro that you want to run and then click the Run button or press Enter to play back all its commands.

Figure 12-6:
Selecting
a macro to
playback in
the Macro
dialog box.

If you assigned a shortcut keystroke to the macro, you don't have to bother opening the Macro dialog box to run the macro: Simply press Ctrl plus the letter key or Ctrl+Shift plus the letter key that you assigned and Excel immediately plays back all the commands that you recorded.

The reason that macros you record in the Personal Macro Workbook are always available in any Excel workbook is because the PERSONAL.XLSB workbook is also open — you just don't know it because Excel hides this workbook immediately after opening it each time you launch the program. As a result, if you try to edit or delete a macro in the Macro dialog box saved in the Personal Macro Workbook, Excel displays an alert dialog box telling you that you can't edit a hidden workbook.

To unhide the Personal Macro Workbook, first clear the alert dialog box and close the Macro dialog box; then click the Unhide button on the View tab (Alt+WU) and click the OK button in the Unhide dialog box while PERSONAL.

XLSB is selected. Excel then makes the Personal Macro Workbook active, and you can open the Macro dialog box and edit or delete any macros you've saved in it. After you finish, close the Macro dialog box and then click the Hide button on the View tab (or press Alt+WH) to hide the Personal Macro Workbook once more.

Assigning macros to the Ribbon and the Quick Access toolbar

If you prefer, instead of running a macro by selecting it in the Macro dialog box or by pressing shortcut keys you assign to it, you can assign it to a custom tab on the Ribbon or a custom button on the Quick Access toolbar and then run it by clicking that custom button.

To assign a macro to a custom group on a custom Ribbon tab, you follow these steps:

1. **Choose File⇨Options and then click the Customize Ribbon tab in the Excel Options dialog box (or press Alt+FTC).**

   Excel displays the Customize Ribbon pane in the Excel Options dialog box.

2. **Click Macros in the Choose Commands From drop-down list box on the left.**

   Excel lists the names of all the macros created in the current workbook and saved in the PERSONAL.XLSB workbook in the Choose Commands From list box.

3. **Click the name of the custom group on the custom tab to which you want to add the macro in the Main Tabs list box on the right.**

   If you haven't already created a custom tab and group for the macro or need to create a new one, follow these steps:

   a. *Click the New Tab button at the bottom of the Main Tabs list.*

      Excel adds both a New Tab (Custom) and New Group (Custom) item to the Main Tabs list while at the same time selecting the New Group (Custom) item.

   b. *Click the New Tab (Custom) item you just added to the Main Tabs.*

   c. *Click the Rename button at the bottom of the Main Tabs list box and then type a display name for the new custom tab before you click OK.*

   d. *Click the New Group (Custom) item right below the custom tab you just renamed.*

   e. *Click the Rename button and then type a display name for the new custom group before you click OK.*

4. **In the Choose Commands From list box on the left, click the name of the macro you want to add to the custom group now selected in the Main Tabs list box on the right.**

5. **Click the Add button to add the selected macro to the selected custom group on your custom tab and then click the OK button to close the Excel Options dialog box.**

After you add a macro to the custom group of a custom tab, the name of the macro appears on a button sporting a generic icon (a programming diagram chart) on the custom tab of the Ribbon. Then, all you have to do to run the macro is click this command button.

To assign a macro to a custom button on the Quick Access toolbar, follow these steps:

1. **Click the Customize Quick Access Toolbar button at the end of the Quick Access toolbar and then click More Commands on its drop-down menu.**

   Excel opens the Excel Options dialog box with the Quick Access Toolbar tab selected.

2. **Click Macros in the Choose Commands From drop-down list box.**

   Excel lists the names of all the macros created in the current workbook and saved in the PERSONAL.XLSB workbook in the Choose Commands From list box.

3. **Click the name of the macro to add to a custom button on the Quick Access toolbar in the Choose Commands From list box and then click the Add button.**

4. **Click OK to close the Excel Options dialog box.**

After you close the Excel Options dialog box, a custom button sporting a generic macro icon (picturing a standard command flowchart) appears on the Quick Access toolbar. You can choose a different icon by clicking the Rename button below the Customize the Ribbon box. To see the name of the macro assigned to this custom macro button as a ScreenTip, position the mouse pointer over the button. To run the macro, click the button.

Figure 12-7 shows the Quick Access toolbar and Excel Ribbon after adding a custom button that runs the Company_Name macro described earlier in this chapter. I added the custom button that runs this macro to the end of the Quick Access toolbar and to a custom group named Simple Macros, which I added to a custom Ribbon tab named Macros.

Figure 12-7:
The Excel
Ribbon
and Quick
Access
toolbar
after adding
a custom
macro
button.

Custom macro button

Sharing Worksheets

Excel 2010 makes it easy to share your spreadsheets with trusted clients and co-workers. You can use the Save & Send panel in Backstage View to e-mail workbooks to others who have access to Excel on their computers. If you have access to a collaborative online Web site, such as a Microsoft SharePoint Web site or use Excel Services, you can save your workbooks to these Web resources from this panel.

If you maintain a Windows Live SkyDrive storage site, you can share and access your spreadsheets online by logging on to this site and then uploading copies of your workbook files to this Internet location. Additionally, you can review or edit the workbooks you save on your SkyDrive when you're away from your office and the computer to which you have access doesn't have a compatible version of Excel installed on it. You simply use that computer's Internet access to log on to the My Documents folder of your SkyDrive containing uploaded copies of your spreadsheets, and then use the brand new Excel Web App (that runs on most modern Web browsers) to open and then review and edit them.

Sending a workbook via e-mail

To e-mail one of your workbooks to a client or co-worker, choose File⇨Save & Send⇨Send Using E-Mail (Alt+FDE). When you do this, a Send Using E-Mail panel appears with the following five options:

- ✔ **Send as Attachment** to create a new e-mail message using your default e-mail program with a copy of the workbook file as its attachment file.

- ✔ **Send a Link** to create a new e-mail message using your default e-mail program that contains a hyperlink to the workbook file. (This option is available only when the workbook file is saved on your company's or ISP's Web server.)

✔ **Send as PDF** to convert the Excel workbook to the Adobe PDF (Portable Document File) format and make this new PDF the attachment file in a new e-mail message. (Your e-mail recipient must have a copy of the Adobe Reader installed on his or her computer in order to open the attachment.)

✔ **Send as XPS** to convert the Excel workbook to a Microsoft XPS (XML Paper Specification) file and make this new XPS file the attachment in a new e-mail message. (Your e-mail recipient must have an XPS Reader installed on his or her computer in order to open the attachment; this reader is installed automatically on computers running Windows 7 or Windows Vista.)

✔ **Send as Internet Fax** to send the workbook as a fax through an online fax service provider. You will need an account with a service provider as well as the Windows Fax and Scan Windows feature installed.

After selecting the e-mail option you want to use, Windows opens a new e-mail message in your e-mail program with a link to the workbook file or the file attached to it. To send the link or file, fill in the recipient's e-mail address in the To text box and any comments you want to make about the spreadsheet in the body of the message before you click the Send button.

Sharing a workbook on a SharePoint Web site

If your company maintains a SharePoint site to facilitate different kinds of online team collaboration, you can save the workbooks to which various teams need access directly on this special Web site. When saving a workbook to a SharePoint site, you can save a static copy so that the teams can simply review and refer to its data or you can save a more dynamic copy (using Microsoft's Excel Services server technology) that enables teams to make changes and do certain types of online analysis in their Web browsers.

To save a copy of your workbook, choose File⇨Save & Send⇨Save to SharePoint and then click the Save As button. Excel opens the Save As dialog box where you replace the suggested filename in the File Name text box with the URL of your SharePoint site before you click the Save button.

Excel then connects to your SharePoint site (on some systems, after prompting you for your User Name and password, if the site is hosted) and displays the Site Content page in the Save As dialog box. You then select the SharePoint document library, sub-site, or workspace in which to save the workbook by double-clicking its icon or clicking the item and then clicking the Open button. When you click the Save button after selecting the location, Excel saves a copy of the workbook directly on the SharePoint server.

Uploading workbooks to your SkyDrive and editing them with the Excel Web App

Microsoft offers several free online apps and services as part of its Windows Live Essentials suite. And if you maintain a SkyDrive (the file storage and sharing component of Windows Live; the first 25 GB of storage is free), you can easily upload copies of your Excel workbooks to this drive for sharing.

1. **Choose File➪Save & Send➪Save to Web (Alt+FDK).**

   The Save to Windows Live panel displays. Your options are to learn more about Windows Live, sign-in with a Windows Live ID, or to sign up for a new account.

2. **Click the Sign In button to sign in with your Windows Live ID.**

   After you sign in, you can choose to create a new folder or select an existing folder.

3. **Select a shared folder, and then click the Save As button.**

   Excel contacts the SkyDrive service and then displays the Save As dialog.

4. **Type a name for the workbook and then click Save.**

   Excel saves the workbook to SkyDrive.

If you maintain copies of your spreadsheets on your SkyDrive, you can give other clients and co-workers access to them (using their Windows Live IDs). Additionally, you can edit these worksheets in your Web browser using the brand new Excel Web App (part of the Office Web Apps, which also include a Word and PowerPoint Web App, all of which are available free to users with Windows Live IDs).

The great part about using the Excel Web App to edit a copy of your online workbook is that this Web App runs successfully under Microsoft's Internet Explorer 8 and under the latest versions of other popular Web browsers, including Mozilla Firefox for Windows, Mac, and Linux as well as Macintosh's Safari Web browser.

To edit a workbook you've uploaded to the My Documents folder of your SkyDrive, you follow these simple steps:

1. **Open the My Documents page of your SkyDrive and then click the file icon of the workbook you want to edit.**

   A Web page showing information about the Excel file you selected appears.

2. **Click the Edit link to the immediate right of the View link on the command line.**

   Windows Live then opens the selected workbook in Excel Web App in your Web browser (see Figure 12-8 for an example).

3. **Edit the contents of the cells in the worksheets of the open workbook and the workbook's formatting if necessary (using the tools on the Home tab of the Excel Web App Ribbon).**

   To change the text or number in a cell or to edit its formula on the Formula bar, click the cell to make it current and then click in the Formula bar. To edit the cell contents within the worksheet, make the cell current and press F2.

   To modify the layout or formatting of a cell selection, click the appropriate command button in the Font, Alignment, Number, or Cells group on the Home tab of the Ribbon.

Figure 12-8: Editing an Excel 2010 workbook that was uploaded to the My Documents folder of SkyDrive with the new Excel Web App.

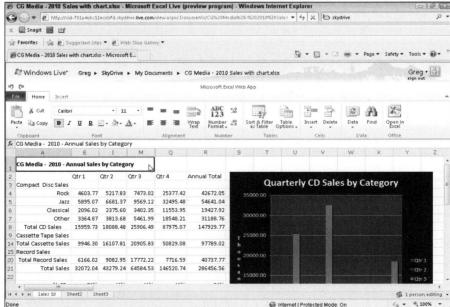

4. **When you finish editing the workbook, save your changes by choosing File⇨Save As and then editing the filename that appears in the text box of the Save As dialog box before you click Save. (Or click the Overwrite Existing Files check box if you want to save the changes under the same filename).**

The Excel Web App is pretty handy when it comes to making simple editing, formatting, and layout changes to your spreadsheet data. However, the Web App is completely incapable of dealing with any type of changes to charts and other types of graphics that you've added (even though they do appear in the worksheet online). To make these types of modifications to your worksheet, you have two choices: Open the workbook in a local copy of Excel (assuming that the computer you're using has Excel 2007 or later installed on it) by clicking the Open in Excel button at the end of the Home tab on the Ribbon. Or, download a copy of the workbook to your local office computer (where you do have Excel 2010 installed) by choosing File⇨Download a Copy and make the more advanced edits to this downloaded copy of the file once you get back to the office.

Part VI
The Part of Tens

The 5th Wave   By Rich Tennant

"I started running 'what if' scenarios on my spreadsheet, like, 'What if I were sick of this dirtwad job and funneled some of the company's money into an off—shore account?"

In this part . . .

Finally, you come to the fun part of this book where the chapters all consist of lists with the top ten Excel 2010 tips on this, that, and everything in between. In homage to David Letterman (Indiana's favorite son), you'll find lists of the top ten features in Excel 2010 and the top ten beginner basics. And, in homage to Cecil B. DeMille, Moses, and a much higher power, I've included a chapter with the Ten Commandments of Excel 2010 that, although not written in stone, when followed faithfully, are guaranteed to give you heavenly results.

Chapter 13

Top Ten Features in Excel 2010

*1*f you're looking for a quick rundown on what's cool in Excel 2010, look no further! Here it is — my official Top Ten Features list. Just a cursory glance down the list tells you that the thrust of the features is graphics, graphics, graphics!

In case you're interested in more than just a brief feature description, I've included a cross-reference to any place in this book where I cover the feature in more detail.

10. **Conditional Formatting & Sparklines:** Conditional formatting in Excel 2010 gives you the ability to define formatting when the values in cells meet certain conditions. You can now instantly apply one of many different Data Bars, Color Scales, and Icon Sets to the cell selection merely by clicking the set's thumbnail in the respective pop-up palettes. When you apply a set of Data Bars to a cell range, the length of each bar in the cell represents its value relative to the others. When you apply a set of Color Scales, each shade of color in the cell represents its value relative to the others. Additionally, when you apply one of the Icon Sets, each icon in the cell represents its value relative to the others. See Chapter 3 for more on using different types of conditional formatting to add dynamic formats to specific sets of worksheet data.

    Sparklines are the newest graphic addition to Excel. They are tiny charts (so small they fit within the current height of a worksheet cell) that visually represent changes in ranges of associated data. You can use sparklines to call attention to trends in the data as well as to help your users quickly spot high and low values. See Chapter 10 for more on how to add these exciting new charts to your worksheets.

9. **Cell Styles:** Comparing the six measly and bland cell styles offered in versions of Excel prior to 2007 to the more than 40 colorful ready-made styles offered in Excel 2010, I'm here to tell you that in Excel 2010 you finally have cell styles. Moreover, these are styles you can preview in the worksheet with Live Preview (see Number 1 that follows) to see how they look on the data before you apply them. You apply a cell style to the cell selection by quickly and easily clicking its thumbnail in the Cells Styles gallery (see Number 4 in the list). Take a gander at Chapter 3 for info on applying ready-made styles and creating some of your own.

8. **Formatting and Editing from the Home tab:** The Home tab of the Excel Ribbon (see Number 2 that follows) literally brings home all the commonly used formatting and editing features. Gone are the days when you have to fish for the right button on some long, drawn-out toolbar or on some partially deployed pull-down menu. Now all you have to do is find the group that holds the command button you need and click it — what could be easier! See Chapter 3 for more on using the formatting command buttons in the Font, Alignment, Number, and Styles groups on the Home tab. See Chapter 4 for more on using the editing commands in the Clipboard, Cells, and Editing groups on this tab.

7. **Charts from the Insert tab:** Charts have been a part of Excel since I first wrote this book for Excel 4 back in 1993. Nonetheless, it feels like charts have finally come into their own in Excel 2007/2010. Excel 2010, like its immediate predecessor, retires the Chart Wizard and offers you direct access to all the major types of charts on the Ribbon's Insert tab. Simply select the data to chart, click the command button for the chart type on the Insert tab and then select the style you want for that chart type. And with a little help from the many command buttons and galleries on the Design, Layout, and Format tabs on its Chart Tools contextual tab, you have a really professional-looking chart ready for printing! See Chapter 10 for details on creating charts in Excel 2010.

6. **Format As Table:** This feature is a real keeper. By formatting a table of data with one of the many table styles available on the Table Styles drop-down gallery, you're assured that all new entries made to the table are going to be formatted in the same manner as others in similar positions in the table. Better yet, all new entries to the table are considered part of the table automatically when it comes to formatting, sorting, and filtering. By the way, filtering the table's data is easy with the addition of filter buttons to the top row of column headings. See Chapter 3 for more on formatting a range as a table. See Chapter 11 for more on sorting and filtering data.

5. **Page Layout View:** Page Layout View in the Excel worksheet is just what the doctor ordered when it comes to visualizing the paging of printed reports. When you turn on this view by clicking the Page Layout View button on the Status bar, Excel doesn't just show the page breaks as measly dotted lines as in earlier versions but as actual separations. Additionally, the program shows the margins for each page, including headers and footers defined for the report (which you can both define and edit directly in the margin areas while the program is in this view). As an extra nice touch, Excel throws in a pair of horizontal and vertical rulers to accompany the standard column and row headers. Couple this great feature with the Zoom slider and the Page Break Preview feature and you're going to enjoy getting the spreadsheet ready to print. See Chapter 5 for details on using Page Layout View and defining headers and footers for your printed reports.

4. **Style Galleries:** Excel 2010 is jammed full of style galleries that make it a snap to apply new sophisticated (and, in many cases, very colorful) formatting to the charts, tables and lists of data, and various and sundry graphics that you add to your worksheets. Coupled with the Live Preview feature (see Number 1 in the list), Excel's style galleries go a long way toward encouraging you to create better looking, more colorful, and interesting spreadsheets. See Chapter 3 for ideas on how to use styles to add real style to your worksheet.

3. **Document Information and Printing in Backstage View:** The brand new Backstage View in Excel enables you to get all the properties and stats (technically known as metadata) about the workbook file you're editing (including a thumbnail of its contents) on one pane simply by choosing File⇨Info (Alt+FI). This new Backstage View also makes it a breeze to preview, change settings, and print your worksheet using its new Print panel by choosing File⇨Print (Ctrl+P or Alt+FP). See Chapter 1 for more on getting at-a-glance information about your document in the Backstage View. See Chapter 5 for details on printing the worksheet using the new Print panel.

2. **The Ribbon:** The Ribbon is the heart of the new Excel 2010 user interface. Based on a core of standard tabs to which various so-called contextual tabs are added as needed in formatting and editing of specific elements (such as data tables, charts, pivot tables, and graphic objects), the Ribbon brings together most every command you're going to need when performing particular tasks in Excel. Check out Chapter 1 for the lowdown on using the Ribbon.

1. **Live Preview:** You simply can't say enough about Live Preview, including how much easier it makes formatting the worksheet. Live Preview works with all the style galleries (see Number 4 in the list) as well as Font and Font Size drop-down menus in the Font group on the Home tab. It enables you to see how the data in the current cell selection would look with a particular formatting, font, or font size before you actually apply the formatting to the range. All you have to do is mouse over the thumbnails in the drop-down menu or gallery to see how each of its styles will look on your actual data. As an extra nice feature, many of the larger style galleries sport spinner buttons that enable you to bring new rows of thumbnails in the gallery into view so that you can preview their styles without obscuring any part of the cell selection (as would be the case if you actually open the gallery by clicking its More drop-down button). When you finally do see the formatting that fits your data to a tee, all you have to do is click its thumbnail to apply it to the selected cell range.

Chapter 14

Top Ten Beginner Basics

● ●

*1*f these ten items are all you master in Excel 2010, you'll still be way ahead of the competition. When all is said and done, this top ten list lays out all the fundamental skills required to use Excel 2010 successfully.

10. **To start Excel 2010 from the Windows 7 or Vista taskbar,** click the Start button, type **exc** in the Search Programs and Files text box and then with Microsoft Excel 2010 selected in the Programs section, press Enter. To start the program from the Windows XP or 2000 taskbar, click the Start button, highlight All Programs on the Start menu, and then highlight Microsoft Office on the All Programs continuation menu. Finally, click Microsoft Office Excel on the Microsoft Office continuation menu.

9. **To launch Excel 2010 automatically when you open an Excel workbook that needs editing** (in the Documents window in Windows 7 and Vista or My Documents window in Windows XP), simply locate the folder containing the Excel workbook you want to edit and double-click its file icon.

8. **To locate a part of a worksheet that you cannot see onscreen,** click the scroll bars at the right and bottom of the workbook window to bring new parts of the worksheet into view.

7. **To start a new workbook (containing three blank worksheets) using the Excel default template,** simply press Ctrl+N. To open a new workbook based on another template, choose File⇨New or press Alt+FN and then select the template to use in the New section of the Backstage View, where you can select a template or download one from Office. com. To add a new worksheet to a workbook (should you need more than three), click the Insert Worksheet button to the immediate right of the last tab at the bottom of the Worksheet area.

6. **To activate an open workbook and display it onscreen** (in front of any others you have open), click the Ribbon's View tab, then click the window to activate in the Switch Windows button's drop-down menu (or press Alt+WW followed by the window's number). To locate a particular worksheet in the active workbook, click that worksheet's sheet tab at the bottom of the workbook document window. To display more sheet tabs, click the sheet scrolling arrows on the left side of the bottom of the workbook window.

5. **To enter stuff in a worksheet,** select the cell where the information should appear; then begin typing. When you finish, click the Enter button on the Formula bar (the one with the check mark) or press Tab, Enter, or one of the arrow keys.

4. **To edit the stuff you entered into a cell already,** double-click the cell or position the cell pointer in the cell and press F2. Excel then positions the insertion point at the end of the cell entry and goes into Edit mode (see Chapter 2 for details). When you finish correcting the entry, click the Enter button on the Formula bar or press Tab or Enter.

3. **To choose one of the many Excel commands on the Ribbon,** click the Ribbon tab, locate the group containing the command button, and then click the button. (Or, press the Alt key to display the hot keys on the Ribbon and then type the letter of the tab you want to select followed by the letter(s) of the command button to use.) To choose a command in Backstage View, choose File and then click its menu option or press Alt+F followed by the option's hot key letter. To choose a command on the Quick Access toolbar, click its command button.

2. **To save a copy of your workbook on disk the first time around,** click the Save button on the Quick Access toolbar or press Ctrl+S. Next, designate the drive and folder directory where the file should be located, replace the temporary `Book1.xlsx` filename in the File Name text box with your own filename (up to 255 characters long, including spaces), and then click the Save button. To save a workbook so that older versions of Excel can open it, click the Save As option on the File tab, then click the Excel 97-2003 Workbook (*.xls) option in the Save as Type drop-down menu.

1. **To exit Excel when you're done working with the program,** choose File⇨Exit or press Alt+F4 or Alt+FX. If the workbook you have open contains unsaved changes, Excel 2010 asks whether you want to save the workbook before closing Excel and returning to Windows. Before you shut off your computer, be sure to use the Shut Down command on the Start menu to shut down the Windows operating system.

Chapter 15

The Ten Commandments of Excel 2010

* * *

*W*hen working with Excel 2010, you discover certain do's and don'ts that, if followed religiously, can make using this program just heavenly. Lo and behold, the following Excel Ten Commandments contain just such precepts for eternal Excel bliss.

10. **Thou shalt commit thy work to disk** by saving thy changes often (clicketh the Save button on the Quick Access toolbar or presseth Ctrl+S). If thou findest that thou tendeth to be lax in the saving of thy work, thou shalt maketh sure that thy AutoRecover feature is engaged. Chooseth File➪Options➪Save or presseth Alt+FTS and then maketh sure that the Save AutoRecover Information check box hath a check mark and that its text box is set to no more than 10 minutes.

9. **Thou shalt nameth thy workbooks** when saving them the first time with filenames of no more than twelve score and fifteen characters (255), including spaces and all manner of weird signs and symbols. So, too, thou shalt mark well into which folder thou savest thy file lest thou thinkest in error that thy workbook be lost when next thou hast need of it.

8. **Thou shalt not spread wide the data in thy worksheet,** but rather thou shalt gather together thy tables and avoideth skipping columns and rows unless this is necessary to make thy data intelligible. All this thou shalt do in order that thou may conserve the memory of thy computer.

7. **Thou shalt begin all thy Excel 2010 formulas with = (equal)** as the sign of computation. If, however, ye be formerly of the Lotus 1-2-3 tribe, thou shalt haveth special dispensation and can commence thy formulas with the + sign and thy functions with the @ sign.

6. **Thou shalt select thy cells before thou bringeth any Excel command to bear upon them,** just as surely as thou doth sow before thou reapeth.

5. **Thou shalt useth the Undo feature (clicketh the Undo button on the Quick Access toolbar or presseth Ctrl+Z)** immediately upon committing any transgression in thy worksheet so that thou mayest clean up thy mess. Should thou forgeteth to useth thy Undo feature straightaway, thou must select the action that thou wouldst undo from the pop-up menu attached to the Undo command button on the Quick Access toolbar. Note well that any action that thou selectest from this drop-down list will undo not only that action but also the actions that precedeth it on this menu.

4. **Thou shalt not delete, nor insert, columns and rows in a worksheet** lest thou hath first verified that no part yet undisplayed of thy worksheet will thereby be wiped out or otherwise displaced.

3. **Thou shalt not print thy spreadsheet report lest thou hath first previewed its pages by clicking the Page Layout View button** (the middle button of the three to the immediate left of the Zoom Slider on the Status bar) and art satisfied that all thy pages are upright in the sight of the printer. If thou art still unsure of how thy pages break, clicketh the Page Break Preview button to its immediate right on the Status bar to seeth how Excel doth divide thy pages.

2. **Thou shalt changeth the manner of recalculation of thy workbooks from automatic to manual** (clicketh Formulas⇨Calculation Options⇨Manual or presseth Alt+MXM) when thy workbook groweth so great in size that Excel sloweth down to a camel crawl whenever thou doeth anything in any one of its worksheets. Woe to thee, should thou then ignoreth the Calculate message on the Status bar and not presseth the Calculate Now key (F9) or clicketh Formulas⇨Calculate Now before such time as thou mayest print any of thy workbook data.

1. **Thou shalt protecteth thy completed workbook and all its worksheets from corruption and iniquities** at the hands of others (clicketh Review⇨Protect Sheet or Protect Workbook). And if thou be brazen enough to addeth a password to thy workbook protection, beware lest thou forgeteth thy password in any part. For verily I say unto thee, on the day that thou knowest not thy password, that day shalt be the last upon which thou lookest upon thy workbook in any guise.

Index

• *G* •